PENGUIN BOOKS

# CASSOWARY CROSSING

David Astle is the author of two novels – *Marzipan Plan* (1986) and *The Book of Miles* (1997). His shorter fiction has appeared in such places as *Picador New Writing*, *Behind The Front Fence* and *Heatwave*; and his feature articles in *Sunday Life* and *Inside Sport*. He co-wrote *One Down, One Missing*, an inside account of the hunt for the killers of two policemen, which was published in 2003. He lives in Melbourne, composes cryptic crosswords, and can't hit the road without his family for another two years.

# CASSOWARY CROSSING

A guide to **offbeat** Australia

## DAVID ASTLE

Penguin Books

PENGUIN BOOKS

Published by the Penguin Group
Penguin Group (Australia)
250 Camberwell Road, Camberwell, Victoria 3124, Australia
(a division of Pearson Australia Group Pty Ltd)
Penguin Group (USA) Inc.
375 Hudson Street, New York, New York 10014, USA
Penguin Group (Canada)
90 Eglinton Avenue East, Suite 700, Toronto, ON M4P 2Y3, Canada
(a division of Pearson Penguin Canada Inc.)
Penguin Books Ltd
80 Strand, London WC2R 0RL, England
Penguin Ireland
25 St Stephen's Green, Dublin 2, Ireland
(a division of Penguin Books Ltd)
Penguin Books India Pvt Ltd
11 Community Centre, Panchsheel Park, New Delhi – 110 017, India
Penguin Group (NZ)
Cnr Airborne and Rosedale Roads, Albany, Auckland, New Zealand
(a division of Pearson New Zealand Ltd)
Penguin Books (South Africa) (Pty) Ltd
24 Sturdee Avenue, Rosebank, Johannesburg 2196, South Africa

Penguin Books Ltd, Registered Offices: 80 Strand, London, WC2R 0RL, England

First published by Penguin Group (Australia),
a division of Pearson Australia Group Pty Ltd, 2005

10 9 8 7 6 5 4 3 2 1

Text copyright © David Astle, 2005

Text design by David Altheim © Penguin Group (Australia)
Cover design by Jo Hunt © Penguin Group (Australia)
Maps by Damien Demaj
Typeset in 9.5/12.5 Nimbus Novus by Post Pre-press Group, Brisbane, Queensland
Printed in Australia by McPherson's Printing Group Pty Ltd, Maryborough, Victoria

National Library of Australia
Cataloguing-in-Publication data:

Astle, David, 1961– .
    Cassowary crossing: a guide to offbeat Australia.

    Includes index.
    ISBN 0 14 300169 8.

    1. Voyages and travels – Planning. 2. Australia – Description and travel – Guidebooks.
    3. Australia – Miscellanea. I. Title.

919.404

www.penguin.com.au

To Iris, Boris and Doris
For going the miles
And holding your ground

# CONTENTS

**Introduction: offbeat and away   ix**

# INTRODUCTION: OFFBEAT AND AWAY

Welcome to a book that celebrates the curious, a guide to the things most tourists miss. *Cassowary Crossing* combines travel information with trivia, pop culture, crime, science, art . . . and that's just the first few pages.

Most tourists go to the obvious places, and who can blame them? The obvious places are usually fine, if a little crowded. Why not dodge the droves and take a few bizarre side-trips along the way? Just to be different, this book ignores the well-sung features of the Great Barrier Reef. They're the job of mainstream guides. Instead we dive into koala hospitals, organic golf, a windmill museum, whale chairs, pistol teapots – from Airborne to Zany with a hundred or so other chapters in between.

With *Cassowary Crossing* under your wing, you carry an alternative way of seeing Australia. Take a place like Bondi, for example. How many of the beach's million visitors per year know about the missing mermaid on the northern point (see Rocks) or realise why the traffic poles up the road (see Poles) are unique?

That's how the book was born. Personally, I have no gripe with Bondi or anywhere tourists go. As a matter of fact, I'd trade this desk for a surf right now. See you there. But before you go – go anywhere in Oz – a dip in these pages will offer you another way of taking the day, ahem, on board.

That's the fun of *Cassowary Crossing*, and the promise. It offers you treasures off the radar. Pack your standard maps and guides to get you from A to B. Pack this book as well and you're guaranteed a tangent. Heading north to Alice Springs, why not call by Stuarts Well and meet Dink, the singing dingo? Or take a side trip to see the four meteorite holes in Henbury. Each entry comes with an invitation, a chance for you to enter the strangeness somehow: a street name, a touchstone, a secret trail off the beaten track.

Writing this book was two parts research, three parts dashboard and four parts word-of-mouth. Over a year I visited a thousand small towns across the country. I drove to Minnamurra, north of Kiama in New South Wales, to find Bionic Ear Beach, and along the way found the purple dinosaur of Mollymook. Both appear in these pages, along with other curios I mined and sourced and saw with my own eyes.

Seeing wasn't just believing – it was vital to the writing. I know from experience how travellers tire of third-hand reports or a list of budget fleapits an easy walk from the station. Tell us what we don't know, and tell us like you know it: that was the mantra to fuel those 50 000 kilometres, and it saw me quizzing almost as many people along the way.

To be fair to this offbeat continent, the job of writing such a maverick guide is never truly done. No doubt I have missed as many marvels as I have found, and welcome suggestions for future editions and for the benefit of fellow offbeat travellers. Likewise, if you find a glitch or meet a change in details, let us know.

In the meantime, both book and road beckon. Enjoy yourself. And keep your eyes out for cassowaries.

## HOW TO USE THIS BOOK

*Cassowary Crossing* is a unique breed of travel guide. From the armchair, the pleasure lies in discovering condom trees or bushranger sausages on the next page. From the glovebox, you have several ways of making the book enrich your trip.

Airborne? Arty? Where do you start? It really depends on you and what you're using the book for. There are nearly 1500 entries, divided into themed chapters such as Arty, Ghosts, Music or Vertigo, to name but four. Many of the chapter headings will explain themselves, namely Bridges or Walls. Others (such as Irony or Urghh) may require a browse before you get the idea.

So how to find your way around – or, more importantly, find out what there is to see? If, say, your passion is trees, then the chapter

Trees is the logical place to start. Go there, and among the twenty or so entries you'll learn of many remarkable trees across Australia, from the snappy gum of Onslow (WA) to the three-way tree of Tewantin (Qld). But that's not all: you can also look up trees in the General Index, which will tell you that, for example, there's also a prison tree in Derby (WA) and a Tree of Knowledge in Barcaldine (SA). Of course, you can also expect to find a few curious trees in Gardens, and so on.

Use the book, in other words, according to your topics of choice. If art is your bag, visit Arty. And why not pop over into Literature, Crafty, Film or Visions, all of which have arty undertones? Or try the General Index, where you'll find helpful entries such as Aboriginal art, craft, and sculpture. In other words, let favourite themes steer your way through the pages, and open up roads to fresh destinations.

But theme is not your only way around. Another tack is geography, and here the Regional Guide on (page 405) comes into play: it identifies the continent's main regions and lists for each all the towns mentioned in the book. Imagine you're touring the Barossa Valley northeast of Adelaide in SA: aside from vines and vistas, what else can you see? In the regional guide you'll discover that towns of interest there include Angaston, Williamstown and Nuriootpa, which you can then look up in the Index of Places to find out why. Turn to the relevant chapters for further details, and suddenly your trip has taken on a welcome kink.

Unlike orthodox guides, *Cassowary Crossing* is designed to be enjoyed in and for itself. To read of the quandong liqueurs of Tanunda (another listed attraction in the Barossa region, lurking in the Sweet chapter) is almost as good as tasting the rarity yourself. Almost. There's nothing like going there and swirling the sensation across your own palate. This book is your chance to experience both the vicarious and the real in the world of the unusual.

Cheers.

## PRICES AND CONTACT DETAILS

Access and contact information, prices and opening hours are, if relevant, provided at the end of entries. All details were correct at the time the book went to press, but if you're planning a visit it's advisable to check ahead as things may have changed.

Prices are set out as follows:

$10/$5 (= adult/child) **or** $10/$7.50/$5 (= adult/concession/child) **plus** family rates if applicable.

Every effort has been made to check all the information, but this was not always possible and we would be glad to hear of any omissions or inaccuracies.

## ABBREVIATIONS AND CONTRACTIONS
## USED IN THE BOOK

| | | | |
|---|---|---|---|
| ACT | Australian Capital Territory | Pde | Parade |
| Ave | Avenue | Pt | Point |
| Ck | Creek | Qld | Queensland |
| cnr | on the corner of | Rd | Road |
| Dve | Drive | SA | South Australia |
| ha | hectares | St | Street; Saint |
| Hwy | Highway | TAFE | Technical & Further |
| kg | kilograms | | Education |
| km | kilometres | Tas. | Tasmania |
| m | metres | Tce | Terrace |
| Mt | Mount | Vic. | Victoria |
| NSW | New South Wales | WA | Western Australia |
| NT | Northern Territory | | |

# AIRBORNE

*(Being a squadron of un-plain planes,*
*dynamic dynamics and unorthodox up-things)*

## WINGS OF DESIRE

**BELLINGEN, NSW**  Flying foxes are either creepy, smelly, nasty vampire things, or they are splendid navigators of the night, depending on your point of view. No matter what your opinion, stand on Lavender Bridge over the Bellingen River and prepare to be amazed. Oh, I should add that dusk is the time and the warmer months the season, when the smelly/sublime colony starts to multiply (from November). The bridge is the ideal viewing point, as the valley effectively funnels the bats directly overhead. True enthusiasts can stay at the caravan park (02 6655 1338), which offers exclusive access to Bellingen Island, where the bat colony hangs out. There are also some remarkable photos by bat-fancier Vivien Jones in the local galleries. **[Viv can be buzzed on (02) 6655 2213 or check out www.bellingen.com]**

A town in the middle of Australia is named after a wing flap. **Aileron (NT)** is roughly 100 km north of Alice Springs. Reasons for the aerodynamic name are literally up in the air. Did a plane part fall from the sky? Did truck driver Bill Clarke win a pub by learning to fly at his first attempt? Feel free to fly the theories in the pub when you get there.

## THE GIRLS OF HELL

**BROOME, WA**  Eva, Loris, Sally, Maud, Madge, Fiona-Gwenda, Trixie, Karen . . . no, not the Pearl Queens of Broome, but a sequence of cyclones – and that was just the 1970s. You can learn about the whole family of devastating sheilas (and a few chaps), as well as cyclone monitoring and the Aboriginal 'wheel of seasons', at the Bureau of

Meteorology on Gus Winckel St beside the airport. The free tour concludes with the release of a data-collection balloon into the upper atmosphere. **[Phone (08) 9192 1211 to book. Tours run weekdays, except public holidays, or visit www.broome.wa.gov.au/bom/]**

> If the surf (or your spirit) is flat, you can always join the circus in **Byron Bay (NSW)**. Trapeze training is offered daily, for $40 per two-hour session, at the Byron Bay Beach Resort on Bayshore Drive. Call 0417 073 668 and get swinging, or visit www. flytrapeze.com.au. Or, if your hunger is aerial, call 1300 888 938 and ask about kite-boarding (three-hour sessions weigh in at $250, maximum two people); you can also visit www.byronbaykiteboarding.com.

## JUST THE TICKET

**CHINCHILLA, Qld**    The first passenger to fly Qantas was an 84-year-old farmer named Alexander Kennedy. 'Be damned to the doubters,' the game geezer was heard to yell. Dressed in leather cap and goggles, Mr Kennedy boarded a mail run between Longreach and Cloncurry in 1922. A copy of his ticket is on display in the Chinchilla Museum. Looking at the ticket closely, you'll be gladdened to see how little has changed: part of the small print reads, 'the company hereby expressly stipulates and provides that it will not be responsible and shall be exempt from all liability'. **[Villiers St. Open Wed.–Sun. 9a.m.–4p.m. Entry $5/$3. Phone (07) 4662 7014]**

## SPLATDOWN

**ESPERANCE, WA**    At first, Roger Graham thought he'd hit a tree stump. He hopped off his tractor to check. What he found, lying in the soil, miles from the nearest civilisation, was a cylindrical air-conditioner. It turned out to belong to Skylab, the American space station that lost its battle with gravity in 1979 and fell piecemeal over the Nullarbor Plain. Other farmers, and space-junk fossickers, found fridges, lockers and oxygen tanks. Teaspoons and T-shirts were made to celebrate the shower.

More by luck than NASA knowhow, a fragment that weighed 77 tonnes landed in the Indian Ocean. When a member of the US State Department called by Esperance some months later, a Council warden issued him with a $400 fine for littering. **[Esperance Museum, cnr James and Dempster Sts. Open daily (except Christmas Day and Good Friday) 1.30p.m.–4.30p.m. Entry $4/$3/$1. Phone (08) 9071 1579]**

The Roulettes, the famous aerobatic squadron, are to be found in **Sale (Vic.)** – twice. The first is the life-size version that flies out of the RAAF base near town. The second is the mini-version, flown by the Sale Model Aeroplane Club. The model 'Roulette-ettes' can be seen most Sundays on the back Maffra Rd, in a paddock called Desailly Flats.

## SCENIC STRIP

**GERROA, NSW**   The view alone is worth the detour. But this is also where a man in goggles, in a plane not much bigger than your modern-day kitchen, took off from Seven Mile Beach heading for New Zealand. It was 1933 and Charles Kingsford-Smith was making the first commercial flight across the Tasman. Above the beach stands the Kingsford-Smith Memorial Lookout, where a three-quarter scale outline of the *Southern Cross*, his plane, is traced around the memorial. **[Cnr Crooked River Rd – the main coast road – and Headland Rd]**

## ETERNAL THERMALS

**MANILLA, NSW**   Mt Borah is recognised as one of the best launching pads in the world for paragliders and hang-gliders. Not only are the benevolent thermals God-given for the sport, but the summit offers a clear 'runway' on all four compass points. As proof of the perfect conditions, the world-record distance for a paraglider (a giddy 335 km) was achieved by local instructor Godfrey Wenness, from Mt Borah. Every February, the Big Sky Festival descends on the town to push the envelope even further. **[Call Godfrey Wenness on (02) 6785 6545 for paragliding details or visit the Manilla Sky Sailors at www.mss.org.au]**

In the western **Brisbane (Qld)** suburb of Moggill there is a firm that exports Spitfire aircraft to their land of birth, Britain, and elsewhere. Supermarine (don't let the name fool you) sell these slightly scaled-down flying machines as DIY kits for dogfight diehards around the world. **[388 Hawkesbury Rd. Phone (07) 3202 9619. This is a private factory. Alternatively, check out the babies on www.supermarineaircraft.com]**

## FRIGHTFULLY NICE FLIGHT

MELBOURNE, Vic.   Her nickname is the Gooney Bird. Her real name is DC-3 (Douglas Commercial Model 3) and this particular model was used by the RAAF during two wars, carrying A-list ambassadors, senators and chiefs of staff from one (war) theatre to the next. Martini in hand, you can be the next VIP on the Silver Clipper dinner flight: don your glad rags for a flight above the Melbourne foreshore at 800 m. The joy-ride lasts for 75 minutes; the joy itself, a fair bit longer. [Flights leave Essendon Airport most Saturdays, at a cost of $199 per person. Bookings at Shortstop Jet Charter on (03) 9379 9299, or visit www.shortstop.com.au]

## ON THE WRIGHT PATH

NOWRA HILL, NSW   Lawrence Hargrave was a brave so-and-so. All you need to do is see the flimsy canvas wings to appreciate his grit (or lunacy). Hargrave jumped off dunes in Stanwell Tops in the 1870s, leaving the ground for fathoms at a hop. His brinkmanship, years before the Wrights got their act together, advanced the cause of aviation in leaps and bounds. In the Museum of Flight a replica of the Icarus kit hangs beside one of Ansett's first planes – a Lockheed 10 – as well as an intervening link: the French engine responsible for Australia's first powered flight in 1910, by none other than escapologist, Harry Houdini. [At HMAS *Albatross*, south of Nowra. Open daily 10a.m.–4p.m. Entry $10/$7/$5, family $24. Phone (02) 4424 1920 or visit www.museum-of-flight.org.au]

## CHINESE TAKE OFF

**MERREDIN, WA**   Seems odd, a wheat town of 3000 people having two massive runways at the aerodrome. The paving was sponsored by China Southern Airlines, which operates a flying school out of the Merredin hangars. Currently the CSWAFC (or China Southern Western Australian Flying College) subjects some 70 Chinese nationals to 100 flying hours in featherweight German Grobs. Once they earn their wings, the pilots graduate to Jandakot Airport, south of Perth. **[No tour as such, but you'll find Merredin Airfield 7 km south of town, heading for Narembeen. Phone (08) 9041 3193 or visit www.cswafc.com.au]**

## AIRLYNE

**ROSE BAY, SYDNEY, NSW**   Few people realise that Sydney has three airports. Let's count them – Mascot, Bankstown and the ocean off Lyne Park, in Rose Bay. Once upon a time, back in 1938, flat-footed Catalinas would lift off the harbour en route for London, a ten-day journey, stopping for fuel (and nibbles) at airfields across the globe. A plaque down by a children's play-ship tells you more, while the charter seaplanes bobbing beside the jetty can help you relive the experience – although, instead of London they whisk you off to Palm Beach, Gosford or Newcastle. **[Parking in Vickery Ave off New South Head Rd. Take a look at www.sydneybyseaplane.com or seaplanesafaris. com.au for inspiration]**

## SAUCERY

**TULLY, Qld**   Arguably the first 'crop circle' observed on our planet was at Horseshoe Lagoon near Tully in 1966. George Pedley, a sober banana farmer, heard a hissing noise and next saw 'a blue-grey vapour-like saucer' lifting from the lagoon. After the UFO shot through, Pedley found a nest of flattened reeds, a perfect circle 9 m across. Other farmers confirmed the phenomenon and there have been independent UFO reports over the years. Indeed, in Tully an earthling can't move for bumping into an ET yarn. Sadly, Horseshoe Lagoon is out of bounds to the public, but keep your eyes peeled for low-flying cigars.

# APTONYMS

*(Being a glossary of people and places
with perfectly appropriate names)*

## SEEMLY

CESSNOCK, NSW   An obelisk outside a supermarket celebrates the discovery of coal at Greta Seam, back in 1886. Originally the obelisk stood at the seam itself, behind the hill on Vincent St, but local Rotarians opted to move the marker for more exposure – and, presumably, fewer rockfalls. And the supermarket? Coles, of course. **[Cnr Charlton Ave and Cooper Sts]**

## THE PENNY DROPS

HOBART, Tas.   On 1 April 1955, a Park-O-Meter was planted outside the Commercial Bank of Australia. For sixpence (roughly 5 cents) our country's first meter allowed you to occupy the space for half an hour. Nowadays the Commercial is the Commonwealth Bank, and the rate is 50 cents according to meter number 175, which roughly occupies its ancestor's space. As for the maiden meter's first customer in 1955, who else but the Lord Mayor of Hobart, Mr Park. **[81 Elizabeth St]**

At Vaucluse House, in **Vaucluse, Sydney (NSW)**, lies the earliest known headstone in Australia. The plot originally lay on George St, where the first Australian cemetery sputtered out, and dates back to 1788. The corpse in question was a boatswain's yeoman on the HMS *Sirius* named George Graves.

## DRIPS AND DREGS

LAKES ENTRANCE, Vic.   The earliest evidence of oil on mainland Australia was found on the shores of Lake Bunga, in 1924. A midget rig stands on the actual site, along with a diluted history of geosurveys, limestone crusts and something called 'gas ebullition'. In fact the mother lode was lurking offshore, some 20 km into Bass Strait. Explorations were probably cursed from the word go, however: one of the pioneering Bunga riggers was the son of a Ballarat miner, Keith Scarce. [About 3 km east of town, turn down Old Bunga Rd, not the adjoining road to Lake Bunga]

## ENCHANTED DELL

**OBERON, NSW**   This alpine . . . er . . . hamlet was named after a fairy in William Shakespeare's play *A Midsummer Night's Dream*, long before her townsfolk twigged that the surrounding soil is alive with mushrooms. From late January to early May, local pine plantations are pimpled with such fairy favourites as saffron milk caps and succulent bolets. The Cobweb Craft Shop in town (named after another *Midsummer* sprite) has an excellent mushroom guide for the puckish, sorry, peckish among you. [The shop is (02) 6336 1895 or try www. cobwebcraftshop.com.au]

Small wonder that **Coober Pedy (SA)** appeals as a film set (it's hosted such films as *Mad Max*, *Priscilla* and *Red Planet*). Coincidentally, the town's legendary mailman for more than 20 years, braving the arduous Birdsville Track every two weeks, was none other than Tom Kruse. See Tom's epic exploits in the film *The Bank of Beyond*, available at the tourist centre.

## MINNIE DISASTER

**WARRNAMBOOL, Vic.**   A young teacher lies in the Catholic section of Warrnambool Cemetery. Her headstone tells how she tried to save a young girl from drowning. Sadly, the girl, Minnie Deveraux, and her rescuer became tangled in a snag and drowned. The name of Minnie's would-be saviour was May Day. [Main entrance is on Otway St. Row 5, Grave 30]

# ODDITIONS

◎ A sign on Napier St in **Deniliquin (NSW)** advertises 'Short's Electrical Supplies'.

◎ In **Bathurst (NSW)**, the last roundabout before Charles Sturt University is called Brilliant St.

◎ What better names for gold towns – Lucknow (NSW) and Rushworth (Vic.)?

◎ Just west of Yass, along the Hume Hwy, speed cameras are a regular sight at **Bookham (NSW)**.

◎ William Orr was a foremost investor in the Mt Lyell mine, **Queenstown (Tas.)**. While the surveyor who opened the road from Queenstown to Strahan was none other than F.A. Cutten.

◎ **Warrnambool (Vic.)** is a fishing town. As a clue, the main drag is Liebig St.

◎ Wuruma Dam blocks the Nogo River, just northwest of **Eidsvold (Qld)**.

◎ **Rockhampton (Qld)**, which labels itself as the Beef Capital of the World, is crammed with bull statues. Upholding the theme, the Turnbulls run the Criterion Hotel, next-door to the office of the local paper, *The Bulletin*.

◎ In the tropical spirit of things, one of the main drags in **Kuranda (Qld)** is Thongon St.

◎ The glass pyramid on The Esplanade in **Perth (WA)** is loaded with cycads and fan palms. The conservatory pays homage to a long-standing town clerk – Allan Green. Pop inside and lose a litre of sweat between 10a.m. and 3p.m. any day.

◎ Twenty-four km from **Kempsey (NSW)**, the town responsible for the famed Akubra hat, is the promontory that Captain Cook named over a century before: Hat Head.

◎ The world's first beauty pageant involving bathing costumes took place on Maroubra Beach in **Sydney (NSW)**, back in 1920. The winner was a 14-year-old named Edith Pickup.

◎ An artery of **Manjimup (WA)**, a town that relies on logging for its lifeblood, is Chopping St.

◎ Yes, the law firm on Wharf St in **Forster (NSW)** specialises in personal injury claims, as you'd expect with a name like Stacks.

# ARTY

*(Being a palette of insane installations,
barmy busts and objets outrés)*

## A SAWREY STORY

**DALBY, Qld**   Bush artist Hugh Sawrey started life on a small farm at Kogan, a blip on the back road to Chinchilla. The story goes that his mum drove the 50 km to Dalby every week, back in the 1960s, selling eggs to make ends meet. When Dalby publican Mary Barry heard about this she offered Mrs Sawrey free bed and board each time she visited and Hugh decided to paint a canvas in gratitude. The rear lounge in which the magnificent gift, *Clancy on the Condamine*, hangs is the very room where Sawrey worked at his easel. 'Makes me laugh,' recalls Mary, the publican for 51 years. 'Hugh came back years later to fix the horse's ears, but I wouldn't let him.' See what *you* think of them. **[Commercial Hotel, Cunningham St]**

## LAURA AURA

**LAURA, Qld** – For information about Split Rock, a stunning art site 13 km north of town, go to the Ang-Gnarra Aboriginal Corporation Caravan Park. Split Rock sits above a steep ridge in the heart of Quinkan country. Quinkan is a spirit figure, a gangly magician with droopy earlobes who bobs up often in the rock gallery, along with the frumpish Anurra, a sorcerer with pretzel legs. No less eerie are the post-contact images of rifle-bearing white men. **[Ang-Gnarra is on the Peninsula Development Rd. Phone (07) 4060 3214. You need about two hours to meander the rock]**

## ALIEN LIFE FORM

**LYNDHURST, SA**   Dutchman Cornelius Alferink, aka Talc Alf, roamed the outback as a geologist's assistant and fell in love with talc and its potential as a sculpture medium. When Alf found the deposit at Mt Fitton in the northern Flinders Ranges, he stopped wandering. His open-air expo at the Talc Alpha Rink Republic Art Gallery is a lexicon of talcum letters: A is a phallus, and stands for Adam; the tipped-over B is a set of breasts and therefore woman – and Beautiful; C represents Child and Creation; D denotes Death, Doom and Destruction. $E = mc^2$, but that's another theory altogether. No less fascinating are Alf's other creations, among them a pedal-powered washing machine, and his mansion – a Nissen hut used on the A-bomb fields of Maralinga. **[Railway siding beside the Ghan railway line. Open daylight hours. Free entry]**

A surreal tribute to a century of **Newcastle (NSW)** steel hangs in the SwillnGrill of the Stag and Hunter Hotel, on the corner of Hanbury St and Maitland Rd in the suburb of Mayfield. The collage by Danielle Palmer, with its medley of smelter diagrams, BHP hardhat and toy helicopters, says more than 1000 words.

## WHOLE HAVEN

**NOWRA, NSW**   An estate called Open Country, in Murrumbeena, now a Melbourne suburb, was home for early members of the Boyd family – the illustrious dynasty of potters, painters, sculptors, writers and architects. In 1968, hungry for new open country, Arthur Boyd and his wife Yvonne pottered to the Shoalhaven River, where they found a beautiful property called Bundanon. It became their home, studio and rural retreat, which they eventually bequeathed to the nation: 'You can't own a landscape' was how AB put it. Bundanon is now a residence for artists, by scholarship or by invitation. This unique live-in workshop, with a massive art collection and 3-D landscape paintings anywhere you look, is open on Sundays. **[Bundanon Rd, off Illaroo Rd. Owing to such a narrow road, trustees suggest you arrive between 10.30a.m. and 1p.m., and leave between 1.30p.m. and 4p.m. Phone (02) 4423 0433 or try www. bundanon.com.au]**

## ROCK-STEADY HANDS

**PETERBOROUGH, SA**     More than 1700 hours went into making the Federation Quilt, a seamstress's snapshot of the region, which hangs in the Town Hall's foyer. By contrast, roughly 17 minutes went into the painting of Uluru that hangs beside the hall's stage and which eccentric Aussie entertainer Rolf Harris whipped up in 1992. Amazingly, the Rock shifts colour as you walk past the picture – just like the real McCoy out in the desert. **[Main St, next to council offices, not to be confused with the YMCA Hall. At weekends, ask at the Visitors Centre in the railway carriage. Phone (08) 8651 3566]**

## DEFENDANT DREAMING

**DARWIN, NT**     The Pintupi people of outback Australia existed for millennia without a police force. Instead they had The Law Enforcer, or Kadaitcha Man. This cosmic figure of multiple auras is depicted in a painting by Ronnie Tjampitjinpa that hangs outside Interview Room 2 in Darwin's Supreme Court. Nearby, outside Court 1, hangs a car door wrenched from a wreck in Utopia (NT), the duco decorated by Elsie Kemarre. Yet the brightest blast of hope lies in 700 000 pieces on the foyer floor – a galactic mosaic called Milky Way Dreaming, by Nora Napaltjari Nelson. **[State Square. Open weekdays 9a.m.–5p.m.]**

## NEEDFUL THINGS

**WALCHA, NSW**     Sculptor Stephen King's metal fountain Weather Signs was installed in McHattan Park in 1996. Its popularity galvanised the shire into strewing the town with other pieces, of which there are now 25, among them a giant orange chair, a sea monster, and a tallow-wood tuning fork. Grab a sculpture guide from the Visitors Centre in Fitzroy St, and make sure you stroll the river levee, as well as investigating all four entries into town. If you time your visit for winter, you'll see King's fountain become an ice sculpture. **[Phone (02) 6774 2460]**

## DOBELL PRIZES

**LAKE MACQUARIE, NSW**     Sir William Dobell, triple-winner of the Archibald Prize for portraiture (including for the controversial 'caricature' of poet Joshua Smith in 1937), lived on a peaceful finger of land,

called Wangi Wangi, poking into the lake. His original home is open
Sat. and Sun. 1p.m.–4p.m., or call (02) 4975 4115. But any day of
the week you can see his modest lakeside memorial at the bottom of
Dobell Place.

## ODDITIONS

◉ **West Wyalong (NSW)** is possibly the only town in Australia with a
dog-leg for its main street. Painter Russell Drysdale captured the
kink in 1949, taking the perspective from the corner of Monash and
Main Sts. The viewer's eye looks towards Meagher's Store – which
is now Target. In a fit of artistic licence, Drysdale preferred to omit
the road's tar surface, in place at the time.

◉ Painters such as Russell Drysdale and Brett Whiteley have captured
**Sofala (NSW)** on canvas. Noted artists such as John Olsen and
Donald Friend have found inspiration in the contours of nearby
Golden Gully. And the same town, allegedly Australia's oldest
surviving gold settlement, was dubbed 'Paris' in Peter Weir's first
major-release feature of 1974, *The Cars That Ate Paris*.

◉ Van Gogh would cough (with shock) if he had lived to see his sun-
flowers magnified to industrial size on Australia's biggest easel, in
**Emerald (Qld)**. You can live the still life in Morton Park, just near
the Visitors Centre.

◉ The rugger buggers of **Vincentia (NSW)** have a cultural streak. The
local football team, with a gory ear as logo, is the Vincentia Van
Goghs.

# BARKING

*(Being a pack of curious canines and one or two memorable maniacs)*

## WEE JOCK ROCKS

**BALLARAT, Vic.** To date, very few animals have received the Purple Cross, an award devised by the RSPCA to celebrate a creature's loyalty and heroism. One recipient is a Glen Innes kelpie called Boots, who ran a mile with news of his master's heart attack tucked into his collar. In Ballarat the super-pet was Wee Jock, a terrier who attended the Eureka Rebellion in 1854, when miners battled police and the military over hikes in licence fees. Wee Jock's master (The Pikeman, an Irish digger) copped a killing blow. Wee Jock guarded the body for hours, until the death cart came. **[The statue stands outside the Eureka Centre in Eureka St, cnr Rodier St. Phone (03) 5333 1854 or visit www.eurekaballarat.com]**

## LIVING ON THE SHEEP'S BACK

**CASTERTON, Vic.** Not just a statue, the kelpie of Casterton warrants his own heritage trail, with multiple statues along the way (and more than a few websites). Destined to be the future darling of Aussie farmers, the breed allegedly began in the late 1860s when Irish stockman Jack Gleeson swapped a horse for the offspring of farmer George Robertson's black-and-tan dog, which he had seen perform miracles with a flock of sheep. The breed went on to kick serious woollen butt in the first sheepdog trials of 1872. **[Outside the Town Hall. There's a kelpie festival each June. Warrock homestead, Robertson's property, 31 km north, tells more. Open daily 10a.m.–5p.m. Entry $6/$2. Phone (03) 5582 4222 or visit www.kelpies-casterton.org]**

## SEE RED DOG RUN

**DAMPIER, WA**   Red Dog embodies the spirit of every restless male. Born in Paraburdoo (WA), the result of a kelpie–heeler consummation, the mutt's real name was Tally Ho. When his owners moved to Dampier, Tally became known as Red Dog, a vagrant of the first degree. He learnt how to catch the Hamersley Iron work-bus. He rode on ore trains, fathered several mongrels and cadged meals from back doors. Once, a family took Red Dog to Perth for a holiday and lost him on the beach. Anguished, they drove the 1500 km back to Dampier, only to find the dog had arrived before them. There are plenty more yarns documented in *Red Dog – The Pilbara Wanderer* by Beverley Duckett. Even Louis de Bernieres, of *Captain Corelli* fame, wrote a book on this offbeat Aussie pooch. The bronze statue of Red Dog, gazing out at the roadside from the town's information bay, was erected after his death in 1979.

## HAMMER AND FARCICAL

**KATHERINE, NT**   Germorgen Sergeef was a virtuoso violinist as well as a keen astronomer. In 1929 neither activity was paying too well, so the former Cossack took up peanut farming in Katherine. The story goes that he became more and more obsessed with sputniks, and with the possibility of enemy agents trying to poison his food. Thus the man known as The Galloper limited himself to tinned sardines. Afterwards he cleaned the cans and hung them on strings as a kind of mobile planetarium, which is displayed in the Skillion Building at Katherine Outback Heritage Museum. One feature of this firmament is the image of a god-like being, which Sergeef found in an old magazine – Elvis Aaron Presley. [Gorge Rd, opposite hospital. Open Sat. 10a.m.–1p.m., Sun. 2p.m.–5p.m., weekdays 10a.m.–4p.m. Mar.–Oct., or 10a.m.–1p.m. other months. Entry $3.50. Phone (08) 8972 3945]

A hokey legend surrounds Dog Rock on Middleton Road in **Albany (WA)**, where a spaniel speared by Noongar Aborigines is said to have been transmogrified overnight into a granite boulder (see the rock and you'll see why the legend has legs.). However it got there, this mystical dog head is a fetching sight.

## THE QUICK AND THE DEAD

**KEW, MELBOURNE, Vic.**   A skinny metal greyhound lies on the grave of Thomas Serrell in Kew (Boroondara) Cemetery. One story has it that the real dog maintained a devoted vigil here, starving on the spot, and so was given his place in perpetuity by Serrell's admiring next-of-kin. According to another theory, the loyal hound died before his master. Whatever the case, the dog's nose has become a bit like the toe of the St Peter statue in St Peter's Church in Rome, with all manner of visitors rubbing the protuberance for luck. **[High St]**

## BIG BLUE

**MUSWELLBROOK, NSW**   The situation is best described as a dog's breakfast. Two towns claim to be the historic home of the blue heeler, and essentially both are right – and wrong. Thomas Hall began the breed back in the 1840s, on a property called Dartbrook, 12 km north of Muswellbrook (or a few km south of Aberdeen, depending where your loyalty lies), when he mated a dingo with a 'blue merle' British cattle dog. The outcome was the 'bluey' we know today, a hardy, efficient drover and a recognised breed in its own right. But where did the union occur? In Muswellbrook, or in Aberdeen a bit further north (as claimed by Aberdonians)? At this stage Muswell-brook could be said to be winning the dogfight, with a bronze of bluey on Bridge St.

The Dog's Refuge boarding kennels border Australia's first pet cemetery, a hectare of marble tablets in **Shenton Park, Perth (WA)**. The first loyal customer was buried as far back as 1935. **[Lemnos Rd. Open daily 11a.m.–4p.m. Phone (08) 9381 8166]**

# ODDITIONS

Some notable dog statues:

⑤ Outside E Shed in **Fremantle's (WA)** docklands is a wide-eyed new immigrant with suitcase and model ship coming face to face with the Australian reception committee – a dingo/heeler cross in the pounce position.

◎ Rabid mongrels once guarded the isthmus of **Eaglehawk Neck (Tas.)** against Port Arthur escapees. Back in 1832, dogs were also stationed as sentries on platforms offshore, just in case the runaways swam. Now the same isthmus is occupied by a bronze cur no less fearsome.

◎ A bronze kelpie stands in mustering pose in **Ardlethan (NSW)**, the breed's contested birthplace. (See Casterton entry in this section.)

◎ Another brazen kelpie stares daggers at two merinos outside the Town Hall in **Hallet (SA)**.

◎ The giant wooden dog guarding Fairfield station in **Melbourne (Vic.)** originally barked at passing trains, a hidden sensor setting off a woof-woof recording in his chest. Now debarked, the Mutt of Troy seems as happy eyeballing commuters. **[Cnr Station and Wingrove Sts]**

◎ A swagman and his bronze heeler are cooling their heels outside the Council Chambers in **Linton (Vic.)**.

# BRIDGES

*(Being a crisscross of bridges old, odd and otherwise)*

## UNDERBELLY

**BENDIGO, Vic.**   In Rosalind Park (named after the cross-dresser in *As You Like It*), you'll find a stormwater channel that would seem to warrant a second glance. Clamber down if your knees allow it. The subway is not just a skateboard mecca, but the underbelly of Australia's widest bridge. Early Bendigo was low-lying and flood-prone, obliging settlers to cover the creek with 100 m of stonework. Modern history, on the other hand, tells us that *GABI LUVS SPIDER*. **[On Pall Mall, close to Queen Victoria's statue]**

## TALE OF TWO BRIDGES

**DARLINGTON POINT, NSW**   In 1905, the first bridge to cross the Murrumbidgee River near Griffith was a bascule, a counterweighted drawbridge that lifted when a steamboat needed to pass. Council engineers replaced the rarity with a concrete job in 1979, leaving the old scaffold to rust on the riverbank. Ten years later, Professor Ron Fraser from the University of NSW passed by. He took a shine to the ironwork and allocated semester time to reviving the bridge. A majestic reconstructed section is mounted in the Darlington Point Riverside Caravan Park – a redundant gateway across an absent river. **[Park is on the Griffith side, about 30 km south of that city]**

## UNFATHOMABLE

**HOME HILL, Qld**   Driving north, you'll cross the marvel that is the Burdekin Bridge, known as the 'Silver Link' by locals. In length alone it pips the Sydney Harbour Bridge by roughly 500 m, but in depth it beats any bridge in the world. When chief engineer H.A. Lowe sank piers into the riverbed in 1948, he couldn't find a bottom: below the sand was more sand and so on, *ad infinitum*. Ten years later, and at a cost of $6 million, the aborted piers were replaced by a series of caissons (pontoons), making the Silver Link one of the biggest floating bridges in the world. [There's a walkway on the eastern edge. Take a look at the swamped alternative downstream. There's more information at the diorama near the bridge]

## IDERAWAY HIDEAWAY

IDERAWAY, Qld   An orchard patch northwest of Gayndah, Ideraway doesn't get much passing traffic. No doubt you'll double the annual mean if you pay a visit to its remarkable bridge. Technically, the bridge is listed by architectural historians as a 'steel/timber deck-type with pin-jointed fishbelly trusses', but the good folk of Ideraway prefer to call it 'The Upside-Down Bridge'. Built in 1902, the 45-m span is all belly and no crest. Unlike your average bridge, the supporting scaffold dangles in the gully below, giving you the impression that the whole thing has capsized. Luckily the goods train from Monto, which presently comes through once a week, doesn't seem fazed by this. [From Gayndah, head for Mundubbera, turning right after 7 km. Next turn right at the big silos, then left across the railway tracks. The bridge is lurking 400 m to your right down Mingo St]

Tom Ugly's Bridge spans the Georges River in **Sydney (NSW)**, linking Blakehurst and the suburb of Sylvania. Though if the Roads and Traffic Authority had its way, the bridge would be known as something more genteel. No way, say locals: Tom may be Ugly but he's our Tom. Curiously, the name is thought to derive from an early resident called Tom Huxley, a name that Aboriginal tongues struggled to pronounce. (Then again, Theory 2 concerns a one-armed, one-legged chap the natives knew as Tom Wogul, meaning One.)

## MEGA-MECCANO

LAKES ENTRANCE, Vic.   'Historic Trestle Bridge' is the sign you'll see 20 km east of Lakes Entrance, heading for Orbost. But that's akin to calling the Sydney Opera House a Notable Cultural Centre. Stony Creek Trestle Bridge is guaranteed to wow. Built in 1916, the bridge is a massive grey-box and ironbark web nearly 20 m high and more than 250 m long. Trains used to run along it, except in 1964 when one fell off. Bushfires in 1980 almost razed the woodwork, but the boggy ground saved the timber from burning. Fewer bums on train seats spelt the bridge's doom in 1988. Cyclone fencing prevents you from walking across the old sleepers, but you can walk below and crick your neck. **[For those interested in having a good look at some nearby bushland, a 3-km dirt road runs through state forest north of the highway]**

## SALUTING PRIVATE JONES

**MT MORGAN, Qld**    Victor Jones, a paymaster at the local goldmine, was the first Australian to be killed in the Boer War of 1899–1902. Jones passed over to the Other Side in 1900 via a fatal wound. A century later, in the soldier's honour, sappers strung a remarkable suspension bridge across the River Dee. The tribute sways at the end of East St, beside a weatherboard hall named Footbridge Corner. The hall hosts anything from Emotions Anonymous to the local chess club. The adjacent bridge could carry that load and more. **[Entering from Rockhampton, turn left after crossing the Dee]**

## SWAN PRODUCTION

**NORTHAM, WA**    The longest suspension footbridge in Australia hangs across the Avon River. The wobbly wonder has a 117-m span and can supposedly support 400 people if they are adequately spaced out (geometrically, not hallucinogenically, speaking). From the bridge you can see wild white swans, a rarity Down Under. Black swans occur in many WA pockets, including the Swan River, but the white version (the original cob and pen hailed from England in 1896) only seems content in Northam and is now protected. Cygnet production has dwindled lately, and a special breeding compound has been established upriver, with graceful studs imported from a Melbourne golf course. **[Bridge is behind Visitors Centre on Minson Ave. The swans are fed daily at another bridge, near Newcastle St. Breeding pond cnr Heaton Ave and Peel Pde]**

Westgate Bridge in **Melbourne (Vic.)** is the biggest cable-stayed girder bridge in the world, admittedly a pretty technical category. Yet in 1970 the bridge made headlines for darker reasons. A park on the Yarra's west bank, below the bridge, pays tribute to the 35 riggers and engineers killed when Span 10–11 fell into the drink. The toll doesn't include a bloke like Des Gibson, who survived the fall, only to die from his fourth stress-related heart attack, aged 32. **[Cnr Hyde St and Douglas Pde]**

## HIS COMICAL EMINENCE

**ROSS, Tas.**   Convict mason Daniel Herbert, with his ex-burglar foreman James Colbeck, crafted Australia's oldest bridge (1836). They took the opportunity to sculpt Celtic gods, plus a local publican, into the bridge's stones. Eventually the men won a pardon from the governor of the day, George Arthur. Not that they showed much gratitude: the drunken face staring from the arch furthest from town, on the right-hand side, is a caricature of Arthur himself, though it's said His Eminence never realised the parody.

## SWING MUSIC

**SALE, Vic.**   The father of composer and pianist Percy Grainger was also nimble with his hands. In 1883, John Grainger built the state's first movable bridge, an elegant scaffold that pivots on a central turntable, much like a vinyl recording on a phonograph. Back then, Sale was a prosperous port, receiving steamboats via the massive lake system. The Latrobe River proved a navigational headache, however, for which the treatment was a hand-dug extension from McArdell's Gap – known as Sale Canal. Silting and disuse condemned Mr Grainger's swinger to relic status for many years until loving restoration began in 2003. **[Head out to Yarram, 5 km along the South Gippsland Hwy]**

## GETTING THE POINT

**SWANSEA, Tas.**   A canny farmer called Shaw seized his chance back in the 1840s. For years the Progress Society had been lobbying for a bridge across an uneven gully in the Rocky Hills district, but the local superintendent, Major de Gillen, kept knocking back the proposal. One night Shaw chauffeured the major home after a civic meeting, driving the cart full-bore through the offending spot and taking special care to ride over the biggest bumps he could see. In the end, the deep-set bruises on his viceregal buttocks encouraged de Gillen to see reason. By 1844, a gang of convict workers had built the echidna-like Spiky Bridge. **[4 km south of Swansea, opposite Spiky Beach]**

Built in 1892, Pyrmont Bridge at Darling Harbour in **Sydney (NSW)** is one of the first electric swing-span bridges in the world. Amazingly the mechanism relied on juice from the Ultimo Powerhouse (now the Powerhouse Museum) years before Sydney's streets had electricity. You can usually see the marvel pivot on weekends and public holidays at 10.30a.m., noon, and 1, 2 and 3p.m.

# ODDITIONS

⊚ The Giblett brothers, Hubert and Walter, used axes and axemen's nous to land a giant karri tree clean across the Donnelly River in 1904, so creating One-Tree Bridge, 22 km west of **Manjimup (WA)**. The original log has perished, but a reconstructed tribute remains.

⊚ When pre-cast pre-stressed concrete was all the rage, around 1964, the Gladesville Bridge in **Sydney (NSW)** was the longest concrete arch in either hemisphere. The mantle was eventually stolen in 1980 by the Krk Bridge in Croatia.

⊚ The original McKillops Bridge west of **Tubbut (Vic.)** was destroyed by the Snowy River in full flood back in 1934, a scary thought when you see the 250-m-long sequel, poised 18 m above the gorge.

◉ Kirwans Bridge in **Nagambie (Vic.)** is a clinker-built boomerang of 313 m, which needs crossing in order to be believed. The deck was laid in 1896 and now, thanks to termites and fatigue, it can't bear the weight of the local school bus.

◉ Montezuma footbridge is a steel suspension bridge near **Renison Bell (Tas.)**. It crosses over rainforest, cheek-to-cheek with Tasmania's highest waterfall.

◉ Batman's Bridge in **Sidmouth (Tas.)** is one of the world's first cabled truss bridges. Note the majority of strain is borne by the Tamar's firmer west bank.

# BRRR

*(Being a floe of freezing follies and icy idiocies)*

## SLIP, SLOP, SLIDE

**THEBARTON, ADELAIDE, SA**   In the height of summer, Adelaide can be a kiln. One way to shrug off the heat is to zip up the parka, pack the skates and head for the Ice Arena – even though in this state sub-zero temperatures are rarer than snowballs in Hell. **[23 East Tce. Open daily Mon.–Fri. 10a.m.–4p.m., Wed. 7a.m.–9.30p.m., Sat. and Sun. 12.30p.m.–4p.m. Entry fee of $12.50 includes skate hire. Phone (08) 8352 7977]**

## GET THE DRIFT

**ALBURY, NSW**   In the summer of 2001, Tammy van Wisse braved bees, snakes, logs, rips and snags to swim the Murray – all 2438 km from alpine Corryong (Vic.) to estuarine Goolwa (SA). To sample her feat the lazy way, you can borrow the surge below Hume Weir to drift into Albury. The epic drift begins at Waterworks Bridge, opposite the airport on the Riverina Hwy. Life jackets are advisable, and inner tubes luxurious. Follow the current – if it's not *too* freezing – to the former corroboree grounds of Mungabareena Reserve. If your body allows, keep going around Doctor's Point, under the Hume Hwy, and onto the sands of Noreuil Park, some 5 km away. This summer pastime is pretty much a secret known only to locals – until now.

## FLYING DOCTOR'S FLUE

**ALICE SPRINGS, NT**   Before fridges were invented, Australians relied on a box covered with damp hessian, known as a Coolgardie safe. (Trivia note: the safe was not invented in Coolgardie, but by a bloke in Ballarat who apparently felt the name Coolgardie sounded cool.) Back in Alice Springs, flying doctor John Flynn applied the same cool principle to Adelaide House, central Australia's maiden hospital: below the wards is a tunnel draped in wet sacks that filter and cool all incoming air. Flues in each room are disguised as side-tables, while the 'dampening hatch' is in the tea-room. A cut-out diorama in the stairwell shows how the hospital became so hospitable. **[Todd Mall. Usually open Mon.–Fri. 10a.m.–4p.m., Sat. 10a.m.–noon. Entry $4/$3.** Phone (08) 8952 1856]

Market gardener Ah You grew weary of the heat. So he sliced a dozen kerosene cans into diamonds, and used fencing wire to construct a harlequin-pattern mesh cloak to screen his shanty from the brunt of the rays. The cool innovation now dangles upstairs at the **Barcaldine (Qld)** Historical Museum. **[Cnr Beech and Gidyea Sts. Open daily 7a.m.–5p.m. Entry $3.** Phone (07) 4651 1724]

## KNOCK, KNOCK

**GUNDAGAI, NSW**   Who the hell was knocking on the door of the cafe at midnight? 'You're too late, mate!' shouted Jack Castrisson, the owner, through the glass. 'We're shut.' The visitor looked familiar. He wore round spectacles. 'I'm hungry,' said the caller, 'and I'm freezing. Can you do anything to help?' Strewth, it was the Prime Minister, John Curtin, realised Jack. This was 1942. War was on, and here was the PM wanting a cup of tea. Jack opened up. In came Curtin, as well as former PM Artie Fadden, and future PM Ben Chifley, who tucked into T-bones and eggs in the kitchen. Tea was scarce, thanks to war rationing, and in gratitude Chifley pledged to up the Niagara Cafe's quota. The faces of other famous diners beam above the booths, including the knightly trio of Sir Robert Menzies, Sir Donald Bradman and Sir Charles Kingsford-Smith. **[Sheridan St. Open daily.** Phone (02) 6944 1109]

## CABBAGE PATCH

**HOBART, Tas.**   No matter what the weather is like outside, you will need a polar-fleece to inspect the Sub-Antarctic Plant House. Constant mist and a blast to mimic the polar winds keep the temperature flirting with zero, which is just how the cushion plants like it. Ducts in the ceiling seep a desirable drizzle, keeping the room's humidity to 98 per cent.

Despite being 1500 km from home, the Macquarie Island cabbage is thriving (whalers used to eat the leaves for Vitamin C). There's a polar panorama to make the hairy rushes and helmet orchids feel even more comfy, but watch out for the buzzy – a cunning little burr that can spot an explorer's sock from 50 m, so they say. The house is the only one of its kind in the world, and the liverworts love it. **[Royal Tas. Botanical Gardens, Queens Domain. Gardens open daily from 8a.m., closing at 5p.m. in winter months, and later when warmer. Admission free. Phone (03) 6236 3050]**

## ESK ESKY

**AVOCA, Tas.**    Senior Constable Terry Crichton works in a 'coolroom that isn't so bloody cool in summer'. The original cop shop, down by the Esk River, got torched by 'certain parties from the neighbourhood' in 1991. Ever since then, the lone Avoca lawman has relied on a corrugated demountable, much like a shipping container with a chequered blue stripe to signify authority. But you have to knock before entering – Terry will need to shunt the desk sideways to let you in. **[You can't miss this icebox, on the western edge of town]**

Every midwinter (usually in late June), knit-wits rule the streets of **Alice Springs (NT)**. The Beanie Festival has been growing since 1996, taking to new creative heights the hallowed head-gear traditionally favoured by ferals, surfies and footy fans. If you're lucky, women from the Ngaanyatjarra Pitjantjtjara Yankunytjatjara Women's Council will show you how to knit kangaroo paws (the plant) into your creation. Check out the 'purlers' on www.beaniefest.org or mingle among the artisans when the weather takes a turn for the fresh.

## PARAFFIN RISING

**MAPLETON, Qld**    Jackie Stilla is the daughter of a thermometer maker. Eric Mitchell, her dad, launched this curious career in Melbourne after

World War 2. They moved to the Qld hinterland in 1977, bringing the mercury and glass-blowing kit along. Did I say mercury? That's in fact a myth, I discovered – most thermometers hold dyed paraffin, not mercury. While the factory floor is off-limits, at least you can say you've visited Australia's only thermometer plant – a sleepy farm in Queensland. **[Technitherm, 26 Delicia Rd, off Obi Obi Rd. Open weekdays 8.30a.m.–4p.m. Entry free.** Phone (07) 5445 7175]

## REVERSE SHRINKAGE

**BONDI, SYDNEY, NSW** In summer, lifesavers save lives; in winter, they get restless. So back in 1929 a bloke called Snow Stewart started up the Icebergs Club, an association of masochists who met each week to swim the winter's cobwebs away at the Bogey Hole, at the southern end of Bondi. Handicap races spiced the meet, as did belly-flop tournaments and lobster quests. A splinter group, the Coogee Penguins, came and went, but the Icebergs have remained rock-solid and now they warm up afterwards in the revamped clubhouse located in the four-storey palace that ad-man John Singleton funded in 2002. For all the mod cons and lobster mornays, the club still initiates new swim members by hurling them into the water in full clothing, in full-on winter. **[1 Notts Ave. Entry to the cool eight-lane pool is $4/$3.60. The building is also national HQ to the Surf Lifesaving Association. Phone (02) 9130 3120 or dive into www.icebergs.com.au]**

## DEVONIAN TEAS AVAILABLE

**YANKALILLA, SA** Between Yankalilla and Victor Harbor is one of the largest glacial boulders in the world. Though don't get your hopes up. As ancient rocks go, Selwyn's Rock is fairly plain to the lay eye – but geologists go ape over the Cambrian Kanmantoo quartzite, unquote. The slab is a nudge over 500 million years old. **[Open daily. Free access. Iceberg lettuce available at Glacier Rock Restaurant. Phone (08) 8558 8202]**

# ODDITIONS

◎ Crystal Trout Caravan Park, on the New England Hwy in **Guyra (NSW)**, claims to be the highest van park in Australia. At 1320 m above sea level, the accommodation is undoubtedly top-of-the-range.

◎ **Stanthorpe (Qld)** is one of the few towns in that state where you can see snow. At 915 m above sea level, this fruit and veg centre celebrates the big chill each winter with the Brass Monkey Festival. Part of the fun is a running bet called How Low Will You Go?, where punters can lodge a wager on the overnight temperature.

◎ With a yearly average temperature of 7–8°C, **Cabramurra (NSW)** is the dry continent's coldest town (outside seasonal resorts and chairlift villages). Drop by the post office and you can get a special postal stamp for your correspondence to confirm your altitude.

# CLASHES

*(Being a melee of stirring strikes, rousing rumbles
and unusual uprisings)*

## DIGGERS IN BATTLE

BRANXTON, NSW   In 1929, a workplace dispute at the Rothbury Colliery turned into a year-long strike, described by one modern unionist as 'the bloodiest clash in the industrial history of Australia'. The *annus horribilis* was known as the North Coal Lockout, with hundreds of miners on the outer, and scabs in the same number agreeing to keep working the seam. The worst clash was in December, when mounted police confronted the strikers: one miner was killed and there were dozens of serious injuries on both sides. **[A coal-black plaque marks the site, cnr Main Rd and Reid St, as you head towards Cessnock]**

## FLOOR SHOW

BRISBANE, Qld   Merle Thornton and Rosalie Bognor marched into the Regatta Hotel on a hot Wednesday afternoon in March 1965. They asked for beers and were refused: in those days, women were banished to 'ladies lounges' (also known, by some boors, as sow pens), where men couldn't stray unless accompanied. In protest, Merle and Rosalie shackled themselves to the bar's footrail while their husbands issued anti-discrimination pamphlets. The police appeared, bolt-cutters in hand, and the 'two female persons' were escorted off the premises. Liberated actor Sigrid Thornton believes her mother played a major part in the sea change that led to unisex boozing. **[The footrail persists at 543 Coronation Dve, close to the radical hotbed of Queensland University. Phone (07) 3871 9595]**

## MANN AMONG MEN

COCKBURN, SA   For a while there in Broken Hill, more miners were threatened by police truncheons than by pit collapses. In 1892 two dozen police, bayonets raised, burst into the Theatre Royal Hotel to arrest the leaders of the miners' Labour Defence Committee. Banned from speaking, red-blooded 'disruptionist' Englishman Tom Mann accordingly assembled his 3000 fellow strikers and proceeded into the Flinders Ranges of SA, some 50 km west, choosing Coburn Hotel for his tub-thumping. **[Phone (08) 8091 1634 to strike up a chat at the pub]**

## SURFACE TENSION

**KALGOORLIE, WA**    Back in 1934, the various ethnic groups of Kalgoorlie were living a few bars short of harmony. So when a fireman named George Jordan died as a result of a brawl with hotel barman Claudio Mattaboni, violence erupted and mobs descended on the 'wog end of town' as the vernacular of the day went. Three buildings were torched (at least ensuring work for Jordan's old colleagues) and the Home from Home Hotel – now Hannans – was trashed. When fire brigades arrived, they used their hoses as water cannons to repel the crowd. As for the All Nations boarding house, where the Midas Motel now stands, the original building might have been saved if rioters had not axed the hose. **[Read more in Hannans at 400 Hannan St, or across the road at Amalfis, once the Italian enclave known as the Kalgoorlie Wine Saloon]**

## OYL OVER TROUBLED WATERS

**LEURA, NSW**    Boofhead was a comic-strip that ran in Sydney's *Daily Mirror* during the 1940s and 50s. And that's where the dill should stay, think many of the Leura locals obliged to consider a 4.5-m statue of the idiotic hero, along with Olive Oyl of Popeye fame. The giant figurines occupy one of the most spectacular clifftop blocks in the Blue Mountains, erected by landowner Clive Evatt in 1992. The barrister denies he installed the loony icons to annoy residents after serial complaints plagued orchestral performances on the block. Nor is it a dig, he says, at the local council for ludicrously declining an offer of the land as a gift back in 1984. The wind-gauge on Boofhead's head, much like a propeller cap, is to keep the dill guano-free. **[Cnr Olympian Pde and Balmoral Rd. A $2 turnstile allows you nearer the view, though Boof and Olive are visible from the street]**

## A RED-LETTER DAY

**PORT HEDLAND, WA**   Although they helped develop the vast pastoral industry of the northwest, Aboriginal station hands were treated as little more than vassals. Their pay was poor, as were their living and working conditions, and they were subject to strict curfews. In 1942, the year Japan bombed Darwin, a white campaigner for Aboriginal rights, Don McLeod, persuaded jackeroo Dooley Bin Bin and his mates to strike. Clancy McKenna, a friend of Bin Bin's, cycled around the Pilbara to issue calendars with the strike day circled in red. When push came to shove, strikers were placed in neck-chains and taken to jail. On the first of May in 1946, 800 black station workers walked off the job and gathered outside Port Hedland where the Tjalka Warra community is now based. The bosses caved in and the New Deal, where the land is leased rather than owned by white pastoralists, still holds good today. **[See the heroes' cast-iron silhouettes in a park on the cnr Wedge and Anderson Sts]**

## SEEDS OF DISCONTENT

**TORRUMBARRY, Vic.**   A tomato nearly stopped Torrumbarry Weir from being built. Back in 1919, two waiters on the Murray River site started hurling tomatoes at each other. A chef intervened, and in turn got pelted. You'll find a red-splattered specimen commemorating the melée (known locally as the Great Tomato War of Torrumbarry) in the riverside interpretative centre. This eclectic exhibit also features Yorta Yorta creation stories, and glam-shots of the Miss Torrumbarry Lock Beauty Pageant. **[20 km west of Echuca. The weir turnoff is past Torrumbarry township]**

## FOOTY FEVER

**WALLANGARRA, Qld**   Every year, when the State of Origin rugby series dominates the airwaves, the town of Wallangarra is even more divided than usual. Poised on the border with NSW, this Qld town has a ludicrous stand-off with its adjoining town, Jennings, in NSW. But the publican of the Wallangarra pub is a passionate NSW fan while Terry Holzwart, owner of the Jennings equivalent, is mad for the more northerly Maroons. Each fills his hotel with treasonous balloons – the wrong colour in the wrong state – and they have been known to scowl at each other across the painted borderline on Wallangarra's railway station. (In some strange twist of fate, Jennings is the only town in NSW to possess a Queensland postcode – 4383)

## LOADED TO THE EYEBALLS

**WELLINGTON, NSW**    The Lion of Waterloo, claimed to be the oldest pub building in Australia, was serving grog in 1854, just like any other year, when a scuffle erupted between Dr Samuel Curtis and magistrate B. Sheridan. The two adjourned across the road, close to the one-time ferry crossing, for Australia's last-recorded pistol duel. Neither man was hurt: it seems that the shots served up at the Lion had far more impact. **[Plaque to be found in Teamsters Park, a jay-walk from the Lion]**

## KILLER PUNCH

**YOUNG, NSW**    Lambing Flat represents no proud chapter of Australian history. In 1861 a band of Young (and not so young) locals launched an attack on Chinese miners. Scores were wounded on both sides, but the lone fatality was a bystander, William Lupton. A Punch-and-Judy puppeteer with a visiting circus, Lupton was simply in the wrong place at the wrong time. On Gordon St, above the battlefield, there's a simple park bench known as Lupton's Lookout. Down the hill, at the Young Museum, you can see the bellicose banner ('No Chinese, Roll Up, Roll Up') used in the skirmish. **[Campbell St, at the Wagga exit. Open daily 10a.m.–4p.m. Phone (02) 6382 2248]**

# CLAUSTRO

*(Being a shoebox of tight squeezes)*

## NO SHOUTING, PLEASE

BEVERIDGE, Vic.   Imagine a pub so small that you need to slide away the television set on its retractable perch if you want to play darts. The Beveridge Tavern, built in 1840, boasts a dozen seats, including a pew for the drinking faithful. Mein host Ian Rankin, no relation to the Scottish thriller writer, takes pride in his room-warm Guinness, his horse brasses, his stuffed boar, the giant hare mounted on the wall (it's actually a kangaroo), and the stirrup cup of mead he distributes at the seasonal fox-hunt. [Take the Beveridge turnoff from the Hume Hwy. Follow the blue 'Historic Pub' signs up the hill. Phone (03) 9745 2363]

## 'TWAS THE NIGHT BEFORE CHRISTMAS

DARWIN, NT   A sign on the door of 'The Black Room' warns survivors of Cyclone Tracy that the sound effects inside may reawaken nightmares. Tracy was savage, killing 62 Darwinians and demolishing nine out of 10 houses. Eerily the sound effects bring the horrors back to life. It isn't just wind or rain or hail, but also the sound of a thousand sheets of corrugated iron and other bits of domestic detritus dragging along bitumen in excess of 200 kph. Father Ted Collins taped the cacophony on that fateful Christmas Eve – hence the carol occasionally audible during the recording. [Museum and Art Gallery of the Northern Territory, Conacher St. Open Mon.–Fri. 9a.m.–5p.m., weekends and public holidays 10a.m.–5p.m. Admission free. Phone (08) 8999 8201]

## BEST CELLARS

GREAT WESTERN, Vic.   A thousand wines are stored along the 2.5 km of tunnels beneath this Seppelt vineyard. The winery hired a crew of gold-miners to gouge the first tunnel (or drive) in 1868. A few years later a leaky barrel caused an outbreak of the black mould that now dangles from every ceiling, making the cellars resemble the inside of a gargantuan vacuum cleaner. A million-plus bottles lurk in the catacombs, including ex-PM Malcolm Fraser's own cellar in the elite Brandy Room. [Open daily 10a.m.–5p.m. Cellar tours Mon.–Sat. (and Sun. during holidays) at 10.30a.m., 1.30p.m. and 3p.m. for $7.50/$3. Phone (03) 5361 2239 or visit www.seppelt.com.au]

Chubby managers need not apply to the bank in **Shackleton (WA)**, between Quairading and Bruce Rock. The branch measures only 3×4 m, with an impossible two rooms within. Best avoid that extra slice of cheesecake if you're planning to visit. [**Open Fridays 3p.m.–4.30p.m.**]

## DOWN THE GURGLER
**MT GAMBIER, SA**   Well-shafts are not for the phobic. The same applies to elevators built *within* well-shafts . . . And if that's not bad enough, the lift's only stopping point is a cement tunnel with disco-neon strips fixed to the wall. The tour of the Blue Lake's underground aquifer is a great way to have a close encounter with the unique crater lake. In summer, Blue Lake lives up to its name, turning a deep azure as sunlight reflects in the calcite crystals produced in response to the warmth of the water. (In winter, the water reverts to steel-grey.) But down below, only midget trout and tortoises can survive the food-poor clarity. [John Watson Dve, on the city side of crater. Tour prices $6/$3. For tour times phone (08) 8723 1199 or visit www.aquifertours.com]

## EXIT STAGE RIGHT
**MARIAN, Qld**   Despite the fact that there's a 'Melba House' in this small sugar town, Dame Nellie herself (née Helen Porter Mitchell, then Armstrong during her marriage to a Marian mill manager) wasn't here for long. Being a Melbourne girl, perhaps she was put off by the facts of tropical life, such as leeches, toilet frogs, bedside snakes and mildewed pianos. Her son George was born here in 1883, but Nellie lasted less than a year. Before the end of the decade she had embarked on her stage career in Europe. [**Eungella Rd, open daily 9a.m.–3p.m.** Free entry. Phone (07) 4954 4299]

## CRUISE CONTROL

**TOWNSVILLE, Qld**   In classical Greek stories, Pandora's box contained all the evils in the world plus a left-over scrap of hope. In true sea stories, 'Pandora's box' was a jerry-built cell that contained 14 mutineers from *The Bounty* (who had no hope at all). HMS *Pandora* was a British frigate carrying Captain Bligh's rebel crew members back to England for trial. In August 1791, after five months at sea, the ship ran aground on the Great Barrier Reef and sank off Cape York, and several of the prisoners drowned. 'Ten minutes of Hell', the life-size display of the shipwreck and its captives, delivers what it promises. [**Museum of Tropical Queensland, 70–102 Flinders St. Open daily 9.30a.m.–5p.m. Entry $9.50/$6.50/$5.50. Phone (07) 4726 0606 or visit www. mtq.qld.gov.au]**

# ODDITIONS

⊚ Capricorn Caves, north of **Rockhampton (Qld)**, offer down-and-dirty tours for the more adventurous cave-goer. Not for the squeamish, however, if a name like Fat Man's Misery is any indication.

⊚ No longer a bank, the ANZ cubicle in **Bridgeport (SA)** must rate as one of the tiniest branches Down Under. Not even a branch – more a twig!

⊚ Paris is famed for its grand Cathedral of Notre Dame. Closer to home, Paris St in **Australind (WA)** claims the smallest church in Australia. Once a worker's cottage, the church of St Nicholas is only 8.2 m long and 3.6 m wide, far too small for the real St Nick to sit inside.

⊚ The Black Hole of Magic Mountain, above **Merimbula (NSW)**, is a rarity among water slides. Not only does this evil chute complete a 360° loop, it does so underground. [**Open daily 10a.m.–4p.m. in high season. Park entry includes all rides. Phone (02) 6495 2299 or visit www.magicmountain.net.au]**

⊚ The smallest witness box in Australia is at **Injune (Qld)**. The minuscule cubicle stands in the grounds of the police station.

# CRAFTY

*(Being a patchwork of novel needlework,
headlining hobbying and the odd wiliness)*

## OBJETS OUTRÉS

**BOWNING, NSW** Priscilla (a table) has stiletto heels on her wooden legs. Nearby is a candelabra wrought from the tails of two iron peacocks. Countless other canny creations occupy Crisp Galleries, whose owner and chief artist, Peter Crisp, is also a maestro of slumped glass: his vases and highball glasses suggest exotic jellyfish left to bake on a hot dashboard. The 2 ha include a lavender garden which reverberates your softest whisper, plus Michael Murphy's bronze swan dashing across a lake, leaving metallic splashes in its wake. A magical place. **[14 km south of Yass, off the Hume Hwy. Open daily 10a.m.–5p.m. Phone (02) 6227 6073 or visit www.petercrisp.com.au]**

Who needs a map of the Blue Mountains when a flight of stairs at the **Glenbrook (NSW)** Visitors Centre spells out each community, from lowly Lapstone to the peak of Katoomba, and down to Blackheath on the other side? A way to shift altitude without your ears popping.

## FUN PARK

**EMU PARK, Qld** One room in the Emu Park Museum (the former courthouse of nearby Yeppoon) holds three outlandish treasures. First are the sand jars of the late Arthur Combett, who trickled the grains into the form of griffins, ducks and palm trees. (Several designs still baffle sand-artists today, for Arthur took his techniques to the grave.) Next-door is a high chair by Anon., built entirely of cotton spools. Opposite is a pedestal that Mrs W. Coade wangled from spigots, fobs, door-knobs and bottle-openers. **[17 Hill St. Open weekdays 10a.m.–4p.m., Sun. 10a.m.–2p.m. Entry $3/50c. Phone (07) 4939 6080]**

Bull kelp has 1001 uses, and Betty and Bevin Collins of King Island Kelp Craft in **Grassy (Tas.)** have found new ways to manipulate the local variety. First they shrink the fronds, so ridding the kelp of its knockout reek. Next, they craft brooches, belts and Ned Kelly figurines. [**6 Currie Rd.** Phone **(03) 6461 1464**]

## CHANGING HORSES MIDSTREAM

GYMPIE, Qld   Gympie blacksmith Richard Ambrose had a lifelong passion for horses, and from the late 1890s he developed a reputation for custom-making convoluted horseshoes. Elsewhere, an array of 11 horseshoes would spell out UUUUUUUUUU, but Ambrose's set in the Gympie Gold Mining Museum gives you O8UUODUTUU$\Omega$. He eventually switched to veterinary science, but kept on with his equine orthopaedics as a sideline. [**In the museum's main building, 215 Brisbane Rd. Open daily 9a.m.–4p.m. Entry $6.60/$4.40/$2.20, family $8.80. Phone (07) 5482 3995 or visit www.gympiemuseum.com**]

## QUILT BY ASSOCIATION

NORTHAMPTON, WA   Airing of the Quilts© probably doesn't warrant a © after its title, but it's better to be sure. The idea emerged from the local Patchwork Group in 1997: why not dangle our doonas from the windowsills and revive the town's spirits in the process? A bee began. Quilters went berserk. To inaugurate what is now an annual custom on the last Saturday of Term 3 school holidays in WA (usually Oct.), 150 quilts flagged the main street. Since then the number has doubled, with all the needlework locally made. And don't just expect bedspreads if you chance on the mining town – there are maypoles, floats, the whole sewing kit and caboodle. Down the road, the people of Dongara flash their patchworks every two years in what is known as The Hanging of the Quilts – quite a separate concern.

## THERE ARE BEARS IN THERE

TAMBO, Qld   The team at Tambo Teddies has made over 25 000 bears in less than 10 years. All the wool and leather is home-grown, all the artisans local, and all the bears individually named. Goliath, the biggest of the ursine critters, is the bouncer at the shop door and isn't for sale. Nor is Mary's debut bear – a plastic-sealed character on the top shelf, which took nearly a month to make. You won't miss the studio – there's a teddy-bear silhouette on the pedestrian sign out the front. **[Open weekdays 8.30a.m.–5.30p.m., Sat. 9.30a.m.–12.30p.m. Bears also on sale at Fannie Mae's Cafe next door. Phone (07) 4654 6223 or windowshop at www.tamboteddies.com.au]**

Australian Weird and Wonderful Novelty Teapot Collection has to be the most drawn-out business name for a craft shop. This store in **Morpeth (NSW)**, teeming with tea trappings from edible pots to teapot key-rings, belongs to one of the biggest craft precincts in Oz. Nestled on the Hunter River, Morpeth has more than 60 knick-knack emporia, whose names (Grandma's Feather Bed and Teddy Bears Downstairs, to name but a few) tell all.

## FILIGREE FABULOSO

**WOOLLAMIA, NSW**  Just as well Gary, the Woollamia postie, isn't arachnophobic: five days a week he has to slip letters into the tail of a redback spider. The creepy-crawly is the brilliant work of a local metallurgist called Sampson, who's also made his gate a spiderweb for the redback and its baby to cling to. The rest of the fence is less venomous, featuring brolgas, tongue-poking frogs, dragonflies and brumbies. In the garden perches a mermaid with a pink monokini. People don't need to say '300 Woolamia Rd': most Shoalhaven dwellers know it as the place with 'that fence'. **[Between Huskisson and the Princes Hwy]**

# CRASHES

*(Being a logjam of smashing smashes
and colourful collisions)*

## SKYMASTER DISASTER

BEVERLEY, WA   The worst civilian air crash in Australia's history occurred on private land between York and Beverley in 1950. The 29 lost souls found in the debris of the DC4 Skymaster included the Bishop of the Riverina. The story of the crash, plus one of the plane's landing struts, can be found in the Beverley Aeronautical Museum. **[139 Vincent St. Open daily 9a.m.–4p.m. Entry $2, kids free. Phone (08) 9646 1555]**

## IMPACT STUDY

FREMANTLE, WA   John Button was 17 when in 1963 he and his sweetheart, Rosemary Anderson, had a tiff. Rosemary walked home in a huff and John drove alongside in his Simca Aronde Fiat, trying to plead his case, but to no avail. He gave up and drove home, only to discover next morning that Rosemary had been the victim of a hit-and-run. Button was arrested, tried and sentenced to 10 years' jail for manslaughter. A serial killer called Edgar Cooke later confessed to being responsible for the girl's death, but Button was kept in jail for five years before being paroled. He was only exonerated 37 years later, thanks to a series of crash tests. A Simca with dented bonnet stands in the corner of the Motor Museum, with a nearby petrol bowser showing footage of the crash-test impact. **[B Shed, Victoria Quay. Open daily 9.30a.m.–5p.m. Entry $9.50/$8/$5. Phone (08) 9336 5222 or visit www.fremantlemotormuseum.net]**

## TWELVE GOOD MEN

INGHAM, Qld   On 18 December 1942, an American B-24 bomber disappeared, having last been seen heading away from Townsville into stormy skies. A year later, Aborigines on Hinchinbrook Island, about 150 km north, found cindered American dollars on the slopes of Mt

Straloch in the island's south. It was not until 1944 that a search party found the wreck, just below the summit at some 900 m. A propeller and a memorial plaque can be found in the Ingham Memorial Gardens on the mainland. Using binoculars, you can pick out a steel cross on the slopes of Mt Straloch. Nimbler pilgrims can do a four-hour boulder-hop up a marked path to the crash site. **[Gardens cnr Jane and McIlwraith Sts, Ingham. For more information phone Qld Parks and Wildlife Service in Cardwell, also on the mainland, on (07) 4066 8601, or Ingham's Information Centre on (07) 4776 5211]**

One truck swiped two parked cars on 16 December 1989, bang outside the BP service station in **Euroa (Vic.)**. Quick as a flash, a cashier used a disposable camera to chronicle the fireball, while a roadhouse patron grabbed a fire extinguisher from a wall bracket. Amazingly, nobody was killed. You can see images of the incident – and of the floods that arrived at the pumps four years later – near the indoor loos.

## A SLIM HOPE

**LAURIETON, NSW**     Setting lobster pots near the mouth of the Camden Haven River in 1944, Bunny Wallace spotted two seaplanes flying past. One got lower by the minute, smoke belching from the engine, and finally crashed belly-first onto the sand-bar. Bunny went to the rescue: the first man he fished from the sea was American comedian Bob Hope. The iconic comic was part of a troupe returning from a wartime laugh-fest in Qld when the trouble struck. In gratitude, Hope performed two shows at the local School of Arts, and bought the repair crew a box of Canadian whisky before being motored south. **[There's no plaque, but the School of Arts, now the Neighbourhood Centre, stands cnr Bold and Laurie Sts]**

## SOUTHWEST PACIFIC STOP

**MACKAY, Qld**     Australia's worst aviation disaster during wartime exclusively involved Americans. It happened in 1944 at Bakers Creek, south of Mackay. A propeller by the Bruce Hwy approximates the spot where the USAF Flying Fortress lost control, killing 40 of its 41 crew. The plane's battered 'honeypot' (crapper) has been salvaged by the Mackay Regional Museum, as has a grisly telegram from the US Secretary of War. One reason for the plane crash being unsung is due to the obtuseness captured in the US government's message – your son 'died in the SW Pacific' stop. [Beside Bruce Hwy, about 10 km south of Mackay]

## DELIRIUM TREMORS

NEWCASTLE, NSW    On 28 December 1989, at 10.26a.m., a clock fell off the wall in a Lake Macquarie home, south of Newcastle. The time is important, because it marks the peak of the Newcastle earthquake that brought down three understoreys of the Workers Club on King and Union Sts, killing nine members. Three other Novocastrians died under a shop awning in nearby Hamilton. The frozen clock is just one exhibit in the quake memorial at the Regional Museum. Other relics include church spires, cracked cake-stands and the marble shoes of a World War 1 soldier who fell off his plinth in a city park. [Cnr Wood and Hunter Sts. Open Tues.–Sun. 10a.m.–5p.m. Entry is free. Phone (02) 4974 1400 or visit www.ncc.nsw.gov.au]

## GARLICK CRUSHER

MAROUBRA, SYDNEY, NSW    Phil Garlick liked to drive fast. From 1925, the year the Olympia Motor Speedway opened in Maroubra, the driver dominated the concrete banks in his supercharged Alvis, blurring at speeds over 160 kph. But the 'killer track' deserved its dark nickname. Garlick overshot the sloped corner and crashed in surrounding dunes. The speedway was demolished in the 1940s, but Garlick survives in the form of an extraordinary statue in South Head Cemetery. Higher-profile clients lie in the lot, including the Packer ancestry, but Garlick's headstone, depicting a marble champion gripping a steering wheel, wins the day. 'A most popular, highly skilled, sporting devotee . . .', runs his epitaph. [On the junction of New and Old South Head Rds. The grave sits roughly in the lot's centre, close to a black marble vault belonging to the Hodoba family]

The horseshoe on display at the Melbourne Exhibition in 1854 was made from a meteorite. Finding a precise date for the giant rock that once smashed into **Cranbourne (Vic.)**, a suburb on the southeastern edge of Melbourne, has stumped astronomers. So far over 8 tonnes in 12 pieces have been found. The horseshoe has been lost, but replica space-chunks sway in the breeze cnr Camms Rd and the South Gippsland Hwy.

## DERAILING

**GRANVILLE, SYDNEY, NSW**   Eighty-three roses rained onto the railways tracks on 18 January 1997, the twentieth anniversary of Australia's worst train disaster – a rose for each life lost. The location was the Bold St Bridge in the suburb of Granville, which at 8.12a.m. was struck by a commuter express which had left the rails en route from the Blue Mountains to Sydney's Central Station. The bridge collapsed on impact, crushing two of the carriages. A discreet plaque can be found on the fence at Railway Pde. Across the road, musical cherubim and a memorial roll-call bear witness. **[Take Bold St off Parramatta Rd]**

## BIG BANG THEORY

**TANAMI DESERT, NT**   Noted American geologist and astronomer Eugene Shoemaker visited Australia regularly to examine 'impact craters' caused by falling meteorites. On 18 July 1997, 650 km along the Tanami Track, near the private road to Tanami Mine, he died as the result of violent impact in the form of a car crash. Shoemaker made many astrogeological discoveries over the years, and his name was given to the comet Shoemaker-Levi 9, which he identified a year before it collided with Jupiter in 1994. He also identified 1125 asteroids, as well as convincing Arizona that the 'volcanic' crater in Barringer was in fact a meteor crater. Shoemaker's ashes were sent into orbit from the Lunar Prospector exactly one year after his death.

## CULTURAL CLASH

**BROOME, WA**   It was on the Great Northern Hwy in 1999 that art critic and author Robert Hughes, in a hired car, collided head-on with an oncoming vehicle on the only discernible bend for hundreds of kilometres. Hughes was in a coma for five weeks, and one of the three men in the other car was severely injured. After a lengthy and bitter legal battle, Hughes (in absentia) was banned from driving in WA for three years, though this may not have worried the critic unduly, as he had recently suggested that someone tow Australia 'out to sea and sink it'. **[Roughly opposite the Telstra tower, 120 km south of Broome. No plaque marks the spot]**

# CREATURES

*(Being a zoo gang of far-fetched fauna
and bedazzling beasts)*

## HIPPER FLIPPERS

**GLENELG, ADELAIDE, SA**   Mohawk is a bottlenose dolphin with a scar across her blowhole. She made herself known to Stephen Waites in April 2001 when she swam into his Holdfast Shores Marina. The next year, Mohawk had a calf that Stephen called Jade, after his own daughter who worked with him on the family's charter boat. Mohawk and Jade represent just a fraction of the pod that frolics in the mouth of the Port River. The Waites's catamaran cruises include dolphin swims, among the world's most urbanised bunch of 'wild' cetaceans. And should the pod fail to drop by, you get your 'swim' money back, promise the Waites. **[Trips usually leave at 8a.m. and return by 11.30a.m. Dolphin watch $58/$38, dolphin swim $98/$88. Call Stephen on 0412 811 838 or visit www.dolphinboat.com.au]**

## URSINE WINE

**ANGASTON, SA**   Six generations of Smiths have worked this soil, from Sidney Smith to Robert Hill Smith, making Yalumba the oldest family-owned winery in Australia. As for the Russian black bear standing waiter-like in the tasting room, it is the prized catch of Tiger Smith, vintner number three; a souvenir from his travels in Europe early last century. The bear featured in Yalumba ads during the 1950s, with the tagline 'Bear in mind'. How could you forget? **[Eden Valley Rd. Open Mon.-Sat. 10a.m.-5p.m., Sun. noon-5p.m. Phone (08) 8561 3200 or visit www.yalumba.com]**

## WADERS OF THE LOST ARK

**BROOME, WA**   Lord Alistair McAlpine is a peer with few equals. The former pearl farmer fell in love with Broome during the 1980s, buying up a large chunk of Cable Beach and building a zoo for endangered animals. His vision was to skipper an Ark of the North, but ebbing finances saw the proposed passengers exported elsewhere. All that's left, zoo-wise, of the Lord's 30 ha is the Old Zoo Café, occupying the one-time feedhouse. Here you can read the many bird placards salvaged from the dismantled aviary while you enjoy scrambled eggs. **[2 Challenor Dve, Cable Beach. Open 7a.m. till late, bookings appreciated. Phone (08) 9193 6200]**

## CALM BEFORE THE GALE

**DENHAM, WA**    One of two things will occur when you stand at Eagle Bluff, on the road to Denham. Either you will see the most dugongs you've ever seen in your life, or you will be blown inside-out. That the boardwalk here overlooks the largest sea-grass meadow in the world, nourishing a whole eighth of the world's dugong population, seems almost irrelevant when your shirt is last seen kiting towards Lharidon Bight. Conservation and Land Management (known, ironically, as CALM) has set out silhouette boards to help you distinguish a dugong from a reef shark, assuming the day is calm enough for spotting. Most days aren't – the Shark Bay region endures some of the strongest winds in WA. **[Eagle Bluff is off the Denham–Hamelin Rd, 20 km south of Denham. The approach road is sandy but generally sound for 2WD vehicles]**

The tiny marsupial mouse known as a dibbler was considered extinct for 50 years, until a couple turned up in 1967 and breeding subsequently began at Perth Zoo. Now 41 zoo-bred dibblers have been released in Peniup Nature Reserve in **Jerramungup (WA)**, about half with radio collars. The same territory is also home to other endangered locals such as the mallee fowl and the ground parrot.

## IN POD WE TRUST

**EDEN, NSW**    Old Tom, Hooky, Humpy and Stranger were killers extraordinaire, or killer whales to be precise. The four orcas were famous at the turn of the last century for helping whalers herd and catch passing baleen whales in Twofold Bay. Their methods varied from tail-slapping, so alerting the fleet of the pod's arrival, to capsizing the harpooned baleens to hasten asphyxia. The victims' lips and tongues were the killer whales' reward. **[See Old Tom's skeleton at the Killer Whale Museum, 94 Imlay St. Open Mon.-Sat. 9.15a.m.-3.45p.m., Sun. 11.15a.m.-3.45p.m. Entry $6/$2. Phone (02) 6496 2094 or check out www.killerwhalemuseum.com.au]**

## BREATHTAKING DISCOVERY

**GAYNDAH, Qld**    You're camping by the Burnett River and you hear a sudden intake of air. Do you (a) panic, (b) look for the drowning person, (c) vow to stop drinking or (d) marvel at the life cycle of *Neoceratodus forsteri*? In fairness, all four may be the correct response, though (d) is closest to the mark. Because we should marvel – the Qld lungfish is a living fossil, one of few fish in the world that needs, on occasion, to breathe from the surface. The fish has a mullet brow, boned fins for bed-crawling and a rudder-like tail. It breeds only in the Burnett and Mary Rivers, and can live for up to 80 years. Back in 1869, William McCord salted the first two specimens known to white settlers. He sent them to his cousin called Forster (as in *Neoceratodus forsteri*) at the Sydney Museum, who was suitably impressed by the rarity. The whole story plus a few living specimens are captured in the Gayndah Museum. **[Simon St. Open daily 9a.m.-4p.m. Entry $3/$1. Phone (07) 4161 2226]**

## HARRY POTTER MEETS HEDWIG

**KURANDA, Qld**    Spectacled flying foxes can be seen only in the skies of tropical Qld – and they'll only be there for as long as they avoid barbed wire, feral cats, electrified wires and campervans. But if there is a mishap, Pam Tully and her bat hospital come to the rescue, nursing the mammals back to strength in a Kuranda backyard. Some are orphans. Some are refugees from amateur zoos. All are endearing and, thanks to those spectacles, quite bookish. **[Batreach, Jungle Walk off Coondoo St. Open Tues.-Fri. 10.30a.m.-2.30p.m., Sun. ditto. Entry free, though donations welcome. Phone (07) 4093 8858 or visit www.batreach.cairns.tc]**

## ZZZZZOO

**MELBOURNE, Vic.**   Roar and Snore at Melbourne Zoo is a chance for animal lovers to sleep with a wildebeest or an Asiatic golden cat. Or *try* to sleep – the raucous chorus of cats and birds and pachyderms goes on way past bedtime. Your accommodation is a wall-free tent on the pampas and the deal includes a barbecue (guaranteed to tantalise the lions), plus a torch-lit tour of the inmates and a spot of silhouette-guessing. All you need to bring is a sleeping bag, a pillow and, if you're smart, camouflage pyjamas. In the morning you're invited to escort the keepers to several exclusive zones to see how the creatures start their days. **[Sleepovers run Sept.–May, Fri. and Sat. nights. Cost is $125/$99. Inquiries on (03) 9285 9355 or www.zoo.org.au]**

Four big pigs run Rundle Mall, the shopping artery of **Adelaide (SA)**. Sculptor Marguerite Derricourt is the brains behind the swine – Augusta, Horatio, Truffles and Oliver, the last standing on his hind legs rooting through the bronze trash that pokes from a council bin. Officially called 'A Day Out', the meeting place is known simply by locals as 'The Pigs'. **[Opposite Stephens Place and Rundle Mall]**

## LIKING THE VIKING

**NORSEMAN, WA**   There can't be too many towns named after a horse – let alone *founded* by one. As surely as there can't be too many gee-gees who have found a gold nugget with their hoof, the feat said to have been performed by Laurie Sinclair's horse in 1894, so sparking a gold rush to the area. (Norseman was named after Sinclair's own home town in the Shetland Islands.) Alfred Hitchcock's nephew, Robert Hitchcock, has sculpted the mare in mid-strike, standing cnr Roberts and Ramsay Sts.

## ACRONYM BY A NECK

**PORT LINCOLN, SA**   Bluefin tuna have secured this town's future, creating the most millionaires per capita in any Australian country town.

But thanks to Tony Santic, a second animal has ensured the town's longevity, namely dual Melbourne Cup winner Makybe Diva, who galloped home in both 2003 and 2004. The name is an acronym of sorts derived from the names of five girls who work for his tuna-processing company, Tony's Tuna International – Maureen, Kylie, Belinda, Diana and Vanessa. **[Most of the original Makybe divas work in the plant, on Pine Freezer Rd]**

## SHORT AND CURLY

**PORT MACQUARIE, NSW**   Jean Starr cruised the highways in 1973 looking for concussed koalas, nursing them back to health if possible. Her Samaritan ways inspired the Koala Hospital a few years later. Instead of beds the marsupials are housed in eucalypts, with the John Williamson Wing open to critical cases. The admission charts are revealing: road trauma, dogs, bushfires and chlamydia (a bacterial infection responsible for eye and/or venereal disease) are the chief koala curses. Perhaps the most touching aspect of the 'healing zoo' is the pair of memorial stones within the main yard: the first is to 'Pebbles' and the second to her personal physician, Professor Kenneth Phillips. **[Roto Place, off Lord St. Open daily. Feeding times 8a.m. and 3p.m. Entry by donation. Phone (02) 6584 1522]**

## ODDITIONS

◎ **Ororoo (SA)** has a rifle range, and to good effect. A local by the name of Addison won a prize shooting targets in Canada. His bizarre trophy, antlers and all, hangs in the Town Hall.

◎ Training rams sounds as easy as nailing jelly. But the Australian Woolshed in Ferny Hills, **Brisbane (Qld)** has eight obedient studs which model their wool onstage and listen to the shearer-cum-ringmaster. **[Four daily sessions at 148 Samford Rd, 14 km northwest of town. Phone (07) 3872 1100 or visit www.auswoolshed.com.au]**

◎ The community hall in **Bonargo (Qld)** must be the only civic building in Oz dedicated to a spineless creature – the odd councillor excepted. Cactoblastis Hall salutes the advent of a South American moth introduced to eradicate a prickly pear plague in 1924.

# DÉJÀ VU

*(Being an echo chamber of eerie resonance,*
*repeat performances and reverberations)*

## KNEE-DEEP IN TROUBLE

**AUGUSTA, WA**   The alarm was sounded at 7 a.m. on a midwinter day
in 1986, when a beachcomber found 114 false killer whales stranded
on the beach, not far from town. Rescue workers included paramedics,
Greenpeace, and the nicely named group called ORRCA (Organisa-
tion for the Rescue and Research of Cetaceans in Australia). One by
one, the whales were corralled into a safety pen, and all up 96 were
returned, the best-ever 'rescue ratio' for any such event, according to
Project Jonah. Two years later 60 sperm whales became stranded on
a more remote section of the beach near Ledge Point, and another
year on 18 dolphins were also stranded near White Point, but in both
cases only around half were saved. **[Flinders Bay is signposted en
route to Cape Leeuwin. The boat ramp was the heart and soul of
operations]**

## DRINKING HABIT

**DONGARA, WA**   In 1881, farmer William Criddle won the licence to
open a 'wayside house with bagatelle table' – the second pub in the
area and soon a popular haunt for travellers crossing the Irwin River.
Criddle sold the property to a group of Dominican nuns from New
Zealand, who took up residence in 1899. The building later became
a boarding school for girls (the alma mater of federal politician Car-
men Lawrence), until in 1971 Cyclone Mavis caused the Irwin to flood,
wiping out the terraced gardens and the tennis court. It clearly put a
damper on the nuns as well, for they moved to Perth the following year
and the priory lapsed back into a pub – minus bagatelle table. But
the sisters are not forgotten: a short stroll from the carpark leads you
to a monument recording the 35 nuns who passed away during their
tenure. **[Priory Lodge, 11 St Dominics Rd. Phone (08) 9927 1090]**

## DOUBLE DIPPING

**GERALDTON, WA**   WA Airways Ltd flew the first mail run in Australia, pipping Qantas by a year. The maiden flight in 1921, between Geraldton and Derby in the far north, was a flop, however. The Bristol Tourer biplane plunged into saltbush near Murchison House Station, killing both pilot and mechanic and delaying that first airmail delivery by a week or more. To celebrate this noble service, which eventually resumed without a hitch, a commemorative flight took place in a replica biplane in 1992, retracing the original route. But you can guess, can't you? The replica crashed too – though this time, happily, the pilot walked away from the wreck. **[The restored replica hangs in the brilliant Western Australian Museum, 1 Museum Place. Open daily 10a.m.– 4p.m. Entry by donation. Phone (08) 9921 5080]**

## TANKS A MILLION

**MERIMBULA, NSW**   In May 2001 the fire brigade received a mayday call from the local aquarium. This was creepy: the building had already burnt down in 1998, losing all but the prawn family, although a major rebuild and re-stock had since taken place. This time there was a lethal lack of water, as heavy seas had dislodged the aquarium's inlet pipe off Long Point and the pumps had conked out. The finny inmates were running out of fresh water and oxygen. The firemen used a mobile pump to suck up 20 000 litres of brine into a holding tank, and drop by drop the water resuscitated the conger eels, blind sharks and one-spot pullers (they're fish, not nightclubbers), to name but a few. **[End of Lake St. Open daily 10a.m.–5p.m.: feeding time is 11.30a.m. weekdays during school holidays; Mon., Wed., Fri at other times. Entry $8.80/$5.50/$4.40. Or just drop by the Wharf Cafe upstairs. Phone (02) 6495 4446]**

February 1893 was a bad month for floods, when the **Brisbane River (Qld)** spilled its banks not once but three times. The first and worst deluge, which occurred on 5 February, left three ships (the gunship *Paluma*, the *Elamang* and the *Mary Evans*) stranded in the city's Botanical Gardens. Engineers were still pondering how to return the beached fleet to the water, when the river flooded again on 19 February and the craft were relaunched. **[No plaque records the event, but the story forms part of a free garden tour. Inquiries (07) 3403 0666]**

## THE HUNGRY SEA

MILLICENT, SA    It was a dark and stormy night in 1876 – truly. An iron barque, the *Geltwood*, took on water in Rivoli Bay near Beachport and sank, with the loss of all 31 lives. The only two recovered bodies were buried on the beach, then dug up days later and buried in Millicent – but when the cemetery was moved to a larger site, the two drowned sailors were left stranded near the present-day museum. As for the wreck, it too was lost until abalone diver Mick Galpin found it in 1982 and supervised a salvage operation. In 1985, in a cruel twist of fate, Galpin and a crewmate disappeared at sea. **[Living History Museum on Mt Gambier Rd has the anchor and other relics. Open weekdays 9.30a.m.–4.30p.m. in summer and 10a.m.–4p.m. in winter, weekends 10a.m.–4p.m. Entry $9/$7/$4.50. Phone (08) 8733 3205. The park next door houses the stranded graves]**

## STOPPING A NATION

CLAREMONT, PERTH, WA    When Damien Oliver won the Melbourne Cup on Media Puzzle in 2002, he blew a kiss to the sky as he passed the post, a gesture aimed squarely and tenderly at his brother, Jason. Also a jockey, Jason Oliver had died during a race trial in Perth less than a week earlier. Jason was only 34, one year older than his father, Ramon, when the latter died in 1970 while riding in Kalgoorlie's Boulder Cup. The single burial plot evokes one of the sport's sadder coincidences. **[The graves of Jason and Ramon are on Lawn 9 in the Catholic section in the cemetery off Railway Rd in nearby Karrakatta. The grave number is 319]**

## GRIM FERRY TALE

**PORT MACQUARIE, NSW**    The coastal steamer TSS *Wollongbar* sank in Byron Bay in 1921. Then in 1943 its more grandiose namesake, *Wollongbar II*, which ferried supplies to Sydney, sank off Crescent Head when torpedoed by a Japanese submarine. The captain of a passing Catalina flew to Port Macquarie, and six local men took off in a fishing boat. Of the 32 aboard the stricken steamer, only five survived. Flotsam from the wreck has been found over the years and is displayed in the Maritime Museum, including a sick-looking set of bagpipes – perhaps a relic from the Glasgow yard where the ship was built. **[6 William St. Open daily 10a.m.–4p.m. Entry $4/$2, family $10. The *Wollongbar* story is in the Mermaid Cottage. Phone (02) 6583 1866]**

# DERIVATIONS

*(Being a glossary of obscure origins and
merry meanings behind towns and places)*

## BALL'S IN YOUR COURT

BALLA BALLA, WA    All that's left of this Pilbara ghost port are scraps of lumber – and a linguistic puzzle. The latter all started in the 1960s when anthropologist Count Karl von Brandenstein, studying the area's Indigenous languages, observed that many Aboriginal words appeared to have been borrowed from Portuguese. The local word *balla*, for instance, signifies a spherical stone found near Whim Creek, the same word meaning 'cannonball' in Portuguese. Giving linguists even more ammunition, the Portuguese navy under King Manoel I in the early sixteenth century used round stones as cannonballs. So, which came first? Or is this conundrum a load of ballocks ballocks? **[East of Whim Creek along a dry-weather road]**

## EATING ON THE RUN

CORINNA, Tas.    A baker in his civilian days, the light-fingered Alexander Pearce was transported to Hobart Town in 1819. The Pieman, as he became known, escaped from the penal settlement at Macquarie Harbour with seven other convicts. When Pearce was eventually nabbed, the other escapees had vanished. The Pieman escaped from prison again, this time with only one companion, Thomas Cox. The story became a *cause célèbre* in Hobart when Pearce was recaptured and found to have a morsel of Cox in his pocket: he had eaten the poor wretch, just as he'd eaten most of his earlier fellow escapees. **[You can tour the serene Pieman River with Pieman River Cruises, and hear more of the omnivorous Pearce during the voyage, for $50/$25. Phone (03) 6446 1170]**

Engelbrecht Cave, the limestone system that sprawls below **Mt Gambier (SA)**, isn't named after the cave's first explorer but after its principal polluter. Karl Engelbrecht came to Australia in 1857. The German-born distiller lived in an old flour mill close to the cave's mouth and for years dumped his unwanted whiskey casks and bottles down the sinkhole. **[Jubilee Hwy West. Tours daily. Phone 0418 133 407]**

## BAGMAN

**GLADSTONE, Qld**   Seldom can you point to a given object and say *that* is why doilies are called doilies (or leotards leotards, and so on). But in Gladstone you can see the very Gladstone bag that belonged to globe-trotting 19th-century British PM, William Gladstone, after whom the useful luggage item was named. Peter Gladstone, the PM's great-grandson and a world-renowned deer farmer, bequeathed the cowhide container to the port during a visit in 1988. Teasingly, 'W.E. Gladstone' is gold-stamped under the pocket flap, out of view – at least, that's what the plaque tells us. It *has* to be the original, doesn't it? **[Regional Art Gallery, cnr Goondoon and Bramston Sts. Open weekdays 10a.m.–5p.m., Sat. and holidays, 10a.m.–4p.m. Entry free. Phone (07) 4976 6766]**

## GURU ON THE MOUNTAIN

**NIMBIN, NSW**   Most lexicons source the name Nimbin to a phrase meaning 'big stone' or 'place of many rocks'. But the Age-of-Aquarians who invaded the dairy town for an alternative-lifestyle festival in 1973 latched onto a legend from the Minyaligoh-Walloh people of Lismore. King Morgan, an elder of those people, described a long-haired psychic called Nymbngee who was kidnapped by two jealous giants. They hid Nymbngee in a mountain cave, but he used his energies to burst through a fissure and escape. This wizardry petrified the giants, literally: the sacred site known as the Nimbin Needles, which looks down on the hippie hamlet, is said to embody their frozen forms. **[On the road to Georgica. Only members of the Indigenous community can access the area]**

## OCEANS APART

**OCEAN GROVE, Vic.**    Okay, the town is called Ocean Grove because it's a grove near the ocean. I mean, how obvious can you get? But wait, there's a twist: the original grove is by the Atlantic Ocean, in New Jersey, USA (not far from TV mobster Tony Soprano's lucrative esplanade). Back in 1887, two Wesleyan missionaries from there tried to establish a grog-free, inter-denominational town beside God's blue sea in Australia. The experiment failed miserably, but the name survived. And nowadays you can raise a glass at several booze outlets.

## UNDER THE LAKE

**SUBIACO, WA**    Father Joseph Serra was a Spanish monk who studied in Italy. He came to Perth in the mid-1800s to plant olive trees and sow the word of God. His travelling companion was Father Salvado, with whom he had sworn his monastic vows back in Subiaco (literally 'under the lake'), a Benedictine monastery west of Rome. That's how the railway station got its name when the Fremantle line came through in 1881. A century later, in 1980, a city park was planted with olive trees in tribute, by (ahem) R.V. Diggins, the then-mayor of Subiaco. Flourishing, the trees perhaps owe their ongoing health to the fact that the plot was once the typhoid graveyard for Victoria Hospital down the road. [Park is on Hay and Jersey Sts]

A close encounter of the furred kind? When Ludwig Leichhardt first passed across the **Darling Downs (Qld)** in 1844, he took the Aboriginal name for the cypress pine, *jinchilla*, to be spelt the same way as the South American critter valued for its fur – chinchilla. That's why an exotic rodent happens to double for a sleepy town on the Warrego Hwy.

## JIM'S CAVALCADE

**SURFERS PARADISE, Qld**    Appropriately enough, this hedonistic haven owes its name to a pub. English Channel swimmer, Jim Cavill, who bequeathed his name to the city's chief mall, came to Oz in 1923 to teach swimming, then stayed on and built a hotel in what was then the seaside village of Elston. He called his mock-Tudor tavern the Surfer's Paradise Hotel, from a casual remark made years earlier by surveyor Thor Jensen: 'This is a real surfer's paradise.' Elston was the official name until Cavill and a few local entrepreneurs (including Bruce Small, the Malvern Star bicycle tycoon) lobbied the council for a more enticing moniker. The council finally acquiesced in 1933, since which time Jim Cavill's vision has become set in concrete. **[The former site of Jim's pub is close to where Cavill Mall meets the highway]**

According to local folklore, a bullock driver and an Afghan cameleer were complaining about the heat of the Eyre Peninsula. 'By Allah,' swore the cameleer, 'it's hot.' 'Why Allah?' the bullocky asked. 'You should blame the Devil.' And so the name **Whyalla (SA)**, was born. Believe it or not.

### HOME SHORT HOME

**WINTON, Qld**    Pelican Waters was Winton's original name. Locals maintain that the name change came about because the town's first postman, Robert Allen, was too lazy to keep writing it on documents and envelopes (he was lucky he didn't live in Central Mt Stuart via Pmara Jtunuta). The suggested alternative, Wallace's Camp, was no shorter. So Allen, who once lived in the building that is now the National Bank, insinuated the name of his home suburb in Bournemouth. The name Winton bobs up in several Australian states, but the Qld version has the most unexpected origins.

## ODDITIONS

◎ Yes, it's beautiful, but **Beauty Point (Tas.)** in fact owes its name to a bullock called Beauty who died thereabouts . . .

◎ . . . meanwhile, Beauty Point in **Mosman (NSW)**, the multi-million-dollar headland jutting into a northern stretch of Sydney Harbour, is a real-estate translation for the same spit, which was once called Billygoat Point.

🌀 An extension of **Bunbury (WA)**, the settlement of Australind is a hybrid of the names Australia and India. The name was hatched in the hope of developing a strong trading relationship between the countries – especially trade in the famous NSW 'walers' (robust horses used as cavalry chargers).

🌀 **Great Western (Vic.)** is not named after some classic cowboy flick, but in honour of what was once the largest luxury steamship in the world. The town's street names honour the liner's shipwrights and maiden skipper.

# EXPLOSIVE

*(Being a report on loud noises,
deafening disasters and kinky kabooms)*

## A SHORE THING

**BEACHPORT, SA**   The 240 people who died in Darwin during the Japanese bombing raid of 1942 were not the first casualties of World War 2 on home soil. That grim laurel belongs to Able Seamen Danswan and Todd in 1941. A mine had been found by a fisherman at sea and was towed 2 km into the shallows off Beachport. Danswan and Todd attached a demolition charge and retreated behind trees. Unfortunately, according to Issue 20 of *Wartime*, a truck severed the wires and so new ones had to be fitted. But the new ones didn't work. So waiting the regulation 15 minutes, Danswan and Todd went to investigate the very instant the device exploded. It's thought a wave rolled the mine, causing one of its horns to be activated. **[A monument and plaque stand atop a high dune at the eastern end of the surf-beach carpark, Millicent Rd]**

## ALL HAIL THE RAINMAKER

**CHARLEVILLE, Qld**   Clement Wragge was an optimist. He'd heard of such things as hailstorm-diverting cannons being used in Europe, and thought that perhaps similar weaponry could elicit rain at home. No doubt the people of arid outback Qld were prepared to give anything a go. So in 1902 Wragge set up several Steiger Vortex Rain Guns around Charleville. Alas, the explosions were a damp squib in the downpour stakes, though a photo of one of Australia's worst hailstorms – a whiteout in Charleville in 1947 – which hangs in the Hotel Corones foyer, suggests that perhaps Wragge's artillery did work, if slowly. Two of Wragge's guns are still in place. **[Guns stand in front of scout hall south of town in Graham Andrews Parkland, Matilda Hwy. Photo hangs in the pub foyer, on Wills St]**

No need to panic. That German mine sitting in the middle of **Robe's (SA)** main roundabout has been defused. The evil egg was a gift from the merchant ship *Narvik*, which planted at least 13 mines around the time of Pearl Harbor. **[On the Royal Circus round-about]**

## MAGAZINE SHOP

**STAWELL, Vic.**   Thomas Brown had a bustling business back in 1870. His hardware store on Goldreef Mall sold shovels and pans to the diggers, while out the back he stored gunpowder for the mining companies. Brown's shop has been demolished, but the dome-shaped powder magazine, once the most dangerous structure in Stawell, now harmlessly inhabits the supermarket carpark. Which supermarket, you ask? Safeway. **[In the middle of Church St, parallel with Goldreef Mall]**

## DOZING ON THE JOB

**TENNANT CREEK, NT**   If a bus brings you into Tennant Creek, take a minute to find the sign just outside the transit centre. Fifty years ago a fire broke out at the general store nearby. One man was killed and seven were injured, but the toll could have been much higher if it hadn't been for quick-thinking locals Bert Fairchild and Sergeant Jim Manion. When they saw the flames approaching petrol pumps and the gelignite shed next door, they seized a bulldozer and pushed the inferno holus-bolus onto the safety of the plain, winning British Empire medals for their efforts. **[Near cnr Paterson and Stuart Sts]**

## COAL COMFORT

**WOLLONGONG, NSW**   In a small cemetery at Mt Kembla, the nation's worst mining disaster comes sadly alive. Ninety-six miners were killed when an explosion ripped through the nearby coal-mine in 1902. A Royal Commission determined that a roof collapse had produced a gust of flammable gases that exploded on contact with the miners' lights. The church is a memorial to the lost workers, as is an archway fabricated from coal. (Near the church you can see one of the last chunks of coal ever mined at Mt Kembla, salvaged in 1971.) An obelisk among the graves lists the 96 victims, with a terrible poignancy in the last entry, 'George Youngman'. **[Leave the freeway at Unanderra and turn right on the old Princes Hwy. Go right again at Cordeaux Rd. The church is a block on from the Mt Kembla pub]**

## ODDITIONS

- A sign near the Big Winch in **Coober Pedy (SA)** reads 'Stop Here Only If Your Car Is Dynamite-resistant'.
- A road sign near **Bajool (Qld)**, halfway between Rockhampton and Gladstone on the Bruce Hwy, knows the secret of keeping motorists in line. 'Caution', it reads, 'Trucks Carrying Explosives Turning in Next 500 Metres'.

# FAKES

*(Being an assembly of semblances
and scintillating simulacra)*

## CONIFERS

**GLEN OSMOND, ADELAIDE, SA**   Outside a Mobil petrol station are six real pine trees and 11 fake ones. The fakes are concrete works of art commissioned to celebrate the oldest fossils known to man – a pre-Cambrian batch uncovered in the area in 1940. Tony Bishop is the visionary involved; he enlisted local artists such as film director Scott Hicks (*Shine* and *Hearts in Atlantis*) to create their own bogus botany. **[Cnr Glen Osmond and Portrush Rds]**

## CABIN FEVER

**HOBART, Tas.**   Roger Bastone has a thing for the *Titanic*, and it shows in one of the rooms in his Battery Point Guest House. The Empire Suite, all 4½ stars of it, is a painstaking replica of a stateroom from the ill-fated passenger ship that sank off Newfoundland in 1912. A carriage clock on the mantelpiece is frozen at 1.36a.m., the minute the White Star liner was swallowed by the Atlantic. There's even a *trompe-l'oeil* porthole, with a seahorse swimming past. At the end of the day you can settle down for Titanic-label port. The wallpaper, the mirror – every detail is true to history (except the telly, hidden in the sideboard). **[77 McGregor St, above Kelly Steps. No public viewing, but for $170 a double the room is all yours. Phone (03) 6224 2111]**

Compressed air and a covert computer (hidden in a rain-tank) provide a shocking shake-up in the Pumping Station Museum in **Cunderdin (WA)**. The Richter force equates to the 1989 Newcastle earthquake nightmare of 5.5. Amazingly, the 1968 Cunderdin quake, centred in Meckering, was even stronger at 6.9. **[Open daily 10a.m.–4p.m. Entry $4/$3/$1.50, family $9. Phone (08) 9635 1291]**

## WORKMANSHIP

**MAROOCHYDORE, Qld**    James Cook may only have sailed two-thirds of the way around the world if he'd skippered the scale model near Maroochy River Resort. That's the reduction ratio used by Bill Goodchild when constructing his honourable fake. Seaworthy she may not be, but Goodchild's *Endeavour* is certainly lagoon-worthy and is moored off the Waterfront Hotel. **[Visible, though not visitable owing to termites in residence, on David Low Way, Eudlo Creek]**

## THE ITALIAN JOB

**NOOSA, Qld**    His first name is Richard, but being a gondolier, he prefers Ricardo. His gondola, a picture-perfect imitation of the Venetian McCoy, plies Noosa River and its offshoot canals. The boat takes up to six people, with sunset cruises particularly popular. And you can have a peek at how the Queensland Medicis live as you slide past their holiday homes. **[Half-hour cruises cost $70, one hour $100; a seafood cruise also available. Bookings essential. Phone Ricardo on 0412 929 369]**

If you're agnostic, you'll no doubt think blessing a fleet of fishing boats, as happens in **Ulladulla (NSW)** each Easter, is a bit strange. And even if you're religious you might well wonder where the scarecrows lining the streets and shop windows come into it. In fact they're part of a charity drive that operates in sync with the blessing ceremony. And believe me, the Milton-Ulladulla-Scarecrow-Blessing-of-the-Fleet-Festival is fun on a stick.

## BRICKS AND WATER

**WOLLONGONG, NSW**    If you stand near the water at the North Beach Surf Sheds and look inland, you'll see a warship apparently emerging from the sheds' outline, complete with a shark siren fixed to the mock-funnel. Built in 1938, with the world at war, the ship-shape sheds were seen as an additional defence against any offshore enemies, albeit a token defence. Uphill, in a grassed emplacement, three cast-iron cannons point at the breakwater, aiming to quell the Russian hordes thought to be about to invade in 1893. **[Top end of Cliff Rd]**

There is a figurehead replica in the hotel foyer of the Heritage Resort in **Dampier (WA)**. The original was found north of Cape Peron in 1989, by a dugong researcher. A Norwegian barque, the *Gudrun*, sank in 1901 after the ship's carpenter, a man with a few screws loose, drilled holes in the keel on a voyage to the Cape of Good Hope.

## AS GOOD AS GLASS

**ZEEHAN, Tas.**    The West Coast Pioneers' Museum has 100 bizarre minerals, but two stand out. The first is a mustard sea-urchin called crocoite, which was adopted in 2000 as Tasmania's mineral emblem. The second exhibit is tektite, resembling a windscreen fragment and otherwise known as Darwin glass. Tektite, it's believed, formed on the slopes of Mt Darwin in southwest Tasmania about 730 000 years ago. Geologists can be fairly sure about the date, as the mineral was created when a giant meteorite plummeted into the quartz bed, the extreme heat melting the rock into ersatz glass. Aborigines found various uses for this mineral, from cutting to trading. For many years, historians were baffled as to how the West Coast people had come across glass long before European settlement. The answer lay in the stars. **[Main St. Open daily 9a.m.–5p.m. Entry $9/$8, family $20. Phone (03) 6471 6225]**

# ODDITIONS

◉ Stonehenge may stand on Salisbury Plain, but there's a valiant replica on a dairy farm at 387 Gap Rd, between **Teven (NSW)** and Alstonville. Unlike the Druid original, this marvel has shorter steles (pillars) but massive horizontals.

◉ No need to brace yourself as you cross the cattle grid near the

Minjina Roadhouse, close to **Wittenoom (WA)**. The 'iron bars' are merely a series of painted white stripes, though they seem to deter nomadic cattle all the same.

⊚ On the banks of Swindlers Creek, below the bottom station of the Blue Ribbon Chairlift on **Mt Hotham (Vic.)**, is a fake cattleman's hut. It was erected for *The Silver Brumby* (1993), a kids' movie starring Russell Crowe as The Man.

# FARMS

*(Being a collective of properties
with a big-D Difference)*

## SMITH BY NAME, SMITH BY TRADE

ARDROSSAN, SA    Back in 1877, Richard Smith and his entrepreneur-ial brother Clarence took out a patent on the stump-jump plough, which henceforth made the stump-strewn terrain of the Yorke Peninsula's mallee plains more malleable. Up until then, local farmers had to grub out the pesky roots by hand or risk toppling their top-heavy ploughs from the Old Country. A prototype model is parked near East Tce, while the Historical Museum has a series of the Smiths' design doodles on stretched linen. **[Fifth St, open Sun. and holidays 2.30p.m.–4.30p.m. Entry $2/50c. Phone (08) 8837 3213]**

## A LOYAL FOLLOWING

CANBERRA, ACT    Canberra was created in 1909 to stem the ego battle between Sydney and Melbourne, who both fancied themselves as a federal capital. An empty space between the rivals was chosen – a paddock with a ready-made population of 20 000 (the sheep belonged to Duntroon, a pastoral run). Bizarre names proposed for the nas-cent city ranged from Gonebroke to Swindleville. While it's not hard to imagine the unruly flocks of yesteryear, especially in the vicinity of Parliament House, you can relive the capital's pastoral past by pop-ping into Blundell's Cottage on Lake Burley Griffin, or walking the City Walk in Civic where sculptor Les Kossatz has moulded a ewe and ram. Sitting on a throne, the ram is intended to evoke evicted farmer James Ainslie, formerly prime minister of all he surveyed. **[Cottage is on Wendouree Dve, Parkes. Open daily 11a.m.–4p.m. Entry $4/$2, family $10. The Civic bleaters can be viewed free of charge]**

## BIG DIG

COLEAMBALLY, NSW    One of the youngest towns in Australia, Coleambally was born in 1968 to service a brand-new irrigation area.

Guarding the town's entry is a trench-digger on steroids – the 130-tonne Bucyrus Erie Class III Dragline. The monster arrived at 3 km per hour in 1978, putting the water channels in place. It's parked in Lion's Park on the Jerilderie–Darlington Pt Rd at the edge of town, and it ain't budging.

## POSEIDON'S PANTRY

**CURRIE, KING ISLAND, Tas.** Dennis and Peta Klumpp (I kid you not) have pioneered some tasty ways to use King Island's bull kelp, an ultra-weird weed more than 8 m long and growing up to 12 cm a day. Their products include Hot Kelp Pickles and Hot and Spicy Kelp Sauce, based on a traditional Klumpp family recipe, though using kelp was Dennis's idea. As an industrial chemist, he is well aware of the elements involved. [**Produce inquiries on (03) 6463 1151. Most of the weedy wares are available in Currie's food stores, and at King Island Produce, or online at www.kip.com.au**]

Two centuries ago, it was the custom at weddings to present the brand-new spouses with a marriage jug. There's a farm-proud example in **Dongara (WA)**, belonging to John Wilton and Mary Marklove Fishpool, whose names are inscribed above a conjugal doggerel that warrants quoting:

*Let the wealthy and great*
*Roll in splendour and state*
*I envy them not I declare it.*
*I eat my own lamb,*
*My chicken and ham,*
*I shear my own fleece and I wear it.*

Whether the couple's farming life flourished or wilted goes unnoted. But their jug is as new as the day it was baked. [**Irwin District Museum, 5 Waldeck St. Open weekdays 10a.m.–4p.m., Sat. 10a.m.–noon. Entry $2.50/$2/50c. Phone (08) 9927 1323**]

## TUTTI FRUTTI

**EMMAVILLE, NSW**   Why settle for a lemon tree when a single plant can bear mandarins, navels, lemons, limes and tangelos all at once? James and Kerry West are the orchard boffins behind these freaks, which they developed through years of patient grafting. Colder weather is better for the 'multi-nashi', a sort of pear supermarket with four species ripening over different months. Splashes of paint can help growers identify which branch will offer blood plums and which one peaches. [Fruit Salad Tree Company, 2369 Gulf Rd. Phone (02) 6734 7204. Mail order possible. Check out www.fruitsaladtrees.com]

## NO FLIES ON FORTH FOLK

**FORTH, Tas.**   In the opium business, the world has two triangles: the Golden Triangle of Thailand, and the Forth Triangle of Tasmania. The poppies here were planted around 1964 by a Hungarian chemist called Janos von Kabay, who devised a method to extract morphine from the green poppy straw. Today the market is blooming. Drive from Devonport to Forth in high summer and you'll be dazzled by the silvery bulbs on display, plus paddocks of yellow daisies. A cousin crop, the daisies yield pyrethrum, a basic ingredient of many insecticides. Unwind the window and inhale if you don't believe me.

Deer-O-Dome and Guinea Pig World, close to **Albany (WA)** Airport, supports more than 250 red and fallow deer. Tours are available, as are antler creams and venison sausages. But the farm's sideline is the country's largest free-range herd (yes, that *is* the collective noun) of guinea pigs. [**Link Rd. Open Thur., Fri., Sun., Mon. (Sun.–Fri. in school holidays) 10a.m.–4p.m. Feeding times 10.30a.m., 11.30a.m., 2p.m. and 3p.m. Phone (08) 9841 7436]**

## SILVANBERRY FIELDS

**SORELL, Tas.**   Given the right month, strawberries are almost ho-hum at Sorell Fruit Farm. At Australia's most diverse berry plantations you can pluck loganberries, tayberries and silvanberries, as well as the usual stone-hearted suspects. Check www.sorellfruitfarm.com to find out which brambles are blooming, or try your luck at the gate. [**174 Pawleena Rd. Turn left 150 m past McDonald's. Phone (03) 6265 2744**]

## TROPICS IN A BOTTLE

**TI-TREE, NT**   Shatto Mango is a tin shed on a 9-ha oasis along the Stuart Hwy. It boasts 1700 mango trees which yield more than 60 tonnes of fruit. Most of the succulent darlings are trucked interstate, but a good number are pulped on the premises and made into wine (try their tongue-numbing liqueur, Mango Moonshine). No pesticides are used on the farm, and only bore water is used. Check out the website for a myriad of mango recipes, including boosters, smoothies, milk shakes and mango cheesecake. [**Open daily 9a.m.–7p.m. Free entry. Phone (08) 8956 9828 or try www.redcentrefarm.com**]

# ODDITIONS

◎ There are bigger wind farms, but the mills at Cargoar Dam, near **Blayney (NSW)** have the longest blades (47 m in diameter) on record. [**Cargoar Dam turnoff between Blayney and Cargoar**]

◎ If you have a taste for less common wine varieties, take an offbeat odyssey through the **Hunter Valley (NSW)**, stopping at Calais Estate (for Zinfandel), Honeytree Estate (for Clariette), Rothbury Ridge (for Durif) and The Boutique Wine Centre (for Viognier).

◎ A team including one-Test batsman Paul 'Dasher' Hibbert is growing 17000 English willow trees in **Wood Wood (Vic.)**, beside the Murray River. One day the trunks will become cricket bats across India, the West Indies and home. [**35 km northwest of Swan Hill, along the Murray Valley Hwy. For more see www.cricketbatwillow. com.au**]

◎ Table Cape Tulip Farm in **Wynyard (Tas.)** has exported over a million bulbs to the Netherlands. The same farm, all 90 vivid ha atop an extinct volcano, harvests daffodils, Dutch irises and onions. [**363 Lighthouse Rd. Open daily 10a.m.–4.30p.m., late Sept.–mid Oct. Entry $5. Phone (03) 6442 2012**]

# FEATS

*(Being a tribute to heroic hauls
and enigmatic endeavours)*

## WONDERLAND IN ALICE

ALICE SPRINGS, NT   Back in Holland during World War 2, humanitarian forger Henk Guth secretly removed Stars of David from Jewish passports. After the war, he migrated to Australia and was smitten by the desert around Alice Springs. In 1975, after setting up a massive circular scaffolding, Henk and fellow countryman Fritz Pieters spent six months painting the world's biggest desertscape. Now housed in a special octagonal loft, the work took 33 linen sheets and 680 kg of paint. [Panorama Guth, 65 Hartley St, a block from Todd Mall. Open Mon.–Sat. 9a.m.–5p.m., Sun. and holidays noon–5p.m. Entry $6.50/$4.40. Phone (08) 8952 2013 or visit www.panoramaguth.com.au]

## LOGS OF ACCLAIM

BALLINA, NSW   Spaniard Vital Alsar was convinced that flotillas of Americans had crossed the Pacific in ancient times with the express intention of reaching Polynesia. To prove his theory, Alsar harvested 27 balsa trees and built three rafts. In 1973 the fleet set sail from Ecuador, bound for Mooloolaba in Qld. After 178 days and one anticyclone, *Las Balsas* reached Ballina (wayward currents dashed the Queensland plan). The two surviving rafts were cannibalised to produce the remarkable craft now housed in the Naval and Maritime Museum – without a nail, screw or rivet to be seen. [Behind the Visitors Centre, Regatta Ave. Open daily 9a.m.–4p.m. Entry by donation. Phone (02) 6681 1002]

The world's biggest fruitbowl, in the **Proserpine (Qld)** Historical Museum, was gouged on a single lathe five years ago. The timbers involved (or should that be revolved) are cedar and mango-wood. The bowl has a

2.6-m diameter and a total of 25 glued layers. [Bruce
Hwy. Open Mon.–Fri. 9a.m.–4p.m., Sun. 10a.m.–4 p.m.
during the tourist season. Entry $4.50/$2.50. Phone
(07) 4945 3969]

## INTO THE ABYSS

BEACHPORT, SA    Murray McCourt had a swamp on his farm taking
up valuable pasturage. So in 1957 he cut a ditch, which became a
trench, which became a chasm . . . Finally, with the aid of Dick McIntyre
and some gelignite, Murray made his very own canyon via which the
swamp water could escape. A kilometre long and some 33 m at its
deepest, the Woakwine Cutting is one of the seven artificial wonders of
the world. [10 km north along the Robe Rd]

## BLAZING SADDLE

DORRIGO, NSW    A plain plaque commemorates an extraordinary
journey. Bushman R.M. Williams challenged his Canadian pal Dan
Seymour to blaze a trail down the Great Dividing Range – all 5330
km of it. Dan took the bait, and in 1973 loaded up his pack-horse and
rode from Melbourne to Cooktown, with a few loops along the way.
So it was a Canadian who set down the template for our Bicentennial
National Trail, the longest marked track on the planet. With so many
tranquil ridge towns to choose from, Dan plumped for Dorrigo, where
he passed away in 2001, aged 78. [The plaque is in the Heritage
Gardens of the Pioneer Park]

## PLATYPUS GALORE

HEALESVILLE, Vic.    The first platypus to be hatched in captivity was
Corrie, who was born in 1943 at Healesville Sanctuary. The birth triggered front-page headlines in the *New York Times* – not bad going for
wartime. Although successful breeding seemed henceforth assured,
the next Healesville offspring took another 56 years to appear, in the
form of twins Barak and Yarra Yarra. [Badger Creek Rd, off Maroon-
dah Hwy. Open daily 9a.m.–5p.m. Entry $19/$14.50/$9.50. Phone

(03) 5957 2800 or check out www.zoo.org.au. There's nowhere you'll get up closer or more personal to these animals]

Near **Weipa (Qld)** you can watch sunrise over one sea (the Coral) and sunset on another (Arafura). The journey from Iron Range National Park, where your daylight starts, is a genuine day trip, following Frenchman's Rd to the Developmental Hwy and on to Weipa. (Rivers Pascoe and Wenlock, both tricky crossings and for 4WD vehicles only, will make sure you earn that icy sundowner at the Albatross Hotel.)

## RETIREMENT BERTH

**HUSKISSON, NSW**  *Lady Denman* wasn't made especially for the open sea. The 97-tonne ferry, built in Huskisson early last century, served her days in Sydney Harbour until the scrapheap loomed. But the people of Huskisson offered her ladyship a reprieve. A lock was built, new channels dug, and the ferry tugged home in 1983. Piece by piece an entire maritime museum was built around her. **[Woolamia Rd. Open daily 10a.m.–4p.m. Entry $8/$6/$4. Phone (02) 4441 5675]**

## SILVER BIRD NEST

**LONGREACH, Qld**  Operational birthplace of Qantas back in 1921, Longreach saw a different kind of stork land in 2000. Almost all 3750 inhabitants crammed the streets on 16 November to watch a Qantas 747 land in a compacted paddock, where it was to become the prize exhibit of the airline's museum. Two hangars were moved to allow enough landing space. Captain Mike Fitzgerald tested his mettle on a flight simulator before confronting the paddock for real, and the big bird coasted calmly to a halt to become a permanent landmark. **[Qantas Founders' Outback Museum is at the airport, Sir Hudson Fysh Dr. Open daily 9a.m.–5p.m. Bookings essential for the $12 Jumbo tours. Phone (07) 4658 3737 or visit www.qfom.com.au for more]**

## YOU UP FOR IT?

**MIRROOL, NSW**    Robbie Mills from Darwin did it first – in bare feet. Then Geelong legend, Billy Brownless, hit the heights on his way to a wedding (he's reported to have missed the grand occasion). Now it's an annual event at the Royal Hotel: who can kick a ball clear over the 32-m silos (kids get to kick over stacked oil drums). **[Usually held on second Sun. in Oct. Phone (02) 6974 1237 for the next showdown, or just lob in – and lob]**

## ODDITIONS

◉ The only dairy town in the Australian tropics, **Malanda (Qld)** is the start of the world's longest milk run. Trucks leave frequently from Eacham Shire heading to Darwin, some 3800 km away. Other runs include Townsville, Alice Springs and Papua New Guinea.

◉ Harold Gatty from **Campbell Town (Tas.)** required not 80 but 8 days, 15 hours and 51 minutes to fly around the world. This was in 1931: a model of *Winnie Mae*, the mosquito-like aircraft, perches atop a globe on the northern edge of town.

# FILMS

*(Being a set of cinematic locations
and Hollywood associations)*

## BISONTENNIAL

**ADELAIDE RIVER, NT**  Crocodile Dundee needs no introduction. Armed with knife and lopsided grin, Mick charmed the world – and a big water buffalo – in 1984. The buffalo involved was Charlie, the horniest walk-on in Hollywood history after Errol Flynn in *The Case of the Curious Bride*. Sadly, Charlie died in 2000. If not for the front-page obituary, the owners of the Adelaide River Inn might have opted to sneak in a body-double, but a stuffed carcass has to suffice. The buffalo stares knowingly into the famous .303 Bar. **[Behind the BP station]**

## AMONG THE STARS

**BROOME, WA**  Cyclone Eva almost cancelled the movies in Broome (WA) in 1970. The winds were so strong that the outdoor screen tilted at 45°. But the locals kept watching. They'd been through worse – like the annual king tides, the dog fights in the stalls, and the termites. The Sun Cinema is the world's oldest picture gardens, and warmly recommended. Just don't panic when the Virgin Blue jet interrupts the first act. **[Weld St. Movie hotline (08) 9192 3199]**

Perched at the top of Chifley Tower in central **Sydney (NSW)** is Forty One Restaurant, a sky-room of Thai silk and Tasmanian myrtle. You may recognise the decor from the original *Matrix* movie. It's where Cypher and Agent Smith (Aussie Hugo Weaving) locked horns and basically ignored the view. **[Take a peek at www.forty-one.com.au, or at dare to dine by calling (02) 9221 2500]**

## VINLAND

**COOBER PEDY, SA**   Aliens haven't landed in the opal fields, just Americans. The Hollywood team were here in 1998 making the Vin Diesel sci-fi flick *Pitch Black*, leaving behind a spaceship in the car park of Umoona Opal Museum as a token of gratitude. Across the road, behind the Lions Information Board, is another cinematic memento – a *Priscilla* triptych. **[Main drag of Hutchison St]**

> Old **Adaminaby (NSW)** is the original, flooded version of New Adaminaby. The town was relocated in 1956 to allow Lake Eucumbene to sprawl during construction of the Snowy Mountains hydro scheme. Some municipal relics persist, though, including the racetrack on the Rosedale road, where many of the racing sequences for *Phar Lap* (1983) were filmed.

## QUEENS OF THE STONE AGE

**KINGS CANYON, NT**   Queens adore Kings Canyon, southwest of Alice Springs, where key scenes of the cross-dressing smash-hit *The Adventures of Priscilla, Queen of the Desert* were filmed. To reach the movie's greatest touchstone – the V-like cleft that led our transvestites towards the Garden of Eden – follow the blue arrows on the Rim Walk, heading for the Northern Wall, till you pass the sign announcing Ancient Sandbars.

> Most of the bowls bowled in Mick Molloy's film *Crackerjack* were slung at the Melbourne Bowling Club, at 138 Union St, **Windsor (Vic.)**. But the storyboarding was done at the **Richmond (Vic.)** Union Bowling Club, 2 Gleadell St. **[Phone (03) 9428 1951]**

## CALL THAT A PUB?

**MACKINLAY, Qld**   Before 1986, it was the Federal. But then Sue Charlton, the naïve Yank reporter played by Linda Kozlowski, wandered into Mick Dundee's lair at the Walkabout Creek Hotel, and the pub has adopted the cinematic name ever since. Licensee Paul Collins plays the movie trump to the max, with cinema posters, croc murals and a film-set façade for Never Never Safaris. **[Matilda Hwy, open daily]**

## DOUBLE FEATURE

**PARACHILNA, SA**   The town has a population of seven, but that multiplies dramatically if a film is being shot in the adjacent Flinders Ranges. Over the years the area has hosted such productions as *Gallipoli*, *Holy Smoke*, *Kings in Grass Castles* and *Rabbit-Proof Fence*. The Prairie Hotel, base camp for most of these, is also home of feral cuisine, offering such morsels as camel sirloin and rack of goat. **[For more on the film and feral fronts, try www.prairiehotel.com.au or call (08) 8648 4844]**

Without giving too much away, there's a crucial scene in *Lantana* where a phone call is made outside a roadhouse on a lonely highway. Pie in the Sky is that roadhouse, a cult cafe overlooking the Newcastle Fwy, near **Cowan (NSW)**. The lonely road is the Old Pacific Hwy, by far the most rewarding route to Gosford, unless you happen to be Anthony La Paglia fighting for his . . . oops. That's enough of that.

## WILD WEST SHOOTING

**SILVERTON, NSW**   The ultimate location for outback locations is this town 25 km northwest of Broken Hill. It has played backdrop to *Mad Max 2*, *Mission Impossible 2* and *Priscilla* too. Midnight Oil and INXS have made classic clips here also.

## AGRICULTURE

**LOWER WONGA, Qld**   Gary King has always been a believer in alfresco cinema. He ran the projection room in Mt Isa as a 16-year-old and now runs Australia's only boutique drive-in, a twin-screen farm-o-plex off a dirt road. The set-up is super-casual, though Gary relies on a quorum of four vehicles – which happens most nights – before the feature gets rolling. [Take Wide Bay Hwy north of Gympie for 12 km, turn left at Bell's Bridge, then turn into Abel Rd and continue for 3 km of gravel road. Phone (07) 5486 1201. Screenings Fri. and Sat., $10 a carload]

*Social Salvation*, claim various film scholars, was the world's first feature-length movie, made in **Melbourne (Vic.)** in 1898. Shot by the Salvation Army in Australia's first film studio, it most resembles a televangelistic variety show. **[Stills and footage can be seen beside the Army's City Temple in Westwood Place, off Bourke St. Open weekdays 10a.m.–4p.m. Entry is free (ring bell). Phone (03) 9639 3618]**

Redruth Jail in **Burra (SA)** has evolved from a co-ed prison to a girls' reformatory school to a filmset for *Breaker Morant* (1980). The movie was shot, like its noble hero, against the grim stone walls. **[Off Barrier Hwy, 2 km northeast of town. Open daily 9a.m.–5p.m. Entry by Burra Heritage Passport ($15/$11) from Visitors Centre. Phone (08) 8892 2154 or log onto www.visitburra.com]**

# ODDITIONS

⊚ Back in 1970, Mick Jagger did much of his *Ned Kelly* thing in the Royal Mail Hotel of **Braidwood (NSW)**. For trivia nuts, Ian McKellen (now Sir Ian) was offered the role first, but the producers opted for the Jagger swagger.

⊚ *Paperback Hero* helped kick-start Hugh Jackman's film career. The pub on screen is the Nindigully Hotel in downtown **Nindigully (Qld)**, about 35 km south of St George.

⊚ *The Shiralee* (1957) was remarkable for being a simple homespun tale on a major Hollywood budget. Many scenes were shot in

**Binnaway (NSW)**, accounting for the beaming faces of Peter Finch and Elizabeth Sellars above the bar of the Royal Hotel.

◎ When the big-screen crew came to **Robertson (NSW)** in 1994 to film a chatty little pig called Babe, they thankfully managed to keep the town's Big Potato out of frame.

◎ Park Avenue Bridal on Level 3 of Westfield Shoppingtown in **Parramatta (NSW)** is the place where Muriel Heslop aspired to become Mariel Heslop-Van Arckle. The film, of course, is *Muriel's Wedding* (1994).

◎ The Gothic vaulted car park beneath the South Lawn at the University of Melbourne in **Parkville (Vic.)**, with a pair of bluestone gods at the entrance, was picture-perfect as the Police Garage in *Mad Max 2: The Road Warrior* (1981).

◎ **Creswick (Vic.)** was turned into a vampire village in 2003 for the US miniseries, *Salem's Lot*, starring Donald Sutherland, Rob Lowe and Rebecca Gibney. The RSL became Grazioso's Funeral Parlour on the same occasion.

◎ In **Bermagui (NSW)** you can charter the actual fishing boat that exploded in *The Man Who Sued God*. Comedian Billy Connolly was the captain of the fireball, but since the film the Tarpin's licence has reverted to Keith Appleby on (02) 6493 4451.

# FREAKS

*(Being a sideshow of special specimens
and individual individuals)*

## STONE THE CROWS

**ALBURY, NSW**   Bush stone curlews are rare and endangered, which is strange because they are camouflage experts. A whole curlew family can lie prone in a litter of leaves and sticks, and you'd think the aviary empty. Take up the challenge at Aussie Wildlife, just north of town, which *alleges* it is home to four of these invisible birds. Much more obvious is the zoo's albino kangaroo. **[Hume Hwy. Open daily 9a.m.– 5p.m. Entry $10/$8/$5, family $25. Phone (02) 6040 3677]**

## NEW-WAVE THINKING

**AVOCA, NSW**   Mark Sainsbury ('Sanga' to his mates) innovated and perfected the dump floater, a radical surfboard manoeuvre involving a lateral drift across a wave's broken back. This trick gave him the Pro Junior title in Narrabeen in 1985, and arguably helped him win the World Amateur title in England in 1986. But the fairy-tale wiped out in 1992, when Mark rode his last monster off Avoca Rocks. There's a memorial plaque level with the breakline, along the rock platform.

Dook (rhymes with spook) is a chicken with three legs, who lives in the Lambing Flat Museum in **Young (NSW)**. Sharing the collection is a pickled white piglet with an elephantine trunk. **[Campbell St, on the Wagga exit, opposite St Mary's Church. Entry $4/$3/$1. Open daily 10a.m.–4p.m. Phone (02) 6382 2248]**

## A CROSS TO BEAR

**BROOME, WA**   Irishman Jim Clark showed the freak oyster to his wife Bessie in 1874. She crossed herself and said, 'Take it to the Holy Reverence at once'. (Jimmy took it to a Roebourne pub instead.) It was incredible – seven pearls welded to the shell in shaft formation, with another poking from either side. Pearl broker Bob Sholl purchased The Southern Cross oyster for £90. Now, many believe, it resides in the Vatican. See the photo, and read of other mutant pearls, in the Broome Historical Society Museum. **[Robinson St. Open daily Nov.–June 10a.m.–1p.m., weekdays Jul.–Oct. 10a.m.–4p.m. (weekends till 1p.m.). Entry $5/$3/$1.** Phone (08) 9192 2075]

## BULLDUST

**DONALD, Vic.**    Botanists call it a 'parasitic excrescence' but locals know the lumpy box-tree as the Bullock's Head and the resemblance is certainly uncanny – horns, snout and puckered brow. The tree stood for years in the bed of the Richardson River, but succumbed to rot in 2003 and keeled over. **[Turn towards the river off the Sunraysia Hwy. The resurrected tree is on Byrne St, parallel with the highway]**

**Dunmarra (NT)** seems as far from the sea as geographically possible. Yet this Tanami Desert roadhouse enjoyed a rainstorm of fish in February 1994. (Small-scale compared to Cyclone Tracy, of course.)

## A TALE OF TWO TAILS

**NANA GLEN, NSW**    Hiding in the hinterland north of Coffs Harbour (just like paparazzi-shy actor Russell Crowe) is a two-tailed lizard known to local Aborigines as Nana. He's hard to find – inhabiting just a narrow strip from Coffs to Grafton – but is represented in murals on the Nana Glen Memorial Hall and the primary school. Jeff and Jean Maher warmed to the reptile so much that they named their winery Two Tail Wines. **[963 Orara Way. Open daily 11a.m.–5p.m., closed Mon. during school terms. Phone (02) 6654 3633]**

At Vance's Bar, a part of the Potshot Resort in **Exmouth (WA)**, a few chilling photos record the devastation of the 1999 Category 5 cyclone Vance. Outside Grace's Bar cnr Murat and Pelias Sts, a twisted piece of iron has been lodged in a gum tree ever since.

## SNOW WHITE RAINBOWS

**PLENTY, Tas.**   It's a toss-up to name the rarest rarity at Salmon Ponds. Tails, it's the swarm of albino rainbow trout; heads, the wild platypus that commutes from the Derwent River next door. Australia's oldest fish farm, Salmon Ponds started to breed Atlantic salmon way back in 1864: the eggs were shipped across the Indian Ocean in beds of moss, but the experiment faltered and the farm now concentrates on fishing not breeding. [Open daily 9a.m.–5p.m. Entry $6/$4, family $16, which provides entry to grounds and museum. Fish food extra. Phone (03) 6261 5663]

# FURNITURE

*(Being a suite of special effects,
including ineffable tables and offbeat seats)*

## STRIKING SIT-DOWNS

**BARCALDINE Qld**   The Tree of Knowledge is a ghost gum in Barcaldine, where striking shearers rallied in 1891, so sowing the seeds of the Australian Labor Party. Across the road, the park bench near the newsagency is nicknamed the Seat of Knowledge, a tribute to the assorted doyens who gather on the woodwork each morning to await the *Morning Bulletin* from Rockhampton. **[Oak St]**

## INDELIBLE STAIN

**CHARTERS TOWERS, Qld**   In 1901 the manager of a local gold-extracting plant, David Brown, found that his weekly wage had slumped from £8 to £6. Not happy, he pulled a revolver at a shareholders' meeting in the hope of unmasking his undoer. When temporary chairman Graham Haygarth refused Brown's request to see the minutes from the last board meeting, Brown shot him dead, and then shot himself – but survived. An eerie souvenir of the incident is the table with a noticeable stain at one end, plus a painting of the grim scene on the facing wall. **[Upstairs in the World Theatre giftshop, 82–90 Mosman St. Ask at the counter to see the crime scene. Phone (07) 4787 8472]**

## SHOT ACROSS THE BOWS

**GOULBURN, NSW**   Australia's oldest surviving brewery (built in 1836) has a Viking ship within its walls. Salvaged from the Fjord Room of Sydney's Menzies Hotel, the ship serves as a smorgasbord and carried finger food for the 175th anniversary celebrations of the great trek of explorers Hume and Hovell in 1999. **[23 Bungonia Rd. Open daily from 11a.m. Entry fee and tasting $5.50/$4.40/$2.20. Phone (02) 4821 6071]**

The elegant mirror in the foyer of the Palace Hotel in **Kalgoorlie (WA)**, was a gift from mining engineer (later US president) Herbert Hoover to the hotel barmaid. It came with a DIY poem that is a model of alliteration (I give you 'murmurous mellow music' by way of example). **[Cnr Hannan and Maritana Sts]**

## A DROP IN THE OCEAN

NOWRA, NSW   On 10 February 1964, the Australian warships *Voyager* and *Melbourne* collided off Jervis Bay, killing 82 sailors. A fisherman from Currarong found a grey chair bobbing in the South Pacific a few days later, and presented it to the Australian Museum of Flight 30 years down the track. Identified as belonging to the *Melbourne*, the chair is one of a few keepsakes of the collision. Was it jettisoned during hijinks before the accident, or thrown into the water as a makeshift life preserver? **[Part of the museum display at the naval base, Nowra Hill, south of town. Open daily 10a.m.–4p.m. Entry $10/$7/$5, family $24. Phone (02) 4424 1920]**

## WITHNELL AND I

ROEBOURNE, WA    Emma Withnell was the first European woman to settle in the state's harsh northwest, now known as the Kimberley. She arrived in 1864, heavily pregnant and with two young boys at her knee. Husband John did his best to make her comfortable, scrounging bones from the whaling station on Rosemary Island and fashioning them into a chair. No nail in sight, the chair has a vertebra as a base, ribs as arms, and a whale clavicle for a back. An unreal replica stands in the Old Roebourne Jail, Emma's original throne having been seconded by the National Trust in Perth. **[Queen St. Open winter weekdays 9a.m.–5p.m. and weekends 9a.m.–3p.m., summer weekdays 9a.m.–3p.m. Entry by donation. Phone (08) 9182 1060]**

In 1836 South Australia's first governor, John Hindmarsh, arrived aboard HMS *Buffalo*, which anchored in Holdfast Bay off **Glenelg (SA)**. Four years later the Calcutta-built ship sank off New Zealand, but she still haunts Glenelg in replica form: as a floating restaurant in Patawalonga Creek; and (off-limits to the public) as a 2-m-high chair, made from *Buffalo* spare ribs, in the Holdfast Shire Council offices.

## LOOK BUT DON'T BUY

**WANGAN, Qld**   Geoff Donald runs a post office, service station and tea room all in one. The last is packed with 50 years' worth of works in timber inlay, created by Geoff's grandfather, John Oliveri, who worked in a mill. Averse to waste, he started fashioning the offcuts into all manner of things, including 400 trays and decorative veneer work depicting marlins, the shire council, even a buzz-saw in profile. When the Oliveri garage overflowed, the tea room reaped the benefits. [**Donald's Duck In adjoins the Esso service station on Meyers Ave. Open daily 5a.m.–7p.m. Free entry. Phone (07) 4064 2265**]

# ODDITIONS

◎ Park benches along Marine Pde in **Coolangatta (Qld)** have been customised to mimic surfboards.

◎ Potential winner of the Freakish Furniture final is the century-old cedar wardrobe, clad in kangaroo skin, which stands in the Centenary Cottage, part of the folk museum of **Tenterfield (NSW)**. [**Logan St. Open Wed.–Sun. (daily during school holidays) 10a.m.–4p.m. Entry $3/$1. Phone (02) 6736 2844**]

◎ Outside Blue Gum Gallery, an arts and craft shop on the main drag of **Merriwa (NSW)**, is an elegant bench bearing the inscription 'Bored Husbands' Seat'.

◎ Salvaged from the Green Lizard, a legendary dance hall in **Albany (WA)**, is a hat rack with petrel beaks for hooks. [**You can see this barbaric treasure at the Patrick Taylor Cottage Museum, 31 Duke St. Open 1p.m.–4p.m. Phone (08) 9841 5403**]

# GADGETS

*(Being an intermesh of gizmos, inventions and assorted brainchildren)*

## STAGE PROP

**ALICE SPRINGS, NT**   Chances are you'd have no plans to visit Lake Hopkins, a saltpan in a trackless part of the Tanami Desert. Mineral surveyor Kurt Johannsen learnt of it in 1950, landing there with his mate Jimmy Prince to refuel. On taking off again, their plane nose-dived and smashed its wooden propeller. Kurt found a knife in his box of tricks and started whittling the prop until the blades were in miniature but, they hoped, maybe still good. Leaving Jimmy behind, Kurt fired up the engine and took to the sky, chasing the eagles to find the thermals. **[See the improvised prop in the Central Australian Aviation Museum, part of the Cultural Precinct on Memorial Ave, off Larapinta Dve. Open weekdays 9a.m.–5p.m., weekends 10a.m.–5p.m. Entry $8/$5, family $24, for all 10 facilities. Phone (08) 8951 5686]**

The 30-sail windmill called Steel Wings, on Lake **Jerilderie (NSW)**, is among the largest windmills in the world. Made in North Sydney in 1910, Steel Wings is the only operating example of its type and brings to mind a boat propeller from a fish's point of view. Over 15 m tall and 7.6 m in diameter, it's hard to miss. **[Powell St, Luke Park]**

## HAUL OF FAME

**BURRA, SA**   Cornish miners burrowed for copper here in the 1850s. But there was a snag: water in the shafts, and not a decent pump to be found. So the company imported an engine from Cornwall – essentially a pump about the size of Liechtenstein. This created another problem: there was no vehicle big enough to haul the 15-tonne contraption inland. Hence necessity mothered the mother of all jinkers, a 10-m monster, the road train of its day. Weighing over 4 tonnes and requiring 72 hauling bullocks, it remains one of the biggest rigs from the colonial era. **[Parked on Market St, near the town centre]**

## PROTO-BLOWER

**CAMPBELL TOWN, Tas.**   Alfred Barrett Biggs made the first long-distance telephone call in Australia. In 1876, having cribbed Alexander Bell's design from *English Mechanic* magazine, Biggs rigged his wooden receiver onto the railway's telegraph line. He next rubbed a pencil over the receiver. 'Did you hear that?' he asked the stationmaster far off in Launceston, about 70 km away. The reply was unforgettable: 'Like a locomotive moving on a bridge!' **[Both receivers stored in the Heritage Hwy Museum. Open Mon.–Fri. 9a.m.–4.30p.m., Sat. 9.30a.m.–3p.m. Gold coin donation. Phone (03) 6381 1353]**

## A SUCKER IS BORN

**ELDORADO, Vic.**   The three Vic. towns that used the most electricity during the early 1950s were Melbourne, Geelong . . . and Eldorado (population 337 in 1947, and still falling). The reason for the big consumption figures in such a small town is that it's home to the largest, heaviest dredge in the southern hemisphere. This 110-bucket leviathan, used for large-scale gold mining, may weigh 2142 tonnes but it *floats*. The dredge operated until 1954 and is now a registered historic structure marooned on the edge of town. **[Off Byawartha Rd]**

## OUT OF THE BOX

**KALGOORLIE, WA**   The tyranny of distance heightens the call to improvise. This fact is embodied in a wooden bike created by Mulga Bill, a subsistence miner on the Kalgoorlie goldfields in the 19th century. The deft digger used packing boxes for wheels, meat tins for tyres, mulga for spokes and bullock hide for the chain. Legend has it that Bill *pushed* the contraption from Mt Barker to Southern Cross, a distance of some 500 km over soft and treacherous terrain. You'd like to think he pedalled part of the way as well. **[Kalgoorlie-Boulder Museum, top end of Hannan St – look for the towering headframe. Open daily 10a.m.–4.30p.m. Entry by donation. Phone (08) 9021 8533 or visit www.museum.wa.gov.au]**

On display at the Police Station Museum in **Mt Barker (WA)** there's a vintage, pump-action Star vacuum cleaner. Every breeding season a striated pardalote returns to make her nest in the dust compartment. **[Albany Hwy. Open weekends and public holidays 10a.m.–4p.m. But it's always worth checking for signs of life during the week. Entry $5]**

## PRESS REPORT

**LANGHORNE CREEK, SA**   When grapes first flourished on the Murray river plains, most wineries used hand-worked presses. Except the Potts of Bleasdale: a century or so back, Frank Potts II made a red-gum exaggeration of the European screw press. It's a monster, the lever alone weighing 3.5 tonnes, and the twin barrels capable of holding almost the same in grapes. All bolts and rivets were forged at the vineyard, following which the press groaned to life in 1892. The contraption, one of the largest wine presses in the world, ceased work in 1962. It was used again in 2000, but only for a 150th anniversary squeeze. **[Wellington Rd. Open daily 10a.m.–5p.m. Ask at the cellar door to view the beast. Phone (08) 8537 3001 or visit www.bleasdale.com.au]**

That kowtowing stork outside the service station in **Carmila (Qld)** is a marooned Texan oil pump.

## THE ANSWER, MY FRIEND

**MORAWA, WA**   Malcolm Walter reckons his official title is 'molinologist' (from the Latin), though you and I might prefer to call him a 'windmill nut'. Proof of his mania crams a whole shed in the local museum. At last count, Malcolm's collection numbers 23, but he recently bought a dozen DIY models from South Australia and he's always on the hunt for more. These aren't just your run-of-the-mill local Southern Crosses, but English models, Webbs and Duxes, the US Climax, the Altona Defiance, and the very first oil-bath engine. Don

Quixote would have a field day. [Cnr Prater and Gill Sts. Open seasonally on demand. Entry by donation. Phone (08) 9972 2051]

## REINS ON THE PLAIN

PARKES, NSW    Between horse-drawn ploughs and tractors at Pioneer Park Museum stands the Fowler Rein Drive. Picture a mechanised harness racer with a motor where the horse should be, and reins as the steering wheel. A bloke named Murnane from Melbourne invented the contraption, and Fowler Industries in England developed the model from army surplus in 1913. Only two were imported Down Under. One is lost and the other is parked in Parkes. [Dubbo end of town. Open Mon.-Sat. 10a.m.-3.30p.m., Sun. 10a.m.-2p.m. Entry $5/$2. Phone (02) 6862 5388]

## PULLING POWER

STANTHORPE, Qld    Stoves fashioned from kero cans, gate hinges from bottles, grape dusters from packing cases, meat safes from cotton reels. But the pièce de résistance is Charlie Mandelkow's Mystery Overland, a home-made tractor of which he made three during the 1920s. For want of a welder every joint is bolted, while the carburettor is a syrup tin with a horsehair filter. [Stanthorpe Historical Museum, 12 High St. Open Wed.-Fri. 10a.m.-4p.m., Sat. 1p.m.-4p.m., Sun. 9a.m.-1p.m. Entry $5/$2. Phone (07) 4681 1711]

Suffering insomnia? The jitters? Then look no further than the Automatic Medical Battery in the Barossa Historical Museum, in Tanunda (SA). The device is said to bring relief from headaches and paralysis by increasing your Electrical Vitality. No longer working, the battery was patented by the same London company that gave us the essential Electropathic Corset. [47 Murray St. Open daily 11a.m.–5p.m. Entry $2/$1. Phone (08) 8563 0507]

# GAMES

*(Being a toybox of remarkable recreations
and amazing amusements)*

## MONEY SPINNER

BEVERLEY, WA   Tell me, would you trust a bloke called Sport? Hundreds did during the 1940s, giving the wily farmer money for the chance to spin a plough disc. If the disc stopped on a white wedge you lost your money, which hundreds did owing to the weights secretly soldered to its base. Not that Sport Richards was a venal profiteer – all monies went to help build the nearby Morbining Hall. **[The crooked piece of engineering sits in the Dead Finish Museum, cnr Morrison St and Hunt Rd. Open Sun. 11a.m.–3p.m. Mar.–Nov., or by request through the Tourist Bureau. Phone (08) 9646 1555]**

## GREEN FEES?

COOBER PEDY, SA   Here the golf links are downright lunar. The hills mimic mounds of ice-cream. A carpet patch is the tee-off point. 'Green' is a misnomer: a thick coat of dieselene helps you recognise what's rough and what supposedly isn't. The greenkeeper is responsible for checking the course daily and, so goes the gag, pulling out any blade of grass he finds. Ten dollars give you unlimited playing time, though heat and dust are likely to hasten you to the 19th hole. **[4 km out of town along 17 Mile Rd. Phone (08) 8672 5965]**

Bill Knight's idea of paradise is watching the cricket in summer while sipping on a cool beer. The trouble is, Bill runs a corner shop in **Maryborough (Qld)**, offering takeaway food and country wares, and often a customer will interrupt his viewing pleasure. 'If I miss a wicket falling,' growls Bill, 'then that's inconvenient.' Hence the shop's name – The Inconvenience Store. **[Cnr Ferry and Macadam Sts]**

## LONG SCYTHE OF THE LAW

**KULGERA, NT**   Not a big town, Kulgera. At last count, going by the tipping competition in the only pub, the population is 16, including Sergeant Jack Clifford. In 2002, Jack had the job of quelling a snake plague with a household mattock. The poor bugger had to trudge the paddock opposite the pub, belting what serpents he found. In the middle of the carnage, his mind began to wander. A golf course would keep the grass shorter, he reckoned. And reptiles can't hide in short grass . . . So it was that a working bee turned the snaky wilderness into the Territory's first (or last, depending which way you're heading) golf course. [The pub-cum-roadhouse is 20 km north of the SA border]

## FOR THOSE WHO GIVE A TOSS

**GLEN INNES, NSW**   The Standing Stones of Glen Innes, a cryptic array of 38 granite blocks erected in 1990 by the Celtic Council of Australia, is the only such arrangement Down Under. The stones spell out compass points and solstice shadows, and from the air they capture both the Celtic and Southern Crosses. Every May, on the first weekend, the stones are the setting for a Celtic festival, complete with a competition to extract the Excalibur sword at the fringe of the circle. [Centennial Parklands, Watson Dve]

Train workers created the sport of trugo (from the phrase 'true go') around the 1920s, when you had to make your own fun. It's a sort of lawn bowls played with a sledgehammer. Everything has train connections: the grass court is the length of a carriage and the goal is the width of a train door. You can do your own trugo training at 219 Esplanade East, Port Melbourne. [Explore the website www.portphillip.vic. gov.au for more information]

## ZINFANDEL FOR INFIDELS

**MARGARET RIVER, WA**   Don't know a burgundy from a burger? Think a palate is something a forklift uses? Then Wine for Dudes is your kind of outing. Run by Cat Willcock, who grew up among grapes, the tours sidestep the elitism that dogs many cellar doors. Features include tastings, perhaps a bit of vineyard volleyball, and an International Wine-Spitting Tournament, where accuracy is all. **[Tours operate daily, with variations according to your bent. The going rate is $60, including barbecue or picnic lunch and five vineyard stops. Phone Cath on (08) 9758 8699 or check out www.winefordudes.com]**

## COARSE OUTING

**ONSLOW, WA**    Cyclone Vance in 1999 wreaked no perceptible havoc on the Onslow golf course, mainly because it already resembled a bomb-site. The Salt Lakes Golf Coarse (*sic*) has diesel-soaked greens and triple-decker tyre stacks for 'natural hazards'. A termite mound known as Carton Hill obstructs the first fairway. 'Hit the hill and have no fear,' threatens the poem on top of the ant nest, 'You will be buying a carton of beer.' **[Opposite the salt works a few km short of town. Members play for free. Visitors can chip in $2 (honesty tin) for a swing]**

A massive log outside the Plough Inn in **Bulahdelah (NSW)** owes its arrival to a guessing competition. The brush box fell early last century, was carted onto the banks of the Myall River and estimates were invited. Reputedly, the correct weight is 38 tonnes.

## LIFE AT THE SHARP END

**TIMBOON, Vic.**    Between Peterborough and Allansford, travelling the Great Ocean Rd, you'll be tempted by the Boggy Creek Pub. Once the hub of a thriving less-than-legal distillery, the Boggy is now hosting the longest game of darts in the world. No, the darts aren't thrown any great distance, but every week the pub's players test their eye against players in the Cadogan Arms, a corner snuggery in Chelsea, London. Scores are confirmed via a live phone hookup. **[Curdie Vale Rd. Look for the four-rifles emblem. Phone (03) 5566 5223]**

## CRICKET MERCHANDISE

**URALLA, NSW**    Kent Mayo is a curator extraordinaire. As overseer of McCrossin's Mill, a gem among regional museums, Mayo has packed all three storeys with fantastic stories as well as more conventional memorabilia. Part of the exhibit 'It's Just Not Cricket!', a lump of rock on the first floor, dated c. 3000BC and salvaged from Stonehenge, is believed to be the world's maiden cricket bat. Beside it, a bat with hinged flaps is an Opening Bat. A camouflaged bat with gunstock and trigger is obviously a Combat. And so on. **[Salisbury Rd. Open daily noon–5p.m. (10a.m.–5p.m. on public holidays). Entry $4/$3/$1.50. Phone (02) 6778 3022]**

Should you be reading this in heavy south-coast rain, marooned in a beach house with an eternal week in front of you, rest assured the library in **Kiama (NSW)** has more than 150 jigsaw puzzles, and every one can be borrowed. **[7 Railway Pde. Open daily from 9.30a.m., except Sun. Phone (02) 4233 1133]**

## ON A WHIM

**WHIM CREEK, WA**    The Whim Creek Hotel's speciality is 'ring on a string', which involves a brass ring, a string and a hook on the wall. While you're waiting for a game, look around for the numbered beams from the pre-fab kit that produced the building in 1886. This is the quintessential outback pub, and was so long before imitators 'invented' the genre. It's had a juicy murder (all 13 witnesses died before the hearing), a mischievous ghost, and a camel called Camelot. It's also a consulate for Hutt River Province. **[Between Roebourne and Headland. Open daily from 7.30a.m.]**

## ODDITIONS

- ⑥  South down Todd St in **Alice Springs (NT)** is a ten-pin complex called the Dust Bowl . . .
- ⑥  . . . in cane country, **Innisfail (Qld)** has its very own Sugar Bowl.

◎ *Night Watch* by Rembrandt takes pride of place among 100-plus jigsaws in the **Bridgetown (WA)** Visitors Centre. The Brierley Jigsaw Gallery treats puzzles as artwork, hanging the completed versions on the wall. **[154 Hampton St. Open daily 9a.m.–5p.m. Phone (08) 9761 1740]**

◎ Near Noah Beach in **Daintree (Qld)** National Park you'll find the dried pods of the aptly named cannonball mangrove. When cracked, the pods were used by the Kuku Yulanji people of Cape Tribulation as 3-D jigsaws.

# GARDENS

*(Being an abundance of arboreta
and hard-to-forget-mes)*

## ALL FENUGREEK TO ME

**ADELAIDE, SA**   Cumin stops lovers from being fickle, and borage encourages courage. Find out more herbal hokum at the Museum of Economic Botany. If a shrub has a by-product, then the pods and seeds and folkloric tidbits are here. You'll also get to see a disconcerting double coconut as well as crab's eyes and Indian pudding pipes. **[In the heart of the Botanical Gardens. Museum closed for restoration during 2005 but expected to reopen Jan. 2006. Free entry. Phone (08) 8222 9311]**

## GREEN GEOMETRY

**BALLARAT, Vic.**   Origami turned to glass. That's one description of the Robert Clark Conservatory in the Botanical Gardens, designed by Peter Elliott. The zigzag glasshouse stands 13 m high and has six angular folds on each flank. Robert Clark, the newspaper editor who seeded the project, squints in statue form near the door. Westward stand more busts – a chronological avenue of Australian prime ministers. **[Open daily 9a.m.–5p.m. Free entry, except Mar.–Apr. when admission to Begonia Festival is $3/$2/50c. Phone (03) 5320 7444 or visit www.ballaratbotanicalgardens.com.au]**

## MINE, ALL MINE

**BIGGENDEN, Qld**   Cooper's Ridge sounds more like a mine, or a wine, than an eccentric garden. Its owner has warmed to the prospecting theme, with shovel heads littering the tanbark, and a mine trolley entering the slab hut. Across the road, where surplus artefacts fill a paddock, a sign declares the spot to be Cooper's Overflow. **[60–62 Edward St. Look for the four palm trees]**

## COLOSSUS OF RHODOS

**BURNIE, Tas.**   Inland from Burnie is the world according to rhodo-dendrons. North America fringes the car park. Taiwan hems the middle lake. The lower lake is nicknamed The Sea of Japan, thanks to the tea-house, the arched bridge and all the Kyoto bloomers teeming its banks. Maurice Kupsch is the green thumb and engineering brain behind the 13 ha at Emu Valley. **[Off the Ridgley Rd. Open daily 10a.m.–5p.m., Aug.–Feb. Entry $5, kids free. Phone (03) 6433 0478]**

## JURASSIC PARKLANDS

**CAIRNS, Qld**   When you hear words like Gondwana and Triassic and Neozoic, your eyes can be forgiven for glassing over. It's hard to comprehend geo-time. But in the Flecker Botanic Gardens, the only wet tropical botanical garden in Australia, an evolutionary trail has been laid out to explain the millennia through flora. It begins with blue-green algae (Quaternary) and culminates in the Age of Angiosperms (now). **[94 Collins Ave, though the evolution sector is cnr Collins and McConnell Sts. Open weekdays 7.30a.m.–5.30p.m., weekends 8.30a.m.–5.30p.m. Phone (07) 4044 3398]**

What better place for an Aboriginal medicine garden than in the grounds of **Mt Isa's (Qld)** underground hospital on Joan St? Nature offers the anti-flu conker-berry, snappy-gum antiseptic and the wart-thwarting sap of the caustic bush.

## UNDER A BUSHEL

**COFFS HARBOUR, NSW**   Bernie Hyland was rootling in the rainfor-est on Bartle Frère, the highest mountain in Qld, when he found an unfamiliar nut and knew he'd discovered a new tree species. That was in the 1960s. The plant in question proved to be a cousin of the elusive nightcap oak, a tree rife in Gondwana times but now reduced to fossil traces. A second specimen was later found in northern NSW and the species has been propagated in the Botanical Gardens here. Don't expect one of the world's rarest trees to be flamboyant – modesty has been its secret for centuries. **[Open daily 9a.m.–5p.m. Free entry. To see the nightcap oak, walk down the central path to the Endangered Species section.** Phone (02) 6648 4188]

## THE BEAU AND THE BEAUTIFUL

DUNGOG, NSW    Retired circus worker and boxer Beau Hancock does the finding and putting up, and wife Betty does the painting. Gas cylinders and petrol tanks have become sharks and robots in this paddock of a garden. Fairground gear has been reborn into spaceships. A cow made of milk cans grazes by a sign that reads '4U2C'. A rainbow turnstile near the main gate costs nothing for visitors to spin. **[Fosterton Rd]**

## SURPRISE BY THE YARD

MIDDLE SWAN, WA    A Hills Hoist festooned with stiff clothes blown by an imaginary wind is one of dozens of installations in Gomboc Gallery and Sculpture Park. Every month or so a new exhibition fills the gallery, while over time the statues tend to become the garden furniture. **[50 James Rd. Open Wed.–Sun. 10a.m.–5p.m. Closed Jan. Entry free. Phone (08) 9274 3996 or visit www.gomboc-gallery.com.au]**

## PARMA KARMA

MOUNT WILSON, NSW    True garden buffs go to Yengo. This sanctuary of beeches, oaks and cedars is one of Australia's oldest surviving gardens, laid out in 1877. It's also the world's first reserve for the endangered Parma wallaby. Dozens of these dwarfish marsupials mooch among the European giants and bronze gazelles. Should the grounds around Cherry Cottage (next-door) be open for a stroll, be sure to see the Moon Gate, a miraculous circle of stacked stones. **[Yengo is open weekends Apr., May, Oct., Nov. 10a.m.–5p.m. To check exactly when, phone (02) 4756 2002. B&B also available]**

Robert Field's oldest cactus, over 100 years old, is the size of a golfball. There are 2000 other cactus varieties in the garden of his property Whiora in **Tennyson (Vic.)**, from agave (source of tequila's ancestor, pulque) to the Old Men of Peru (planted in 1927).

November is blooming time for many species. **[Field's Cactus Centre, 2064 Prairie Rd, between Rochester and Echuca. Entry $4/$2. Phone (03) 5488 2244]**

## DATE WITH DESTINY

TOWNSVILLE, Qld    Palmetum is a Lewis Carroll sort of word, being a marriage of palm and arboretum. Planted in Australia's bicentennial year, this palm-only garden is an oasis within an oasis. One of only two such plantations in the world (the other is in Tenerife in the Canary Islands), it boasts more than 350 species, from lipstick to fishtail, from rainforest to desert plants. An added feature is a memorial to a collision between two Blackhawk helicopters, which occurred near here in 1996, killing 18 soldiers. **[Off Nathan St in the southwest suburb of Douglas. Historic tea-room open Wed.–Sun. 10a.m.–5p.m. Gardens open every day. Phone (07) 4727 8330]**

## PUTTER CUPS

WANNEROO, WA    Vision and elbow grease turned 2 ha of crumbling dunes near Perth into a sanctuary of ponds and shade. It took Theo and Hanneke Puik seven years to re-create a little piece of their native Netherlands in the Wanneroo wastelands. Waterfalls, a pavilion, terracing and, finally, 36 putt-putt holes, were interwoven through the grounds. Botanic golf, as the Puiks called it, is a unique distraction for garden-lovers. A billiards–golf challenge was added in 1998. **[25 Drovers Place, 26 km north of Perth. Open Tue.–Fri. 9a.m.–4p.m. (weekends till 4.30p.m.). Entry $13.50/$11/$8.50 includes both courses. Check www.botanicgolf.com.au for other times, or phone (08) 9405 1475]**

The Botanic Gardens in **Wagga (NSW)** are both verdant and varied. The Tree Chapel has trees and shrubs of biblical significance set into the side of the hill. There is also a rough-hewn cross and altar. Though lovestruck locals are as liable to tie the knot in the nearby Shakespearian knot garden.

## THE NAMES OF THE ROSES

YORK, WA    I never knew that tea roses are so called because they first arrived in Chinese tea clippers. Or that Christian soldiers returned from the Crusades in the 12th century with damask roses from Damascus. That's the sort of information you can glean at the Avon Valley Historical Rose Garden. **[Osnaburg Rd, off Ulster Rd. Open Nov.–Jan. in good flowering seasons. Entry by donation. Phone (08) 9641 1469]**

# ODDITIONS

◉ Look twice at the couple tending the municipal gardens in **Halifax (Qld)**. The she-mower and the he-tiller were created courtesy of a Rural Arts Grant.

◉ Eight little green men stand around a tiny tin spaceship on the east edge of **Terowie (SA)**. Ex-sailor Kevin Hancock has also added Ned Kelly and an ironing woman for good measure.

◉ Pathways and benches in this tiny garden in **Ballan (Vic.)** have been inlaid with mirrors, marbles, broken tiles and teacups. Littered quotes from Jimi Hendrix and Michael Leunig make a call for peace. **[111 Inglis St. There's a visitors' book on the veranda]**

# GHOSTS

*(Being a séance of spectral appearances
and addresses)*

## HIGH SPIRITS

**ALBION, BRISBANE, Qld**   The original owner of the Breakfast Creek Hotel, William Galloway, drank more than his fill in 1895. His mates sent the publican upstairs to dry out, only for the bloke to climb from his window, slip and fall to his death on the cobbles. The staff tell visitors (who have included Mikhail Gorbachev) that William still clambers the rafters – presumably in search of a good drop. **[2 Kingsford Smith Dve. Phone (07) 3262 5988]**

## RESTLESS SLEEPER

**ACTON, CANBERRA, ACT**   Somewhere in the vaults of the National Film and Sound Archive, formerly the city morgue, sleeps the Pyjama Girl. Long nameless, this murder victim from Albury (kept here briefly en route to a Sydney autopsy), was eventually identified as Linda Agostini, and the killer was found to be her husband. But the case being resolved didn't still the victim's spirit and Ms Agostini has been heard upstairs by the occasional ghost tour. Coincidentally, and creepily, among the massive film archive is a movie on the Agostini mystery, *The Pyjama Girl* by Gabrielle Jones. **[McCoy Circuit. Open weekdays 9a.m.–5p.m., weekends 10a.m.–5p.m. Free entry. Phone (02) 6248 2000 or visit www.screensound.gov.au]**

## BUTLERS IN ATTENDANCE

**CARDWELL, Qld**   Renee Wright, curator of the Heritage Centre (originally the telegraph station) has often heard the floor sensors trip off a display's commentary, only to find an empty space when she ventures from her office. Renee believes that the invisible visitors are Thomas and May Butler, who ran the station for many years. Even stranger, tin panels covering the phone-exchange sockets randomly pop open to reveal a numbered phone line. Renee is hoping for the day when she gets a full eight numbers, for her Tattslotto ticket. **[This excellent museum is open Mon.–Fri. 10a.m.–1p.m., Sat. 9a.m.–noon. Free entry. Phone (07) 4066 2412]**

## SCANDAL SHE WROTE

**CHARTERS TOWERS, Qld**   Julie Loughrey, the owner of the Park Motel, was poked in the ribs near Room 29. She turned around, but nobody was there. A muscle twinge, she thought. But later the cleaners said they'd only fix Rooms 28, 29 and 30 in pairs. Room 30 is where Bridget Clancy swallowed rat poison after Watson Nixon, her brother-in-law, was killed in a mining accident in 1904. Hang on, her brother-in-law? Locals had the same misgivings. A request from Bridget's suicide note didn't dispel any doubts: 'Bury me aside or on top of Nixon,' she wrote. **[Cnr Lissner and Deane Sts. Phone (07) 4787 1022]**

Frederick Baker (also known as Federici) was the tenor in an 1888 production of *Faust* in **Melbourne (Vic.)**. Descending into Hell, via a trapdoor on the Princess Theatre's stage, he suffered a heart attack and died. You can hear about his pesky afterlife on White Hat Tours. **[Phone 0500 500 655, visit www. whitehat.com.au or keep your eyes peeled at the theatre, 163 Spring St]**

## CLAPPED OUT

**CUE, WA**   Ghost towns around the gold fields are more common than fools' nuggets. But Big Bell, 26 km northeast of Cue, is a bit of a special case. Why? Probably because it all happened relatively recently. Houses and gardens and the Palais Theatre sprang from the promising clay in 1936, with the opening of the Big Bell Mine and the prospect of long-term employment. Churches, an iceworks, the railway, a power station, a drapery, a library, an air-raid shelter all followed ... but the mine folded, and the populace departed in 1955. The modern visitor will find a grand two-storey shell once known as the Big Bell Hotel, and a grid of red streets in a stony wasteland. A few signs across the plain explain where and how 850 people once lived here.

## CREEPY CRAWLEY

**JUNEE, NSW**    Beware, gentlemen. A starched collar could lead to blood poisoning, as Christopher Crawley learnt to his peril in 1910. Aggrieved, his widow converted the upstairs storage room into a chapel and, it's said, left the house only twice until she died in 1933. Not long after Reg and Olive Ryan bought Monte Cristo 30 years later, they drove home to find all the lights on – though the power was yet to be connected. Touring 'the most haunted house in Australia', small children in particular are often 'blocked' while trying to climb the stairs. Ryan's own son, Lawrence Legend, a motorbike stunt-rider, has seen his share of apparitions while leaping cars near the garden maze. **[Monte Cristo Rd, 2 km west of town. Open daily 10a.m.–4p.m. Entry $9.50/$7.50/$4.50, family $20. Phone (02) 6924 1637 or visit www.montecristo.com.au]**

Warwick Moss, once the husky host of TV's *The Extraordinary*, nominated the old copper settlement of **Kapunda (SA)** as the most haunted in Australia, with over 38 eerie addresses, including the cellar of the Sir Sidney Kidman Hotel and the former girls' reformatory. **[Cnr Main and Crase Sts. Phone (08) 8566 2205]**

## PARANORMAL PROPERTY

**OAKABELLA, WA**    Loretta Wright, a blond Irish–North American Indian, is the hostess with the mostest ghosts around the coast, she boasts. Loretta co-manages an 1851 estate north of Geraldton, with a spooky stash of paranormal snaps, including perceptible images of a beheaded Aboriginal, a Scottish terrier, and a boy with a candle. In some rooms, your camera may refuse to operate, which happened the day I was there. So if you want to sense a spirit, and wolf down a fresh scone, the ouija board is spelling out OAKABELLA HOMESTEAD. **[Some 30 km north of Geraldton, off the North West Coastal Hwy on Starling Rd. Open daily 9a.m.–4p.m. for a $6 tour. Phone (08) 9925 1033]**

## PICKED ON

**PICTON, NSW**    Liz Vincent writes history for *The Macarthur Chronicle*, but she walks it – with ghosts – every even weekend of the month. Most tours commence with a feed in the haunted post office. Next, you may see a phantom horse, a pirate grave or the murdered shoemaker. One of the spookiest sites in town is a disused railway tunnel, built in 1867. It's now occupied by mushroom farmers, but that doesn't stop train victim Emily Bollard from frequenting the line. Keep your senses peeled for bizarre lights and unexpected breezes. **[Call Liz on (02) 4677 2044 or visit her website www.lizvincent.com.au. Tour prices from $25 (dinner tour $50, supper tour $35). Kids' ghost tour also available]**

# ODDITIONS

⊚ The first explorers to enter the **Hunter Valley (NSW)** lost a good horse called Cockfighter in the boggy sand of Wollombi Creek. Legend says the same noble nag haunts the Putty Rd, close to a winery called Cockfighter's Ghost. **[Milbrodale Rd. Phone (02) 9667 1622]**

⊚ Ghost tours of **Windsor (NSW)**, take in the oldest pub in Australia, a man hanged without trial from the banisters, an obscure bushranger, several good psychic yarns, and Mary the freaky fire phantom. **[For a tour, call John and Beryl Miller on (02) 4577 6882]**

⊚ So livable a city is **Melbourne (Vic.)** that even the dead choose to stay on. You may meet the odd loiterer through Melbourne Haunted Ghost Tours, run by occult author Drew Sinton, owner of the Haunted Bookshop. **[Tours on Sat. at 8.30p.m. from 15 McKillop St. Prices around $20/$18, depending on tour. Phone (03) 9670 2585 or visit www.haunted.com.au]**

⊚ The Dusthole is the solitary cell beneath the Penitentiary Chapel in **Hobart (Tas.)**. Guests on the chapel's two-hour ghost tour report having heard a woman wailing and invisible men singing, and camera batteries have been known to cut out. **[Bookings can be made on 0417 361 392]**

# GRAFFITI

*(Being a spray of scurrilous scrawls
and eccentric etchings)*

## PASSING COMMENTS

**ARAMAC, Qld** The coach company Cobb & Co was the Greyhound Bus Company of its day. Museum junkies will find the odd stray carriage, but no site better preserves the hearts of the paying passenger than Gray Rock. The outcrop was a spelling point on the road to Clermont, chosen for its Wayside Hotel and the natural enclosed pasture of Mailman's Gorge. Cooling their heels, those in transit took time to inscribe the soft sandstone with their initials and occasionally dreams – 'I'm the greatest cook in the world,' claims one client. **[Gray Rock is 35 km east of Aramac – look for signs. The Wayside Hotel has fallen by itself]**

## CAESAR WOZ ERE

**BROAD ARROW, WA** – A bloke called O'Meara (or O'Mara), so it's said, scratched arrows onto trees to blaze a trail to a patch of gold north of Kalgoorlie. Fifteen thousand souls followed, and sank some 1000 shafts into the open plain. Thus the town of Broad Arrow was born and it soon boasted a stock exchange, eight pubs, two breweries, and a fever hospital. The rush fizzled in the first years of the 20th century. Now just one pub stands – the BAT, or Broad Arrow Tavern, a place with more graffiti than O'Meara could have scratched in a lifetime. Inside, virgin surface is at a premium. Pre-texta, the pub was used for the movie *The Nickel Queen*, starring Googie Withers. **[38 km north of Kalgoorlie. Open daily from 11 a.m. Phone (08) 9024 2058]**

## PETROL HEADS

**DELORAINE, Tas.** In 1993, Karl and Tracey Mansfield opened a shop selling bubble-headed petrol bowsers and period oil cans. Soon the obsession picked up speed, warping into their Lost in the 50s Diner that rewrites *American Graffiti* with an Aussie twist. The joint features an ice-cream stand wrought from a Cadillac hood. The legs on the tables of the Chevy-chic booths are made from crankshafts. [2 Railway St. Open Sat.–Thur. 10a.m.–5p.m. Phone (03) 6362 2978]

## INTERNATIONAL MAN OF MYSTERY

MARREE, SA    The mystery man is an Aboriginal hunter 4 km long and 28 km in circumference, carved into the Finnis Plateau east of Marree. In 1998 a fax arrived at the local pub claiming the 'geoglyph' (aka Marree Man) to be twice the size of the largest Nazca etching in Peru, and 24 times bigger than any UK chalk giant. A later fax, sent from an Oxford hotel in England, spoke of a plaque buried near the hunter's nose. Dug up in secret, this hidden container allegedly carried an American flag plus vague references to the Branch Dravidian movement. A big red herring for a big graffito, or a farewell gesture from the missile boys of Woomera? While heavy rains have erased the carving somewhat, it is still clear from the air, assuming a recent no-fly zone is lifted. [Check for progress at the Progress Association Inc., care of the Marree P.O., on (08) 8675 8351]

## HARING TO GO

COLLINGWOOD, MELBOURNE, Vic.    The New York subway was Keith Haring's studio and, by and large, New Yorkers loved his work. Before dying of AIDS in 1990, this Matisse of the Metro collaborated with Andy Warhol, Timothy Leary and William S. Burroughs on various projects. If you can't travel to the Big Apple, pop down to the Northern Metropolitan TAFE where you'll find a two-storey orgy of dynamic bodies under a computerised caterpillar. Haring travelled Down Under in 1984.

## TWISTED SISTERS

STAWELL, Vic.    The local council was peeved by the number of names being sprayed on Sisters Rocks, a granite outcrop just south of town. So 10 years ago the alderpersons painted the rocks purple – which only refreshed the canvas for the amateur Michelangelos. The original sisters were the Levi girls, who camped out here during the gold-rush of the 1850s. It seems their fame has been eclipsed by the likes of Sniff, Ali, Wozza et al. As for K. Moller (1957) – how the hell did you get up so high? **[Western Hwy, about 5 km south of town]**

## YOURS ETERNALLY

**SYDNEY, NSW**   Arthur Stace was a man on a mission. In a word, his mission was 'Eternity'. The reformed alcoholic, a man in God's thrall, saw his purpose as scrawling the one-word motto all over Sydney during the 1940s and 1950s, in elegant chalk, which lent his message a touch of magic, not to say impermanence. Though one place where Eternity may fulfil its promise is on Argyle St in The Rocks. Look down at the opening of the lane, near the Argyle Centre's gate, and you'll see the famous copperplate written in cement. Is it the real McCoy? Historian Wayne Johnson calls it an each-way bet. 'Cement was never Stace's medium, and the 'y' has an added flourish,' he says. But the jury remains out.

## MOUNTAIN MYSTIC

**TOWNSVILLE, Qld**   Forty years ago a group of engineering students celebrated year-end by painting a stick-figure saint, complete with halo, on the city-facing side of Castle Hill, some 250 m above sea level. The initial public reaction was irritation, but four decades have helped to endear the artwork to Townsville hearts. A recent web-poll in the *Townsville Bulletin* voted 69 per cent to retain the figure. Climbing clubs acknowledge the graffito in their 'Saint & Sinner' route to the summit. And in November 2002, a phantom abseiler spiced the debate by adding a pink smile to the character. **[One of the better spots to see the saint is cnr Gregory and Kennedy Sts, en route to the Castle Hill Lookout]**

# ODDITIONS

- ⊚ Down at Parsley Bay in **Sydney (NSW)**, a 1920s advertisement, inscribed in a sandstone boulder close to the loos, reads: 'Lunch Costumes Boiling Water and Tables at Kiosk'.
- ⊚ On the road between **Nimbin (NSW)** and Mullumbimby, the hippie heartland of Australia, is a sign identifying 'Tweed Shire, A Place of Contrasts'. But the first T is missing.

◎ Honeymooners began the trend during the 1950s, daubing the boulders with valentines and their own brand of optimism. Evidently the craze caught on. Now the Vee-Wall on Wellington Dve in **Nambucca Heads (NSW)** brags more names than rocks.

◎ Down Austin St, the main drag of **Cue (WA)**, you may notice an antiquated shopfront at Lot 5 that spells out the treacheries of gold-seeking. The façade is meant to read 'PROSPECTING SUPPLIES', but some wag has erased the first half of the second word.

# GRAVES

*(Being a subplot of gravestones, gallows humour and various memorials)*

## CENTRAL PLOTS

**ALICE SPRINGS, NT**   Spend some time in the Pioneer (or Memorial) Cemetery, now home to notables such as artist Albert Namatjira and hapless gold-seeker Harold Lasseter. Down the back are camel-drivers' graves, and a pruned tree marking the accidental death of a young man. Was he killed by falling timber or does the sapling signify a life cut short? The colourful Olive Pink, who created the town's Botanical Gardens with the help of Johnny Jambijimba Yannarilyi in 1953, is also planted here. **[Part of the Cultural Precinct on Larapinta Dve. Phone (08) 8951 1120]**

## MIXED ENDEAVOURS

**FORBES, NSW**   There's a fair bit of history hiding in the Church of England section of Forbes Cemetery. Residents include Rebecca Shield, the grand-niece of Captain Cook (she reached the rosy age of 86). Twenty paces away is Kate Foster (nee Kelly) who managed to rack up 36 years before drowning in a lagoon on the Condobolin Rd. (Her big brother Ned is a tad more famous.) And further on is Ben Hall (27), who led a life of highway robbery before being shot by police near Billabong Creek. His body was aired outside the Albion Hotel as a lesson to all aspiring knaves. **[Take Bogan Gate Rd. Turn third left once you're inside the cemetery]**

## NO ISLANDER IS A MAN

**HERVEY BAY, Qld**   Kanakas, as Pacific Islanders were dismissively known, were seen as cut-rate navvies for the Queensland canefields. From 1863 to 1906, many were head-hunted by sugar barons in a custom known as blackbirding. The story is enshrined in a 'noble savage' statue in Polsen Cemetery, around which names like Sampson Swallow and Tom Lamato echo the era. The last grave belongs to Willy

Wondunna, otherwise known as Turramon, an Aboriginal trooper who assisted in Ned Kelly's arrest in 1880. **[Polsen Cemetery, Corser St, at Point Vernon. Inscribed on the main gate, the story behind the cemetery's name is also a gem]**

## SEMPRE RICORDATA

**INGHAM, Qld**    The Italian pioneers of Ingham have claimed a spot in Australia's sugar history, as witnessed by the breathtaking 'new' cemetery amid the cane. The mausoleums commemorate the Novellis, the Paganonis and the Puccios of the region. Most of the graves carry cameo portraits *'in cara memoria'*, as well as Pietas and Madonnas in Perspex. The first mausoleum, built for the Mammino family, loomed in 1952. The largest – holding the Prestipinos – occupies eight plots and boasts its own portico. By comparison, the Anglican section looks decidedly low-rent. **[Look for signs off the Townsville Rd. And watch out for the elbow turn at the end of Cemetery Rd – could it be a ploy to recruit more customers?]**

You know you're a champion of champions when the governing body of your chosen sport modifies the rules just to give somebody else a chance of winning a game. Such was the dominance of Walter Lindrum in the world of billiards (his record break of 4137 points in 1932 is still unbroken). The maestro's grave in Melbourne General Cemetery in **Carlton (Vic.)** sports a marble billiard table with vases for the pockets.

## SCOUT'S HONOUR

**MOLONG, NSW**    Yuranigh, escort on Major Thomas Mitchell's treks to the tropics, could well be the first Aboriginal to be afforded a European-style grave. Yuranigh had the knack of sourcing water or food wherever he travelled. 'His intelligence and judgment rendered him so necessary to me,' wrote the major in his journal, 'that he was ever at my elbow . . .' After the treks Yuranigh returned to obscurity as a stockman in Boree Creek, near Wagga. When he died in 1850, Mitchell spurred the governor, Sir Charles FitzRoy, to preserve about a square kilometre for a circle of carved ceremonial trees and the carved marble headstone. **[Just south of Molong, some 2 km off the aptly named Mitchell Hwy]**

## NEIGHBOURHOOD VIGIL

**PORT STEPHENS, NSW**    Cecilia Cromarty would roll in her grave if she could see what surrounds her these days. She and her captain husband were granted 300 acres (around 121 ha) of Port Stephens foreshore in 1842, predating the collapsible clothesline of 10 Seaview Crescent (private property) by a long chalk. Cecilia spent 20 years on Soldier's Point, now a bustling borough of beach-lovers with surf-skis and Perrier umbrellas to the fore. The grave's situation is bizarre, plunked as it is beside a plain-brick letterbox and suburban driveway. If not for a wetlands corridor rescued by the Mambo design company in nearby Salamander Bay, Cecilia's entire prospect might be the sprawl of progress. **[Off Foreshore Ave, Soldier's Point]**

## HEY, WAIT FOR ME

**SARINA, Qld**    Spare a thought for John Curran, formerly of Plane Creek. When he died in 1903 he joined the marbled ranks of Sarina's Catholic churchyard. Alas for John, the church moved some time later, relocating most of its graves in the process. Not Mr Curran's, however. While the reasons remain vague, his is the lone grave in the Sarina Showgrounds, right beside the gymkhana jumps and mud-racing circuit. **[A few km north of town, along the Bruce Hwy. You can see the grave from the road, jammed against the fenceline in the northwest corner]**

## CITY OF BONES

**LIDCOMBE, SYDNEY, NSW**    Established in 1868, Rookwood Necropolis is the largest cemetery in Australia, and one of the largest in the world. (Name another necropolis with its own branch line from a city's main train station.) Close to a million deceased persons call this graveyard home – among them shipwreck victims, typhoid patients, bank robbers and jilted brides, to name just a few – and the complex covers 283 ha, roughly the size of an amalgamated shire. You can stroll the subdivisions, or choose a theme tour (Heritage, Murder and Mayhem, Plague and Pestilence, Convict, Irish) that suits your appetite. **[Main gate is off East St. Closest railway station is Lidcombe. Different tour each month. Cost $12 for a half day, $20 full day. For details phone (02) 9499 2415]**

## DYING TRADE

**WARWICK, Qld**    Bill Frater belongs to a vanishing breed. The personable Scot is one of few in Australia who can rely on his naked eye, his steady wrist and his immaculate spelling, to engrave headstones serif-perfect. After 40 years of monumental masonry, Frater has marble in his veins. The Italian mausoleums of nearby Stanthorpe are largely his toil, as are hundreds of graves in Warwick. The workshop site has been a headstone hive since Federation days, at one stage employing 20 artisans. The manual crane in the yard was used to build St Mary's Church. **[Cnr Percy and Canning Sts. Phone (07) 4661 1359]**

## Y MARKS THE SPOT

**WYE RIVER, Vic.**    In 1891, as smoke blurred the air from rampant bushfires, an iron barque named the *W.B. Godfrey* crashed into rocks. Though the ship, carrying tonnes of American timber, sank, no lives were lost. Three salvage attempts later, however, five sailors had drowned, including a man named Victor Godfrey, believe it or not. The victims rested in shallow graves above the wreck site until the Great Ocean Rd was put through in 1930, on top of the makeshift cemetery. A memorial tablet was installed not far from nearby Godfrey Creek, and at low tide you can discern the *W.B. Godfrey*'s winch and anchor. **[Some 5 km east of Wye River]**

# ODDITIONS

- ⑥ The pioneer cemetery on McLeod St in **Cairns (Qld)** has 96 residents with the surname Ah – from Ah Boo to Ah You.
- ⑥ One grave in the bleak cemetery just outside **Wittenoom (WA)** tells it like it is. The headstone, belonging to an asbestos worker called Peter Pas, is 'In Loving Memory Of My Father Taken By The Dust'.

# GREEN

*(Being a salad of eco-green variations)*

## SUNNY ONE DAY, SUNNY THE NEXT

BRISBANE, Qld   The Hall Chadwick Building is one of Australia's greenest skyscrapers, earning a 4.5-star rating from the (Efficient) Powers That Be in 2001. The sun does most of the work, thanks to the nation's first 'solar voltaic roof'. Every few seconds, the LED screen outside flashes data on the meagre greenhouse gases emitted by the building (some 1600 tonnes, less than your average city tower). Giddy with all this excess energy, a sun-run pinwheel spins above the main entrance. **[120 Edward St, or see www.hassell.com.au/projects for the new-age slide show in the corporate sector]**

## BAGS THE LIMELIGHT

COLES BAY, Tas.   New Year's Eve 2002 attracted a swarm of revellers to Coles Bay. The litter they left took a week to clear. Ben Kearley, the local baker, aired the problem with a passing customer called John Dee, who happened to be the founder of eco-lobby Planet Ark. By April 2003, plastic bags were banned in Coles Bay and residents were issued with calico bags. Great Oyster Bay never looked greater, and another bonus was a bit of spin, every bag bearing the boast: 'Coles Bay. Australia's First Plastic Bag Free Town'.

A 7-ha patch of scrub in Hunters Hill, **Sydney (NSW)** known as Kelly's Bush, earmarked for luxury townhouses, inspired the world's first 'green ban', when the Builders Labourers Federation forbade any sod from being turned on the site. After a decade of wrangling, the land stayed intact. **[Cnr Nelson Pde and Alfred St, with amazing harbour views]**

Pandas, please note: at Belli Bamboo Parkland, west of **Noosa (Qld)**, you can learn the difference between a runner and clumper, and brush shoulders with 90-plus species of bamboo (including Malay Dwarves and Colombia's Revenge). **[1171 Kenilworth Rd. Open Mon.–Sat. 7.30a.m.–4.30p.m. Phone (07) 5447 0299 or visit www.bamboo-oz.com.au]**

## LONG SHOT

SWANSEA, Tas.    Australia's largest billiards table sprawls in a cosy seaside museum, between a Tasmanian tiger trap and a leather blackboard. Made from a slab of uncut slate, the table is 63.5 mm longer, and 38 mm wider than your standard full-size model. An entire fiddleback blackwood tree went into the monster's legs. You can wield a cue for a nominal fee. [Glamorgan Swansea Museum, 22 Franklin St. Open Mon.–Sat. Entry $3/$2. Phone (03) 6257 8215]

## PALM SUNDAYS

TIONA, NSW    If Tarzan and Jane ever tied the knot they'd say their vows in the Green Cathedral. The setting is idyllic, with a dreaming touch of Gilligan's Island about it. Halved logs are the pews, pebbles make up the altar, and the lectern is a sea-worn piece of timber. Overhead, a hundred palm trees thrash or whisper, depending on the weather. A sign out on the road identifies the median strip as Refuge Island but it could well refer to the Green Cathedral, which is open all hours and provides a refuge even for the heretic. [On the lake side of Tiona Park Caravan Park, along The Lakesway. Phone 1800 808 900]

A block of green-grey granite sits outside a quarry in **Jerramungup (WA)**. This unique shade of stone was selected for the construction of the Australian war memorial in London's Hyde Park. Very few places on the planet yield such green granite. **[21 km towards Albany, down Marnigarup East Rd for 6 km]**

## WATCH THIS SPACE

**WESTBURY, Tas.**   Lieutenant Governor George Arthur conceived the idea of including a village green among the civic plans – a rarity in Australia. Back in 1828, Arthur mapped out some 200 km of streets for the new settlement, and only managed to establish tent barracks, a jail, a church – and the green – before the grand vision went to seed. Nowadays we take parks for granted, yet here is a town which embraced greenery from square one.

# ODDITIONS

⑥ At 98 Queen St, the main street of **Berry (NSW)**, a massive wall of privet conceals an excellent cafe. In a bid to attract both punsters and gourmands, the cafe goes by the name of Hedgehogs. **[Phone (02) 4464 3051]**

⑥ With a trunk nearing 2 m in diameter, the grapevine of **Chiltern (Vic.)** is registered by *The Guinness Book of Records* as the biggest in the southern hemisphere. Endless tendrils double as the old Star Hotel's roof, cnr Main and Conness Sts.

⑥ When flood waters in 1968 prevented beer trucks from reaching **Birdsville (Qld)**, diehard patrons in the town's only pub resorted to a cobwebbed crate of crème de menthe. Hence the name for the hotel's lounge area: The Green Lizard Bar.

⑥ Instead of lawn, one home-owner in Medindie, **Adelaide (SA)**, has opted for crushed green glass. Fetching the paper barefoot in the morning can be a challenge. **[Cnr Klamps Rd and Dutton Tce. This is a private residence]**

⑥ **Gympie (Qld)** is run by nuts. Their unique Macadamia Cogeneration Facility aims to burn nearly 10 000 tonnes of nutshells a year to generate electricity. **[Visit www.ergon.com.au]**

⑥ Mt Shadwell in **Mortlake (Vic.)** is alive with olivine, a green crystal that commonly occurs in a teardrop formation – or 'bomb'. A decent sample sells for $75 a carat, with rock colours ranging from khaki to Midori.

# HANKY-PANKY

*(Being a tryst of notable nookies
and nefarious nooks)*

## BELOW THE NAVAL

BOWRAVILLE, NSW   Leading Seaman Kevin Moloney developed a passion for tallies, those ribbons that sailors wear on their caps. You know the ones – usually gold letters on black, declaring the ship's name. The strangest of the 500-plus ribbons he collected, which are on display in the Folk Museum, belongs to HMAS *Snipe*. Allegedly a prank played by crew members, the tally doesn't spell Snipe but rather an anatomical anagram. No, the word isn't Spine, but you're in the right ballpark. **[High St. Open Tues. and Sat. 10a.m.–3p.m., Wed. and Fri. 10a.m.–noon, Sun. 11a.m.–3p.m. Entry $1.10. Phone (02) 6564 7251]**

## HONKY-TONK WOMEN

ECHUCA, Vic.   In the historic port precinct you'll come across what was once a notable knocking shop, one of few 'historically significant' brothels in Australia. The trade only lasted 20 years, servicing the needs of wharf workers and honky-tonk enthusiasts, before the Licensing Court stepped in. 'But we don't employ high-kickers,' protested the Murray Hotel's publican. 'We hire female pianists.' The jig was up. **[Now an art and souvenirs shop. Upstream from the cnr Leslie St and Murray Esplanade]**

## AT A BRANCH NEAR YOU

FITZROY CROSSING, WA   In 2002 the Nindilingaari Cultural Health Centre went out on a limb to combat the upsurge of sexually transmitted diseases in the Kimberley. (With only 2 per cent of the state's population, the region accounts for nearly half of its cases of syphilis and gonorrhoea.) Patrick Davies helped to get the plan off the ground, hanging gratis condoms in PVC tubes from the lower branches of several river gums, where the local Aborigines traditionally congregate for shade. After the initial mild shock, the rubbers started disappearing

and the current outflow is 3000 a month, among a population of 3500.
[Outside the Crossing Inn on Skulthorpe Rd]

University is for learning, not carnal yearning, according to Sir Langdon Bonython in 1936. To see his credo illustrated, visit Bonython Hall at the University of Adelaide, in **Adelaide (SA)**. A stipulation of the press baron's grant was to install a sloping floor to preclude dancing.

## BILBIES IN HEAT

**HUNGERFORD, Qld**    A bilby pregnancy only lasts for 12 days – barely enough time for a shower tea. They begin breeding from around six months of age, typically have a litter of two and live to the ripe old age of eight. This, you'd think, would see the tiny bandicoot rule the world, but the opposite is true: it's extinct in three states, and only just holding its ground in Qld. Enter wildlife crusaders Dr Peter McRae and Frank Manthey, alias the Bilby Brothers, who with help from volunteers and sponsors have erected 25 km of steel fence in Currawinya National Park, a mulga patch central to the bilby's hunting range and now their private kingdom. Kingdom is the word too, each male bilby bragging a harem of nine long-eared concubines in the 2900-ha playground. [North of Hungerford. Or learn more at www.wildlife.org.au]

## RUBBERNECKING

**KALGOORLIE, WA**    Langtrees 181 was the first brothel in the world to offer tours of the premises. Get set to enter 12 bedrooms unlike any other. There's the Boulder Shaft Room, with 'infinity mirrors' on either side of the bed, a Boxing Ring, the muralled Roman Orgy Room, and the Holden On Room where motor-racing champ Peter Brock has autographed the boot of an EK Special. Gutted to accommodate a mattress, the car comes to life when moaning is detected by a voice monitor, with wipers and tail lights jumping into action. [**181 Hay St. Tours run daily at 1p.m., 3p.m. and 6p.m. for $35 per adult – which naturally you need to be. Phone (08) 9026 2111 or visit www.langtrees.com**]

## CASE OF THE MISSING MACE

**EAST ST KILDA, MELBOURNE, Vic.** Amid the graves in St Kilda Cemetery allegedly lies the body of Caroline Hodgson, better known to clients as Madam Brussels. Described by the press as 'the wickedest woman in Melbourne', the madam ran a busy bordello on Lonsdale St, granted protection (you'd think) by her cop-husband and customer base of politicians. The latter rumour was strengthened when the state parliament's ceremonial mace went missing and was later traced to a little house off Lonsdale St, where other less civic usages were likely being explored. **[Cnr Dandenong Rd and Hotham St. Hear about Caroline, Alfred Deakin or Pickle the Spy on the regular tours. For more information, visit www.vicnet.net.au/foskc]**

Four years of foreplay between boy and girl jabirus (aka black-necked storks) finally paid dividends in June 2003 at the Rainforest Habitat Wildlife Sanctuary in **Port Douglas (Qld)**, home to the world's first jabiru born in captivity. **[Port Douglas Rd. Open daily 8a.m.–5.30p.m. Entry $28/$14. Phone (07) 4099 3235]**

## RESOLVED SEXUAL TENSION

**NARACOORTE, SA**    Nowhere else in Australia can you sit in front of a television and watch live bat sex. Or bat bickering. Or a bat crèche. The TVs are linked to infra-red cameras in four chambers below your feet. Some 33 000 bentwing bats 'perform' for the monitors on the Bat Cave Tour. In colder months, when the bentwings hibernate, the guides provide a highlights package from the raunchier summer. **[Wonambi Fossil Centre, on the Penola side of town. Open daily 9a.m.–5p.m. Prices $11/$8.50/$6.50, family $29. Phone (08) 8762 2340]**

## STEAMY SURF

**WAMBERAL, NSW**    Wendy Brennan is a glamorous grandmother whose pen-name is Emma Darcy. She's written over 80 romance novels, most under the Harlequin Mills & Boon label, which have sold in excess of 65 million copies. You might say she's our own Barbara Cartland, with a drop more sauce. For those with an interest in libido or Wamberal, her 2003 novel *The Blind-Date Bride* is set on the sands of Spoon Bay, just north of town. It was the biggest-selling romance in America for March 2003.

## CAMEL LOT

**WAUCHOPE, NT**    Twinkles was born in Port Augusta. The young camel travelled by car to Darwin, where she outgrew the garden quick-smart. So the calf was sold to a Mildura woman, who ran out of money driving back to Victoria. In order to pay an ugly fuel bill she hawked the beast to Lee Richard, manager of the Wauchope roadhouse, south of Devils Marbles. Unwary travellers get the fright of their lives when Twinkles sneaks up to their campervan to steal a gingernut biscuit. Come mating season, Twinkles has been to known to corner a ute carrying sleeping swags (either one hump or two) and yank the nearest bundle to the floor for a rigorous workout. As for Mystery, the companion donkey who believes Twinkles to be her mum, she's been seeing an analyst in Alice Springs.

## ODDITIONS

- Rub the boar's nose. Make a wish. Drop a coin at his trotters. That's the protocol at Il Porcelito, the little pig perched outside Sydney Hospital on Macquarie St, **Sydney (NSW)**. But there's another appendage that seems to attract as many well-wishers.
- Trevor John Dixon lies below the sand at Andamooka Cemetery east of **Roxby Downs (SA)**. Written on the headstone (courtesy *Monty Python*) is the opal miner's nickname: Biggus Dickus.
- The Criterion Hotel in **Townsville (Qld)**, alias The Cri, claims to host the longest-running wet-T-shirt competition in Australia. The spectacle unfolds every Sunday, with the winner receiving $800 in cold hard cash.
- Nib in shape and surfboard in length, the whale's penis hanging in the Ningaloo Reef Resort Hotel in **Coral Bay (WA)** would probably kill the barmaid if the organ slipped its ropes.

◎ The ideal venue for the next Bachelors and Spinsters Ball to be held in **Jerramungup (WA)** would have to be The Rootpickers Hall. The name derives from settlers who harvested mallee roots as firewood to raise funds for the hall.

◎ The Viper Room in Yeerongpilly, a suburb of **Brisbane (Qld)**, is the first brothel in Oz to offer pensioner discounts. Only 5 per cent mind you, but that'll buy a jumbo tube of denture glue. **[945 Fairfield Rd, or phone (07) 3392 7070]**

# HEROES

*(Being a cavalcade of unsung saviours
and a few sung ones too)*

## LEND AN EAR

**ADELAIDE, SA**   War memorials marble our continent for good reason. But none compares with the Chorus of Stones, opened in 2001 beside a surf shop at the Holdfast Shores Marina. Granite and bluestone fringe a ceremonial pool, though the real innovation is in evidence between 10a.m. and 7p.m. every day: stand by the speakers to hear the stirring words of men and women recalling the sorry impact of war. **[Very end of Anzac Hwy, Glenelg]**

Paddy Bugden earned his Victoria Cross in World War 1, for courage under machine-gun fire. His World War 1 deeds are listed beside the remarkable statue on Bugden Ave in **Alstonville (NSW)**, which shows a man dragging his wounded mates into the fountain, its watery jets representing enemy fire.

## GOLDEN HANDSHAKE

**BUNINYONG, Vic.**   In 1880, market gardener Simon De Soza stumbled across one of the richest gold reefs this side of Sovereign Hill. Flushed with wealth, De Soza assembled the poor in this, his village, and gave each person a carat, earning him the nickname the Gold King of Buninyong. A park with a poppet-head and surreal crushing wheel bears his name. **[10 km south of Ballarat, past Sovereign Hill]**

Open regular hours, the **Derby (WA)** Library displays a 1953 Coronation Medal awarded to Larry Kunamurra, better known as Tracker Larry. This remarkable character was once a juvenile 'hostage' of the outlaw 'Pigeon' (Janadamarra). Hit by crossfire between Pigeon and the police in 1913, Larry recovered on Oscar Range Station where he was recruited as a tracker and became one of the best the Kimberley has known.

## IMPOSSIBLE POSITION

**FREMANTLE, WA**    'The position has become impossible,' wrote C.Y. O'Connor in 1802. C.Y. was the genius who designed the Golden Pipeline, the 600-km tube that still carries water uphill from Mundaring Weir to the gold mines of Kalgoorlie. Sick of bureaucrats and doom-sayers, he rode his horse into the sea before the ceremonial tap was turned in the goldfields. A remarkable sea-girt statue of man and steed stands off Robb's Jetty, near the hulk of South Fremantle Power Station. **[Look for signs off Cockburn Rd, heading to Rockingham]**

## RAFT TO THE RESCUE

**GUNDAGAI, NSW**    Before such things as dams and irrigation, the Murrumbidgee was a notorious flooder. In 1852, after three weeks of rain, the low-lying town of Gundagai became an island, lapped by the river and Morley's Creek. All up, close to 100 people lost their lives in one of the nation's most lethal floods, though the toll was contained by Yarri, a local Aboriginal who, in pitch dark, managed to rescue 49 souls in his bark canoe. Another local, Jacky Jacky, fished out 20. They were each awarded a gorget (hero shell) to wear around their necks and henceforth were accorded the right to request a sixpence from anyone in town. **[Yarri's grave lies in the Catholic section of the North Gundagai Cemetery. His gorget is in the museum, a short stroll up from Yarri Bridge, alongside Yarri Park]**

## ENGULFED

**LINTON, Vic.**    On a hellish December day in 1998, five firemen from Geelong West headed into scrub to save the town of Linton. They never returned. A flame-shaped monolith in town salutes the courageous quintet, and deeper in the bush, 2 km past the cemetery down Kelly Rd, a pentagonal sculpture marks the spot where the men's water tanker was entrapped by the evening wind-change. **[Off Snake Valley Rd, just beside the township monument]**

Parliament House in **Darwin (NT)** sits on the site of the old Post and Telegraph Office, which suffered major damage during the Japanese bomb-raid of 1942. Nine postal workers died, plus young Iris Bald, the postmaster's daughter. Portraits of the victims hang in the main reception hall, along with biographies and a piece of shrapnel salvaged from the blitz.

## LEFT CROSS, RIGHT CROSS, CELTIC CROSS

MAITLAND, NSW    Les Darcy had the world at his laced-up boxing boots, and by the time he was only 20 'the Maitland Wonder', as he was known, had won 22 fights straight. At the outbreak of World War 1, Darcy was too young to enlist without his mum's okay. When he subsequently took off for a middleweight tour of America, he was labelled a deserter. Bizarrely, he died in Memphis, as the result of an abscessed tooth. A statue of Darcy stands in a black marble ring in a park outside the East Maitland Bowling Club on Bank St. His grave, complete with Celtic cross, is in the East Maitland graveyard. **[Statue cnr Bank St and the Pacific Hwy, also known as Les Darcy Dve. To find the grave, head for Raymond Tce, past the golf club. In the Catholic section, Darcy's cross stands close to the railway line]**

## A PEALING TRIBUTE

MT MORGAN, Qld    Lord Baden-Powell was a household name back in 1900. The soldier was instrumental in defending Mafeking against the Boers in 1899, and later founded the Boy Scouts movement. He is commemorated by a unique bell outside the Mt Morgan scout hall. Children donated copper pennies to create the bell's shell, while the clanger was cast from fob-watches sacrificed by the older citizens. **[Lower end of Morgan St, off the main drag]**

Lest humans forget, a plaque in **Ballarat (Vic.)** reads: 'This horse monument is dedicated to the 985 600 horses and mules killed in World War 1, including the 196 000 to leave these shores never to return.' Below is a horse eulogy by poet Adam Lindsay Gordon. **[Cnr Sturt and Lyons Sts, five blocks uphill of the Visitors Centre]**

## COURT IN THE ACT

**ROMA, Qld**   Harry Redford (alias Captain Starlight) was a cattle-stealer of the first water. In 1870, he herded thousands of cattle from a property called Bowen Downs (around half a million ha near modern-day Muttaburra) and drove them across 2000 km of unmapped saltbush, from Longreach to SA. He survived the trip (as did the cattle), but was nabbed the following year, tried and found guilty. He was, though, later acquitted by the grudgingly admiring Governor of Queensland. **[The new courthouse in Roma, built in 1907, tells more of the remarkable trial]**

## ROSE BY ANY OTHER WEIGHT DIVISION

**ROSEDALE, Vic.**   Russell Heathcote, who runs the Rosedale Hotel, once dabbled in the noble art. As a result, two boxers now strike poses at the public bar – Johnny Famechon and Muhammad Ali. Both fighters have been sculpted from logs by local baker Rex Sheehan, who also has 1968 world title-holder Lionel Rose guarding his bakery down the road. But most eyes turn to Ali, largely due to Cathy Freeman's signature on his wooden trunks. **[29 Lyons St. Phone (03) 5199 2504]**

# HIDEYHOLES

*(Being a stash of secretive sites
and abstruse addresses)*

## ARCH RIVAL

**ABERCROMBIE CAVES, NSW**   The Grand Arch at Jenolan Caves is a magnet for tourists and photographers. Yet not so far away, halfway between Bathurst and Goulburn, Archway Cave, while far less well known, brags the biggest arch in Australia. More than twice the size of Jenolan's parabola, the Archway leads into the biggest limestone tunnel in the southern hemisphere. Inside you'll find a sprung dance floor built by revellers in the 1880s. Now the cave plays occasional host to string quartets. **[Between Trunkey Ck and Tuena, off the Bathurst–Goulburn route. Open daily 9a.m.–4p.m. Self-guided tour of archway available. Phone (02) 6368 8603]**

> Fresh and filthy rich from The Great Train Robbery of 1963, UK fugitive Ronald Biggs spent many quiet suburban hours in Hibiscus Rd, North Blackburn, in **Melbourne (Vic.)**. The wily bird flew to Rio a day before the boys in blue came knocking. **[East of Middleborough Rd, in a grid of streets with equally horticultural names]**

## 100-ACRE NATIONAL PARK

**BRAIDWOOD, NSW**   Winnie the Pooh is living in a cave on a hairpin bend on the Kings Hwy between Nelligen and Braidwood. The cave was created in 1942, under orders from the Australian Defence Forces, the idea being to load the cave with TNT and detonate it, so denying access to the nation's capital should the Japanese invade. This never happened – instead, a painted Pooh with reflectors for eyes occupies the grotto, complete with honey jars from passing well-wishers.

## OVERHANG HANGOVER

BROOKLYN, NSW    Postal voyeurs can join 'Australia's Last Riverboat Postman' on the mail-boat run. The tour takes some four hours, puttering about the Hawkesbury, delivering phone bills (and groceries) to estuary residents. One port of call is a rock platform well known to thirsty fishermen. Painted pink, Blotto Grotto is the perfect cave for a riverside six-pack. **[Prices $38/$33/$20, family $85. Phone Hawkesbury River Ferries on (02) 9985 7566]**

## TIGER, TIGER, FADING FAST

CHILTERN, Vic.    For the Duduroa people Mt Pilot was a sacred place, where meetings and ceremonies were held. The clan spent winter (*myer*) here, hiding from the snow-winds in the outcrops. Closer to the peak, a rock-art gallery celebrates the spirit of the Tasmanian tiger, though most of the paintings have faded (heritage controls forbid any sort of makeover). Along the Yeddonba trail there's an A-shaped cave where Duduroa boys underwent initiation. **[About 12 km from Chiltern heading for Beechworth, off Tovey Forest Rd. The trail leads left from the picnic area. There's also a fire tower in the area, on Old Coach Rd]**

## CAVE WITH A VIEW

GRIFFITH, NSW    Little is known about Valerio Recitti. It is thought that he migrated to Oz when he was 17, then cut timber, worked on riverboats, and ended up travelling to Griffith. A storm forced the young Italian to shelter in the hills, where he remained for over 25 years. Elaborate pathways led to his stone bedroom, a garden, a kitchen. He fashioned his own catchment basin, and kept a candle burning in his private chapel. A random swastika on his newspaper-wallpaper led security to think Recitti a spy, and he was impounded at Hay during World War 2, after which he returned to the cave. He died in 1952 on his only return visit to Italy. **[Over 2 km past Pioneer Park on Scenic Dve, below Dudley De Chair's lookout]**

A cave on **Booby Island (Qld)**, a green speck west of Thursday Island, acted as a larder for much of the 20th century. Mariners in good times stocked the grotto with salted meat and fresh water for future crews in tougher times. Later, Post Office Cave earned its name as a storehouse of mail and messages for corresponding sailors.

## HEAVY TRAFFIC

**LORNE, Vic.**   Boggaley Creek is a blink-and-miss-it bridge about 15 kg west of Lorne. Did I say kilograms? A Freudian slip, as one of Australia's biggest drug busts occurred here, with close to $220 million worth of heroin being seized. The cargo came aboard the Pong Su, a North Korean ship that struck bad weather in April 2003. Federal police located 75 kg in nearby scrub, and staked out the spot. No one came, though 34 Korean nationals were eventually charged. Should you find a snow-white bundle under a mulberry bush, please smile for the cameras.

## BC SUITE

**MT VICTORIA, NSW**   Rent-a-cave is not a Flintstone gag. For a minimum two-night stay, the cave can be yours and you can explore the pagoda rock-stacks next-door as well as World Heritage escarpments. Mark O'Carrigan, who runs Hatter's Hideout, keeps the cave's precise locale a secret, issuing a map to guests on their arrival. A four-star lodge is part of the package, but why not take the million-stars option? **[Rates vary. Phone (02) 6355 2777 or visit www.hattershideout. com.au]**

## QUEEN'S RETREAT

**ROSS, Tas.**   A tease, I'm afraid, but worth the telling. South of Ross, off the main highway, lurks Mona Vale, once home to Robert Kermode, whose likeness is sculpted within Ross bridge (see Bridges). Known as a calendar house, the only one in Australia, Mona Vale boasts 365 windows, 52 rooms, 12 entrances and seven chimneys – and one private owner with a private road who won't let passersby pass by. HM Elizabeth II has been known to lodge there during her colonial sorties. **[Abercrombie House in Bathurst (NSW) offers travellers the next best thing to a calendar house: see Kingdoms]**

## KEARNEY'S CRANNY

SANDSTONE, WA     A raw red outcrop has an L-shaped cave in its core, hand-carved in 1907. Not a mine, but a beer cellar once run by Irishman J.V. Kearney. Water was pumped from a well sunk above the cave, serving the brewery on the upper level. Gravity saw the beer trickle to the vats below. They say the Black Ranges Pale Ale was the best in the shire, though it didn't travel well (which suited the local population anyway). **[You can find Kearney's cranny on the excellent Heritage Trail, south of the Mt Magnet–Leinster highway, along with a natural basalt arch known as London Bridge]**

# HOLES

*(Being a selection of dazzling depressions*
*and puzzling pits)*

### FLYNN STONE

**ALICE SPRINGS, NT**   Sneak a peek into the John Flynn Memorial Church on Todd Mall. On the rear wall is a collage of all Flynn's good works, from Christian missions to the Royal Flying Doctor Service. But the mural's image of note is a navigator's compass through which a hole has been pierced. In times gone by, before the mall trees grew, a laser-like sunbeam shone through the hole close to 25 November, Flynn's birthdate in 1880, illuminating St Andrew's Cross. To check you're in the right place, take a closer look at the smaller windows – the rectangular designs mimic the initials JF. [**Todd Mall. Open within Adelaide House (opposite) hours, though you may need to ask for a key**]

### HIP, HIP, HYPIPAMEE

**ATHERTON, Qld**   Not only is Mt Hypipamee hard to pronounce, but it has a crater that's hard to explain. The signs on the viewing deck, mounted on the lip of the 60-m drop, suggest that a turbulent build-up of gases blew a hole through the earth's crust. But some geologists are less convinced, mainly due to the crust being of relatively impenetrable granite. Another theory implicates the nearby Barron River as the principle burrower. Whichever way Hypipamee's Hole was created, the vertigo holds good. [**Between Atherton and Ravenshoe, off Kennedy Hwy**]

### COSMIC CLOUT

**HENBURY, NT**   It's halfway between Alice Springs and the SA border, but there's no township, just a sign. After following 15 km of reasonable dirt road, you can wander the rims of four connected craters pounded into existence by a nickel-iron meteorite that split into separate projectiles some 4000 years back. The dividing walls of the craters were gradually eroded away. Scientists including Eugene Shoemaker (see Crashes) marvelled at the regmaglypts (okay, thumb patterns) imprinted in the scattered space rock.

## THAR'S WATER IN THEM HILLS

**KINGSTON, SA**    When the goldfields of Bendigo and Ballarat were booming in the 1850s, thousands of hopeful Chinese headed for the Great Southern Land. But a £10 landing tax dissuaded most from docking in Melbourne, and they sailed instead to Port Adelaide or Robe in SA, thence backtracking the 300 km or so on foot. Many parties hired a guide for the journey, a £50 precaution that tended to erode the penny-wise purpose of the march. The travellers dug a well, which became a popular way-station on the trek. Fittingly, perhaps, a ranger named Phil Hollow was a prime mover in preserving the site, where you can still see traces of paths and market gardens. **[Chinaman's Well is 68 km from Kingston, along the Princess Hwy]**

An uxorious lighthouse-keeper carved a bath for his arthritic wife on Gantheaume Point, just out of **Broome (WA)**. The circular cavity lies at three o'clock from the dinosaur footprints (replicas, in fact) that also dimple the Gantheaume rocks. The footprints lie at the end of the stone pathway. Time your visit, if you can, for sunset, when the day is cooler and the sky staggering.

## WORKING DOWN THE SHALLOW END

**LONGREACH, Qld**    Ancient History, for recent Longreach students, was not just Xerxes and the Punic Wars, but distributor caps and Christmas lights too. These are just some of the artefacts their archaeological dig (now completed, but another planned) unearthed in the old town pool. Abandoned in 1962, the pool served as a cooling tank for the adjacent powerhouse until a leak called for landfill, which took the form of layers of coal, dirt and domestic detritus. Some excavated items are on display around the pool. **[Part of Powerhouse Museum on Swan St. Open daily 2p.m.–5p.m. in winter, weekends Nov.–Mar.**

2p.m.–5p.m., and Jan. 4.30p.m.–7.30p.m. Entry $6/$5/$2, family $15. Phone (07) 4658 3933]

## A FLOOR IN DESIGN

**MARYBOROUGH, Qld**   When Qld was promoted from colony to state in 1859, Maryborough became a principal port for European immigrants, and for some prized cargo. The Bond Store on Mary River was used to hold such excise goods as rum, cigars and opium. But the stronghold had one serious flaw – its only doors opened inward, and during the floods that regularly hit the town the kegs would often drift off their rails. When the waters ebbed, the goods would block the doors. Hence the trapdoor at your feet in the Bond Store Museum – a hole for the skinniest exciseman to slip through, and restore order. **[Wharf St, open weekdays 10a.m.–4p.m., weekends 10a.m.–1p.m. Entry $7/$5, family $15 (includes entry to Customs House). Phone (07) 4190 5730. And check out the flood level on the side of the building]**

## UNCANNY SORT OF FEELING

**MOUNT GAMBIER, SA**   Way back in the 19th century, a pretty lake vanished into the earth. The leftover sinkhole was an eyesore, so in 1884 local resident James Umpherston added trees, terracing and a sailboat. The sinkhole subsequently sank into disuse until locals revived it in the early 70s with floodlights, palm trees and cascades of creepers. 'The hole creates an uncanny sort of feeling,' wrote a journalist back in 1886, 'not unmixed with enjoyment.' The description still applies. **[Umpherstone Sinkhole, Jubilee Hwy East. Free entry. Floodlit till 1a.m. Take an apple for the possums]**

## MAJOR UNDERTAKING

**NEWCASTLE, NSW**   Major James Morrisset, the military commander of Newcastle, didn't fancy paddling in the wild Pacific. So in 1819 he had a convict gang dig him a bath. The chosen spot seems downright foolhardy, a rock platform level with the pounding sea, but what were a few convict casualties in the final wash-up? The 'Bogey Hole' was later allocated for public use, and despite its perils in rough weather few can resist the pool's allure. Come January, the local Greek community congregate there to throw a crucifix into the water, as part of their Epiphany celebrations. **[A steep but rewarding walk down from the junction of Shortland Esplanade and York Dve. Take extra care on the peripheral rocks, and check for sea conditions]**

## WATER MUSIC

**QUOBBA POINT, WA**   The blowholes here don't rely on heavy seas – even a mild swell can get this pit and its five radial vents hissing, whistling and vomiting better than a bunch of soccer hooligans. (No question, these are the 'sickest' blowholes in Australia.) While you're in the vicinity, continue east along the track to 'Shack City', a ghetto of caravan outgrowths with rain tanks and whalebone weathervanes that fishermen call home for seasons on end. **[80 km from Carnarvon. Turnoff is 19 km north on highway. At the coast, the blowholes are a short distance left from the T-intersection]**

## VOLCANO ADVENTURE

**SKIPTON, Vic.**   Our largest lava cave is on a merino stud farm. Once a guano gold-mine, the cave then became a provincial ball-room in the early 1900s, though 'fall-room' seems closer to the mark: the clay floor is treacherous, especially after rain, and the chamber pitch-black. For eeriness there is no trumping it. You'll definitely need a torch, plus pre-loved clothes and an acute sense of direction. **[Mt Widderin property, 6 km south on the C172 to Lismore. This is a private property: please phone for permission on (03) 5340 2018. Entry $5/$3]**

## PUSSY'S IN THE WELL

**THE ROCKS, SYDNEY, NSW**   There's a disused well in the Gumnut Tea Garden in The Rocks. Archaeologists made a grisly find during the 1990s while checking the ground before development began, unearthing 14 rooster legs (with spurs) in the well, along with several cat skeletons. The popular theory is that the courtyard, where five terrace houses once stood, was used for illegal cockfights during the 1870s. Dog fights too – with bound cats as bait. **[28 Harrington St. Open daily from 8a.m. Phone (02) 9247 9591]**

# ODDITIONS

- An aperture on the southern side of the inlet's mouth in **Narooma (NSW)** is known as Australia Rock. At a certain angle, in a certain light, the hole resembles this fair continent – though a puma's head is just as eligible.

- Much like a stamp, the imprint of a baby's foot helps to identify a load of pioneer bricks on display at the Mulgrave Settlers' Museum in Gordon St, **Gordonvale (Qld)**. **[Open Mon.–Sat. 10a.m.–2p.m. Entry $3/$2/$1. Phone (07) 4056 1810]**

- Ten hours of diligent chainsawing have turned a karri tree near **Pemberton (WA)** into a walk-through archway. **[Near Beedleup Falls, west of town along Vasse Hwy]**

# HUMBLE

*(Being an offering of lowborn localities
or unbelievable beginnings)*

## HOME OFFICE

BATHURST, NSW    Hard to imagine a more modest suburban house, but 10 Busby St was declared 'an historical place' by the Hon. E.G. Whitlam, QC. Train sounds would have orchestrated young Ben's dreams, and indeed the boy grew up to be an engine driver and co-founder of the Australian Federated Union of Locomotive Employees. But Chifley (for it was he) had higher stations in mind and became Prime Minister in 1945. His working-class ways coloured his initiatives, which included legislating for maternity benefits, green-lighting the Snowy hydro-electricity scheme, and attempting to centralise the country's banks. This last campaign derailed his career, however. **[Take Havannah St, off the hwy at the eastern end of town. Property is called Chifley Home. After 1 km, turn left into Brilliant St. Open Sat.–Mon. 11a.m.–3p.m. Entry $5/$3, family $12. Phone (02) 6332 1444]**

## CHEZ KELLY

BEVERIDGE, Vic.    The world's most cinematic bushranger sure knew what daub-and-wattle meant. Beard-free, Ned Kelly grew up in this ramshackle shack on the corner of Kelly and Stewart Sts, long before the road names existed. 'Please Keep Out', reads the cyclone fencing. 'Unsafe Premises'. No doubt, back in 1860, before the family shifted to Greta, the same warning would have applied.

His given names are Mark Anthony, but Hollywood knows him as Baz. His father, Leonard Luhrmann, ran a petrol station in the one-highway town of **Herons Creek (NSW)**. *Romeo + Juliet*, his breakthrough film of 1996, has a gas station in Scene 1, a tribute to those days. Young Mark served burgers, sold aquarium fish and ran a local radio station, on which he played Wagner and cha-cha.

## HAWKE'S NEST

BORDERTOWN, SA    The nose is missing, but the eyebrows tell all on this bronze memento of the 'silver bodgie' P.M. Robert James Lee Hawke was born here in 1929 and once, reputedly, terrorised the town on his Panther motorcycle. It's hard to say whether our 28th leader will be remembered for his feats in office or those at Oxford, where he allegedly sculled two and a half pints of beer in 12 seconds. [Woolshed St, outside the Tatiara District Council offices, which feature the Bob Hawke Gallery in the lobby. Around the corner is the family home, once a bank, at 63 Farquhar St opposite the Apex Park]

## CURTIN SHOWER

CHARLTON, Vic.    Though John Curtin was born in Creswick in 1885, he learnt how to smoke in Charlton. That's what his statue tells you. Aged 11, the future PM also learnt to ring the church bells, shrug a football tackle, and act – skills that came in handy during wartime. Press the button behind the bespectacled head to hear an excerpt from his 'Yellow Peril' address. [Outside the new Caravan stopover on High St]

With art-deco fanlights and ersatz marble columns, the Delta Cineplex on Queen St, **Ayr (Qld)**, has been revamped with a slice of Karrie Webb's golf earnings. It's owned by her mum and dad, Evelyn and Rob. Karrie's grandfather, Mick Collinson, owned the local toy shop, where the future No.1 player acquired her first set of plastic clubs as a four-year-old.

## TIME IS A TRAVELLER

TENTERFIELD, NSW    Peter Allen went from a saddle shop on 123 High St to a nightclub stage at Studio 54 – via Rio. The mercurial songwriter bared his heart in his song 'Tenterfield Saddler', a tribute to his grandfather, George Woolnough, who worked in the saddlery from 1908 till 1960. At 15, Peter went to Sydney, ditching the name Woolnough for Allen. One-time wife Liza Minnelli beams from the saddlery walls, reflecting how diverse was his journey. [Tenterfield Saddler open daily 10a.m.–4p.m. Gold coin donation. Phone (02) 6736 1478]

## MAN OF THE MANGROVES

**TWEED HEADS, NSW**   Sir Neville Bonner, Australia's first Aboriginal senator, was born under a cabbage palm in 1922, on a tiny mangrove island called Ukerebagh. Bonner's path from 'Camp Mosquito' on the Tweed River to Canberra's House on the Hill was an extraordinary climb. You can retrace his early steps via a 250-m boardwalk that threads through the mangroves facing his birthplace – a haven that Bonner, once in office, helped to preserve. [Part of the Minjungbal Aboriginal Cultural Centre. Kirkwood Rd, off the Pacific Hwy. Open weekdays 9a.m.– 4p.m. Entry $15/$7.50. Phone (07) 5524 2109]

> Olympic champions once wore Floaties too. Petria Thomas, Commonwealth record-holder in the 100-m butterfly, earned her wings at the Memorial Baths on Jubilee Ave, **Mullumbimby (NSW)**. Though these days, the Memorial Baths has a new name – the Petria Thomas Pool. Her mum and dad still live around the corner.

## WE LIKE SPIKE

**WOY WOY, NSW**   His real name was Terence, but he will always be Spike to his millions of adorers. Co-creator of *The Goon Show*, singer, jazz trumpeter and novelist, Spike Milligan was born in Ahmadnagar, India, in 1918. His family soon migrated to Woy Woy, a town the comic described as the only above-ground cemetery known to man. For all his snipes in the past, Woy Woy loves its prodigal goon and celebrates his life each October with Spikefest. The keynote event embraces Spike's song 'I'm Walking Backwards for Christmas', with half the population reversing their clothes and strolling the main drag. The local library also has a reading room named in honour of the man who wrote *Puckoon* there. [Library on Blackwall Rd is open seven days, including Sun., 1p.m.–4p.m.]

# ODDITIONS

◎ The building on the Sydney side of the **Tarcutta (NSW)** Café, a famous exchange point on the Hume Hwy for Melbourne- and Sydney-bound truckers, is the shell of Roche's Butchery. Born in 1945, Tony Roche won 15 Grand Slam titles and went on to coach a future No. 1 in Czech/US star, Ivan Lendl.

◎ Cruise past the grass courts on Townsend St in **Albury (NSW)**. Coached here by Wally Rudder in the mid-1950s, Margaret Court (née Smith) went on to win 62 Grand Slam titles and remains Australia's greatest female player. The pavilion named after her is often open.

◎ Snugglepot and Cuddlepie, the gumnut babies of May Gibbs' children's fiction, germinated on a patch of earth 10 km from **Cowell (SA)**, on the Cleve Rd. Gibbs arrived in Australia in 1881. A plaque and tree mark the site of her first home.

◎ You can scoff a veal parmigiana in the Valentino Café in the **Perth (WA)** suburb of Northbridge and marvel at how far Hugh Jackman has come. The Sydney-born X-Man dished up lasagne here in 1992, to help make ends meet. **[Cnr Lake and James Sts. Phone (08) 9328 2177]**

# ICONS

*(Being an embrace of cultural keepsakes
and mythic memorabilia)*

## DOCTOR GRANGELOVE

MAGILL, ADELAIDE, SA  Penfolds Grange is considered by many as the Rolls-Royce of red wines. A 6-litre bottle of the 1998 vintage fetched a cool $64000 in 2003. The Grange itself still exists, a cottage in the midst of Adelaide suburbia and now engulfed by the descendants of Dr Christopher Penfold's French cuttings, planted back in 1845. **[Tours of the Magill Estate at 78 Penfolds Rd start daily at 11 a.m., 1 p.m. and 3 p.m. for $15. You can visit the Grange itself with four to six friends for $150, to meet the coopers and tour the winery as well as tippling. Phone (08) 8301 5569 or visit www.penfolds.com.au]**

## COSTLY BLUE

BALLARAT, Vic.  The symbol of the Australian fighting spirit – the Eureka flag – was reputedly designed by a Canadian. Henry Ross was among the gold miners who, begrudging the licence fees, took up cudgels at the Eureka Rebellion in 1854, and lost 22 men. The flag lives on in a gloomy room in the Ballarat Fine Arts Gallery, the first regional gallery in Australia. The room's absence of daylight has helped preserve all 2.6 x 3.2 m of the banner's midnight blue. **[40 Lydiard St North. Open daily 10.30a.m.–5p.m. Entry $5/$2.50, kids free. Phone (03) 5320 5858]**

## HOWE'S THAT?

BLACKALL, Qld  A Jacky Howe is a woollen singlet worn by bushies, named after the fastest gun shearer of all. Before the days of electric clippers, Howe fleeced 327 merinos in eight hours – close to one every 90 seconds. He was born in Blackall, which boasts a life-size statue of the legend on the main street. But his unmatchable feat was performed further south in Warwick, where a memento in miniature stands above the Jacky Howe Motel (cnr Palmerin and Victoria Sts) and giant scissors surmount huge wool bales in Jacky Howe Park.

## A LINE IN THE SAND

BLACKALL, Qld    One debate on constant simmer is where 'the outback' stops and/or starts. One theory puts its hopes in the charred remnants of a tree that once stood in this town. Used by surveyors as a theodolite perch in 1887, the famous black stump became synonymous with the outer edge of civilisation. The stump now warrants its own niche beside the school oval although, sadly, the original was destroyed by fire several years ago. [Thistle St]

## WILD HARVEST

BROKEN HILL, NSW    Mutawintji National Park, an arid domain nearing 70 000 ha, was handed back to its traditional owners on behalf of the Mutawintji Land Council in 1998. Heritage tours, led by an Indigenous custodian, explore the myriad caves and overhangs in the Byngnano Range, where the Mutawintji people have drawn ochre animals, handprints and (unusually) stencils of feet. [**The park is 130 km northeast of town via a good dry-weather road. Tours leave the camping grounds Wed. and Sat. at 11 a.m., Apr.–Oct. No booking required. Fees $20/$15, family $40. Phone (08) 8080 3200**]

## LAST RESORT

COOLAH, NSW    It seems that at least one town per state has its own burnt bloodwood to mark the margins of Christendom. They include the farming town of Coolah in the foothills of the Liverpool Ranges. About 10 km north of town, heading towards Coonabarabran, is a replica of such a stump, near which a pub called the Black Stump Wine Saloon once offered a 'last resort' for surveyors outward bound. The Gamiliraay and Warijuri people reputedly knew the area as 'Weetalibah-Wallangan', which persuasively translates as 'The place where the fire went out and left a burnt stump'.

Fast food has fast become part of the Australian table – and landscape. For the record, our maiden Kentucky Fried Chicken (KFC) sprang into life in

Guildford (NSW), in 1968. The first McDonalds opened 3 km away, in Yagoona, three years later. (And if you're planning a calorie crawl, the first dinky-di Pizza Hut appeared in Belfield, near Bankstown, in 1970.)

## POLICE SKETCH

ETTAMOGAH, NSW    Dressed in full police uniform, Ken Maynard walked into the offices of *Australasian Post* magazine in 1954. Head artist, Vane Lindsay, thought it was a raid. But Ken had some cartoons to show – pictures of a gaunt horse called Neddy, and his larrikin owner, Ned. Thus the Ettamogah series was born; the back-o-Bourke shanty pub with its attendant drunkards, whisky pilots and blowflies. Maynard grew up in Albury. He hunted rabbits round Ettamogah, about 10 km north of town, where the peculiar pub arose in his imagination, despite the fact the town was pub-less and he was a teetotaller. In 1986, a true-life larrikin, Lindsay (Coops) Cooper, built a pub based on Maynard's chaotic cartoons. Look for the 1927 Chevy parked on the sagging roof. Or the batwing doors that tower above your head. [Burma Rd. Phone (02) 6026 2366]

## PICKUP JOINT

CONARGO, NSW    In case you haven't noticed, every second ute in Australia carries a bumper sticker proclaiming the Conargo Hotel. This jackeroo magnet is full of merino snaps, kelpie pics and loads of AC/DC on the jukebox. Early last century, the pub also boasted a bunyip on the walls, said to have been snaffled in the billabong out the back. Most written accounts divine the catch to be a seal, despite the sea being 1500 km away as the ute drives. [Open Mon.–Sat. 10a.m.–midnight, Sun. 10a.m.–10p.m. Phone (03) 5884 6607]

## GRAND STEAKS

DUBBO, NSW    Muzzled kelpies leap over yard gates. Red-cheeked men in Drizabone coats holler numbers. Agents stalk the catwalk. This is meat country writ large. Dubbo's Regional Livestock Markets are actually the biggest in the southern hemisphere, and onlookers are welcome, but don't scratch your nose or you may end up owning 800 head of Black Angus. [Heading out to Gilgandra, turn right into Boothenba Rd. Sales Mon. and Thur. Entry free]

For a different view of the Sydney Opera House, take the Backstage Pass Tour, which takes you into the back corridors and provides Green Room gossip. You can hear about malfunctioning fog machines and floating garbage bags every Sunday morning when the House is accessible. [Tour price of $140 includes light breakfast; kids must be over 12. Book on Lower Concourse, or call (02) 9250 7250. For more information, visit www.sydneyoperahouse.com]

## LAST LAP

GUNDAGAI, NSW    Despite being born in New Zealand and dying in San Francisco, Phar Lap remains the quintessential Australian champion. Big Red, as millions knew him, won 37 of the 51 races he started, including 14 in a row during the 1930s Depression. His last race was the Agua Caliente Handicap in New Mexico, another handsome win with Billy Elliott on board. Two weeks later the gelding was dead, of unknown causes although speculation was rife for decades. (Scientists now plump for a condition known as duodenitis-proximal jejunitis.) One of the horse-lovers who funded the return of Phar Lap's body was a Gundagai grazier named George Robinson, which is why the champion's ultimate saddlecloth is hanging in Gundagai Museum. [Homer St. Open daily 9a.m.–noon. Entry $3/$2/$1, family $7. Phone (02) 6944 1995]

## BJELKE-PETERSEN CENTRE

KINGAROY, Qld    Born in New Zealand of Danish parents, Sir Joh Bjelke-Petersen was Queensland's premier for 19 years from 1968. His time in office was not without furore, though it's his doomed dash for a federal parliamentary seat that may well achieve posterity, along with his wife

(Lady) Flo's Fabulous Pumpkin Scones. Group tours of the family farm, Bethany, are available (by appointment only), and the property includes cottage-stay accommodation. **[On the town's highest hill, near Kingaroy Airport. For accommodation inquiries, phone (07) 4162 7046 or visit www.bethany.net.au]**

## JUNGLE STORY
**WOLLOMBI, NSW**   On any given Sunday, a dazzling row of motorbikes will be lined up outside the Wollombi Tavern. The pub is a magnet to all road-riders, not only for its idyllic setting, but for the unique elixir served within. Dr Jurd's Jungle Juice, a secret recipe of port, brandy and ingredient X, appears to be an effective elephant repellent, given how few of them have been seen in these parts. **[Phone (02) 4998 3261]**

# ODDITIONS

- In the inner garden at the National Motor Museum in **Birdwood (SA)** is Margaret Dodd's sculpture, *Fossil*. The work depicts the very first Holden FX emerging from stone.
- Don't dress fancy for your visit to the Ridgi Didge Ugg Boot Factory in **Boorowa (NSW)**. Opening hours to the Rye Park plant can vary, so check first on (02) 6227 2126.

# IRONY

*(Being a medley of comical parallels
and bizarre backfirings)*

## FIGHT FOR THE RIGHT

**ALBANY, WA**   Nearly 200 whaling ships once operated out of Albany, many armed with the new-fangled Norwegian contraption called a harpoon gun. Their prized prey was the Southern Right Whale, whose blubber was barrelled by the tonne and its bones customised into corsets and umbrella spokes. Up to 1978, that is, when ecology won the conscience vote, in Australia at least, and the industry was scuttled. The one-time bloodbath is now home to Whaleworld, above Misery Beach. **[Open daily 9a.m.–5p.m. Entry $18/$14, family $45. Phone (08) 9844 4021 or visit www.whaleworld.org]**

The small Riverina town of **Ardlethan (NSW)** has two major claims to fame. First, it is argued to be the birthplace of the kelpie, Australia's famous working dog (see Casterton in Barking for the flipside of that story). It is also where a grazier called Gunn refined a cure for anthrax in the early 1900s. According to the information board in the town's main park: 'A plague (*sic*) . . . commemorating the development of the anthrax vaccine is nearby.'

## POOR-TASTE MENU

**AUGUSTA, WA**   Less than two years old, the Scottish steamship *Pericles* traversed the oceans between Australia and the mother country until, on a clear, placid day in 1910, she grounded on rocks off Cape Leeuwin. All 463 passengers and crew made it to shore, but there's a nice irony in the ship's menu on show in the Augusta Museum. On one side of the menu are clues pointing to the meal choices, and on the facing page lie the answers: 'One too many', for instance, signified

'Tipsy Cake'; and 'What to say to the tax collector' 'Raspberries'. As for 'Bad for ships'? The answer is 'Leeks'. **[Blackwood Ave. Open daily Sept.–May 10a.m.–noon (June–Aug. 10a.m.–noon and 2p.m.–4p.m.) Entry $2/$1.50/50c.** Phone (08) 9758 1878]

## GUNS FOR HIRE

**DARWIN, NT**   At the end of East Point Reserve, just north of town, work gangs erected a gun emplacement in 1941, at the height of World War 2, in case of Japanese attacks. Enter the fortress now and you'll find the turret empty, as in 1959 the guns were sold for scrap – to the Fujita Salvage Company. **[Nearby, at low tide, you can see relics of the world's longest submarine net off Dudley Point]**

**Windsor (NSW)**, along with the nearby towns of Richmond, Pitt Town and Wilberforce, are known as the Macquarie Towns, having been founded by the colony's early governor. His statue graces a park on Moses St, across the road from St Matthews Anglican Church. Note Macquarie's anguished expression, which seems to belie the site's official name: 'The Don't Worry Park'.

## ALLERGY GALLERY

**LAKES ENTRANCE, Vic.**   Twenty-six cypress trees were planted along The Esplanade to salute the fallen in World War I. The trees flourished in the salt air for 70 years or more, until the council decreed their removal because of the threat posed by falling limbs. A local businessman, aptly named Tim Hack, rescued the trees by suggesting they be sculpted into Anzac figures. Chainsaw in hand, sculptor John Brady started shaping, turning six of the sicker trees into Simpson's donkey, a nurse, a walking wounded, and more. Ironically, the sculptor developed a cypress allergy late in the project. He is now based in Melbourne, where he continues to sculpt – but in ice.

## ANOTHER ENGLISH COLLAPSE

**PORT CAMPBELL, Vic.**   British backpacker Kelli Harrison and her Queensland cousin David Darrington had just crossed the spectacular rock formation London Bridge. They had no idea what caused the splash. 'It was very quick,' said Darrington. 'We turned around, and bang.' The bang was several tonnes of limestone hitting the Southern Ocean. The young couple were marooned for three hours on what was left of the arch, until rescued by helicopter. As you'd expect, on 17 January 1990, the day London Bridge fell down, sub-editors around the continent went overboard. **[Just west of Port Campbell, along the Great Ocean Rd]**

# ODDITIONS

◎  Two images stand out in the awesome array of flood photos in the **Katherine (NT)** Outback Heritage Museum: a submerged car-wash, and the Kumbidgee Lodge Tearooms awash with tea-brown water. **[Gorge Rd, opposite the hospital. Open Sat. 10a.m.–1p.m., Sun. 2p.m.–5p.m., weekdays 10a.m.–4p.m. (Mar.–Oct.) or 10a.m.–1p.m. other months. Entry $3.50/$2.50/$1. Phone (08) 8972 3945]**

◎  **Wollongong (NSW)**, one of the largest producers of coal in Australia, also claims the country's first pre-fab lighthouse, the dwarfish beacon at Belmore Basin. But despite the coal riches lurking round the corner, the light was fuelled for its first 13 years with vegetable oil.

◎  Only in Qld could you find a casino occupying the former State Treasury. The money is made (or lost) at the Gibson Hotel, 130 William St, Brisbane.

◎  The massive Farmers and Graziers Woolstore on Smollett St in **Albury (NSW)** is now occupied by fleecing experts of a different stripe: the Australian Taxation Office. (Beware of dags on the footpath.)

# ISLANDS

*(Being an archipelago of idiosyncratic isles
and lonesome locations)*

## SKIN DEEP

**BRISBANE, Qld**   In Moreton Bay, off Brisbane, lies a former leper colony. Its name, bizarrely enough, is Peel Island. A quarantine depot was the first European inroad on Tukrooar, as the Quandamooka people knew the island. Next it was a 'Benevolent Asylum', and from 1907 it became the Peel Lazaret, a community for sufferers of Hansen's Disease (the official name for leprosy, and not to be confused with that ailment which afflicted supporters of Pauline Hansen and her mono-cultural One Nation Party some 90 years later). At its peak, 86 lepers lived on Peel; the colony fell into disuse in 1959.

## TIMBER FELLERS

**DENILIQUIN, NSW**   Prior to 1861, Deniliquin lacked a court but not a sense of justice. Those who overstepped the mark were handcuffed to a log on the Island Sanctuary on Tarangile Creek. The DIY system worked well until a half a dozen hooligans were exiled en masse, and conspired to lift the log and carry it between them to Wyse's Pub for a change of scenery. **[A footbridge leads you to the prison-cum-picnic-spot just off Cressy St]**

During his various treks between 1828 and 1847, Surveyor-General Major Thomas Mitchell would stash his flour sacks for safe-keeping on an islet in the Glenelg River in **Nelson (Vic.)**, which became known as the Isle of Bags. Little did the trail-blazer realise that bark canoes had a range of functions, island-raiding being among them. **[Up North Nelson Rd, turn left on Isle of Bags Rd]**

## BUZZ OFF

**KANGAROO ISLAND, SA**   Honey is forbidden on the incoming ferry across Backstairs Passage. As the oldest bee sanctuary in the world, established in 1885, Kangaroo Island has been the exclusive home of the Ligurian bee, a golden Bologna-based bee that first arrived in 1881. KI, as islanders know it, is home to the last remaining pure stock of this insect, with queens going for a king's ransom around the world. Every bee you see on KI is a direct descendant of denizens of August Fiebig's original 12 hives. **[Sample the difference at Hog Bay in Penneshaw. Phone (08) 8553 1237]**

## GOLF IN THE GULF

**NAMBUCCA HEADS, NSW**   According to the ancient principles of golf, the ideal course is bounded on three sides by water. This club has gone even further, occupying the length and breadth of Stuart Island in the Nambucca River. To reach the links, you need to cross a causeway off Riverside Dve. Please note that the fenced-off area behind the 13th green is a known burial site of the Gumbaynggir people. A series of plaques on the highway side of the channel tells more of the island's ancient links. **[Nambucca Heads Island Golf Club. Phone (02) 6569 4111 for times and fees, or visit www.namgolf.com]**

Coocumbac Island, a low-lying isle in the Manning River at **Taree (NSW)**, enjoys the benefits of having a multinational sponsor. One of the last swampland rainforests on the north coast, Coocumbac is funded by the weed-killing Monsanto Company giant. **[Off Fotheringham Park on River St, just below the bridge]**

## ENTERPRISE IN SPADES

**NOWRA, NSW**   Alexander Berry was the first white man to leave footprints beside the Shoalhaven River, in 1822. Having lost two crewmates trying to row inland from the estuary, and finding the nearby Crookhaven River cut off from the main river by a 200-m spit, he gave four men (including future explorer Hamilton Hume) a fortnight to dig a navigable channel between the two waterways. Time and floods widened the channel that is now the river's new mouth. Though the triumph was bittersweet – Berry found that part of his land grant had been invalidated in the process, as a good-sized chunk was now deemed an island! **[Comerong Channel is some 12 km east of Nowra, along Terrara Rd. A free ferry plies to the island daily, 6a.m. to midnight]**

## NO ISLAND IS AN ISLAND

**PIRRON YALLOCK, Vic.**   Take a time-lapse camera to Lake Pirron Yallock, west of Colac. Otherwise you won't believe that those islands you see, complete with five-storey trees, are on the move. The shallow bowl that forms the lake was once a peat swamp, which around the 1920s suffered both fire and flooding, freeing four whole blocks of peat from the basalt floor. Since nearby roadworks made the swamp a permanent lagoon, the blocks have taken to floating swan-like back and forth across the water. **[17 km west of Colac]**

## ISLE BE DAMNED

**PORT ARTHUR, Tas.**   Henry Savery lies among the unmarked graves assigned to convicts on this promontory's so-called Isle of the Dead. Savery is credited as Australia's first novelist, having written the saga *Quintus Servinton* in 1830, after being transported to Van Diemens Land for forgery. Later freed, he sent for his wife, who had a liaison with a magistrate on the voyage across and was banished back to London. Savery was arrested again for forgery, and his case was tried by none other than the love triangle's third. Savery was sent to Port Arthur, where he died two years later. **[Entry to Port Arthur Historic Site $24/$19, family $52, includes walking tour and harbour cruise; extra fee to disembark at the Isle of the Dead. Phone (03) 6251 2310]**

## BUG BUNNY

**PORT VICTORIA, SA**   That lump of land facing Yorke Peninsula is Wardang Island, site of the first field trial of a killer virus in 1995. All going well, the calicivirus was meant to obliterate the imported rabbit population, leaving all native fauna intact. The bug did its job, but streams of bush flies, it's believed, carried the germ to the mainland

and there caused the deaths of millions of rabbits in the same year.
[Island display is in the Maritime Museum near jetty. Open weekends
and public holidays 2p.m.–4p.m. (plus Tues. and Thur., Oct.–April).
Entry $2/50c. Phone (08) 8834 2202]

One of the most valuable documents in the vaults of
the Mitchell Library, **Sydney (NSW)** is Abel Tasman's
map of Australia. Hand-drawn on Japanese paper, the
original dates back to 1644, the first time our continent appeared in silhouette form, albeit sketchily.
As the original is too brittle to suffer admirers, the
library has implanted an amazing marble version on
the floor of the main vestibule. **[Macquarie St]**

## DRINKING IN ISOLATION

**WOLLONGONG, NSW**    Big, Rocky, Martin, Bass and Flinders are
the five islands off the city of Wollongong, and Michael Bolt, former
hooker of the Illawarra Steelers, has hooked 'Five Islands' for his beer
label. The bar in this remarkably diverse micro-brewery, which faces
said islands, offers 10 home brews on tap, from Lighthouse Light to
Parkyns' Shark Oil. Sampler trays are available, though Bolt advises
saving the smoky Porter Kembla till last. [**Back of Win Entertainment
Centre, cnr Crown St and Marine Dve. Open daily noon–midnight.
Phone (02) 4220 2854 or visit www.fiveislandsbrewery.com**]

## TRANSMIGRATION

**YAMBUK, Vic.**    The latest seal census declares Lady Julia Percy Island
the largest colony in Australia, with a population nudging 20 000. Such
abundant life seems odd for a place once known by local Aborigines as
Deen Maar, 'the island of the dead'. Aborigines describe canoes launching off the Yambuk dunes, carrying the souls of ancestors. You can join
a charter cruise from Port Fairy to see the seals up close, or stand on
top of the 30-m slide near Yambuk Lake and soak up the eeriness. [**For
daytrip inquiries, call the skipper of** _Mary S_ **on (03) 5568 1480, or of**
_Michael J_ **on (03) 5568 2816. Group bookings only**]

# JAILS

*(Being a porridge of stirring stirs
and celebrated cells)*

## OUT OF BOUNDS

**BATHURST, NSW**   Tour professionals Peter O'Malley and Gavin Coles cut their teeth on the Bathurst golf course. It was established in 1894, making it the oldest NSW club outside Sydney. Curiously, the new Bathurst jail was established two years earlier, occupying the rough beside the 16th and 17th holes. Diehard golfers have been known to climb the cyclone fence to retrieve wayward balls, but so far there's been no traffic the other way. **[Orange Rd. Visitors' green fees $17 for nine holes, or $25 for the whole stroll.** Phone (02) 6331 1379**]**

Hard enough that the impoverished Dorizzi family had to live in the old Newcastle jail, in **Toodyay (WA)**, during the Depression. Mum and Dad occupied the warder's quarters, while the three sons had a cell each. Much harder was the loss of all three boys in World War 2. A tribute cell forms part of the museum. **[Clinton St. Open weekdays 10a.m.–3p.m., weekends 10a.m.–4p.m. Entry $2.50/$2, family $5. Phone (08) 9574 2435]**

## INNER LIFE

**BROOME, WA**   You'd walk a long way to see a prison groovier, or more dignified, than Broome Regional Prison. Palms and frangipani grow behind the wires. Along Hamersley St, on the principal wall, twelve panels of Indigenous art add both colour and hope to the address. In Panel 7, Ross Ryder pokes gentle fun at the white man's totems of justice – the emu and the kangaroo. In Panel 9, Jimmy Mosquito tells the pelican story of Kununurra. Lastly, in Panel 12 an elder hurls a boomerang that flies through all twelve murals. **[Opposite cnr Hamersley and Barker Sts]**

## ORGANIC CELL

**DERBY, WA**   And the prize for Australia's Strangest Jail goes to . . . the boab tree outside Derby. This hollow 'bottle tree' was used as a holding cell from 1883 to 1887, when bleaker cells were built in the township proper. White opportunists would regularly impound Aboriginals en route to the Derby jetty. Most of the detainees, usually wearing neck-chains, were being 'blackbirded' for their labour on pearling boats. In happier times, the Indigenous people knew the boab as Larrkardiy, a holder of *malaji*, or traditional magic. Instead of 'blackbirds', two night-jars and a family of grey-crowned babblers now call the prison home. **[7 km south of town. Also look for one of the world's longest cattle troughs lining the layby]**

Across the road from the Spencer St Remand Centre in downtown **Melbourne (Vic.)** is the Break-Out Cafe. While down the road is the Time Out Deli.

## PENMANSHIP

**DARWIN, NT**   The first Aboriginal drawings to be displayed to the world came from Fannie Bay Jail. John Knight, the Deputy Sheriff of Palmerston (as Darwin was known up to 1911) selected the work of four inmates and sent the sketches to the Centennial Exhibition in Melbourne in 1888. The fifth artist, Billy Muck (or Billiamook) was a police interpreter who spent as much time behind bars as those in his keep. Turtles, tomahawks and other images are preserved in Perspex in Cell Block A. **[Cnr Dick Ward Dve and East Point Rd. Open weekdays 10a.m.–4.30p.m. Entry by donation]**

## THE ART OF CONFINEMENT

**FREMANTLE, WA**   As part of the Fremantle Prison tour, you'll come across three extraordinary cells. Cell E28 is the escape-proof box allo-cated to bushranger Moondyne Joe, a cattle thief with a knack for slipping his shackles. The room is walled in jarrah beams studded with dog-spikes from railway lines, and has only a tiny, treble-barred window.

(Joe still escaped.) Further along is E30, home to Peter Irwin Cameron in 1991, the year of the jail's demise. A full-blooded Aboriginal from the desert country, Cameron dot-painted his cell into a Dreamtime fantasy with horizons that stretch for ever. In E33, later used as a storeroom, a broom dislodged some wall plaster and revealed the ethereal figures drawn by currency forger John Walsh, using only his fingernails and the ground lead buttons of fellow inmates. **[1 The Terrace. Daily tours start every half-hour from 10a.m. Day tour is $14.90/$7.50, night tours Wed. and Fri. $18.90/$9.90. Phone (08) 9336 9200]**

## ALL MOD CONS

**COBURG, MELBOURNE, Vic.** Before 1870, a person living in Pentridge might have been either a convicted crim or a law-abiding citizen of Coburg. That's because Coburg was originally named after the bluestone jail that ruled its horizon. Lately the jail has become a desirable address. In a makeover costed at $300 million, razor wire has been replaced with lattice, the exercise yard dubbed a piazza, and some 1500 dwellings outfitted. H Division, once home to Mark (Chopper) Read has been . . . er . . . earmarked as a museum. But first five religious leaders from around the world held rituals in an attempt to flush the ghosts and ghoulish vibes from the walls. **[Learn more at www.pentridgevillage.com.au]**

## LAG GALS

**ROSS, Tas.**   Most women in the so-called Female Factory were teen-agers with illegitimate babies (this was their crime, in some cases). They worked a 10-hour day during which they were required to make eight hankies or 15 inches of stocking, in addition to attending prayer sessions and 'crime classes'. While a cheerless place, the overseer's cottage is the most intact relic of Australia's female-convict history. **[Walk uphill from the tourist office, and down the stone stairs]**

## SEA BLOCK

**SOUTH-WEST ROCKS, NSW**   What other jail in Australia – occupied or defunct – comes with its own coin-operated telescopes and whale-watching pamphlet? Many of the inmates at Trial Bay were 'licence holders', hard cases near the end of long sentences elsewhere, who were brought in to build a breakwater off Lagger's Point. Once that job was done, the jail was closed, although it was briefly used as an internment camp for Germans during World War 1 and boasted a lively Bavarian Theatre Group. **[Cardwell St, Arakoon State Conservation Area. Open daily 9a.m.–4.30p.m. Entry $5/$4/$3.** Phone (02) 6566 6168]

Once a ward for the criminally insane, J Ward is now a museum in **Ararat (Vic.)**. Notice the diagonal corners within the exercise yard, which were introduced after an acrobatic inmate 'chimneyed' his way up the right-angled version. **[Girdlestone St. Open Mon. to Sat. for tours at 11a.m. and 2p.m. Hourly tours Sun. and public holidays 11a.m.–3p.m. Entry $10/$8/$5.** Phone (03) 5352 3357]

## DRY DOCK

**VILLAWOOD, SYDNEY, NSW** 'Villawood Detention Centre', the temporary home of hundreds of detained refugees, is hidden among an industrial block, the smell of rubber and margarine in the air. You can't get past the gatehouse, but just seeing the high-rise cells looming behind the Smith Family depot gives the wayfarer a most peculiar feeling. Thomas Keneally, author of *Schindler's List*, visited here in 2002, and later described the so-called asylum as 'a few stops short on the initial journey to concentration camps'. He wrote *The Tyrant's Novel* as a result of his visits. **[End of Birmingham Ave, parallel with Woodville Rd]**

## WHIRLY JAILBIRD

**SILVERWATER, SYDNEY, NSW** You can't fly near Silverwater Jail, in Sydney. Not since Lucy Dudko hijacked a helicopter joy flight in March 1999, and collected her boyfriend from the exercise yard. (They were retrieved within a week.) Though you can stroll Millennium Park next-door, where 'an anonymous hobbyist' saw his remote-control plane breach the no-fly zone to touch down in the complex in September 2003. **[On Hill Rd, off the Western Hwy]**

# KINGDOMS

*(Being a bloc of private domains, ridiculous realms
and interesting enclaves)*

## BESIEGED

**BALLARAT, Vic.** Keith Ryall is the king of Kryal Castle, a Kamelot gone krazy on the slopes of Mt Warrenheip. The mansion has a torture chamber, an alchemy display, plus falconry at 3p.m. All doors are nail-free, every portal and arch being held up by dowels and tenon joints, as was the medieval practice. A period pedant will commend the architect for the anticlockwise stairs, a spiral allowing the castle's defenders to wave swords freely in their right hands. **[8 km east of Ballarat. Open daily 9a.m.–5p.m. during school holidays, Mon.–Fri. 10a.m.–4p.m. and weekends 9a.m.–5p.m. at other times. Entry $20/$16/$10, family $25. Phone (03) 5334 7388]**

Abercrombie House in **Bathurst (NSW)** hosts a private collection of photos, stamps and coronation trinkets devoted to our more recent British monarchs. The Museum and Archive of Australian Monarchy, alias MA'AM, makes for a majestic acronym.

## ONE MAN'S PARADISE

**EDEN, NSW** Benjamin Boyd created his own bank in 1839, in order to provide himself with some entrepreneurial capital. Soon one of the colony's biggest landowners, Boyd focused his ambition on Twofold Bay, which he dubbed Boyd Town. He made a road from the Monaro plains, he built churches and pubs in the virgin scrub, and he erected a majestic lighthouse. This last never saw use, at least not as a beacon, owing to a dispute between Boyd and the government, the *real* government. **[To see the aborted tower, travel 19 km south of Eden, then 15 km along Edrom Rd]**

## SHARE AND SHARE ALIKE

**GREENETHORPE, NSW**   George Henry Greene is seen as Australia's creator of share-farming, which he introduced here a century ago. The first 20 bushels of wheat were split 50/50 between worker and land-owner, any surplus going to the harvester himself. The deal flourished, for evidence of which you can visit the town the laird created for his workforce in 1908, or take a peek at Iandra Castle, the 57-room palace he called home. [The castle, not open to the public, is on Iandra Rd, 10 km towards Young]

## BREAKAWAY MONARCHY

**HUTT RIVER PROVINCE, WA**   Working for a shipping firm in Fre-mantle, Leonard Casley spent his spare hours reading the Acts of Parliament. Inspired, the young accountant made his move in 1970, seceding from Australia and declaring his mulga acreage (595 km north of Perth) an independent state. The Canberra bureaucracy objected and for three days Prince Leonard declared war on the gov-ernment, mobilising his own defence forces in case of confrontation. The real battle took place in the courts, however, where immunity was granted to His Royal Highness. So it is that Hutt River Province remains tax-free, with its own postage stamps, currency, flag and visas. Leonard is also chancellor of his own Erasmus University, a campus devoted to medical research and spiritual mathematics, and he claims a consulate in Hong Kong. [The turnoff to the prov-ince is 43 km north of Northampton. The road from the east is mainly sealed. Open daily 9a.m.–4p.m. No entry or departure tax; small charge for visas issued on site. Visit www.hutt-river-province.com]

## HOME INSTEAD

**KUNUNURRA, WA**   *Kings in Grass Castles*, the enduring outback saga by Mary Durack, appears as a partial manuscript on the walls of the Argyle Downs Homestead Museum. Argyle is one of seven sta-tions the Duracks established in the 1800s, as Patrick Durack, Stumpy Michael, Long Michael and Galway Jerry opened up the Kimberley. The homestead was moved to its present spot in 1979, to make way for Lake Argyle when the Ord River was dammed. **[Parker Rd, off Lake Argyle Rd. Open daily 7a.m.–4p.m., except during the wet season (Nov.–Mar.). Entry $3/$1.** Phone (08) 9167 8088]

Lutheran cabinetmaker Karl Launer had a bent for castles, such as the metre-high 'Wartburg' that stands in the Barossa Museum in **Tanunda (SA)**. Push a button and the entire Thuringian army rotates around the ramparts, a bell chiming with each lap. The walled realm was donated by a great-grandson aptly called Gerhard Jericho. **[47 Murray St. Open daily 11a.m.– 5p.m. Entry $2/$1/50c.** Phone (08) 8563 0507]

## THAT PARONELLA FELLA

**MENA CREEK, Qld**   How to describe Paronella Park? A cross between Lost Ark and Lost World? Built in the 1930s by a Catalonian cane-cutter, with its own mirror ball and hydro-electric generator, the park is best embodied by creator Jose Paronella's own quote: 'It's always better to ask for forgiveness than permission.' Current owners Mark and Judy Evans have salvaged the castle, fountains, Grand Staircase and Love Tunnel from the effects of fire and flood. **[Old Bruce Hwy, inland from Tully or Innisfail. Open daily 9a.m.–nightfall. Entry $24/$21/$12 (under-fives free).** Phone (07) 4065 3225 or check out www.paronellapark.com.au]

## MY KINGDOM FOR A MALBEC

**MT BARKER, WA**   An elaborate family tree in the tasting room at the Great Southern Region's first vineyard traces the owners' ancestry back to the great houses of Europe. Kings are a dime a dozen. Five Henrys for starters (from II to VI) are painstakingly linked to the grapesters on the Albany Hwy, as are William the Conqueror, Edward the Confessor, Ethelred the Unready and Philip the Long of Spain. **[Open daily 9a.m.–5p.m.** Phone (08) 9851 2150 or go to www.plantangenetwines.com]

In 2000, **Geraldton (WA)** was ruled by a king – for a week. The king was His Royal Boomaroo, alias Edward de Bono, the father of lateral thinking. Invited by the Greenough Shire to flex his regal creativity, for no other fee than the chance to keep his own funky crown, de Bono gave royal lectures, royal barbecues and royal entertainment at Queens Park Theatre.

## AGE OF ENLIGHTENMENT

**CASTLECRAG, SYDNEY, NSW**    Walter Burley Griffin and his wife Marion Mahoney, designers of Canberra, in 1924 conceived a suburb like no other. Street names (The Parapet, The Battlement, The Bulwark) speak of medievalism, as do the castle-like homes, whether Griffin originals (136 Edinburgh St) or post-Griffin strongholds ('Camelot', on The Bastion). Nature was fundamental to the Griffins' vision, as seen in the tranquil amphitheatre known as The Haven on a cul-de-sac called The Scarp. Strolling this suburb is preferable to risking your duco in such tight gauntlets as The Rampart and The Redoubt. **[Lower North Shore off Eastern Valley Way]**

# KITSCH

*(Being an affront of gratuitous gaiety and over-lavish lava lamps)*

## NOT IN MY FRONT YARD

ALECTOWN, NSW   Coral's going to kill me, calling her front yard kitsch, but Coral, please, I use the word kitsch in the kindest way. What other word encapsulates the windmills that hubby Peter has fashioned from old fans, or the blond Elvis and his valentine Priscilla? See if you can spot the piggy bank, the teakettle, the M&M munchkin, and the uncommon housefly. Or look for Coral seeking to strangle the next travel writer who loiters near her letterbox. [Goobang St, alias the Newell Hwy]

## BOHEMIAN SOLUTION

BATCHELOR, NT   Bernie Havlik was born in Czechoslovakia, but lived for the NT. After many years in the Rum Jungle uranium mine, Bernie took to civic gardening. His pride was the park in the heart of Batchelor – and his bane was a large rock outcrop his mower had to skirt. Levers couldn't budge the rocks, so Bernie decided to build a mini-Karlstein Castle on top of the obstacle. In 1990, on the day he died, a miniature wheel was found beneath Bernie's deathbed – the castle's finishing touch. [End of Tarkarri St, along the way to Litchfield Park]

Things are a trifle chi-chi in Bli Bli (Qld). The medieval castle is straight from *Cinderella*, with bedtime dioramas and 350 dancing dolls. You can buy a range of medieval weaponry or visit the toy and doll museum. Great halls and torture chambers conjure up days of yore, though it's a venue more familiar with wedding receptions. [David Low Way. Open daily 9a.m.–5p.m. Entry $12/$9/$6. Phone (07) 5448 5373 or see Snow White and other interiors on www.bliblicastle.net.au]

## TAKING THE MICKEY

**CHILTERN, Vic.**   John Miller, so goes the yarn, was looking for gold in the Chiltern Forest around the 1850s. He spied a golden mouse in the undergrowth instead. Miller dug elsewhere so as not to disturb the yellow-footed antechinus (which isn't a mouse, technically, but a marsupial). Miller got lucky: he struck gold and lived happily ever after. The city abounds with golden-mouse stories. Bushwalkers can even buy a golden-mouse cloth badge ($5.50) at Nanna's Knook and other mouseholes around the town.

> Approaching **Coolgardie (WA)** from Perth, your gaze may be assaulted by a dozen spinning fans, or a tree bearing a crop of enamel mugs. Then again, it's hard to look past two dozen white wheels mounted along a fence, or a bullock skull with the eyes of Marty Feldman. **[Cnr Bayley and Lyon Sts]**

## ELF PROMOTION

**DARDUNUP, WA**   A wishing well with the sign 'There's Gnome News Like Good News' is just the beginning. Numerous other gnome-made gnovelties inhabit Gnomesville, 21 km from Dardanup. The Ward family has filled their acreage with 300 little people: if it's not a gnome fishing, or reading, or snoozing on a mushroom, then it's a guitar quartet called The Rolling Gnomes. **[Wellington Mill Rd, off Ferguson Rd, in the Ferguson Valley]**

## ALPENSTOCK

**LEGANA, Tas.**   In 1981, Dutch supermarket baron Roelf Vos bought 450 ha just north of Launceston and supplanted the paddocks with an alpine village. First a lake, then a storybook chapel, followed by chalets complete with cuckoo clocks. Every stump on the property has been carved into a Grimm-like troll or Smurf-like imp. And the faux-town of Grindelwald Resort even has the Tamarhorn, a knoll as steep as a chunk of Toblerone. **[Waldhorn Dve, off the West Tamar Hwy. Free entry. Phone (03) 6330 0400]**

## MUG LAIR

**MOLE CREEK, Tas.**    The Tiger Bar in the hotel here is the only one in Australia devoted to an animal that became extinct over a century ago. A lifelike thylacine (aka Tasmanian tiger) snarls above the bar. Tiger Woods, Tiger Tyson and Tiger Barassi adorn the walls. Clippings about clones and thylacine cranks choke the cabinets. Pawprints cluster near the door. And of course, that ubiquitous image of dogs playing 8-ball has been usurped by . . . you guessed it. **[Main Rd. Phone (03) 6363 1102]**

Two patient Germans, and plenty of plaster of Paris, has converted an old volcano into a 3-D storyland. Elizabeth and Peter Mayer began adding Aladdin, Alice and Lancelot to Mt Elephant in 1959, making Fairy World in **Anakie (Vic.)** the oldest theme park in Oz. **[2388 Ballan Rd. Open daily 10a.m.–4p.m. Entry $10.50/$5. BYO picnic. Phone (03) 5284 1262]**

## BROLLIES-CUM-LOLLIES

**STRATFORD, Vic.**    Musk-stick pink, it's hard to miss Molly's Lolly Shop. The two-storey building on the main drag was an umbrella factory until drought had the last laugh. Nowadays the candy-plex sells boiled umbrellas, humbugs and Hawaiian crunch. You can even find Pontefract cakes – like liquorice doubloons – among the European imports. **[Molly's is at 23 Tyers St. Open Wed.–Mon. 10a.m.–5p.m. (open Tues. during school holidays). Phone (03) 5145 6620]**

## ANTICLOCKWISE

**SYDNEY, NSW**    An Aboriginal elder walks clockwise past the dioramas. A metre below, a miniature *Endeavour* keeps a steady, anticlockwise course. The Great Australian Clock, the world's largest 'hanging animated turret' timepiece, all four rococo tonnes of it, hangs from the ceiling of the Queen Victoria Building, opposite the Town Hall. It includes 138 figurines and 867 light bulbs. For extra entertainment, drop a $2 coin into the Labrador's head and the uppermost carousel will put on a two-minute turn. [The top balcony gives the best views. Check out the Royal Clock too, beside the ghost piano in the southern wing]

Scooby-Doo, Digeridoo and Hafta Doo – every angle is duly covered by the resident punsters of Doo Town, a colony of shacks on **Eaglehawk Neck (Tas.)**. You'd have to say the only shack defying the cartel's Doo-dogma is Do'lphin Sound. No doubt the owner will be in major doo-doo. [**Part of Blowhole Loop**]

## KITSCH AS KITSCH CAN

**MIDDLE SWAN, WA**    Whether you need bookends, emu magnets or a banksia back-scratcher, the Gumnut Factory is the depot for you. Noah's Ark, with all her seedpod passengers, is moored in Gumnutland. Sleight of hand and dobs of paint have turned gumnuts into owls, frogs and serviette holders. The factory began in 1970, and disseminates its giftware to the four winds. [**231 Toodyay Rd. Open Tues.-Fri. and Sun. 10a.m.-4p.m., Sat. noon-4.30p.m. Tours available. Entry by gold coin. Phone (08) 9274 5727 or visit www. gumnutfactory.com.au**]

## ERSATZ HAMLET

**ARMADALE, WA**    William Shakespeare was born half an hour south of Perth International Airport. At least that's the impression you get when you enter this cobble-perfect replica of an Elizabethan village in the Bedfordale Hills. Quills bristle in the William Shakespeare House, a clone of the bard's Stratford address. Across the hedge is Anne Hathaway's Cottage, with very real-looking thatch. Here's hoping that the accommodation (in the Hamlet Suite) and meals (at Cobwebs Restaurant in the Village Pub) are as you like it. [**Look for the turnoff along the Albany Hwy, about 27 km southeast of town**]

# LILLIPUT

*(Being a smidgen of small and less-than-slight universes)*

## LOOSE LEAF PORTFOLIO

**CHILTERN, Vic.** In the Athenaeum Library Museum you can see Alfred Eustace's rural landscapes, painted on gum leaves. Housed in the same collection is a more familiar art work on a far grander scale, though it must have caused the artist equivalent eyestrain. It's the Federation painting by Tom Roberts – a 3 x 5-m canvas with no fewer than 254 individual portraits. This version is a print: the original of *Opening of the First Parliament of the Commonwealth of Australia by HRH The Duke of Cornwall and York* is owned by Queen Elizabeth II and hangs in Canberra. **[57 Conness St. Open weekends and public holidays 10a.m.–4p.m. Entry $2. Phone (03) 5726 1280 or (03) 5726 1467]**

## MICROFISH

**DARWIN, NT** John Ostara is a carpenter. He met his wife, Helene Pretty, when helping restore her marine ecosystems after Cyclone Tracy in 1974. Ecosystems, not aquaria – the difference is crucial. At their Indo Pacific Marine (which has moved twice since the cyclone), the only fish to be fed are Lucky the Barramundi, and three stonefish. The umpteen other species rely on their own enclosed universes for sustenance. Magnifying sheets are supplied for viewing. A brilliant and rare place. **[Stokes Hill Wharf. Open daily 9a.m.–5p.m., last tickets sold at 4p.m. Entry $18/$6. (08) 8981 1294]**

Ballads and brochures will tell us that the dog sits on the tuckerbox 'five miles from Gundagai'. But fewer impart the fact that Frank Rusconi of **Gundagai (NSW)**, who sculpted the iconic mutt in 1932, later assembled 20 948 marble pieces to make a scale copy of a 15th-century French cathedral. **[The original, Ste Marie, is in Paris. The diminutive likeness is behind a door in the Vistors Centre in Sheridan St. $3/$2/$6 will see the door open]**

## PLATFORM SOULS

**JERVIS BAY, ACT**   The world's longest N-gauge railway system, with more than 40 (scale) km laid out and up to 14 locomotives chuffing about at any one time, Lilliputland is model mayhem. The display was built during the 1970s and originally toured, but Jervis Bay is now its permanent home. Cranes lift. Funiculars trundle. Farms, factories and fairgrounds adhere to a day/night cycle that elapses every 30 minutes. And for the less train-tragic, there's always the dollhouse village called Greenleaf Valley. **[49 Woollamia Rd. Open weekends 10a.m.–4p.m., every day in Jan. and during NSW public holidays. Entry $9/$6, family $24. Phone (02) 4447 8664 or visit www.lilliputland.com.au]**

The Bagot Cup, presented by the people of **Kapunda (SA)** to its popular superintendent in 1859, is claimed to be the first Australian artefact to depict a scale model of a working mine. Atop the lid stand a pumphouse, a winch, a whim and boiler – all in solid silver. **[Kapunda Museum, Hill St. Open daily 1p.m.–4p.m. Entry $5/$3/$2, family $12, includes admission to nearby Bagot's Fortune display. Phone (08) 8566 2286]**

## ALL MOVING PARTS

**KEMPSEY, NSW**   At the flick of a switch, workers at the scale-model timber mill in the Macleay River Historical Museum go hammer and tongs – and axe. The roughcast duplex, built by Dudley Timms from Coffs Harbour, has a staff of bushies lopping, buzz-sawing, cross-cutting, whetting and sweeping. A steam engine chugs at one end, while a sawyer lingers on the thunderbox at the other. **[The museum is beside the Visitors Centre, south of town. Open daily 10a.m.–4p.m. Entry $3.30/$2.20/$1.10. Phone (02) 6562 7572]**

## SHORT REACH

**LONGREACH, Qld**   Clothes pegs, wishbones, seed pods, shells and pillowcases – Pam Anderson can conjure a doll from anything, though porcelain is her material of choice. She and husband Syd run a private museum that is home to the smallest teddy bear in existence, a pregnant Barbie and a three-faced baby, as well as felt, stone and wooden dolls. **[19 Quail St. Open daily 9a.m.–5p.m. Entry $5/$4/$3. Phone (07) 4658 1958]**

## WELL TRAINED

**PETERBOROUGH, SA**   Train-spotters need to approach Peterborough on all four main entry roads in order to see all the mini-locomotives perched by the road. Retired blacksmith Colin Campbell forged the engines on the roads to Broken Hill, Jamestown, Terowie and Ororooo respectively. The replicas celebrate a town that once boasted three separate rail gauges.

## IS THERE A DOCTOR IN THE HOUSE?

**WESTBURY, Tas.**   Felicity Clemons, a surgeon's wife from Launceston, decided to make her daughter a doll's house – though the three-storey mansion wasn't ready till Tonia turned 40 and was living in a life-size house of her own. Pendle Hall, crafted with Dr Clemons' scalpels, stands inside the National Trust property The White House. Minuscule residents, each hand-carved and with jointed limbs, lead a glamorous life in the 21 rooms. Servants mop the parquetry floor comprising a thousand tiny segments. Curtains and cushions are flawlessly stitched. And do take a closer look in the cellar – all those tiny bottles are actually injection ampoules. **[Cnr King and Adelaide Sts, facing village green. Open Tues.–Sun. 10a.m.–4p.m. Entry $7.70. Phone (03) 6393 1171]**

## POW WOW

**WINDSOR, NSW**   Next time you accuse the Australian government of being ninnies, consider the shirt buttons of Windsor, as designed by the Defence Department. The buttons, intended for use by POWs, come in two styles. With the first, two buttons can be balanced one on top of the other, at which the uppermost will rotate and point to magnetic north. The second is a single button that dangles from a string, and when the button stops oscillating its custom-made notch indicates magnetic north. Other compasses here are stashed inside cigarettes, or stitched within clothing. [Hawkesbury Museum, Thompson Sq. Open daily 10a.m.–4p.m. Entry $2.50/$1.50/50c. Phone (02) 4577 2310]

# ODDITIONS

⊚  The smallest marsupial in the world is (barely) visible at East Coast Natureworld in **Bicheno (Tas.)**. The little pygmy possum is one of several star attractions at this seaside menagerie, along with free-range emus and the resident devils. **[7 km north of Bicheno. Open daily 9a.m.–5p.m. Entry $12/$10.90/$6.60, family $34.80. Phone (03) 6375 1311]**

⊚  In a world of Big Prawns, Big Winches and Big Mortgages, its nice to encounter Paul (Heck) Cole's organic fruit shop in **Bowraville (NSW)** – the little banana (all lower case). 'Because really,' says Heck, 'it's the little things that matter in life'.

⊚  With no steeple, no gable and no gargoyle, the church of St John the Baptist in **Murray Bridge (SA)** is classified as the smallest cathedral in Australia. **[Close to cnr Mannum Rd and Clara St. Open by appointment on (08) 8532 2270, or join the Sunday Mass at 9.30a.m.]**

# LITERATURE

*(Being a library of letters, masterly manuscripts
and extraordinary extracts)*

## SWIFT RESPONSE

**CEDUNA, SA**   'It would not be proper, for some reasons, to trouble the reader with the particulars of our adventures in those seas; let it suffice to inform him, that in our passage from thence to the East Indies, we were driven by a violent storm to the north-west of Van Dieman's Land. By an observation, we found ourselves in the latitude of 30 degrees 2 minutes south.' Thus spake Lemuel Gulliver, the footloose surgeon created by Jonathan Swift in 1726. The latitude is roughly that of the Nuyts Archipelago just south of Ceduna, named after the audacious Dutchman Pieter Nuyts, who traversed the Bight in 1627, en route to the Spice Isles. While the coordinates strictly refer to a patch of the Nullarbor Plain, it's probable that Swift had this island cluster in mind for the location of his colony, Lilliput.

## THE WOMAN ON THE $10 NOTE

**CLONCURRY, Qld**   Poet Dame Mary Gilmore lies alongside her husband William and son William in the cemetery here. The younger William was born in Paraguay, South America, owing to Mary's quixotic youth when she joined another William (Lane) on a quest to establish a utopian community there in 1895. When that idyll flopped, all three Gilmores sailed home, where Mary became the first woman to join the Australian Workers Union. She edited the Women's Page of the labour newspaper *The Australian Worker* from 1908 to 1931 and was the founding member of the Fellowship of Australian Writers, all this while running a large cattle station between Cloncurry and Julia Creek.
**[Walk through the main gate on Sheaffe St. Head for the central shelter, turn left and walk for 30 m or so]**

The only Australian to be buried in Westminster Abbey, bush poet C.J. Dennis was born (in 1876) in the back rooms of a pub in **Auburn (SA)**. The pub has been razed and replaced by a Senior Citizen's Club, but a replica in copper stands out the front, along with a bubbler, both dedicated to the so-called Laureate of the Larrikin.

## TRAGEDY OF ERRORS

**COSSACK, WA**    William Shakespeare is buried in a pearling town on the Indian Ocean. Well, William Shakespeare Junior to be exact. The infant fell off a ship in 1862. His nanny, who was minding the poor little mite en route to Fremantle where medical attention was available, was allegedly flirting with the crew in true Rosalind fashion, when the mini-Bard went splosh. A memorial mention is made below the epitaph of William's father, William Shakespeare Hall, a former explorer and mainstay of this frontier port – and allegedly related to the real bard himself. [**Towards Reader Head, of all places, 1 km beyond the ghost town**]

## MR PERCIVAL AND FRIENDS

**EUDUNDA, SA**    Gonunda is not a slang word for bankruptcy but the fictional name for Colin Thiele's birthplace. Author of *Blue Fin* and *Storm Boy*, Thiele recycled Eudunda as Gonunda, most notably in a memoir of his more eccentric family members, *Uncle Gustav's Ghosts*. A bronze silhouette of Gustav meets you coming into town from Kapunda, while down in the town's main park is Thiele himself, taking notes from a pelican.

At Euroke St, on the city side of Waverton Station in **Sydney (NSW)**, you'll find a plaque devoted to poet and story-writer Henry Lawson. Lawson's love of the bottle is well documented, as is his restlessness. According to the plaque Lawson lived in five different houses along Euroke St in the space of seven years.

## MUSE ON A WALL

**KENDALL, NSW**    Uphill from the op shop in this town just south of Port Macquarie is a mural depicting bellbirds and most other rural topics ever tackled by the 19th-century poet who gave the town its name. Living in Camden Haven (the town's original name), Henry Kendall drew many ideas and images from the valley around him. Stroll the streets and you'll find many telegraph poles graced with stanzas by other homegrown versifiers.

## WHY NOT POP IN?

**MARYBOROUGH, Qld**    Helen Lyndon Goff is hardly a familiar name. And nor is her pseudonym, Pamela Lyndon Travers. But Mary Poppins, pretty much a household name, was in fact created by this daughter of a Maryborough banker. There's a biographical plaque on the bank (now a Sport and Recreation office), which stands on the corner of Richmond and Kent Sts. And Mary herself can be seen, umbrella furled, sitting outside the Muddy Waters Cafe at the end of Wharf St. **[Phone (07) 4121 5011]**

## DAD 'N DAVE 'N THE REST

**NOBBY, Qld**    Arthur Hoey Davis was the eighth of 13 kids. He went to school in East Greenmount, where his father ran the forge in the 1870s. At one time an 'under-sheriff', he went on to play polo for Qld as well as writing a rowing column. Sculling inspired the pen-name Steele Rudder, which was abbreviated to Steele Rudd. The scribe later repaired to Nobby, near his childhood haunts, where he began to pen rustic yarns based in 'Snake Gully'. The stories featured Dave and his dad, who were soon joined by Mother, Mabel, Kate and Cranky. A *Dad and Dave* radio series ran for 2200 episodes after World War 2, with Mabel earning the pseudonym Lily White. Why? I don't know. Maybe the answer lies among the Rudd relics that crowd Nobby's Pub, where most of the writing got done. **[Tooth St. Open daily 10a.m.–late. Phone (07) 4696 3211]**

Thanks to a certain dog poem, **Gundagai (NSW)** has been on the literary map for donkeys' years. A glance at the street signs – Homer, Virgil, Sheridan, Byron, Ovid – suggests the town is keen to press the reputation home. As is the motel on West Street, dubbed The Poet's Recall.

## RAIN, HAIL OR MOONSHINE

**TOWNSVILLE, Qld**   Mrs Brooks (no first name provided) lived in Mackay. In 1911 she sent a letter to her daughter in Townsville. With all due diligence the Mackay postal services relayed the letter onto the next steamer (the *Yongala*) bound for Cairns. Aboard the steel ship were 76 crew, 43 passengers and a racehorse called Moonshine. One week later, Moonshine's bloated corpse was the only piece of flotsam retrieved from the missing vessel. That, and a sodden mailbag. When Miss J.H. Brooks of Paxton St, Townsville 4810, received her message intact, the envelope bore the rubber-stamped explanation: 'Found on Seashore on Halifax Bay near Ingham 8-4-11.' Almost 50 years on, the *Yongala* herself was found. **[Maritime Museum, 42–68 Palmer St. Open weekdays 10a.m.–4p.m., weekends noon–4p.m. Entry $5/$4/$2 and family $12. Phone (07) 4721 5251 or visit www. townsvillemaritimemuseum.org.au]**

# ODDITIONS

⑥ Novelist Joseph Conrad (née Korzeniowski) once skippered the ship now rusting in Otago Bay in **Hobart (Tas.)**, though at that time she was a seafaring barque and not (as later) a coal barge working the river. **[Look for Otago Bay turnoff on the B32 to Bridgewater]**

⑥ His epic poems *Bush Christening* and *Clancy of the Overflow* were triggered by Banjo Paterson's time in **Isisford (Qld)**. The local pub, named after the more famous of the two poems, doubles as a shrine to the rhymester. **[Clancy's Overflow Hotel. Phone (07) 4658 8210]**

# LOOS

*(Being a block of peculiar plumbing
and wacky WCs)*

## THE BIG OUTHOUSE

BORDERTOWN, SA  Gold gave birth to Bordertown in 1852, but not through any nugget discovery. Instead the town became a halfway stop for gold escorts returning to SA. The 18 escort runs carried over 328 000 ounces (worth almost a billion dollars nowadays) without a grain lost to bandits or transit. A lock-up was prepared just in case of trouble, though, and a replica now serves as the toilet block behind the Visitors Centre (once the old police station).

## THE PAN OF PAIN

GLEN INNES, NSW  Folk museums are usually good for bottle collections, telephone switchboards and perhaps a board of barbed wire. Well, in the Land of the Beardies, the town's history house, you get *17* barbed-wire boards from around the globe. The thorny specimens include Nadelhoffer's Twist, the Crandall Zigzag, Glidden's Ripple and the Wormsley Y Barb. Trust the Swedes to invent a bright-yellow 'wire' made from plastic. And trust the Aussies to fashion a toilet seat with many of the thorny specimens embedded in the ring. **[Cnr West Ave and Ferguson St. Open weekdays 10a.m.–noon and 1p.m.–4p.m., weekends 1p.m.–4p.m. Entry $5/$3/$1. Phone (02) 6732 1035]**

The Croft Institute is not a lab but a pub. This über-funky bar – off Croft Alley, which is in turn off Little Bourke St in **Melbourne (Vic.)** – is only open late, and later in the week. The laboratory mood is amplified inside, with beakers, pipettes and alembics cluttering the shelves and all liquors lined up pharmacy-style. As for the loos, just look for The Departments of Male & Female Hygiene. **[Phone (03) 9671 4399]**

## TRAILBLAZERS

**KALBARRI, WA**    Among the contenders for the title 'First White Man to Step on Australian Soil' is a pair of mutineers, Wouter Loos and Jan Pelgrom, who beached near Wittecarre Creek, in modern-day Kalbarri, in 1629. For the full story on the *Batavia* mutiny, visit the Western Australian Museum in Geraldton. For the plaque (and the bleak creek), turn seaward on the downtown side of Red Bluff Caravan Park.

> The toilet cubicles in the Cargo Bar, a nightclub in Docklands, **Melbourne (Vic.)**, are totally see-through. But fear not: once the toggle switch has been engaged and VACANT flicks to ENGAGED, the walls turn opaque . . . you hope. [**45 New Quay Promenade. Open daily noon till late. Phone (03) 9670 0399 or visit www.cargodocklands.com**]

## OBSTACLE RACE OF CONVENIENCE

**WINTON, Qld**    The Toilet Duck Australian Dunny Derby, in the Le Mans tradition, starts with all the competitors scrambling across the street to reach their respective conveyances. These resemble rickshaws, each with four men or women in harness and a shameless jockey mounted on the pot. During the 250-m race, jockeys must make mandatory comfort stops, dismounting to collect such essentials as a toilet brush and a newspaper. A celebrity race is also on the cards, with many a politician keen to test new seats. [**Every odd year in Sept. as part of the Outback Festival. Check with Waltzing Matilda Centre on (07) 4657 1446 for exact dates**]

# ODDITIONS

- ⑥ At the National Motor Museum in **Birdwood (SA)**, the toilet block is called the Unfilling Station.
- ⑥ Kronosaurus Korner, the marine fossil display in **Richmond (Qld)** has a toilet block for PreHIStoric and PreHERstoric. (Even the rubbish bins have dinosaur feet.)

◎ 'Stallions' and 'Mares', say the toilet doors in the Thoroughbred Hotel in **Scone (NSW)**.

◎ In name at least, the Gents' room in Langtrees 181, a swank bordello in **Kalgoorlie (WA)**, is known as the Head Office – or the Cockpit at a stretch. The ladies own the Box Office.

◎ The only pub in **Hebel (NSW)**, and arguably the only upright building, features toilet doors painted by Lightning Ridge artist John Murray. Man-goes, says the men's door, and No-man-goes, the ladies'.

◎ The sewage treatment works in **Dorrigo (NSW)** have earned the nickname of Bleak's Turdle Farm. A mounted toilet bowl is the mailbox, while several bowls sprout from a 'lavat'ree' belonging to the subspecies Pissina Flushturdum.

◎ Just west of **Tongala (Vic.)** on the Murray Valley Hwy is the Falcon Hotel. Its eyecatcher is The Downunder Dunny, an upside-down boghouse on the roadside.

◎ Perspex protects a snail fossil found in a marble slab above the men's urinal in the Grand Hyatt Hotel in central **Melbourne (Vic.)**. **[123 Collins St. Phone (03) 9657 1234]**

# MAZES

*(Being a muddle of labyrinths – real, imagined and accidental)*

## NOT YOUR AVERAGE THURSDAY

**BALLINA, NSW**   Mimi Dennett has created a dreamy cardigan. It's pink, with three sleeves, one for each of the tamarind branches the garment enwraps. It can be found on a rainforest walk, along with several other smile-sparking creations including a table setting overgrown with moss. There are nature notes, as well as a tea-tree maze. Naturally enough, the trees belong to Thursday Plantation Visitors Centre, which features far, far more than tea trees. **[Pacific Hwy, 1 km north of Ballina Airport. Open daily 9a.m.–5p.m. Free entry. Phone 1800 029 000 or visit www.tphealth.com]**

## COLOUR CODING

**COFFS HARBOUR, NSW**   Not just a maze, but a maze-in-a-maze, with the added bonus of 10 000 butterflies next-door in their own enclosed forest. In butterfly fashion, the maze is colour-coded, each colour representing a degree of difficulty. **[5 Strouds Rd in Bonville, just south of Coffs. Open Tues.–Sun. 9a.m.–4p.m., with the butterflies busiest between 10a.m. and 2p.m. Entry for maze and butterflies combined is $10/$9/$5.50 or $30 family. Phone (02) 6653 4766 or check out www.butterflyhouse.com.au]**

## WANDERING COWS

**COWES, Vic.**   Twist for twist, the wooden maze at A Maze'N Things is one of the biggest three-D labyrinths in Australia, with a flag to find in each quadrant. At the same address there's also a Puzzle Cafe, a Shrinking Room, an Anti-Gravity Room, a Maxi-Mini Golf Course and Puzzle Island. **[Look for the giant disembodied tap opposite the Koala Conservation Centre. Open daily 9a.m.–6p.m. in summer, 10a.m.–5p.m. in winter. To play all the puzzle tables in the cafe is free. Prices from $15/$10, family $45. Phone (03) 5952 2283 or visit www.amazenthings.com.au]**

Ashcombe Maze in **Shoreham (Vic.)** is noted for the evergreen *Cupressus macrocarpa* that bound its main maze. But also worth a wander in season (Oct.–May) is the rose maze, with 1200 rose bushes in a resplendent helix. **[Red Hill Rd. Open daily 10a.m.–5p.m. Entry $12/$10/$7, family $33.** Phone (03) 5989 8387]

## REVOLUTIONARY

**CULBURRA BEACH, NSW**   Canberra designer Walter Burley Griffin also lent a helping hand with the layout of this seaside town east of Nowra. The job wasn't simple, with lagoons, river and ocean cramping three sides, but Griffin found a solution in semicircles. All is revealed by the map on the Progress Association Hall on Penguin Head Rd – assuming you can find it!.

With more than 1000 creepers, from glory vines to clematis, Tangled Maze in **Creswick (Vic.)** is well named. If the half-hectare puzzle, with its 3-km path, doesn't confound and confuse you, the heady perfume of the firecracker honeysuckle may well do so. There's also a daisy maze and mini-golf. **[4.5 km from Creswick on Daylesford Rd. Open daily 10a.m.– 5.30p.m. Entry to maze $7.50/$7; higher rates apply for the whole experience. Phone (03) 5345 2847 or visit www.ballarat.com/tangledmaze]**

## FROM A TO OM

**DENMARK, WA**   Rob Shaw is the one-time garbo of Denmark (not to be confused with the one and only Garbo of Sweden). Along with his brother Lachlan, Rob has carved a curly maze in a tea-tree thicket. The Shaws call it 'passive ecotourism': the maze is more a meditative amble than a giant conundrum. Come and go as you please. The maze is yours, with a donation tin at the entrance. Inside the thicket are two cheat gates to facilitate a Zen state of mind. **[A few km west**

of Denmark, off the South Coast Hwy, turn into Lapko Rd following the sign to Karma Chalets]

Dense with fences, Oz Maze in **Echuca (Vic.)** is a labyrinthine replica of Australia, with each inner journey starting at the riverboat capital and winding around the map via each state capital. Escapes are positioned along the route for the homesick. **[Cnr Sturt and Anstruther Sts, beside the roundabout at Moama Bridge. Open daily during school holidays 9.30a.m.–4p.m., Wed.–Mon. at other times. Entry $9/$8.50, family $30. Phone (03) 5480 2220 or visit www.ozmaze.com.au]**

## SLATE ARRIVALS

**MINTARO, SA**    Sharon Morris is a naturopath and her husband Mike works at the slate quarry. So it makes sense that they have created an all-natural labyrinth of hedges and stonework, with a tranquil pool at its heart. Maze navigators come as much for the serenity as for the challenge. **[Jacka Rd, down from the football oval. Open Thur.–Mon. 10a.m.–4p.m., daily during school holidays. Entry $6/$4. Phone (08) 8843 9012]**

## CRACKPOT KING

**PROMISED LAND, Tas.**    Recognised by Australia Post as a realm deserving mail collection, Tasmazia is the dream of Lower Crackpot laird, Brian Inder. Set among lavender farms and verdant hills, this complex includes sight gags that help soothe your nerves, such as GST House (with one tenth missing) and a one-way Irish maze. It also includes a replica of legendary Hampton Court Maze, the Great Maze (where you hope to find the Three Bears' Cottage) and The Cage, where you aim for a tribute to the toilet's inventor, Thomas Crapper. **[Staverton Rd, 14 km southwest of Sheffield. Open daily 10a.m.– 5p.m. All-day entry $15/$8. Phone (03) 6491 1934 or investigate www.tasmazia.com.au]**

## DUAL DISORIENTATION

**RICHMOND, Tas.**   If you unfurled the fences of the Richmond Maze you'd reach the middle of Hobart some 26 km away. That should read Mazes plural, one riddled with dead-ends while the second has none. The quickest time for a newcomer to complete both challenges stands at 25 minutes, and roughly 3000 steps. **[13 Bridge St. Open daily 9a.m.–5p.m. Entry $5.50/$3.50. Phone (03) 6260 2451]**

## MOVING HEAVEN AND EARTH

**TANAWHA, Qld**   Three men need three days a week with electric pruners and a mobile scaffold to keep the Bhutan conifers of Bellingham Maze looking trim, and that's assuming they don't get lost in the process. Stan Bellingham planted the puzzle – a unique eight-pointed star with a fountain at its centre – in 1991. **[On the Tanawha Tourist Dve, just north of Superbee, heading to Buderim. Open daily 9a.m.–5p.m. Entry $8.50/$6.50 and family $26. Phone (07) 5445 2979 or negotiate www.bellmaze.com]**

# ODDITIONS

- ⊚ Chris and Lauretta Davis 'launched' Mythic Maze in **Nannup (WA)** in 2003. Their contorted hedge corridors are filled with wood spirits, a Nannup tiger and an obstreperous minotaur. There is also a Camelot Maze. **[177 Vasse Hwy. Open daily during school holidays 10a.m.–4p.m., Thur.–Mon. at other times. Entry $7.50/$5, family $22.50. Phone (08) 9756 2121]**

- ⊚ At the Dismal Swamp Visitors Centre, 30 km southwest of **Smithton (Tas.)** you can hop on a giant slide and enter the world's only blackwood swamp maze. **[Bass Hwy. Phone (03) 6456 7199]**

- ⊚ Three thousand hedges comprise a classic maze in **Westbury (Tas.)**, with an estimated escape path measuring 1 km – if you're lucky. **[10 Bass Hwy. Open daily 10a.m.–4p.m., closed Aug. Entry $5.50/$4.40, family $20. Phone (03) 6393 1840 or visit www.greatwesterntiers.org.au/westburymaze]**

# MIRACLES

*(Being a wonderment of extraordinary events
and objects beyond belief)*

## FUTILITY BELT

**BOWRAVILLE, NSW**   Do you suffer from nervous debility? Perhaps you emit at night due to excessive desire? If so, just drop into the Folk Museum, buckle on Dr McLaughlin's Electric Belt, dip the chain battery in a cup of apple cider vinegar, and activate. Dr McLaughlin has lots more helpful suggestions along pure-living lines, with patient progress to be reported within 30 days. **[High St. Open Tues. and Sat. 10a.m.–3p.m., Wed. and Fri. 10a.m.–noon, Sun. 11a.m.–3p.m. Entry $1.10. Phone (02) 6564 7251]**

## FEATHERWEIGHT BELTS THE HEAVIES

**HEATHCOTE, Vic.**   A telephone is nailed to a wooden ceiling beam in Wild Duck Creek Estate. It doesn't work – it's there to remind David (Duck) Anderson of a call he took in 1997, from an American wine importer. 'Robert Parker has given you 99 points,' said the caller. For those outside the wine game, Parker is hailed as the Million Dollar Nose, the force behind the tippler's bible *The Wine Advocate*, with over 40 000 subscribers worldwide. In 32 years of tasting, Parker wasn't in the habit of giving 99 points – such a score was the stuff of fairytales. Overnight, the price of Dave's 'Duck Muck Shiraz' went from A$20 to US$1000, though a rename was imperative. Even now, you can find Wild Duck Springflat Shiraz 1997 for around A$3000 on eBay. **[Spring Flat Rd, 5 km west of town. Open only by appointment. Phone (03) 5433 3133]**

## TALL STOREY

**KAKADU, NT**   Mimi spirits are so slender their necks might snap in strong winds, goes the legend. Invisible and mischievous, these spirits inhabit rocks and sneak into the dreams of artists from the Bunidj and Murrwan people. A supposed sample of the spirits' handiwork, painted with menstrual blood and the powder of old wasp nests, hovers on an overhang two storeys above the ground. Dreamtime stories say the

Mimi have the power to pull down cliffs, add their signature and replace the stone. Once you go there, you'll be hard pressed to conjure a more rational explanation. **[Part of main gallery at Ubirr, north of Jabiru]**

## LORDS OF THE MANNA

**MURWILLUMBAH, NSW**   Just before Easter, 2000, a semi-trailer smashed its front axle near the Mitsubishi dealership. The truck plunged into the river, along with its load of 40 000 slabs of beer. The driver swam to safety. The load was ditched in order to save the truck. Next day every second male in town duck-dived and breathed through garden hoses to reach the freight. The hospital had never seen so many cut feet in its history. As for the Mustang Under-19s, their season also took a dive. The whole town was in party mode. The pubs were facing bankruptcy. When official salvage diver Terry Semple took a reconnaissance he realised the palettes had been picked clean. **[Crash site is opposite the Ampol service station, Pacific Hwy]**

## FAITH UNDER FIRE

**NEW NORCIA, WA**   As a young monk, Rosendo Salvado was given a painting that he included with his cargo when setting out for the New World, in 1846. One year later the painting, *Our Lady Of Good Counsel*, was placed in the path of a grassfire raging through the new Benedictine colony in this town north of Perth. By all accounts, the fire at once switched direction. You can see the painting, and Salvado's tomb, within the abbey church where the brothers still convene daily. **[Great Northern Hwy]**

## OUR LADY OF ASSUMPTION

**ROCKINGHAM, PERTH, WA**   Patty Powell almost choked on her sandwich when she saw the statue crying. The 70-cm Madonna, made of fibreglass, was a souvenir of a trip to Thailand in 2002. Initial tests revealed the liquid to be a cocktail of rose and vegetable oils. Cynics disagreed – they feared the tears could be weeping resin. Unfazed, Patty sent cotton balls soaked in the tears to needy invalids all over the world – gratis. The statue now stands in Our Lady of Lourdes, in Rockingham, along the road to Mandurah. **[1 Townsend St. Mass on Sat. 7p.m. or Sun. 7.30a.m., 9.30a.m. and 7p.m.]**

## NOT A BAD DROP

**TAREN POINT, SYDNEY, NSW**   Journalist Paul Sheehan wrote a feature in the *Good Weekend* extolling the powers of Unique Water. Dr Russell Beckett, a biochemical pathologist, is the boffin behind the bottle. The doctor found that sheep near Cooma in the Snowy Mountains had been lapping from streams high in magnesium bicarbonate (thanks to the region's rocks) and living longer as well as producing a greater rate of twins. Beckett believes carbon dioxide is responsible, eroding cells and hastening crow's feet. Sheehan is convinced that this drink makes the grass seem greener. **[Factory outlet is at 45 Alexander Ave. Open Mon.–Fri. 7.30a.m.–5p.m., Sat. 7.30a.m.–noon. Phone (02) 9525 3033 or visit www.uniquewater.com.au]**

## WONDERS TO BURN

**THE CAVES, Qld**   Capricorn Caves were once called Olsen's Caves, after the Norwegian caver who tied a rope around his waist and crawled into the abyss in 1882. The names Zigzag Passage, Horse Head and The Flower Pot give you a hint of what he found. But the most remarkable feature occurs only at the summer solstice, 22 December, when near noon a sunbeam funnels down a pothole and spills underground. So intense is the light that a metal dish in the hot spot will incinerate your entry ticket. Stand in the beam and watch your clothing's colours thrown into every corner of the chamber. **[23 km north of Rockhampton. Open Mon.–Sat. 9a.m.–4p.m. Tours run hourly for $16/$8. Adventure tours available. Phone (07) 4934 2883]**

## BIRD OF PASSAGE

**WARRNAMBOOL, Vic.**   In 1878 Charles MacGillivray was strolling along the limestone cliffs edging Bass Strait, when he came across a crate. Inside was a porcelain peacock: designed by a French artist and made by Minton, it was destined for Melbourne's 1880 International Exhibition. Chipped beak aside, the 2-m statue somehow survived the *Loch Ard* shipwreck along with only two of the 54 passengers. Historians and ceramicists are still bemused. **[Perched in Flagstaff Hill Gallery, Merri St. Open daily 9a.m.–5p.m. Entry $15.50/$6. Phone (03) 5559 4600 or visit www.flagstaffhill.com]**

# MISNOMERS

*(Being a bungle of tangled terms and wrongly wrangled names)*

## GENERATION WHY

**EDEN HILLS, ADELAIDE, SA**   This southern suburb fringing Adelaide was no Eden for the 350 Aboriginal children taken from their parents between 1942 and the early 70s, in line with government policy. Colebrook Reserve captures the unspeakable sorrow of the Stolen Generation with the sculpture of a weeping woman at the site of a former 'training home'. **[Opposite 237 Shepherds Hill Rd]**

## GRAPESHOT VICTIM?

**ALBANY, WA**   Very few strawberries ever sprouted at Strawberry Hill. Wheat and clover have been the principal crops on what is viewed as the first true farm in WA, with bullocks, olives, vegetables and many stone fruits – but no strawberries. The man behind the misnomer, Sir (Captain) Richard Spencer, was once a firebrand officer under Lord Nelson. (A letter from Nelson hangs in the hallway, admonishing Spencer for firing at a Cisalpine privateer first and asking questions later.) The bellicose knight incurred several nasty head wounds during skirmishes at sea, which may account for his strawberry-red herring. **[170 Middleton Rd. Open daily 10a.m.–4p.m. (closed mid-Jul. to Aug.). Entry $3.30/$2.20. Phone (08) 9841 3735]**

One of the first things you'll see when you walk into the Lion's Den in **Helenvale (Qld)**, south of Cooktown, is a stuffed giraffe. (Not to mention pickled snakes, bloated barramundi, and spiders.) But even more unusually, this hotel's licence has always been owned by women, stemming way back to the first publican, Annie Ross, in 1889.

## IN THE LOOP

**ALICE SPRINGS, NT**    The only turf at this Turf Club is the patch that aprons the pavilion: the racetrack itself is oil-laced sand. But it was the springboard for two famed names of Australian racing. Jim Cummings – father of Bart, the trainer of innumerable Melbourne Cup champions – rode many winners here. And another jockey, Ted Dixon, entrusted a rookie called Colin Hayes to look after his stable – Hayes' later achievements include two Melbourne Cups, three Cox Plates and, remarkably, all ten winners (a world record) at a single race meeting in 1982. **[South Stuart Hwy, towards airport. Peak times are Apr.–May (Alice Springs Cup Carnival) and Oct.–Nov. Phone (08) 8952 4977]**

## OLD CREAM JUMPER

**BORDERTOWN, SA**    Barry Smith couldn't believe his eyes. Back in 1980, riding a motorbike through mallee scrub, he saw a white kangaroo. He caught the animal and rang his sister, a vet in Bordertown. Four years later a baby white roo was born in the wildlife sanctuary here, followed since then by nearly 50 more. White roos, it must be said, are actually western greys with a dominant white gene – but they're prone to sunburn nonetheless. **[East of town, parallel with Dukes Hwy. You can view the colony gratis from the street]**

## BYO ODOMETER

**LOCH SPORT, Vic.**    Loch Sport's major attraction is the Ninety Mile Beach – which in fact runs for 94.5 miles (152 km), but who's counting? The pedants are, it seems – the same folk who have pooh-poohed other Ninety Mile Beaches (in WA and Brazil) for their gross shortcomings. In fact, the Vic. version has no inlet or headland to interrupt its length, making it the longest unpunctuated beach in the world.

**Monkey Mia (WA)** is famed for its up-close dolphins and daydreaming dugongs, not for monkeys. The inlet is thought to have derived its name from the *Monkey*, a survey ship that passed this way in 1830, combined with *mia*, the Indigenous word for meeting-place.

## JONAH'S REVENGE

**NEWMAN, WA**   In 1957, in their Ford Thames truck (now restored and parked in the Visitors Centre), Stan and Ella Hilditch bush-bashed the unmapped desert hereabouts with compass and pick, looking for manganese. They found iron instead – some 68 per cent pure ore on a nameless whale-like outcrop. Over a billion tonnes of payload later, Mt Whaleback has lost its shape, becoming the largest single open-cut iron ore mine in the world. The 2003 film *Japanese Story* was filmed here, in part, above the pit. To date the hole stretches down, in terraces, some 405 m. **[Needing a quorum of four, you can join the mine tour at 8.30 any morning from the Visitors Centre on Fortescue Ave, for $12/$10/$7, family $30. Alternatively, grab an imperfect peek from Radio Hill Lookout, signposted 1 km east along Newman Dve]**

## MOLEHILL

**WYCHEPROOF, Vic.**   One reason why the view from Mt Wycheproof isn't so commanding is that at 43 m it's not really a mountain. Yet locals insist their hillock is Australia's smallest 'official' mountain, and they claim it to be the smallest registered mountain on the planet. Tellingly, the town's name comes from an Aboriginal phrase meaning 'grass on hill'. **[Turn left into Mount St, off High St]**

## ODDITIONS

◎ At Cactus Jack, on the main drag of **Gladstone (Qld)**, happy hour is 5p.m.–7p.m. daily. You also have a chance to try a XXXX margarita.

◎ Mimosa Rocks, a pocket-sized national park north of **Tathra (NSW)**, has much more heath than mimosa. So why the name? A ship called the *Mimosa* went onto the rocks back in 1863.

◎ **Goondiwindi (Qld)** outlaid $5 million to build a recreational water park. All the facilities were in place on schedule – except the water, thanks to the drought of 2002. But 470 million litres of $H_2O$ have since been delivered.

# MISSING

*(Being a vacuum of things lacking and people vanishing)*

## HOT ICE

BROOME, WA   Midway through the Japanese air-raid on Broome in 1942, a Dutch pilot named Captain Ivan Smirnoff took off from the airport. Three Japanese Zeroes chased his DC3, forcing Smirnoff to crash-land in nearby Carnot Bay. Unbeknownst to the captain, part of his cargo was $15 million worth of contraband diamonds. After the war, local Aborigines found a secret cache of the stones, but over two-thirds of the shipment remains at large. [Pieces of the Smirnoff wreck, and fascinating diamond story, are displayed at Broome Museum on Robinson St. Open weekdays June–Oct. 10a.m.–4p.m. (weekends till 1p.m.), daily Nov.–May 10a.m.–1p.m. Entry $5/$3/$1. Phone (08) 9192 2075]

Heading for Batehaven, near **Bateman's Bay (NSW)**, you'll encounter Hanging Rock Creek, right beside Hanging Rock Family Motel and 100 m shy of the Hanging Rock Reserve. The only catch is that the rock itself didn't hang around for long, being wobbly and so deemed too precarious for these litigious times.

## CAPTIVE AUDIENCE

HAMILTON, Tas.   Ignore the plaque outside St Peter's Anglican church. Instead, circle the building and see if you can work out what's missing. No idea? Well, back in the 1800s, since half the worshippers were convicts, the architect decided to install only one door into the church, and so minimise escape routes. Nowadays the door is unattended and the lock is an octopus strap. [Off Ponsbury St, close to the Hobart end of town]

Unlike Hobart and Sydney, **Launceston (Tas.)** is the only city of its vintage to lack a major reference to Lachlan Macquarie. Why? It may have something to do with the NSW governor scorning Launceston's location back in 1811 and voting for the residents to relocate north to George Town. The people – and their grudge – didn't budge.

## OUT OF OBSCURITY

**LISMORE, NSW**    William Steenson was crushed by a runaway railway carriage in 1901, and buried under a Mason's cross. Then, in 1978, there was a story in Lismore's *Northern Star* complete with photo and the headline 'Why does the cross glow?' Reporters, geologists, hippies and faith healers swarmed the grave. Barium paint was suspected, but no, the red Balmoral granite of which the cross was made appeared to be self-illuminating. Notably, the grave's Balmoral pedestal did not glow, and neither did any grave of the same material. Vandals removed the masonry in 1986 and a replica was erected, but it doesn't, alas, do much to enlighten us. **[Elevated section of North Lismore Pioneer Cemetery, cnr Terania and Wilson Sts]**

## MARY CELESTIAL

**NAROOMA, NSW**    Bermuda has its *Mary Celeste*; Bermagui, the green boat of 1880. The boat washed up on 11 October of that year, in a cove now dubbed Mystery Bay. Inside were two lashed oars, two unused gun cartridges, numerous sacks of stones, a few personal belongings and a series of holes drilled into the hull. The books and bedding were traced to Lamont Young, a Sydney geologist, and his German aide, Karl Schneider. The pair had been investigating a gold-field near Bermagui when they went missing, along with three local policemen. Schneider was cast as prime suspect, yet not one body, or fugitive, has ever been found. **[Turnoff is a few km south of Narooma. A plaque near the swings tells more]**

Taste the tap water in **Castlemaine** or **Maldon (Vic.)** and you may register a difference. The shire is possibly alone in its fight against a state initiative to add fluoride to the water supply. Not that consumers were too partisan – the *Chewton Chat* ran a fluoride poll during 2002 which showed 103 nays versus 97 yays. But the nays carried, as your taste-buds will confirm.

## WHICH BA-K?

**STRAHAN, Tas.**   Now a four-star guesthouse, Strahan Central Suites on Harold St was once The Royal Bank of Avram. Owner of this elite branch was the self-titled Duke of Avram, who made and sold his own coins during the 1980s. Federal police objected to the project, so the duke (aka John) dropped the letter N, dubbing his enterprise The Royal Ba-k of Avram. Even on paper, this made no difference to legislators, who shut the bank in a wink. **[1 Harold St. Phone (03) 6471 7612]**

# MONSTERS

*(Being a menagerie of mythical flora and
fauna, actual and anecdotal)*

## PRECIOUS FOSSIL

**ADELAIDE, SA**   Finding a dinosaur is a remarkable thing. But finding
a plesiosaur that's turned into opal has to rate as a double bonanza.
Such luck befell the Addyman family of outback Andamooka in 1968:
while three flippers and a head are missing, the creature's spine and
ribs are gems, in both senses. Sharing the chamber are more marvels,
from an opalised ichthyosaur to Australia's largest ammonite, a prehistoric prototype of the nautilus shell. **[South Australian Museum, North
Tce. Open daily 10a.m.–5p.m. Free entry. Phone (08) 8207 7500 or
check out www.samuseum.sa.gov.au]**

## LEGENDS ON LEGS

**BENDIGO, Vic.**   Mr Lo On of Hong Kong incorporated 90 000 mirrors
and 6000 silk scales into the longest (and possibly last) imperial dragon,
called Sun Loong. (Imperial here means 'blessed by the emperor', which
accounts for Sun Loong's regal quota of five talons per limb.) The 100-m
beast, stabled in the Golden Dragon Museum, ventures out at Easter only,
a goodwill bid begun by Chinese diggers in 1892. Next-door is Loong,
his shopworn ancestor, the oldest imperial dragon in the world, who
has shrunk 5 m since his birth. **[5–9 Bridge St. Open daily 9.30a.m.–
5p.m. Entry $7/$5/$4, family $20. Phone (03) 5441 5044]**

Little monsters have overtaken the old post office in
the **Melbourne (Vic.)** suburb of Surrey Hills. Visit
www.surreysculpture.com.au and look for the link, or
drop by to meet the macabre menagerie in the flesh.
The studio has been going for 20 years, providing
Greek gods and freak reptiles to Victorian homes. **[609
Canterbury Rd. Open Mon.–Fri. 8.30a.m.–5.30p.m.,
Sat. 9a.m.–1p.m. Phone (03) 9836 9555]**

## SCALES OF JUSTICE

**KATHERINE, NT**    Bolung is not a snake to cross. This massive python, the creation spirit of the Jawoyn people, dwells in the rockpools upstream of Jedda Rock in the Second Gorge, part of the Katherine Gorge chain. The Jawoyn don't swim here, or drink or over-fish, for fear of an angry Bolung striking back. Disaster did strike the movie *Jedda*, Australia's first full-length colour film, which was partially shot in the gorge. As soon as filming was finished in 1955, the celluloid stock was lost in a plane crash. **[A range of activities is available in the gorge. For cruises, canoe hire, etc. contact Nitmiluk Tours on (08) 8972 1253. For details on walking tracks and camping, call Nitmiluk National Park Office on (08) 8972 3945]**

## FERAL PORKIES

**KILCOY, Qld**    Sixteen-year-olds Warren Christenson and Tony Solano were hunting pigs at Sandy Creek in December 1979 when they heard a series of thumps. From nowhere a sulphur smell laced the air. Suddenly a giant creature appeared 20 m away, not a pig but more like a yeti with chocolate-coloured hair. Warren grabbed his rifle and the blast scared the monster back into the scrub. A few days later, the boys escorted their biology teacher and her husband back to Sandy Creek and took plaster casts of the monster's prints. Since then, the only yowie to be sighted in Kilcoy is the statue in Yowie Park, and those chocolates in the supermarket. **[Or get a Yowie T-bone at the Stanley Hotel]**

## BIG CAT COUNTRY

**LITHGOW, NSW**    The amateur video shot in 2003 showed a standard feral cat beside a large black cat with a panther-like silhouette. Seven experts concurred that the latter was 'possibly a panther', although panthers aren't known to befriend other felines. Was this more of the Grose-Vale/Lithgow panther puzzle? Most definitely. Horses have been mauled, sheep killed, and headless goats left in trees. Dogs and small cats don't do that last trick. Ken Pullen, a Grose Vale local, keeps a panther database with over 250 entries, including a driveway pawprint. Conflicting theories persist: maybe you, dear traveller, will be the wayfarer who settles the debate for good.

## BIRDS BEWARE

**MOSS VALE, NSW**    As the name implies, Moss Vale is a dampish spot, which is just how *Petalura gigantea* likes it. So much so that the world's largest species of dragonfly has been calling this part of the world home for some 190 million years. Despite being 11 cm long, 14 cm across and heavier than a fairy wren, *Petalura* isn't easy to locate. But there's good news: the insect hatches in mid-October and doesn't stray far from his patch for three whole months. To give yourself any chance of a glimpse, take a stroll near Wingecarribee Swamp, an offensive name for the largest mountain peatlands on mainland Oz. **[14 km east, towards Robertson. The peatlands surround the headwaters of Wingecarribee River]**

> The high fence around the courthouse in **Bathurst (NSW)**, goes one local yarn, was intended for the 'other Bathurst', in Ghana, West Africa. The two sets of plans got mixed up: the railings were originally intended to ward off elephants.

## COUNTRY PUMPKINS

**ORBOST, Vic.**    The alluvial plains of the Snowy River are said to be as fertile as the Nile Delta. Ah yes, but did the Egyptians ever have such large pumpkins? The photos in the Orbost Museum show innumerable examples of the vast veggies deputising as drays, toboggans and prams. Fred Mundy's pumpkin registered 194 lb (that's around 88 kg in the new money). But pick of the pic show belongs to the family of Walter Rice. The man must have used a shovel to hollow out his prize pumpkin before he set it afloat on the Snowy under the name of 'HMAS Orbost'. On board are seven children. **[Part of the library on Ruskin St, open weekdays 8.30a.m.–5p.m. Free entry]**

## ELLIOTT'S PROOF ROCK

**WINTON, Qld**    Scott Hucknull, a fossil freak from Brisbane Museum, made a special trip to Winton in 2001. Apparently a farmer had found a big bone. Scott sat in the farmer's kitchen, unsure whether he'd driven the 1433 km in vain, when the farmer (who prefers to remain anonymous) produced the biggest dinosaur femur the world had ever seen. Later that year, on 11 September in fact, a team of palaeontologists was probing the site and found ribs and vertebrae belonging to a massive sauropod they named Elliot, a five-storey lizard outweighing five elephants. According to Hucknull, the events in the northern hemisphere that day gave him 'a super sense of perspective'. **[The rear of Corfield & Fitzmaurice Store has Elliot's replica femur. Entry $3/$1]**

## TRIGONOMETREE

**WAUCHOPE, NSW**    Even Einstein would baulk at calculating the 'super feet' contained in the tallowwood log outside Timbertown. The titanic tree is roughly 1000 years old, plus or minus a few growth rings. It's a sad irony that the trunk was too big to fit into the sawmill and so was banished to the role of billboard. But in case Albert's wondering, the easiest way to determine super feet (a log's volume of timber) is to resort to the Armstrong Rapid Calculator in the adjacent museum. The equation is roughly $T + B \times L - P$, where T is Top circumference, B is Bottom, L is Length, and P is the Pipe or central hollow. Please show all working-out. **[Oxley Hwy. Museum open daily 10a.m.–3.30p.m. Gold coin entry]**

## MYTH FOR HIRE

**MURRAY BRIDGE, SA**    Legend says that the Moorundie, the Ngaralta name for the Murray, is occupied by man-eating bunyips. But Murray Bridge, once known as Moop-pol-tha-wong, has its share of doubters. In fact Bertha is the only bunyip around, and she costs a dollar to motivate. Pop a coin into the slot at Sturt Reserve, and lo and behold a pig-snouted, taloned and fanged contraption rises from its pond in a fair impression of a Ngaralta nightmare. **[Off Seventh St]**

Krystyna Pawlowski is better known in **Normanton (NT)** as One-Shot Krys. Evidence of her accuracy is the crocodile basking on the main street, an 8.6-m monster that locals call Krys too, just to make things confusing. The Polish refugee shot the reptile in 1957, while hunting with her husband Ron.

## ME AND MY BIG MOUTH

**PERTH, WA**    In 1976, a megamouth – the world's most primitive living shark, hitherto unknown – bit and became tangled in a silken sea anchor in Hawaii. Twelve years later a 5-m specimen (the first and only one observed in Australia) was spotted by surfers in Mandurah, south of Perth. They took it for a whale, despite the gills and fins. The injured giant beached himself at Mandurah, and museum staff did the rest. Though nine megamouths have surfaced around the world, Perth is your only chance to meet one Down Under. **[Western Australian Museum, James St, Northbridge, north of the main railway station. Open daily 9.30a.m.–5p.m. (Anzac Day 1p.m.–5p.m.). Entry by donation. Phone (08) 9427 2700 or visit www.museum.wa.gov.au]**

## WILD STONE CRAFT

**WOLLSTONECRAFT, SYDNEY, NSW**    On Berry Island, which actually isn't an island but a headland, ancient rock art depicts a fishlike monster which could be a stingray or a Dreamtime spirit. Sadly, none of the Koradjis (wise men) of Sydney's Cammeraygal people is here to answer the riddle, many having succumbed to smallpox within a few years of the First Fleet arriving. In surreal contrast, the silver tanks of the Shell Oil refinery stand on the other side of Gore Cove – rock art confronting modern oils. **[End of Shirley Rd]**

## WOLF IN TIGER'S CLOTHING

**TANTANOOLA, SA**    During 1893 dozens of sheep were mangled by a mysterious clawed creature. The prime suspect was a Bengal tiger which had escaped from a travelling circus in the 1880s. Local Tom Donovan saved the day: he shot the tiger dead and carted the corpse to a taxidermist who pronounced the animal an Assyrian wolf. How did it get to Australia? A shipwreck fugitive, perhaps? The mystery was never solved. **[See the so-called tiger at the Tiger Hotel. Phone (08) 8734 4066]**

## MIX AND MATCH

**ULVERSTONE, Tas.**    The bronze weathervane known as the Wolferdinger Fish, in Apex Park, celebrates the story of Otto and Karl von

Staufen. Otto was a naturalist based in northern Tas. His brother Karl, back in Germany, was a taxidermist who liked to splice assorted animals together to create monsters. The fanciful fish in the plaza is based on a madcap description Otto once sent to Karl, attempting to give a picture of the natural wonders of the New World. **[Across the plaza from Banjo's Bakery, look up]**

# ODDITIONS

⊚ A green tyrannosaurus with yellow spots promotes a plumber's services, on the Princes Hwy just out of **Mollymook (NSW)**.

⊚ Relax kids, it's not a real triceratops. The monster hunched in **Ballandean (Qld)**, just south of the state's apple capital, Stanthorpe, is known as the Fruitisforus.

⊚ A whale was found on the Murray River in **Blanchetown (SA)** in late 2002. The 20-million-year-old squalodont (shark-tooth whale), one of the first to be found in Australia, was lodged inside a riverside cliff.

⊚ In 1997, Mark Duncan took some sunset photos over Lake Bonney, near **Barmera (SA)**. When developed, they showed a mystery object swimming across the lake's surface. Was it a carp? Or Nessie's antipodean cousin? No satisfactory explanation has been offered.

# MUSIC

*(Being a symphony of singular notes and notable singles)*

## VOYAGE IN VANE

**BALLARAT, Vic.** Heroically, the band aboard the *Titanic* continued playing on deck as the liner plunged into oblivion. Legend, and lifeboat recollections, insist the final overture was a dour hymn entitled 'Nearer My God To Thee', though others seem to think that a tune called 'Autumn' got the nod. Whatever the track, the band's courage is enshrined in a bandstand on Sturt St. Look twice – or you'll miss the tribute – the White Star liner cast in silhouette as the gazebo's weathervane. **[Opposite the Visitors Centre]**

## STAND BY YOUR FAN

**COWRA, NSW** Colemane's Country Corner is a one-man country-music museum and Athol Colemane is that man. Athol has Johnny Cash singing in German, a rare recording of Orion ('the greatest Elvis impersonator bar none') and five plaster frogs line-dancing on a stump. In fact, Athol has more crammed into his garden shed than you could wave a Gibson guitar at. **[43 Mulyan St, beside the Cowra–Eugowra railway line. Open daily 9a.m.–5p.m. Entry $3/$1. Phone (02) 6342 1064]**

## SUPERSONIC PERCUSSION

**DARNUM, Vic.** Expect the unexpected at Darnum Musical Village. There's a piano capable of playing a duet with itself, a piano-and-organ hybrid, and a gramophone hidden within a piano stool. Piano crates line the museum's walls to enrich the sound from the 300 instruments, one of which your guide may play. The collector and curator, Albert Fox, bought a church for $100, then moved it here for $1500, to accommodate an 1878 William Anderson pipe organ, which is priceless. **[Darnum–Allambee Rd, off the Princes Hwy east of Warragul. Open daily 10a.m.–4p.m. Entry $9.90/$8.80/$4.40, family $22. Phone (03) 5627 8235]**

## BAND IN A BOX

**GREENOUGH, WA**   What am I? I was built in a factory on Bonaparte St, in Nice, around 1880. I have 80 hammers, a spring motor, a coin slot and a crank. Inside my elegant cabinet you'll find sleigh bells, a tambourine, castanets, a triangle, cymbals, drums and piano wires. I am an . . . automatic piano organ, precursor to the nickelodeon and grandmother of all jukeboxes. Joseph Nallino, my maker, describes me as a street piano that sounds like an orchestra. I entertained the patrons in a Fremantle wine saloon before retiring here. But still worth a gander. **[Pioneer Museum, Brand Hwy, 19 km south of Geraldton. Open daily 10a.m.–4p.m. Entry $4.50/$3.50. Phone (08) 9926 1058]**

> When the wind is right, the bridge connecting Tea Gardens and **Hawks Nest (NSW)** will sing – allegedly. They call it Singing Bridge, but I remain sceptical: the night I stayed there, the wind was a Force 5 gale yet when I climbed the bridge the ironwork kept quiet. Though maybe it just couldn't compete with the songs howling out of the pub on Moira Ave.

## ANY CHANCE OF A DRINK?

**INGHAM, Qld**   The enduring Slim Dusty song 'A Pub With No Beer' will drone from radios long after we've shed our mortal coils. But as to *the* pub, most stories point to the Dawn Day Hotel, now known as Lee's, in Ingham. It was a popular hangout for thirsty troops returning to base in World War 2. Yet so seldom did supply meet demand, thanks to wartime rationing, that owners Eric and Gladys Harvey had to invent ways of keeping the good times flowing. A local wit, Dan Sheahan, put pen to paper and, a decade on, north-coast lyricist Gordon Parsons, in combo with a Kempsey lad named Slim, turned the complaint into a platinum hit. **[There's a plaque outside the pub, which faces the Visitors Centre in Lannercost St. But the Taylors Arms, 26 km west of Macksville in NSW, is also widely seen as the pub in question]**

## DIDGE ON THE RIDGE

**KURANDA, Qld**   Marshall Whyler has played with the London Philharmonic, the London Symphony and the Hungarian National Orchestra – on a didgeridoo. Now he's working in The Ark, a land-locked shopping complex moored in rainforest. The didgeridoo showroom, known as Doongal, occupies most of the Ark. It's one of the best places in Australia to learn how the didgeridoo is painted, cured, waxed and (believe it or not) tuned. **[22 Coondoo St. Open daily 9a.m.–4p.m. Free entry. Phone (07) 4093 9999 or visit www.doongal.com.au]**

## FRET NOTES

**NARRANDERA, NSW**   Robert Palmer of Narrandera (no relation to the late Robert Palmer of pop), as president of the town's Country Music Association, spent 300 hours with plywood, steel and Whipper-Snipper cord to make one of the biggest playable guitars in the world. If you ask politely at the Visitor Information Centre, you may be allowed to have a strum. **[Cadell St on the park. Open weekdays 9a.m.–5p.m., weekends 10a.m.–5p.m. Phone 1800 672 392 or (02) 6959 1766]**

## DINGO STAR

**STUARTS WELL, NT**   The roadhouse Jim's Place will soon be known as Dink's Place if Jim's pet dingo keeps stealing the limelight. Jim's neighbour, Wally, caught the pup with a cat-trap on his station in 2001. Too cute to kill, Dink became a fixture at Jim's Place where the dingo took a shine to eavesdropping Jim's daughters' piano lessons. 'Chariots of Fire' is Dink's favourite track, but the dingo will 'sing' any tune and even play the keys on all fours. **[90 km south of Alice Springs. Just don't ask for an autograph]**

## PAPADAMARAZZI

**WARRNAMBOOL, Vic.**   Most big towns can boast an eatery where a few rock stars hang on the wall. The Hard Rock Café has conquered the world on such a premise. But Malaysia, on Liebig St, is a dif-ferent premises altogether. The sun-blasted snaps in the shopfront testify to every pop icon that's passed though town, from homegrown stars to The Supremes, The Monkees and The Deltones. One band summarises the display: Mental As Anything. **[Uphill from Merri Junction. Phone (03) 5562 2051]**

## CHEESE PLATTERS

**WINDSOR, NSW**    Fairly game I reckon, calling a meal 'Chuck Berry'. But that's the flavour of the Red Rock On Café. Chubby Checker is a double-decker burger. Big Bopper comes with the lot. The memorabilia include a cut-out figure of Australian rocker Johnny O'Keefe. The decor is Deco, the waiting staff is lurid Deltone, and naturally the seafood combinations are called The Platters. **[219 George St, opposite the Coles supermarket. Phone (02) 4587 9997]**

**Binnaway (NSW)** was the home of The White Rose Orchestra, a troupe that regaled the remoter corners of NSW and Qld during the 1940s and 50s. Driving into Binnaway, along Bullinda Rd, there's a memento of TWRO in the form of an upright piano built of chicken wire, standing in the garden of No. 6.

## WIRED FOR SOUND

**WINTON, Qld**    If you're into dirt music then don't miss the singing fence on the former Qantas runway. Fence-posts placed at irregular intervals are strung with five taut wires, which make music when struck with a gidgee stick (or anything you can get your hands on). Other feral percussions litter the airstrip, such as a 20-gallon kettledrum, a hubcap glockenspiel and tubular LPG bells. **[Head for Hughenden and turn right into Colston Rd after the railway crossing. Follow the Qantas signs]**

# MYSTERY

*(Being an entanglement of riddles and enigmas beyond the grasp of definitive solution)*

## AMAZING GRAPE

BASKERVILLE, WA   The seedling vine appeared in 1989, the year Dorham Mann's father died. The first shy tendrils suggested a blond grape combined with the distinctive cabernet leaf. Hang on – white cabernet? Impossible, admitted the Manns. But there it was. By 1993 the mystery vine had produced enough grapes to make 10 bottles. They called the strain *cygne blanc* (French for 'white swan') and told the world in 1998, by which stage the winery had 1000 bottles. Port Robe Estate in SA bought exclusive growing rights for the next 18 years, leaving the Manns to savour their 'silky fine finish'. **[105 Memorial Ave. Open daily 10a.m.–5p.m. while stocks last (usually Aug.–Jan.). Phone (08) 9296 4348]**

## MR BROWN FROM OUT OF TOWN

CHARTERS TOWERS, Qld   Lovers of historic homes will beeline to the restored mansion known as Ay Ot Lookout, to ooh at the hand-painted tiles and aah at the iridescent fanlight. But mystery lovers will get a kick too. Late in the 19th century, Thomas Brown, the mansion's first owner, is said to have lost his estate in a poker game and hanged himself in the cellar the same night. Of the next owners, the Foxleys, every last detail is known, yet scarcely a shred can be found about the unfortunate Mr Brown. Historians believe it was an alias, and rumours abound, though nothing certain is known. As for the curator's grandson, he won't go down into the cellar until the ghost 'dressed like a fireman' has gone away. **[Cnr High and Hodkinson Sts. Open weekdays 8a.m.–3p.m. Single entry $3, double $5, including tea and biscuits. Phone (07) 4787 2799]**

## PYRAMID SELLING

GYMPIE, Qld   Local Dal Berry found a sandstone chunk in 1966 while ploughing on Mt Wolvi. Carved to resemble an ape, the rock seemed ancient and fuelled local conspiracy theorists, who believed that Gympie hosted an ancient civilisation separate from the Aborigines. The ape idol echoed talk of other strange finds (a Macedonian coin, a granite Ganesha, an onyx scarab) in the region. Believers insist that a terraced pyramid lies deep in the forest towards Tin Can Bay, perhaps off Wolvi Rd, and that hewn blocks in Gympie's Uniting Church on Surface Hill came from there. And you thought the Sphinx's riddle was tricky to solve! **[The pyramid is off limits. The ape hunches in the Gold Mining and Historical Museum, 215 Brisbane Rd. Open daily 9a.m.–4p.m. Entry $6.60/$4.40/$2.20. Phone (07) 5482 3995]**

## PACKING A PUNCH

**KENDALL, NSW**    Blair Montague-Drake concocts his unique Norfolk Punch from a secret Benedictine recipe his father stumbled across at Welle Manor Hall in England in 1984. Henry VIII had done much to suppress this potion, along with the monks who drank it. You can sample the curious elixir – a mix of vervain, fennel, alehoof, elder, alder and a good 25 other herbs and spices – on a mountaintop 8 km out of Kendall. Complex, calming, moon-harvested, the non-alcoholic punch has a reputation for reducing life's tensions, as vouched by romance dynamo Barbara Cartland. While there, why not taste their Sweet Dreams Tea or St George's Dragon's Breath Sauce? **[Batar Creek Rd, 8 km from town – 4 km of which are unsealed. Open Mon.–Fri. 9a.m.–4p.m., and first and third weekends of each month 9a.m.–4p.m. Punch line (02) 6559 4464 or visit www.norfolkpunch.com.au]**

## THE WHOLE TRUTH AND NOTHING BUT

**KOLAN SOUTH, Qld**    Owen Murrin, in 1971, was widening his vegetable garden when his plough hit rock. A closer look revealed an entire platform lying beneath his patch. Vanilla white, with a strange ochre stain through it, the platform was pocked by ancient craters – some round, some foot-shaped. Geologists' theories abound, though a visit may not clarify the enigma. **[The Mystery Craters, between Bundaberg and Gin Gin. Open daily 8a.m.–5p.m. Entry $5/$2.50, family $12.50. Phone (07) 4157 7291]**

## FICKLE, THOU NAME IS GEORGE

**LAKE GEORGE, NSW**   One of the mainland's largest expanses of fresh water can vanish one day and miraculously fill without a spot of rain the next. Mystics have their theories, as do hydrologists. In 2002 the lake drained completely, allowing scientists to hunt for aquifers connecting the lake to the Yass River. Their main hypothesis has hidden fissures running below the escarpment that once 'barraged' the lake 27 000 years ago. **[Between Goulburn and Canberra on the Federal Hwy]**

## MY THREE SCARED SONS

**MUNDRABILLA, WA**   In January 1988, Faye Knowles and her three adult sons were crossing the Nullarbor at 4 a.m. when a light appeared on the horizon. Sean, the driver, said the light looked like a fried egg and he thought it was a UFO. When he accelerated, the dish swooped over the car, made a quick U-turn and landed on the car's roof. A smell of rotting flesh pervaded the air. A fine black dust trickled off the chassis. The Knowles heard themselves speaking in slow motion. In a word, weird. The encounter was verified by Graham Henley, a truckie who made an independent sighting of the egg and noted dent marks and dust on the Knowles' car roof when he met them later in Mundrabilla. **[The close encounter occurred between Mundrabilla and Madura]**

## SELDOM SPOTTED

**NANNUP, WA**   Hundreds turned up for the beating in 1971. The idea was to spread out in a straight line and march through Shelley Pine Plantation, hooting and howling and hoping the racket would flush the Tasmanian tiger from hiding. 'The tiger has been spotted!' came the cry from the walkie-talkie, though the joy was short-lived. The so-called tiger was a shorn sheep with spray-painted stripes, dumped by a few lads from the local footy team, the Tigers. Pranks aside, sightings of this 'extinct' creature continue. Headless kangaroo carcasses have spiced the intrigue. A boy called Clarence Hunter photographed a plausible cougar on a field trip. Jimmy Green, who works for the National Parks, has seen the tiger down Gold Gully Rd. The myth thickens. **[A statue cnr Warren and Brockton Sts salutes the hearsay]**

North of **Dubbo (NSW)**, heading for Gilgandra, you may notice a turnoff to Balladeran on your right. If you drive that way for a few km, you'll encounter Old Harbour Lagoon, a perfectly circular waterhole some 2–3 km in circumference. This bird haven is a geological mystery – one theory suggests it is a meteorite crater.

## THE BUS STOPS HERE

**PADDINGTON, SYDNEY, NSW**    Staff at St Vincent's Hospital became accustomed to seeing Karl Kulper snoozing at the bus-stop. Once or twice, in the depths of winter, a sister would nip outside and throw a blanket over the homeless man. He was always polite, a fount of time-table knowledge and full of good cheer. Come the end of night shift, Karl would often escort the nurses to the bus. When the sad day came in 2002, nobody could find a next of kin. The man was a phantom. A wife and child were mentioned, but none came forward. His ashes were interred within the shelter, while the Sisters of Charity funded a plaque by the bench. **[Burton St, behind the hospital]**

## UFORIA

**WYCLIFFE WELL, NT**    Hats, cigars, jellyfish, black balls, triangles – the spooky lights over Wycliffe Wells resemble lots of things, but nobody knows who or what they are. After 20 years of sightings, Lew Farkas's roadhouse is a spaceship shrine, with UFO clippings, bug-eyed Venu-tians and a book of testimonials. Just don't be surprised if the EFTPOS plays up. On the day I was there, the diner's computer started spitting out *;lnonir2ornif2onrobv-co2ubfofonc2[odni2cn2orvb*, but that may have been a software glitch. **[Between Alice Springs and Tennant Creek on the Stuart Hwy]**

## WHIM O' THE WISP

**BOULIA, Qld**    The Min Min Lights are eerie luminous balls that hover on the horizon like the headlights of invisible cars. The epicentre seems to be the derelict Min Min Hotel. Recently Professor Jack Pettigrew of the University of Qld attributed the witchery to an inverted mirage (Fata Morgana), where a layer of cold air bounces light from beyond the horizon to a remote observer. Whatever the cause, the effect is spellbinding. **[The hotel is 100 km east of town. Learn more at the Min Min Encounter at the Tourist Information Centre, Herbert St, in Boulia proper. Open daily 8.30a.m.–5p.m. Entry $12/$7.70/$30 family. Phone (07) 4746 3386]**

# MYTH

*(Being a dreamscape of fantastic folktales
and massive misconceptions)*

## SEVEN SISTERS IN EXILE

**ADELAIDE, SA**   Crabs and fish occupy the night skies – but not just the Cancer and Pisces constellations most of us know. Astronomers at Adelaide Planetarium (the last manually operated one in the world) reveal what the stars spell for Indigenous people. In Ngarrindjeri eyes, for example, the Southern Cross is a stingray chased by two sharks; to the Aranda people it is an eagle's claw. There are also hints of galactic timetables, where the Pleiades signalled dingo-hunting for the Yankunytjatjara, or the crocodile at dawn announced Malay boats in the Gulf. Novelist Henry Miller lamented the finite zodiac in his novel *The Tropic of Cancer*. He should have come Down Under. **[Building P on Mawson Lakes campus of the University of South Australia, 13 km north of town centre. Entry $4.40/$3.30. Book on (08) 8302 3138]**

## HEAD UP

**BATHURST, NSW**   When General William Stewart died in 1854 he was buried standing, it is said – perhaps to allow him to survey his landed wealth, or perhaps (as decreed by the Crown) to mark his wartime courage in Portugal. Or has the powerful laird been capsized, his boots in the air, as a snide slight by one of his 120 tenant farmers of the day?  **[More tales inhabit the 210 squares, 52 rooms and 30 fireplaces of Abercrombie House, the former Stewart home, on Ophir Rd, an extension of Durham St. Open most Sundays at 3p.m. Check with the Visitor Information Centre on (02) 6332 1444. Entry $6/$5/$4, family $15]**

## LIE OF THE LAND

**BELLINGEN, NSW**   Driving into this town from the coast (halfway between Coffs Harbour and Nambucca Heads), you get a few chances to see Nyngala the Sleeping Aboriginal. Not that he's easy to spot:

your best chance is at Fuller's garage on the seaboard side of town, standing in the carpark and facing the mountains just south of the river. The story goes that Nyngala was in charge of guarding the women of his tribe when he fell asleep, for which the Magic Man banished the idler into stone eternity. To see his open-lipped silhouette, just kink your head slightly to the right, and gaze left.

## HISTORICAL BENT

**DUBBO, NSW**    Boyd Schyvesschuurder is not Aboriginal and neither is the boomerang – at least, not originally. At his Jedda boomerang factory, Boyd explains how the oldest known boomerang, some 23 000 years old, was dug up in Poland in 1987. Across the Mediterranean, King Tut had a boomerang as part of his afterlife kit. Hieroglyphs in the tomb of Nebamun from a century later depict a sideways individual about to launch a curved throwing stick. Boyd has a bent for boomerang lore. In fact he's had many return visitors. **[Down Minore Rd, on the Parkes side of town. Throwing lessons $5. To buy and decorate your own costs $8 (plywood) and $16 (mulga). Open daily 9a.m.–5p.m. Phone (02) 6882 3110]**

*The Bunyip*, the local paper in **Gawler (SA)**, was originally printed (1863) with the subheading 'A Gawler Humbug Society Chronicle'. Back then its hope was to explode yowies and other bush myths. Nowadays the paper limits its scepticism to the Gone Fishin' column. **[Available at The Bunyip newsagency on Murray St for $1]**

## WHO SAID ROMANCE IS DEAD?

**KAPUNDA, SA**    Which do you prefer? A lovesick Scottish shepherd who drowned in the Light River in 1846, or a lonely Scottish shepherd who recognised his long-lost love in the shape of the publican's wife and fell off his horse in the throes of eloping in 1847? Both shepherds went by the nickname Scotty. The first was James Burnett, according to the plaque. The second, Craig Scott, as the legend insists. For true romantics, the decision should pose no big dilemma. **[Head to Burra from Kapunda for 7 km.** Scotty's lonely grave sits in a paddock on an unmarked junction to your right, just before the Tarnma turnoff]

## PRANCER'S LOVE CHILD

**MARYSVILLE, Vic.**    Should a wombat ever seduce an elk, the off-spring would resemble a gunni. Don't rush to your dictionary, or your A–Z of Animals, for you won't find 'gunni' there. A wombat in every detail, barring the long tail and antlers, it can be seen in the form of a stuffed specimen in the Visitor Information Centre. Anecdotally, the first gunni was netted by timber-getters in Cambaville, in the Yarra Ranges, in 1967. Since then (wink, wink), diverse sightings have been recorded. **[11 Murchison St. Open daily 9a.m.–5p.m. Phone (03) 5963 4567]**

## TRAVIS RENT-A-DOG

**TILBA TILBA, NSW**    Tom Travis favoured the beer in the Dromedary Hotel to the point where work was an annoying distraction. Tom from the Drom (as he was known) would frequently attend the cattle auctions in Bega in the pre-truck era, leaving the mustering of the herd in the capable paws of his nameless kelpie. The dog would reputedly drive the cattle over 60 km, freeing its owner to adjourn to the Dromedary. **[Man and dog stare from the Drom's wall. Open daily from 11a.m. Phone (02) 4473 7223]**

## HIGH AND DRY

**WARRNAMBOOL, Vic.**    Does 'the Mahogany Ship' exist? Two ship-wrecked sealers claimed they spied the wreck in 1836, but that drifting sands and strong seas slowly smothered the vessel. Allegedly she lies under dunes near Dennington Spit, 9 km west of 'the Bool'. A letter in *The Argus*, dated 1876, tells of how the vessel lay 'high and dry in the humocks'. The same correspondent, Captain John Mason of Belfast (Vic.), mentions a 17th-century rapier being salvaged from the Moyne River near Port Fairy, but such a rumour may well *belong* with the fairies. Look for the turnoff and don't forget to pack your spectropho-tometer. **[Part of the Tower Hill State Game Reserve. Phone Parks Victoria on 13 19 63 or visit www.parkweb.vic.gov.au]**

## BEYOND THE PALING FENCE

**WILGA, WA**   These days 'Woop Woop' means any outpost beyond the black stump, somewhere behind the back of Bourke, but records assert that a timber-milling settlement of this name once stood 10 km northwest of modern-day Wilga. Records tell us that in 1925 it comprised 10 shacks or so, plus a boarding house and office. When the jarrah ran out, around 1927, Woop Woop disappeared – drifting from atlas to dictionary. [**The best directions I could scrounge were 'off Walkers Rd'. Just don't get lost**]

## ALL IS GRASS

**YORK, WA**   Just about every Noongar maiden carried a torch for the young warrior Wundig, the champion spear-thrower of this hill people. But Wundig was in love with Wilura, a girl from the valley clan. As this was taboo, the two lovers eloped, sparking a war between the two groups. Muburum, the wise man of the valley people, intervened and with powerful magic turned the hill warriors into blackboy trees – and the lovers into facing hills. A cluster of grass trees spills along the ridge of Mt Bakewell, the taller hill where Wundig lies, known as Walwalling (place of weeping). The other hill, the embodiment of Wilura, is Wongborel (sleeping woman). The two would never touch again, went the Muburum curse, until the hills crumbled – which almost happened in 1968 when the state's biggest earthquake took place less than 30 km away.

# NAMES

*(Being a lexicon of lyrical and loony places lodged in the landscape)*

## FLORA AND FAUNA

**BARCALDINE, Qld**   North St is the only thoroughfare in Barcaldine that's *not* named after a tree. And a kindred fixation occurs in the towns on either side. First there's Blackall, where Coronation and St Andrew are the only exceptions to a floral theme. In Longreach, all 39 streets nominate birds. One pub yarn tells how a local cop rolled a recovered stolen car into Duck St to avoid having to spell Cassowary (St) on the incident sheet.

## ITCHY-FOOTED BADGER

**BEAUTY POINT, Tas.**   Narawntapu National Park at dusk must be home to more forester kangaroos, wombats and pademelons per square centimetre than anywhere else in Tas. Located 25 km north-west of town, the park has (not surprisingly) enjoyed many more human visitors since losing its original name, Asbestos Ranges. On the subject of animals and names, the park's promontory, Badger Head, remembers an escaped convict named Charlotte Badger, who lived among the Norroundroo people here during the early 1800s. **[Access to park off C740. Entry fees $20 per car, or $10 per individual. Inquiries (03) 6428 6277]**

> Not far from each other in the Pioneer Valley just north of **Mackay (Qld)** are the anagramatic towns of Mirani and Marian. The streets in Mirani are named after girls, while those in Marian honour flowers.

## STORM X

**BOWEN, Qld**   On April Fool's Day in 1958, a devastating cyclone hit Bowen. The final tally was 70 homes wrecked and 800 damaged, power lost and water everywhere. Winds exceeding 200 kph over-turned boats and uprooted trees. Most unusually, so quickly did the weather hit town that it was simply recorded as Cyclone Anonymous. **[Snippets and photos of *all* Bowen's cyclones are found in the His-torical Museum on Gordon St. Open weekdays 9.30a.m.–3.30p.m., Sun. 10a.m.–noon. Closed Feb.–March. Entry $4/$2. Phone (07) 4786 2035]**

## FEDERAL FOLLIES

**CANBERRA, ACT** When Duntroon sheep station was earmarked as the nation's new capital city early last century, the town planners needed a name to evoke this august island of ours. Early suggestions included Cookaburra, Wheatwoolgold and Kangaremu, not to mention such all-inclusive clangers as Sydmelperadbrisho and Meladneyper-bane. Timeless favourites, prompted by the city's designated role, included Swindleville, Gonebroke and Caucus City.

## WHAT'S UP

**MANJIMUP, WA** You may have noticed that a fair few towns and creeks in the continent's southwest end in 'up'. There's Nannup, Boyup and Channybearup, to name but three; even Albany has a suburb called Candyup. The precise meaning of the suffix *up* as used by the original Murrum people is debatable. Many favour 'water' or 'water-ing place', but perhaps it is 'meeting point' or 'place of ceremony'. Business opportunities abound, with software (Startup), coffee bars (Perkup) and rap clubs (Wossup) only a matter of time.

The town called **1770 (Qld)** between Bundaberg and Gladstone, was named for the year James Cook visited in the *Endeavour*. It's the only place in Oz derived from a date, and tends to cause municipal migraines in terms of spelling, alphabetising and credit-card details.

## IRON HORSEMEN

**NEWCASTLE, NSW**    The main streets perpendicular to the railway terminal owe their names to steam engineers. The fact is driven home by an extraordinary plaque on the corner of Hunter and Watt Sts that gives potted biographies of each steamy inventor, including Stevenson (the rocket engine), Newcomen (the atmospheric steam engine), Woolf (compound cylinders), Perkins (high-pressured steam) and Bolton (James Watt's offsider). No prizes for guessing that the plaque's sponsor is the Australian Institute of Engineers (Newcastle division).

## SHOCK AND ORE

**TOM PRICE, WA**    This iron town owes its name to Thomas Moore Price, an executive with the American giant, Kaiser Steel. Born in 1961, Tom Price (the town) doesn't offer heritage features, but you can count on Jarndrunmunhna being there. This iron-rich peak, the highest (car-accessible) mountain in the state, towers above the town at a modest 1128 m. Just don't ask for directions: Jarndrunmunhna is too hard for Tom Pricers to say, hence its alternative name, Mt Nameless. **[You can walk up Nameless, a 2–3 hour return from the Tom Price caravan park – though an early start is recommended to beat the heat]**

### WHAT'S IN A NAME

◎ At 336 m, Bust-Me-Gall Hill, south of **Buckland (Tas.)**, is a steep challenge for touring cyclists.

◎ Be warned: Thank Christ Corner is a track marker en route to **Mt Buller (Vic.)**.

◎ Seldom Seen Creek is a truism close to **Gelantipy (Vic.)**.

◎ Woodenbong is just a stoner's throw from **Mulli Mulli (NSW)** in the state's northern dope belt.

◎ Despite their name, Dagg's Falls near **Killarney (Qld)** are magnificent.

◎ Bergen Op Zoom Creek in **Walcha (NSW)** is up there for strangeness.

## MAKING A STAND

**TOOWOOMBA, Qld**    Precisely how Edward Stanley Brown came by the nickname 'Nigger' has been lost to rugby league historians. While the football star *was* Aboriginal, he had fairish skin with a shock of blond hair, suggesting the nickname was a fond irony coined by his family. Others think the name derives from the Nigger Brown polish he lavished on his shoes after every game. Eighty years on, the name stirs a different reaction, especially in Aboriginal councillor Steve Hagan, who has been campaigning unsuccessfully for years to have the E.S. 'Nigger' Brown Stand at Toowoomba Athletics Oval renamed. Hagan has a history of nomenclature activism, having earlier sought to re-brand Coon cheese. He took the Nigger case to the High Court, where Justice Mary Gaudron ruled against him, prompting his visit to the UN in Geneva. [**The oval is off Lindsay St, opposite Queens Park. Turn off at either Hawthorne or Arthur St**]

During World War 1, the SA government tried to undo its German heritage, changing dozens of Deutschland derivations in the **Adelaide Hills** and beyond. Hahndorf, for instance, became Ambleside; Blumburg turned into Birdwood; and Hergott Springs became Maree. Even Mt Schank came close to losing its label, though the name in fact belonged to a British admiral.

# ODDITIONS

- ◎ The Drip Picnic Area refers to a sporadic waterfall with a rash of rock orchids. It's located about 50 km north of **Mudgee (NSW)**, along the Cassilis Rd.
- ◎ Rainbow Power Company, one of few firms dedicated to renewable energy in Australia, can be found at 14 Alternative Way in **Nimbin (NSW)**.
- ◎ A vegetarian cafe on Bridge St in **North Lismore (NSW)** makes its bloody point about the Great Australian Appetite. Its name, 20 000 Cows, is presumably a death toll.

- ◎ Wineries infest the **Swan Valley (WA)**. Most labels carry names evoking the poetic (Lilac Hill) or the family tree (Houghton). But one vineyard – Highway Wines in Herne Hill – tells it like it is.
- ◎ Okay, the business makes sense when you go there, but Tree Top Canoe Hire in **Nornalup (WA)** does sound ludicrous. Call their bluff on (08) 9840 1107 and skim the Frankland River.
- ◎ Cadibarrawirracanna, a salt lake near **Coober Pedy (SA)**, gets the award for longest place name in Australia. Though an evasive bore also in SA went by the name of *Ardivillawarracurracurrieapparlandoo* (meaning 'reflection of stars in the water').
- ◎ Loon.tite.ter.maire.re.le.hoin.er is not a website but a headland track in **Swansea (Tas.)**. The name derives from the Loontitetiterermairrelehoinner people, with the dots a merciful pronunciation guide.
- ◎ Several towns and suburbs in Australia read the same both backwards and forwards. **Tumut (NSW)**, **Glenelg** (in Adelaide, SA) and **Parap** (in Darwin, NT) are three palindromes. We also feel obliged to tell you there's a small town called Degilbo near Biggendon (Qld)
- ◎ And while reflecting on backward things, a settlement on the Murray River, an hour southeast of **Mildura (Vic.)** and not far from Colignan, is called Nangiloc.

# NEIGHBOURS

*(Being an abutment of amazements and
jaw-dropping juxtapositions)*

## E-NORMITY

**BENDIGO, Vic.**   On the corner of High and Short Sts is an 87-m spire attached to Sacred Heart, one of Australia's most neck-cricking cathedrals. A few doors down Short St (which isn't really) is Bendigo 2, a colossal satellite dish perched on top of the Telstra building and one of the main earthbound stations in the BigPond network. A smaller dish focuses on PanAM satellite No. 2, creeping a degree per day to keep aligned. Religion and science cheek to cheek.

> Far north Queensland has a reputation for extremes, even in the afterlife. At **Tully**, in sight of the town's cemetery, is the Cardwell Shire Recycling Centre. While up the road in Cairns, the main cemetery lies adjacent to the Cairns Revival Centre.

## VICTOR/VICTA

**DARWIN, NT**   The B52G Stratofortress looks as impressive as she sounds. In fact her wingspan (at 56 m) pips her length by a few paces. Known as the *Pride of Darwin*, the American bomber is the only such model in Australia. In comical contrast is the plane parked beneath the bomber's wing: a glorified mosquito with a lawnmower engine, billy-cart wheels and spinnaker wings, the Skycraft Scout is one of the original ultralights made in Australia. [**Aviation Heritage Centre, 557 Stuart Hwy. Open daily 9a.m.–5p.m. Entry $11/$6 and $28 family. Phone (08) 8947 2145 or visit www.darwinsairwar.com.au**]

## SMASH REPAIRS

**MURCHISON, Vic.**   Near the main shops is a narrow strip of greenery called Meteorite Park. The space is devoted to the big lump of space rock that descended upon Murchison back in 1969. Cows panicked, kids gawped, and Mr Keith Gregory, according to the park's showcase, thought the shire was under enemy fire. But fortunately the park's neighbour is the RACV Panel Beating Workshop: 'Dents un-dented while U wait' say the brochures.

> With a $12 billion price tag, the North West Shelf Venture in **Dampier (WA)** is the biggest gas project in Australia. You can visit the centre from 10a.m. most weekdays. Or go down to nearby Withnell Bay for an any-time look at the domes, scaffolds and eternal flames – as well as the X-ray turtles and stingrays, and 5000-year-old rock carvings by the Jaburara people.

## LIFE AND DEATH CYCLE

**ROCHESTER, Vic.**   Sir Hubert Opperman was perhaps Australia's greatest cyclist. He was the first Antipodean to contest a Tour de France, finishing twelfth in 1931. A tribute to this homegrown hero, later Australian ambassador in Malta, can be seen in a statue and the trophy room adjoining Rochester's railway station. Keeping things in perspective, on the museum's northern side is the old town morgue, where outbound bodies were stored until the train came and spirited them away.

## STRIKE POWER

**WOOMERA, SA**   Named after a spear thrower, this town has been hurling rockets and missiles into the air since the Cold War – first with British collaboration and now with American backing at the Nurrungar Joint Defence Facility. It's all very ballistic and hush-hush, but there is a streamlined display of Skylarks and Black Knights at the Heritage Centre. Rather bizarrely, the building's other facility is a tenpin-bowling alley. Just goes to show, you can take the rocket scientist out of Bedrock, USA, but you can't... **[Dewrang Ave. Open daily June–Nov. 9a.m.–5p.m., Dec.–Feb. 11a.m.–2p.m. Entry $3. Phone (08) 8673 7042 or visit www.woomerasa.com.au]**

## LOVE THY NEIGHBOUR, NOT

**TALLANGATTA, Vic.**   In 1952, when the people of Tallangatta had to move their town 5 km down the road to allow for a wider Hume Weir, the uproar was in stereo. What about my home? The church? The pub? The Water Supply Commission kept its cool. Brick homes were dismantled, the wooden church cut in half and loaded on a truck. Piece by piece New Tallangatta was created, with one major plus – several pairs of feuding neighbours could finally choose other streets with impunity. **[See the ghost town on Murray Valley Hwy 5 km east of the new version]**

# ODDITIONS

◉ On the northern NSW coast, beside the Lennox Village Estate ('A Unique Beachside Investment'), is a bora ring, the ceremonial ground for the Nyangabal people. Banksia trees – and an eerie atmosphere – distinguish the site.

◉ An empty swimming pool, once the oasis of **Gwalia (WA)**, is perched only metres from one of the richest gold-yielding pits in Australia. You can see both holes from the excellent museum.

# NUDE

*(Being a centrefold of unusual uncoverings
and astounding anatomy)*

## SLIP, SLOP, SLAP

**ADELAIDE, SA**   Maslin Beach, just south of Adelaide, was the first *official* nudist beach in Australia, spurning Speedos back in the early 70s. Many other hideaways have bobbed up since, but Maslin has continued to catch the headlines with its Nude Olympics every January, staging tugs-o-war, three-legged handicaps and a grand sack race. Swanbourne Beach in Perth began the sporting craze, with Maslin picking up the torch in 1984. **[50 km southeast of the city. Look for turnoffs on the Victor Harbor Rd, before Aldinga]**

## SPARTACUS DOWN-UNDER

**BATHURST, NSW**   Ralph Entwistle, an English convict, was skinny-dipping in the Macquarie River in 1829. He was seen by Governor Darling, no less, who conferred 50 lashes on the naturist's back. This episode prompted a 50-strong band of runaway convicts, led by Entwistle. This time, he wore clothes and 'white streamers in his hat', which caused the rebels to be dubbed the Ribbon Gang. When a magistrate's employee was murdered in 1830, troopers and two army regiments were mobilised. They cornered the gang near Abercrombie Caves, 72 km south of Bathurst, and nabbed 10 of the rebels. Marched back to Bathurst, the convicts were dangled (by ropes rather than ribbons) on current-day Ribbon Gang Lane. **[Near cnr William and Church Sts]**

## COME WHAT MAY

**CHILLAGOE, Qld**   As more towns take up the idea, it must be said that Chillagoe was a nude-calendar trailblazer. The community's ambulance garage was provided courtesy of the Chillagoe Charmers 2001 edition, a year's worth of naked blokes. Chillagoe Chicks (2002) funded some hospital equipment, while the Chillagoe Couples of 2003 had their sights set on funding a heart monitor. Marvel at the municipal nerve and curve in the Post Office Hotel on the main street.

> **Port Stephens (NSW)** has a nudist niche called Samurai Beach. Bardots, the adjacent nudist village resort, has been sold to the local council who don't seem eager to continue the tradition. Samurai, however, continues to thrive – though in the depth of winter don't be shocked to see patrons default to woollens.

## PUBLIC BRA

**HUGHENDEN, Qld**    You can't miss the Grand Hotel. The name is a fair description of this creaky Queenslander on Gray St. But inside there's a touch of the modern. A plank of rubber breasts comes complete with owners' names, such as Pamela, Abigail, Ginger and Xena. If that doesn't titillate the anatomist, a boutique-load of customers' bras adorns the wallspace directly above. Many items are trophies of the pub's bizarre games on a Friday night – Never Ever, The Nail Game and Killer Pool. (Ask at your own risk.)

## CRUDE OIL

**MELBOURNE, Vic.**    Diggers fell in love with her. Before joining the trenches in Turkey or New Guinea, our soldiers would pull up a chair beside the naked Chloe and down a few beers in her company. They'd send her letters from the Front, pledging to return to old Melbourne Town and her loving gaze. *Chloe*, it must be said, is a painting in Young & Jackson's Hotel. Chevalier Jules LeFebvre, the painter, won several awards for his nubile nude in 1876. (Not that his model, a mademoiselle named Marie, embraced the success, swallowing phosphorus soon after her sitting.) The canvas toured to Melbourne as part of The Great Exhibition of 1880, causing column-inches of outrage to appear in *The Argus* newspaper every day. Henry Young acquired the lass for his pub in 1908. Nowadays she lives upstairs in her own eponymous bar, attracting a thousand loyal veterans every Anzac Day. **[Cnr Swanston and Flinders Sts]**

An ambler on Granite Island in **Victor Harbor (SA)** may struggle to find Portrait Rock, Umbrella Rock or The Cradle. Though one boulder needs no name: every detail of Bum Rock is perfect, cellulite included. **[Get there via the raised boardwalk, or ride Australia's only horse-drawn tram]**

## STICK FIGURES

**MENZIES, WA**    Englishman Antony Gormley came to this southern town and asked all 98 residents to strip. Not en masse, but one by one in the shire hall. Behind a makeshift screen, each citizen was swept by an electronic scanner and their anatomy mapped in three-D. Gormley was after their 'inner being', which essence he used to cast 51 steel statues, known as *Insiders*. He then planted the spindly figures on a salt lake 50 km northwest of town. He describes the installation as a field of antennae, an image strengthened by the whispers the statues emit, much like white noise. Sponsored by the Perth International Arts Festival, *Insiders* was only ever intended to stand vigil for six months, but the people of Menzies have grown quite fond of their inner beings and lobbied for the array to stay. In fact, if the budget allows, 49 new souls are due to complete the set.

## RAW TALENT

**OUYEN, Vic.**    Ongoing drought was crippling the wheat town of Ouyen. The crisis inspired sheep farmer Lynne Healy to resort to the time-honoured traditional remedy – a naked rain dance. Her derring-do attracted 500 women from around Australia and the event was scheduled for March 2003 in a secret paddock and under police escort. Publicity skyrocketed and the stunt was picked up by the BBC, Japan, India, CNN, Saturday Night Live and Jay Leno. Most importantly, the dance did the trick, persuading 2 cm of rain to fall during the rehearsal period.

Stadium Nightclub at 234 Quay St, in **Rockhampton (Qld)**, saw life imitate art in April 2002. When Lakes Creeks Meatworks shut its doors for the final time, seven footloose butchers did the full monty for charity – and income. Browse the photos here and you may get an eyeful of Brizzo, Fieldsy or Titmarsh.

## AUSTRALIAN SATURNALIA

**TIBOOBURRA, NSW**   The puritans of Tibooburra were out in force in 1972. They'd never seen such blatant manhood on show. Publican Barney Davie was portrayed as the Greek god Bacchus in a mural painted by Clifton Pugh at the Family Hotel. And if that wasn't bad enough, the naked Bacchus sat astride a naked maiden, riding the girl in bronco fashion (Davie, it should be said, is a rodeo champ in real life). Police insisted on a strategic fig-leaf, which later vanished and was eventually replaced by a clump of maidenhair. Elsewhere in the pub are wall-to-wall works by Russell Drysdale, Fred Williams and war artist Rick Amor. **[Briscoe St. Phone (08) 8091 3314]**

## GALLOP MINUS JOCKEYS

**WARRNAMBOOL, Vic.**   Windy City, as some folk call Warrnambool, is famed for hosting the longest (5500 m) thoroughbred race in Oz. The Grand Annual Steeplechase, held in late autumn, also boasts more obstacles than any other steeplechase in the world. But another race here raises far more eyebrows – namely the Undie 500, a part of the Wunta Festival in February, for which runners strip down and hurtle underclad through the streets.

# ODDITIONS

- The Buffalo Club is one of the original social clubs in **Mt Isa (Qld)**. But its nickname – The Buffs – tends to confuse overseas tourists into thinking that the club's dress code is birthday suits.
- Even well-to-do dowagers with cashmere cardigans know the boulder that pokes from the rock platform at **North Avoca (NSW)**, on

the Terrigal side of the beach, as Cock Rock. It is not hard to see why.

◎ The nudist beach in **Coral Bay (WA)**, known as Skinny Dip Corner, is worryingly located between View Rock and Snapper Beach.

◎ People in clothes are welcome to admire the nude surf carnival that takes place every March on Alexandria Beach near **Noosa Heads (Qld)**. Adam and Eve Social Group Inc. help to stage the pageant.

# OBLIVION

*(Being a vagary of vague episodes, vanishing acts
and the sweet hereafter)*

## ZIP CODE

**ADELAIDE RIVER, NT**   Hurtle Bald was Darwin's postmaster when 188 Japanese planes bombed the city in 1942. He and his family and staff members, along with more than 200 others who died that day, are buried in the only war cemetery on Australian soil, beneath the cypress trees on the Adelaide River, an hour's drive from Darwin. **[Memorial Dve, 1 km behind the pub. The postal zone is on the western boundary]**

## TRACY'S BIG SISTER

**BUCCA, Qld**   Fujita is a rating system for tornadoes, which Australia, thankfully, hasn't had much call to use. But late in the afternoon of 29 November 1992 a Force-3 twister mowed a path through Wangi pine forest as a Force-4 tornado screamed across the dairy hamlet of Bucca. Winds were clocked at 417 kph, twice the intensity of Cyclone Tracy. No lives were lost, but the havoc was stupendous: brick homes were destroyed , cows were lifted and spun, a 3-tonne truck was blown for 300 m, stones were buried in tree trunks. 'It was like God had reached down with a pencil sharpener,' records one witness, describing the conical tops of ravaged trees. **[The town, 30 km west of Bundaberg, still bears some scars]**

*The Book of Extinction*, which lies open in the Tasmanian Museum in **Hobart (Tas.)**, tallies the bounty amounts owed to hunters of the Tasmanian tiger (variously known as the zebra wolf or Van Diemen hyena). The going rate was one pound per pelt, with bonus shillings for a litter. **[40 Macquarie St. Open daily 10a.m.–5p.m. Entry free. Phone (03) 6211 4177 or visit www.tmag.tas.gov.au]**

## FLOCK TOGETHER

**GERALDTON, WA**    You cannot miss the dome on the hill. The HMAS *Sydney* memorial ranks as one of the eeriest monuments in Australia. Six hundred and forty-five sailors lost their lives in 1941, when the cruiser sank in the Indian Ocean. Not a bolt or button was found, and conspiracy theories are rife. But one thing not in dispute is the uncanny event on the anniversary of the tragedy on 19 November 1998. As the 'Last Post' was played at dusk, a flock of silver gulls swooped over the mourners, fulfilling the seafarer's myth of gulls as souls. Sculptors Joan Walsh-Smith and Charles Smith used the myth, incorporating 645 steel gulls in the memorial dome. The obelisk is a stylised ship's prow complete with Plimsoll line.

## THIS WON'T HURT A BIT

**LAUNCESTON, Tas.**    Look twice at the gent descending the stairs in Prince's Park. He's a statue. In fact he's William Russell Pugh, the first surgeon to use ether in Australia, only seven months after the first guinea pig went under in Boston. Pugh modelled his ether spray from a diagram in the *Illustrated London News* in 1847. The operation was performed at St Johns Hospital, though the doctor's surgery faces the park's other corner at 190 Charles St, nowadays a restaurant called Fee & Me. To be fair, perhaps Mrs L., Australia's first ether patient, deserves her own statue too. **[Cnr Frederick and St John Sts]**

## DRAUGHTER SHOCK

**MIRBOO NORTH, Vic.**    Strzelecki Brewery went belly up in 1988. The place lay idle until along came Eric Walters with a Telecom payout package and an eye for a decent drink. Renaming the place Grand Ridge Brewery, Walters and his team have since won global acclaim for their beers, including Grand Ridge Moonshine, which was declared Best Specialty Beer in the World in 2003, out of 581 labels across 81 countries. The strongest beer made Down Under, this pure malt ale packs a wallop at 8.5 per cent proof. **[Sample this, the Natural Blond or the Hat Lifter Stout at Baromi Rd. Bar open daily 11a.m. till late; restaurant open Wed.–Sun. lunch and dinner. Phone (03) 5668 2222 or surf www.grand-ridge.com.au]**

In **Triabunna (Tas.)** a ship-shaped shrine moored to a sandstone block commemorates the dead from naval disasters, capsized crayfishing boats, and the collapse of the Derwent Bridge in 1975 when seven sailors and five motorists died. The six yachties killed in the 1998 Sydney–Hobart race are also remembered. **[Beside the Visitors Centre at the Maria Ferry dock]**

## SECOND HONEYMOON

**MONARTO, SA**    Tammar wallabies breed like rabbits in New Zealand, yet they're extinct in their native Oz, devastated by foxes and guns over the last century. But at Monarto Zoological Park the marsupial has won a second chance in Darwin's tournament of the fittest. In 2003, 10 breeding pairs were brought across the Tasman, drawing on the colony that, ironically, proliferated from a SA gift in 1860. Squat like a pademelon, without a trace of a New Zealand accent, the tammar is showing a liking for the warmer conditions. Catch a zoo bus and tour the whole 1000 ha. **[Princess Hwy, 16 km west of Murray Bridge. Open daily 10a.m.–5p.m. Entry $16/$13/$10, family $52. Phone (08) 8534 4100 or visit www.monartozp.com.au]**

## GOING, GOING, GONZO

**NIMBIN, NSW**    As the name suggests, the Nimbin Museum and Joint Café is devoted to dope. Once upon a time, cows outnumbered humans in the valley, but in the 60s flower children flooded the region and turned Nimbin into Hemp Heights. Dodging the ganja merchants in the museum's portal, you can drift through an organic, hallucinogenic history of the town. Follow the rainbow serpent to meet the purple superhero called Plantem – a comical take on The Phantom. Or read about the CIA, or Cannabis Inhalation Association. A screed on bong etiquette, a transcendental cave, two Kombis, hemp rope and a Mardi Grass (*sic*) program will also enrich your trip. **[Cullen St. Open daily 9a.m.–6p.m. Entry by donation. Phone (02) 6689 1123]**

## BROOME OR BUST

**PORT HEDLAND, WA**   The cargo list was nondescript, barring two items. One was a parcel from Marble Bar, believed to contain a wealth of nuggets. The other was the Roseate Pearl, a gem said to inflict a curse on its owner. Unfortunately for all 147 crew and passengers aboard the *Koomana*, the curse held water: the packet steamer sank in a cyclone north of Port Hedland, on the state's northwest coast, in 1912. After two generations of brine, the pearl has most likely dissolved, but those nuggets keep searchers eager. One attempt, using Orion aircraft and magnetic sweeps in the 1990s, was thwarted by the ample iron deposits off Eighty Mile Beach. For the full story, look for the water tower off McGregor St. The Koomana Lookout also offers one of the best panoramas of the port.

# OBSESSION

*(Being a manic medley of ferocious fixations and
pathological behaviour)*

## OLD KID ON THE BLOCK

**ANGASTON, SA**   'For starters, Lego is pronounced lay-go, the Danish way, not leg-go,' says Tom Lucieer, the Lego Man of Angaston. Brick by brick, he has built the largest private Lego collection in the world, starting in 1973 and still going strong. (Toy Kingdom at nearby Nuriootpa treats Tom like royalty.) Queen Elizabeth II presented a golden carriage to the former railway commissioner as a token of her esteem. It sits among Red Barons, Hogwarts, a Duplo dinosaur, and a ferris wheel that took Tom 12 months to make 'and two seconds for my nephew to blow up'. **[37 Jubilee St, off Schilling St. Open daily 10a.m.–4p.m. (last entry 3.15p.m.). Admission $2 (proceeds to St John's Ambulance). Phone (08) 8564 2714]**

Two tenacious men, Cooper and Hooper, have amassed the world's biggest private collection of teapots, at Bygone Beauties in **Leura (NSW)**. See a fraction of their collection, over 3200 items spanning three centuries, along the upper shelves of every room in Bygone Beautys. **[20–22 Grose St. Phone (02) 4784 3117 or visit www.bygonebeautys.com.au]**

## EVERYTHING, INCLUDING THE KITCHEN CABINET

**BINDOON, WA**   When Dicko and Toppy got married in 1949, they bought a lime-and-cream kitchen cabinet from a blind man called Jim. Dicko, formerly known as John Dickerson, was a clover harvester who roamed the state with Toppy and that cabinet, along with every other stick of furniture they owned. Such a hoarder was Dicko that when he sold the honeymoon cabinet to a bloke in Esperance he then tracked down the buyer to redeem it for twice the price. But in 2002 Dicko finally let go, donating all 3000 items to the Chittering Shire, including pram wheels, fridge magnets, spanners, and a rare photo of the *Enola Gay* in Borneo a few days before it flew on a bombing run to Hiroshima. **[On view at Chittering Museum, Great Northern Hwy. Open Fri.–Sun. 10a.m.–2p.m. in summer, 11a.m.–3.30p.m. in winter. Entry $2/$1. Phone (08) 9576 1044]**

## CHANNEL HOPPER

**CHINDERAH, NSW**   'I know every lighthouse-keeper around Australia,' reckons Ray Evans, in essence the country's biggest beachcomber. 'I've cornered the market in creels, that's for sure.' And fishing floats and crab pots and channel markers – any flotsam you care to name. His antique shop creaks with coastal bric-a-brac, some of which he sells and some he rents to film-makers (Ray's nautical knick-knacks have bobbed up in *Dead Calm* and *The Phantom*). In one corner he has a Portuguese cannon, dated 1650, which came from Arnhem Land. In the other stands a mini-version of Sydney Town Hall, made from 74 000 seashells by a butcher called Sydney Darnley. And that's just downstairs. **[Ray Evans' Chinderah Bay Antiques, cnr Waugh St and Chinderah Bay Dve, next to Tweed River Seafoods, south of Tweed Heads. Open most days 10a.m.–4p.m. Free entry. Phone (02) 6674 0099]**

## NECK AND NECK

**CLUNES, Vic.**   German cordial-maker Ernest Eberhard helped the public associate the town of Clunes with queer-looking bottles. The Lee Medlyn Bottle Collection, the biggest such collection on display in the southern hemisphere, sustains the connection. Medlyn was a sucker for meddlin' in glass depots, rescuing such rarities as Rawleigh's Bloat Ease and the Six O'Clock Stout. He even found a twin-necked Benedictine bottle and a naked-lady-doing-a-headstand bottle. If a diva dared to sing high C the impact in the refitted schoolhouse could be fatal. **[Housed in Visitor Information Centre, Old School complex, 70 Bailey St. Open daily 11a.m.–4p.m. Entry $2, family $5. Phone (03) 5345 3896]**

## BRIC-A-BRAC-A-GO-GO

**COPPING, Tas.** 'When they made my dad,' said Dianne Smith, 'they threw away the mould.' Obviously the mould was the only thing Jack Smith threw out – the old blacksmith was hell-bent on hoarding pistols, kettles, bottles . . . An inventory is unthinkable. Jack also dabbled in robotics, creating (among others) Emily the Ironing Lady and the mechanical donkey. Look for the cyber-cop out front, and the wooden mermaid with a real-life beehive in her tail. **[Arthur Hwy. Open daily 9a.m.–5p.m. in summer, 10a.m.–3p.m. in winter. Entry $7/$6/$2, family $20. Phone (03) 6253 5373]**

## ALL STATIONS TO COWRA

**COWRA, NSW** Ron Horsfall and his fellow bowerbird, Doug Stewart, have put together one of the wildest museums in Australia. For starters, it has model trains zipping across 30 km of track. The complex also brags one whole annexe of period carriages and a long, long wall of platform signs from Abbotsford to Zetland. The same institution claims a wing devoted to Nazi memorabilia. There are also a Falklands Island torpedo and more tractors, tanks and klaxons than a taxman could hope to itemise. **[Fun Museum, on the Mid West Hwy 4 km east of Cowra. Open daily 9a.m.–5p.m. Entry $8/$5.50. Phone (02) 6342 2801]**

## GARAGE BANNED

**DALBY, Qld** Reg Collins kept his car on the street. He owned a garage, but it was always chock-a-block. With what, you ask? If I gave you a checklist we'd be here till Christmas. Suffice it to say that Reg hoarded clothes pegs, Silvo tins, board games, chamber pots, lawnmowers, stubbies and spanners (he had a particular soft spot for spanners). He even kept the cricket balls that sailed over his back fence. Recently Reg shifted his stash into the Pioneer Park Museum, requiring four rooms. The museum is hastily making more space in case Reg's wife Sheila wants to donate her doll and Avon collection down the track. **[17 Black St. Open daily 8a.m.–5p.m. Entry $5/$4/$1. Phone (07) 4662 4760]**

## PIPE DREAMING

**HAHNDORF, SA**   Emil Buring, a dentist from Adelaide, started collecting pipes back in the 1930s. A different type of nicotine addiction, the habit grew quickly into a career. Emil became hooked on hookahs and their like, amassing up to 700 specimens, from corncobs to crab-claw pipes. A fraction of the frenzy appears in the Hahndorf Academy, an excellent glimpse of the town's German origins. But the pipes attempt to steal the show, the showcases sprawling into the second room. **[68 Main Rd. Open daily 10a.m.–5p.m. Entry by donation. Phone (08) 8388 7250]**

You have to wonder how Father Bede Lowery found time for the scriptures, given the time he must have devoted to wrangling bull-ants into glass vials. Twenty-eight jars, each representing a different Australian species, are arrayed in the **Esperance (WA)** Museum, the fruits of Father Lowery's meditations.

## SHUTTERBUG

**HERBERTON, Qld**   The string on the Latvian micro-camera is not only to give the spy the focal length when snapping sensitive documents, it also serves as a garotte should anyone threaten to compromise his mission. That's only one amazing camera among a roomful. Roy Jacques, a former secret agent with the Commonwealth contingent and a part-time paparazzo, has cameras disguised as stopwatches, fobs and beer cans – plus a dagger posing as a crucifix. He has a Russian camera that shoots backwards, a sniper camera, a Tiger Moth camera, a Pearl Harbor camera and the first home-movie camera in Australia. The premises also offer darkroom and computer facilities for touring sharpshooters. **[Camera and Photography Museum, 49 Grace St. Open daily 9a.m.–5p.m. Entry $5. Phone (07) 4096 2092]**

## REBEL WITH A CAUSE

**NABIAC, NSW**   'Where the @#*! is Nabiac?', says the flyer. It's between Buladelah and Taree, if that helps. If not, hop into the sidecar of a biker who knows about the National Motorcycle Museum, and hang on. In this E-shaped hangar you can find every two-wheeled model from Acme to Yamaha – even the home-made 'Battle Wagon', built by Myles Huntley around a rotary-hoe engine. Brian Kelleher, the collection's prime mover, has amassed over 600 bikes. Sir Nigel, a pristine 1000-cc tourer, is one of few Vincent Black Knights in the world. There's a 1940 BSA beast that once raced a Tiger Moth and a 1927 Chrysler around Australia. After three flat tyres, three broken windshields and two crashes, it came second. **[33 Clarkson St. Open daily 9a.m.– 4p.m. Entry $11/$6.60/$3.30, family $27.50. Phone (02) 6554 1333 or visit www.nationalmotorcyclemuseum.com.au]**

## MONSIEUR LASH

**NOONAMAH, NT**   Mick Denigan has whipped himself around Australia seven times, flexing his fire whips and electric whips and doing the famous Queensland cross-over in every corner of the country. Thousands admire his cracks (both the droll and leather kind) on Thursday nights at Darwin's Mindil Beach markets. Mick makes more than 300 whips a year, with such fans as Bill Gates, the Duke of Edinburgh and George W. Bush each owning a Denigan original. Samples of his art (imagine Jackson Pollock with a cat-o'-nine-tails) decorate his host ranch on the plains. You can't miss the place – a giant cyclone-proof bullwhip (the largest stockwhip in the world) looms above the gate, officially opened by former bushman's politician Tim Fischer in 2003. **[Mick's Whips Homestead is off the Stuart Hwy. Phone (08) 8988 6400 for whips or stay-over trips, or visit www.mickswhips.com.au]**

**OOPS**

*(Being an errandum of bungles, oversights
and other ginormous gaffes)*

## PERFECT IMPERFECTION

**BENDIGO, Vic.** Without looking guilty, walk into the Bendigo Law Courts. Go past reception, down the last stairs and then up to a foyer of precise red tiles. But on closer inspection, with the fire extinguisher to your left, you can see that the fourth 'circle' tile in the second line is out of sequence. Deliberately, goes the legend. The Chinese craftsmen responsible for the handiwork saw perfection as godly and so, out of respect, the tilers broke the symmetry just to emphasise they were human. **[71 Pall Mall. Open during session times]**

## LONG OFF

**BOWRAL/BOWRAVILLE, NSW** Bowral is not the same as Bowraville. Although they're both in NSW, the two are 700 km apart, according to one tired crow. The *-ville* suffix came as a result of many postal gaffes, but the capacity for confusion remains. Just ask the English cricket supporters, alias the Barmy Army, who flooded into Bowraville in the summer of 1998–9, eager to see an Australia–England match at the Don Bradman shrine – in Bowral, not Bowraville.

## BLOWN OFF-COURSE

**DEVONPORT, Tas.** Caroline Chisholm came to Australia on a barque called the *Waverley*. Yet the ship seen behind the social worker on the old $5 note is a clipper (which has one mast less). There were in fact two *Waverley*s, but the aforementioned clipper was built 25 years *after* Ms Chisholm immigrated. In other words, the *Waverley* on the money is not on the money – it's the wrong ship, and proof of the Reserve Bank's fallibility. **[Maritime Museum, 9 Gloucester Ave. Open daily except Mon. 10a.m.–4.30p.m. Entry $3. Phone (03) 6424 7100]**

A pallet of Swallows Ariel Biscuits was delivered to Wagner's Store in **Jindera (NSW)** in 1940 – wrongly. The shop never ordered the item. But instead of being returned, the 12-box pile sat unsold in the shop till the business closed. And it still sits there today: wonder what the shelf life would be? **[Part of Jindera Museum. Open Tues.–Sun. 10a.m.–3p.m.]**

## ONE OAR IN THE WATER

**FRASER ISLAND, Qld**   Cyclone Daisy uncovered a shipwreck on Orchid Beach in 1972, but only for one day until the sand and sea resumed control. Thirty years later, historian Greg Jeffreys returned with scuba tanks and magnetometers. The wreck was found in hours, and digging began at low tide. Excitement was contagious. Cannon scraps were found and, while it was too soon to tell, Jeffreys could see strong parallels with Portuguese weaponry of the 16th century. Could this ship predate Cook's *Endeavour* by 200 years? The news spread, features were written and timelines re-written – only for several high-pressure hoses to rain on Jeffreys' parade. The metal was not a cannon piece, but a scrap of superstructure from the *Marloo*, an Italian vessel that ran aground on Orchid Beach, circa 1914. **[Just near Waddy Point]**

## LANDMARK STUPIDITY

**JERVIS BAY, ACT**   Built in 1859, the Cape St George lighthouse was a magnificent sandstone beacon overlooking the Tasman Sea. Was – for the light was built in the wrong spot. The error caused more confusion than enlightenment, especially in daytime when navigators drew false bearings from the tower's location. The only remedy was gelignite, and so down the wonky beacon came. Now the tower resembles a Lego kit in the wake of a toddler tantrum. **[Follow Stony Creek Rd seaward until a signposted trail leads to a viewing deck. More info at Booderee Parks Visitors Centre, on Jervis Bay Rd. Phone (02) 4443 0977]**

## ARMAGEDDON HANDICAP

**MEEKATHARRA, WA**   In 1977, on a barnstorming tour of WA, wooing voters for the upcoming federal elections, the incumbent PM Malcolm Fraser and his 'first lady' Tamie were marooned in the central western town of Meekatharra when their BAC1-11 experienced engine trouble. A chance to secure more Coalition converts, you might think. But Tamie estranged all 2000 residents by describing the gold-mining frontier town as 'the end of the earth'. A year later, the penitent Tamie returned in order to present the trophy at the annual Meekatharra Races – The End of the Earth Cup. (In these PC times, the trophy has reverted to being called the Meekatharra Cup. But Tamie's barb gets a regular mention, and endorsement from drinkers in both pubs.)

Good to know the experts aren't immune from bungling. Look at the first set of showcases upstairs at the Royal Australian Mint in Deakin, **Canberra (ACT)**. Every mis-minted coin has been placed on shameless display, including a younger Queen Elizabeth II with accidental rhinoplasty. **[Denison St. Open Mon.–Fri. 9a.m.–4p.m., weekends 10a.m.–4p.m. Phone (02) 6202 6819]**

## CHALK ONE UP FOR EDITORS

**MT BARKER, SA**   Back in 1830, when Charles Sturt travelled down the Murray – the first white man to do so – he spotted Mt Lofty on the horizon and drafted his map accordingly. One hiccup, though: it wasn't Mt Lofty, which lies some 25 km further west. Sturt had spotted a second mountain, realised Captain Collett Barker a year later – which won him a spot in posterity. **[Lookout lies 11 km east of Mt Barker township, heading for Nairne]**

## CIVIC DISOBEDIENCE

**NOWRA, NSW**   A dual Oops entry in the same city block. First up, the post office steps, on the corner of Junction and Berry Sts, whose angle is so breakneck that one flight has been closed off completely and the other channelled like a sheep-dip to prevent unplanned pratfalls. The second gaffe, around the corner on Berry St, is the foundation stone in the School of Arts building. The tablet declares Prime Minister Sir Henry Parkes as the official opener in 1891. In fact, says historian Alan Clark, Sir Henry didn't attend the ceremony because his sister was ill, but by then the engraver had already consigned the leader to history.

It's believed that a hole-digger named Crisp was buried alive in 1875. They re-buried him under a kurrajong tree and fenced the site. Surveyors failed to see the grave when the Jerilderie road was put in, and hence it sits a body's length from the Newell Hwy. The lonesome plot is between Gillenbah Creek Rd and Gillenbah Creek on the outskirts of **Narrandera (NSW)**.

## LAG LAGOON

**PORT GREGORY, WA**    The town was set for big things. Whales were ripe for the spearing. Off-shore breezes were cooling. Convicts were borrowed from Fremantle and housed in a new hiring depot. Guards were lured from England with the promise of land parcels after seven years' service. Inland mines were in urgent need of roads and harbours to move their precious ore south. What more could a new port need? Well, water, food, transport, medical supplies and arable land for a start. And two major shipwrecks did not endorse the harbour's viability. Within three years, the plans were scrapped: the convicts were shunted off, the guards pensioned off, the entrepreneurs ticked off, and all eyes turned to Geraldton in the south. **[Ruined depot, plus Lynton – the villa of entrepreneur Henry Sanford – lie on Kalbarri Rd, 5 km out of Port Gregory. Open daily. Entry by donation]**

Four o'clock occurs four times a day in **Gawler (SA)**. The reason lies in the eastern face of the post office's clock tower (on Murray St), where a manufacturing error made the VI a IV.

## ROMA CANDLE

**ROMA, Qld**    The history of Roma reflects the twin themes of triumph and tribulation. In the late 1890s, water was in short supply: enter the Intercolonial Boring Company, who found a little water and a lot of 'marsh gas'. The town let the pongy fumes float free for five years until the council determined that the gas – petroleum gas, in fact – might serve as fuel. The town set up a reticulated pipe system in 1906, and Roma became the first town in Oz to be lit by natural gas – for a whopping 10 days, at which point the gas ran out. Another dig in 1908 once again struck gas, which wafted into a steam boiler causing an explosion that melted the derrick. A huge gas flame burnt for 46 days on Hospital Hill, becoming the town's first tourist attraction. Nowadays the lure is the Big Rig (on the highway) or the bore plugs, with plaques, on Hospital Hill. **[To reach the hill, head out of town along Bowen St, and turn left into Whip Rd after the water tower]**

## OIL AIN'T OIL

**SALT CREEK, SA**    Oil, Texas tea, black gold – that's what someone decided was lying around the Coorong lagoons in 1852. The rubbery stuff oozed from the soil, as black as pitch and with a strong kerosene bouquet. As rumours spread, the Coorong Kerosene Company sank Australia's first oil well in 1866. No gushes came, however. Instead, 100 gallons (some 378 litres) of the black stuff was scooped from lagoons and shipped to Scotland for review. The oil boom went bust before you could say coorongite – the scientific name for the gooey algae, a gunk with more potential as paint than petroleum. **[A replica oil well stands in town]**

# PLAYGROUNDS

*(Being a jubilee of notable locations
for fun and games)*

## LAKESIDE CASTLE

**BALLARAT, Vic.** A barrel crawl in the Ballarat Community Playground is called 'The Australian Chamber of Manufacturing', or perhaps that's the barrel's sponsor. Most of the other drawcards – the tyre swing, the conveyor-belt bridge, the swan boat, the spiral slide, the minarets – are inscribed by their donors. Built beside Lake Wendouree, the play-ground attracts as many coots from the nearby lake as kids from the car park. **[Botanical Gardens, opposite the McDonald Gates, on Wendouree Pde]**

## YOUNGER AND UP

**BUSSELTON, WA** As soon as you spot the ersatz lighthouse hold-ing up a water slide, you're getting warmer. The slide, and the FUNK ARTS – sorry, FUN KARTS – are pay-for-play activities on Marine Tce that are well worth a try. The free version, for the younger munchkins, is a block away. Called Yongarup, it offers a tugboat called Lil Toot, a funky steamroller, and a big fish scaffold – all ideal for those with limited attention spans. The older child can go mad and militaristic at Fort Courage (of F-Troop fame) with a flying-fox escape route. **[On Scott Rd]**

## THE HOUSE THAT TRACY BUILT

**DARWIN, NT** The force of Cyclone Tracy (1974) was such that she broke the wind gauge at Darwin Airport. Other wind instruments – think bugles and trumpets – were blown from the army barracks into the Botanical Gardens about a kilometre away. Here a massive Indian raintree toppled in the onslaught, but 30 years on the tree is still grow-ing, the branches shooting upward from the horizontal trunk, among them a splendid three-storey treehouse. **[Behind the Wesleyan Church on the Gardens Rd entrance]**

Victoria Park, at the top of the hill in **Peterborough (SA)**, started life as a cycle track in 1897. Soon after that, the council converted the space to playing fields. Restless again, civic leaders inserted a lake in 1976, adding swans, seesaws, an arboretum and a deer enclosure. Best let the kids run wild soon, before the place becomes a rifle range.

## PAVONINE PRECINCT

**KALGOORLIE, WA**    Peacocks rule the roost in Hammond Park. All pomp and posture, they seem to think the miniature Bavarian castle beside the duck pond is theirs. Lesser birds, the lorikeets and corellas are stuck in aviaries, along with Macca the cockatoo, who rather lowers the tone with his 'Hello's and 'Howyagone's. **[Lyall St, opposite Kalgoorlie Cemetery. Open in the cooler months 9a.m.–5p.m., and till 7p.m. Sept.–Mar.]**

A tiny train weaves among totem poles in Heritage Park, **Lismore (NSW)**. The poles are a medley erected by local schools, local artists and Indigenous groups. The train, a 7-inch-gauge electric express, is a kid-magnet. **[The train runs Thurs. 10a.m.–2p.m., weekends 10a.m.–4p.m. A multi-lap fare will set you back $1.60]**

## IVEY LEAGUE

**PERTH, WA**    Ivey Watson seems the right sort of name to be lent to a garden playground. At the western edge of Kings Park, off May Dve, this place has every piece of juvenile equipment a harrowed parent could desire. Not only can your offspring whack a glockenspiel, ride a fire engine and sail a pirate ship, they can also sit abreast of two siblings and plunge down the triple slide. And a height chart at the gate grants extra privileges to the younger in the tribe. The compound is fenced, but best of all, there's an ensuite cafe called Sticky-Beaks for the multi-tasking child-carer. **[Cafe's number is (08) 9481 4990]**

## PEACHY KEEN

SHEPPARTON, Vic.   With four sons, Geoff Allemand knows all about excess energy and the need to channel it. The Shepparton dad was instrumental in securing the old rubbish dump in 1995. Next came the fruit bins (to form a maze), the Bigfoot slide, the duplex treehouse, the swings and the sandpit. Local boy made billionaire, Richard Pratt, donated the VisyLine miniature train that runs along 600 m of convoluted track. **[SPC Ardmona Kidstown, Midland Hwy en route to Mooroopna. Train runs weekends, holidays and selected weekdays 9a.m.–5p.m. Entry gold coin. Phone (03) 5831 4213 or cruise www. kidstown.org.au]**

## VERY MERRY

MERRYLANDS, SYDNEY, NSW   This suburb lives up to its name. At the Sydney Children's Museum, the hands-on culture of the modern learning centre has gone berserk. Little ones can bend light, turn computer dragons into robots, rearrange magnetic toupees, and appear on TV dressed as ambulance officers. Outside, Walpole St Park has a brilliant adventure set-up, entailing five slides and a suspension bridge. And if the children still have energy to burn, let them ride bikes on the road-safety training track. **[Cnr Pitt and Walpole Sts. Open daily 10a.m.–4p.m. Entry $5.50 for adults and kids. Under-twos free, seniors $4.40. Museum entry allows you to come and go all day. Phone (02) 9897 1414 or visit www.sydneykids.org]**

A playground in **Bairnsdale (Vic.)** can boast an Aboriginal canoe tree, an explorer's cairn, a cable bridge, a BMX track, monkey bars, a 30-m slide, and feral rabbits on the river flats. To highlight the diversity, a 40-m flying fox flings you between the extremes. **[Howitt Park Adventure Playground is on the east side of the Mitchell River, heading towards Lakes Entrance]**

## LET US SPRAY

**TOWNSVILLE, Qld**   Things like crocodiles and box jellyfish can make Townsville beaches a little intimidating. One solution is The Strand's Water Playground. A giant bucket balances on top of the play equipment, constantly filling with water and dumping its load on anyone in range. Adjacent to the harbour, on a spongy rubber floor, the playground includes water bazookas, a perpetual shower, pull-cord water jets and the ultimate commendation: 'Valves and handles are accessible to allow children and adults to throttle and play with water.' Seriously, this is the sort of playground that a kid would design. **[Cnr Fryer St and The Strand. Running most days. No entry fee]**

## FROM FEN TO FUN

**WARRNAMBOOL, Vic.**   Lake Pertobe was more of a swamp until Johnny Johnson, the City Engineer, tackled its overhaul. Now the 20-ha foreshore is the answer to a kid's dream, with a lengthy flying fox, pirate ships, chain bridges, forts, swings, giant slides and a maze. There's also Lake Pertobe, a wetland delight with footbridge, bird hides and lookout tower. **[Head down through the cutting beside Flagstaff Hill]**

# ODDITIONS

- One of the odder sandpits you'll see is in the centre of **Gordonvale (Qld)** where the kids get to clamber on a cement python, giant cane stalks and three oversized toads.

- Pioneer Park, off Olivia Tce in **Carnarvon (WA)**, is a pleasant non-descript sort of sanctuary, with the requisite benches and swings. What sets the place apart are the massive jaws of a blue whale that serve as its gateway.

- Worth a visit is the pool in the Ningaloo Caravan and Holiday Resort at **Exmouth (WA)**, where site tariffs begin at $5. The pool fringes a 4-m aquarium, so the only way you can goggle at the captive fish is by going underwater yourself.

# POLES

*(Being a cluster of unusual uprights and the odd European)*

## TURNING OUT A NEW LEAF

**CANBERRA, ACT** A large Canadian flag flies once a year over Regatta Point on Lake Burley Griffin. For the other 364 days the Aussie version prevails, but the maple leaf is hoisted on Canada's National Day (1 July) to salute the flagpole's origins. You see, back in 1957 a 39-m length of Douglas fir arrived in Sydney as a gift from Ottawa. In makeshift quarantine, the flagpole was submerged in the harbour for three days and later bathed in pesticides. Three trucks combined to haul the trunk south to Regatta Point, where a giant crane did the heavy lifting. **[Off Commonwealth Ave Bridge]**

Take a closer look at the lamp-posts in **Caloundra (Qld)**. Each upper arch has been reinforced, as have most of the poles throughout the Sunshine Coast, so they can withstand the strain of multiple perching pelicans. Weighing in at some 5 kg each, a pair of adult males would snap an unreconstructed version like fresh celery.

## BRANDING EXERCISE

**CORAMBA, NSW** When Bob Murray applied a red-hot branding iron to his pergola in 2003, he liked what he saw. The burnt logo evoked the pastoral past of the area, an era slowly being lost as Coffs Harbour high-rises creep deeper into the hinterland, turning cattle runs into 4-ha blocks. So Bob amassed a few other irons, and the council planted two rows of wooden bollards down Gayle St. The wash-up of the 'Great Branding-Iron Round-Up' is an avenue of heritage hieroglyphs that subvert the world of Big Bananas.

## ENTER MORTALITY

**DARWIN, NT**    If you miss seeing the Tiwi Islands, just off Darwin, let the Tiwis come to you – in the shape of burial poles. The cluster stands in the Museum and Art Gallery of the Northern Territory. The poles tell the Indigenous myth about how death came into being. Purukuparli had a faithless wife who left their baby in the heat of the sun while she cavorted among the dunes with her lover, Tapara. As punishment for the child's death she lives in shame while her lover ended up as the moon – living and dying eternally for the world to see. The Tiwi people use the ornate ironbark poles, called *tutini*, as headstones. **[Conacher St. Open weekdays 9a.m.–5p.m., weekends 10a.m.–5p.m. Entry free. Phone (08) 8999 8201 or visit www.dedsca.nt.gov.au]**

A semaphore pole stands on Mt George, just south of **George Town (Tas.)**. Set up in 1822, the message system was designed to outrace ships down the Tamar River, relaying the news these vessels learned from other colonies or the Crown. A visit will tell you the gossip-code the operators adopted. **[Turnoff is just south of town, heading downriver]**

## FOUR-WHEEL FLY

**KEITH, SA**    Between the two world wars, this part of the world was considered good-for-nothing desert by the state's developers. In fact Keith wasn't called Keith, but Mt Monster. Then research revealed the benefits of adding trace elements to the soil, and a superphosphate cocktail turned Ninety Mile Desert into an arable proposition. Insurance giant AMP joined the land rush, inspiring families to venture east from Adelaide. In tribute to the success of the experiment, beside the Dukes Hwy stands a prefab hut, the typical dwelling back then. To symbolise the conquest of the sands, a Land Rover balances next-door on a pole.

## CABERS GALORE

**MACLEAN, NSW**    Tartan is the new black here, with every second telegraph pole girt by the colours of a Scottish clan. The town is named after Alexander McLean (yes, different spelling), who surveyed the valley in 1862. Its first name was in fact Rocky Mouth, the Scottish connection arising when scads of Scots arrived in the late 19th century. In 1893, the town kicked up its heels in the first Highland gathering. A multi-clan cairn stands on Taloumbi St (*Sraid Thaloumbaidh* in Gaelic), where coats-of-arms blaze bright. And the name of the new development atop the hill? The Highlands, of course. [Look for the cairn sign off Grafton Rd]

> Some 20 km west of **Finke (NT)** stands a solitary flagpole that designates our national centre of gravity. Named The Lambert Centre after cartographer Bruce Lambert, who did many of the necessary geodesic sums, the pole was calculated from over 24 000 points dotted around the continent's coast.

## DON'T WORK

**BELLEVUE HILL, SYDNEY, NSW**   Working on the Sabbath is a Jewish taboo. Orthodox Jews may not ride a bike, drive a car, walk a dog, or push a button at a pedestrian crossing. And they are forbidden to ask a gentile to do the last on their behalf. This particular no-no underpins a robust debate within Waverley Council. Leaders of the faith are lobbying to have several traffic signals along Old South Head Rd lapse into automatic mode during synagogue hours. A spokesperson for the Roads and Traffic Authority has conceded that the switch is unprecedented but technically possible.

# ODDITIONS

- ◎ In the roadside cluster called **Prairie (Qld)**, the publican has erected the figure of a witch slamming head-on into the telegraph pole. If you drink and fly you're a b*@!* idiot.
- ◎ Mangroves have peculiar protuberances called stilt roots, those arthritic offshoots that fan above the mud. The poles on the bridge spanning Tweed River, in **South Tweed Heads (NSW)** mimic the trees to a T.

# PUBS

*(Being a grand procession of
remarkable royals and railways)*

## WHERE TRUTH IS THE FIRST CASUALTY

**AGNEW, WA**    The story goes that the former owner of the 'Agnew Hilton' used to offer fish and chips as a counter meal. Unfortunately the fish comprised a tin of John West sardines, and the chips a pack of Samboys. Any complaints could be directed to the pub's Managing Director, this being the name of the owner's dog. Despite new owners having taken over, the spirit of this all-iron pub hasn't dimmed. Filled with gold miners, the Agnew Hotel is a hybrid of speakeasy and rain-tank (the building is two-thirds corrugated iron). **[Turnoff is close to Leinster, heading west to Sandstone. Phone – what phone?]**

## PITH PALACE

**BALLARAT, Vic.**    There's a prize for naming the rhino on the wall, but the name must fit on the animal's horn. The rhino is concrete, but as lifelike as its genuine zebra hide and springbok horns. The safari library boasts bestial books – *Born Free*, *King Rat*, *Jaws* – with pith helmets and Box Brownies adding to the bwana vibe. But hurry – a Ballarat pub minus pokies is an endangered species. **[The Gamekeeper's Secret Safari Inn, cnr Mair and Humffray Sts, a block from The Black Rhino (no relation) on Victoria St. Phone (03) 5332 6000 or visit www. ballarat.com/gamekeepers]**

Mick, Dino, Curly and Huggy caught two ginormous prawns in Wallagoot Lake in 1998. Their hollowed exoskeletons (the prawns, not the prawners) are on display in the **Tathra (NSW)** Hotel. And further down the bar is the nipper of a Bega River crab (caught by Tank), which I swear could crack watermelons.

## KNICK-KNACKERY

**BERRY, NSW**   A wombat steering a surfboat on the roof is your first sniff of futility. Next is the bottleshop, armoured in hubcaps. On the beer deck, a signpost points to every Olympic city, as well as to Gallipoli, Kokoda and Barry's iconic doughnut van. Inside the Great Southern Hotel, normality is absent. A moose with a goatee holds court in the bistro. A surface-to-air missile hangs above a pair of stools. A wooden Apache admires the wagon-wheel chandelier. And you haven't even got to the public bar yet. **[95 Queen St. Phone (02) 4464 1009]**

## WHAT JOHN DUNN

**COLLECTOR, NSW**   The ruckus arising from the Commercial Hotel was too loud to ignore on 26 January 1865. Gunshots were heard. Boisterous carousing. Blue language. Enough was enough: as keeper of the peace, Constable Samuel Nelson went with two of his eight kids to investigate. He found John Dunn, the lookout for Ben Hall's gang, who turned the constable into a colander. An obelisk (alias Nelson's Column) salutes the lawman's bravery outside the pub which, perversely enough, now trades as the Bushranger Inn (alias The Bushie). **[Shackles and other tackle adorn the pub at 25 Church St. Phone (02) 4848 0071]**

## DAILY, NIGHTLY, MADLY

**DALY WATERS, NT**   A sign out the front says 'Angle Parking, Any Angle'. A set of traffic lights blinks in the dust. Inside, a blackboard offers Toe Stead Samiges (say it aloud). Overhead, a line of g-strings hangs above the bar. Since 1893, the Daly Waters Pub has been humouring drovers, telegraph linesmen and even the airmen from Qantas Empire Airways who relied on the town as a midway aerodrome between Brisbane and Singapore. Nowadays tourists do most of the re-fuelling, but *please* don't fall for the one-hole-golf-course trick. **[Phone (08) 8975 9927 or visit www. dalywaterspub.com]**

> Once upon a time there was a handsome Danish prince who went for a beer in a Sydney local during the 2000 Olympics. There he met a feisty commoner

from Tas. called Mary. The two chitchatted about hairy versus non-hairy torsos in men. From that enchanted exchange, a royal romance began. **[Slip Inn, 111 Sussex St]**

## WALL-TO-WALL DRINKERS

**EDEN, NSW**    Regardless of the hour, the Australasia Hotel is always full. Why? Because every regular has been painted in a crowd scene behind the public bar, better known as The Pit. Brett Ralph, alias Ralphy, is the Michelangelo behind the fresco (he's the suave character at the rear left, with a paintbrush behind his ear). Former publican John Crosby, who commissioned the masterpiece in 2001, is the sandy blond complaining about the free grog. A burly man called Beans was the only regular missing from the scene, an oversight the artist put right by adding a 'Wanted' poster in the background. **[60 Imlay St. Phone (02) 6496 1600]**

## KILLER KARAOKE

**GREENOUGH, WA**    On 11 December 1863, a happy drunk called Willis was singing in the Hampton Arms Inn. A surly drunk called Timlin told him to stop, but the singer carried on. Timlin punched Willis, who fell dead to the floor. The minstrel's murder, in the pub's maiden year, is just one episode emanating from this colonial taproom. The only rival to the number of tales lurking in the woodwork is the sprawling collection of 20000 used books the publican, Brian Turnock, sells out the back. **[Open daily noon–2p.m. and 7p.m.–late. Phone (08) 9926 1057]**

Hotel Kempsey, in **Kempsey (NSW)**, displays diverse collections of beer taps, historical fishing reels, and 200 years of carpentry planes. There's also a showcase of maritime muddle, as you'd expect from a town founded by Enoch Rudder. **[3–5 Belgrave St. Phone (02) 6562 8588]**

## POINT 05 ON THE RICHTER SCALE

MARYVALE, Qld   If the Crown Hotel is not the only quake-proof pub in Oz, it's surely the first. American Matt Keefe (who'd survived the San Francisco earthquake four years earlier) built it in 1912, using reinforced steel and concrete. In keeping with Qld custom, the hotel also has a resident ghost and a bottled taipan. [Off Cunningham Hwy. Phone (07) 4666 1148]

Beer cellars make ideal fallout shelters. That was the thinking in **Moruya (NSW)**, where the town's pub hosted regular evacuation drills during World War 2. Accordingly the Moruya Hotel became known as the Air Raid Hotel, even after the war. There's still a yellow 'Emergency Services' sign on the Vulcan St side. [Cnr Mirrabooka and Vulcan Sts]

## BUSH BASH

NEW NORFOLK, Tas.   'The oldest pub in Australia' is one of the slipperiest claims in the trivia industry. Some pubs change names, change sites, or lapse for a period, yet make the boast regardless. But the Bush Inn gets the gong for oldest continuous licence. The taps have been dispensing since 1825, no less. Inspired by the river view, librettist William Wallace wrote his opera Maritana here in 1838. Dame Nellie Melba, a guest, sang a few numbers from the show in 1924. Now the opera is mounted as two vinyl platters, beside the CD jukebox. [Montague St, on the A10, near bridge. Phone (03) 6261 2256]

## WARTS AND ALL

PORT DOUGLAS, Qld   Ironbar is not a Cluedo weapon, but a pub of note. With corrugated iron on every surface (even the menu is behind corrugated plastic), this hotel is also known for its backroom events. I speak of the fanatical cane-toad races, where Forrest Jump, Fat Bastard, Prince Charming, Ozzie Ozzie Ozzie and Skippy's Love-Child compete for supremacy. [5 Macrossan St. Family show Mon.–Thur. and Sun. 7p.m., adults-only Tues. and Thur. 9.30p.m. Entry $5 (free with dinner). Phone (07) 4099 4776]

Innovation and improvisation keep the Grove Hill Pub upright. Dressed in recycled iron, with not a welding spot to be seen, this galvanised Ritz is 21 km from **Hayes Creek (NT)**, along the Goldfields Loop. It incorporates a museum that tells you about the rush of 1880, but you may well be distracted by the publican's use of water pipes. **[Pub open daily 10a.m.–2p.m., museum 9a.m.–6p.m. Phone (08) 8978 2489]**

## HOG HEAVEN

**PYENGANA, Tas.**   Every time she fancies a Boag's beer, Slops the pig wanders down to the local pub. The journey's a walkover, for the pub sits in the middle of 3 ha. The Pub in the Paddock, once a family home for Mr and Mrs Terry and their 15 bairn, is now a permanent trough for one particular snout. **[Open daily. Phone (03) 6373 6121]**

## YEE-HAA

**ROCKHAMPTON, Qld**   Country-and-western star Lee Kernaghan owns the Great Western Hotel, which is unusual enough, you would think. But what makes the Great Western great is its indoor rodeo ring, where clowns and bulls and cowboys emerge from the dust every month or so, usually on a Friday night. To enter, just line-dance past the gals in chequered shirts and wade through the wails pouring from CTV (Country Television). Bands also play here, and Xtreme motorcross is on the roster if steer-wrangling is not your cup of billy tea. **[39 Stanley St. Phone (07) 4922 3888]**

# ODDITIONS

◎ Have a look at the eastern wall of the **Darkan (WA)** Hotel. The seascape, with resident drinker Noel (Cracker) Brewster cast as voyeur, is reserved as the backdrop for the inland sheep town's annual beach party in February.

◎ The pub in **Wye River (Vic.)** must rate among the best in Australia for surf-watching. If the wind doesn't chill your bones, perch on the balcony and watch the wet-suited waxies carve their stuff.

◎ Whalebone Retreat in **Wonthaggi (Vic.)** is better known as the Whalebone Hotel. Acting as door frame is the jawbone of a 22-m leviathan that washed up on the nearby beach in 1924. **[McBride Ave. Phone (03) 5672 1019]**

◎ Nowadays a blues hub, the Highway Inn in **Plympton**, **Adelaide (SA)** opened the world's first drive-in bottle shop in October 1955. **[290 Anzac Hwy]**

◎ The speedboat in the tree is not the result of a waterskiing disaster, but a gimmick to publicise the Bridge Inn Hotel in **Maindample (Vic.)**. The dummy beside the display has dressed as a bikie chick and a duck shooter, among others, over the years.

◎ There's a whopping great fish lodged on the pub roof. Then again, you wouldn't expect anything less in a town called **Fish Creek (Vic.)**.

◎ The Blumberg Hotel in **Birdwood (SA)** has a West End beer truck parked on its verandah roof, in sympathy with the Motor Museum across the road. Blumberg is in fact Birdwood's former name.

*(Being a susurrus of sound-free samplings
and other luscious hushes)*

## AS THE SUN RISES AND GOETH DOWN

**ALBANY, WA**   The first dawn service to commemorate Anzac Day took place in 1923 in St John's Church on York St. Tailor-made for the job was Padre Arthur White, a former army chaplain who'd served in the Flanders trenches. He labelled the maiden ceremony 'Requiem for the War Dead'. In fact that day White served a *pre*-dawn eucharist, using the very sacraments he'd carted around the European battlefields. After the service, in a ritual later adopted throughout the Commonwealth, the rector led his fold to the war memorial up the hill for the laying of wreaths. In later years, Padre White (as all knew him) would lead the pre-dawn march up Mt Clarence, the last Australian landform seen by outgoing infantry bound for Gallipoli. **[Cnr York St and Peels Place. A plaque, and the wartime sacraments, can be found near the altar]**

## BILLY VILLENEUVE

**BANGALOW, NSW**   In 1995, the day the Pacific Hwy bypassed Bangalow, the town fell quiet. Too quiet, decided the Byron Shire Council, which accordingly devised an antidote. Every May, the town assembles 20-deep along the main street to watch a few hundred billycarts whiz by. Every cart requires a brake, and every Schumacher a helmet, though hay bales beyond the finish line provide a crash barrier if the speed of sound is achieved. This didn't help Wilson Draper one year, according to a feature in *Australian Geographic*, when he careered into the trophy table, smashing every cup. Wilson, it must be said, was 84 years old. **[Byron Visitors Centre, on (02) 6680 9271, can confirm dates, or hop onto www.bangalow.com]**

## NELL'S BELLS

**BENDIGO, Vic.**   Dame Nellie Melba was sleeping in the Shamrock Hotel, or trying to sleep – the bells in the post-office tower kept jolting her awake. If the knelling didn't unnerve Nell, the tick-tick-ticking certainly ticked her off. So next morning, in full voice, the prima donna complained to the local constabulary. For almost a century now, Bendigo's bells haven't chimed from 11p.m. through to 7a.m. **[Shamrock Hotel, Pall Mall. Phone (03) 5443 0333. For $180 you can sleep in the Dame Nellie Melba Suite. Wake-up calls available]**

Samuel Jones, a blacksmith from **Condamine (Qld)**, forged a very large cow-bell in 1868. The clang was so clear that farmers could locate their cattle from three paddocks away. But, as writer Dame Mary Gilmore lamented, it also deafened the cows. Imagine what auditory damage the 2-m bell in Condamine's Bell Park would inflict.

## GRANDPOP – 1
BETOOTA, Qld    Until his death (aged 88) in 2004, the sole occupant of Betoota, acknowledged as the smallest town in Australia, was retired grader driver Simon Remienko. The Polish-born bachelor owned the pub – the only substantial building in town – but didn't like crowds much and seldom answered the doorbell, spending his days watching the clouds drift over the desert and counting the traffic on one hand. And you can forget about petrol: the bowser is empty. But the town *is* a town, not just an attitude. It has a sign and a road and a civic plan. It might be worth knocking at the pub this time round – who knows, the new occupants might be inclined to open up. **[Between Birdsville and Windorah]**

## FOREVER ALIGHT
CHILDERS, Qld    A first-floor room in the Palace Hotel has become a shrine to 15 young backpackers who lost their lives in a fire in June 2000. Downstairs, in the tourist centre, phones ring and brochures vie for attention. Upstairs, the memorial includes a tableau (by painter Josonia Palaitis) of the group of travelling fruit-pickers outside the picking sheds on the eve of the fire. There are also back-lit collections of

family photos for each of the victims. While the pub's shell is being rebuilt into new quarters for the orchard armies the region requires, the upstairs memorial is permanent. **[72 Churchill Hill. Open weekdays 9a.m.–4p.m., weekends 9a.m.–3p.m. Phone (07) 4126 3886]**

## CUPID'S HARROW

**HARROW, Vic.**   The problem with Harrow, according to publican Ange Newton, was the boy/girl ratio in town. The girls were, like, so outnumbered. Harrow has a population of 90, more than half of them blokes and the balance wives and kids, with only a rare unattached female. Short of escaping the shire, bachelorhood was guaranteed. So Ange devised the Beaut Blokes weekend in June 2003, a singles ball with a unique twist. Instead of optimistic boys and gals leaving their farms for a fiesta, the Harrow males held their ground, inviting all them dateless city chicks to the sticks. The response was a deluge. In fact hundreds of girls missed out, with only 80 places having been set aside, to match the 80 shy shearers. The black-tie bash was slated for the Town Hall, with Ange's Hermitage Hotel reserved for the pep talks – and debriefing. **[Ange's Hermitage pub is on Blair St. Phone (03) 5588 1209]**

## SHELL GAME

**MINNAMURRA, NSW**   Graeme Clark was holidaying with his family in 1977. As his kids frolicked on the beach, the professor fiddled with a seashell. His mind was on electrodes, specifically the 20 that a surgical team needed to fix inside the human ear in order for the deaf to hear. As Clark twirled a blade of grass inside the shell, it came to him that a flexible implant would be the ideal means of turning sound waves into pulse patterns. One year after that beach holiday the first patient received a bionic ear, rated by the Royal Society of Medicine as one of mankind's greatest scientific breakthroughs. **[To reach the beach, thread the golf course and then take the narrow one-way underpass beneath the railway lines]**

When Queen Elizabeth II and the Duke of Edinburgh visited **Katoomba (NSW)** in 1954, the populace was worried about the reliability of Echo Point's echo. So a dozen local loudmouths were strategically positioned below the cliff, charged with returning the royal yodels should nature fail. It didn't, of course. That's the whole point of Echo Point.

## FIELDS OF BALI

**PERTH, WA**   Sixteen young sandgropers (as citizens of WA are known by those from elsewhere) were killed by the bombs that devastated the Sari Club and Paddys Bar in Bali in 2002. A memorial stands above Swan River, an eyrie of granite and Kimberley sandstone with a million-dollar view. Remarkably, the axis of the monument is aligned to catch the first sun rays every anniversary (12 October) to light up the victims' names. Equally movingly, 16 balgas (grass trees) have been planted in a commemorative garden. **[Kings Park, Fraser Ave]**

## SUPER CHIC

**POMONA, Qld**   Ron West owns 'the only authentic silent movie theatre in the world', a weatherboard palace in Pomona. The Majestic opened its doors in 1921, switching to talkies in 1930. But then Ron saw the virtue of silence, reverting to his Wurlitzer organ for a soundtrack. Every Thursday night from 8.30p.m. Ron bangs out the chords for *The Son of the Sheik* as his patrons hiss at the villain. The Majestic is the world's oldest operational silent cinema. **[Phone (07) 5485 2330]**

## SHHHHAME

**PORT ARTHUR, Tas.**   Forget the cat. The stocks. The triangle. The cruellest torture in our convict days was silence. The Separate (or Model) Prison at Port Arthur is a prison-in-a-prison reserved for the gnarlier inmates. Each man was locked in isolation, with talking or wall-tapping forbidden. The guards patrolled in kid slippers. The only 'relief' was the blinkered pew where on Sundays they listened to the pastor's pronouncements, then back to silence. **[Two-day pass to entire compound $24/$19/$11, family $52. Inquiries on 1800 659 101]**

# REBORN

*(Being a renaissance of renewed life-forms,
refits and reincarnations)*

## I KNOW WHERE YOU SLEPT LAST SUMMER

**ALICE SPRINGS, NT** Snow Kenna was the motion-picture man of Alice Springs. In 1942 he built an open-air cinema which he called the Pioneer, and the outback was hooked. But television saw the sacred site slide into financial ruin, the institution fading into a flea market. More recently it has become a youth hostel. Hot-air-ballooning ads are pasted on the 'Now Showing' board. Inside, the big white screen overlooks the hostel rooms and the projectionist's box holds cleaning supplies. **[Cnr Parsons St and Leichhardt Tce, off Todd Mall. Phone (08) 8952 8855]**

## CELL-TAUGHT

**BALLARAT, Vic.** Students at Ballarat's School of Mines are given a solid grounding. If it's not a geology lecture in the old brewery complex, it's a game of pool in the old jail The jail shut down in 1965 and was reborn only recently. Bushranger Captain Moonlight once escaped these walls, an achievement that is now the fantasy of undergraduates. On the site of a dozen hangings is the vocational guidance office. **[End of Lydiard St, beyond the diamond-shaped Sugg Lamp on the Dana St roundabout]**

It took 10 years for four men to convert a water tower in **Gunnedah (NSW)** into a four-storey folk museum. From the top of the internal spiral stairs, you get the best view in the district. The official opening hours are weekends 2p.m.–5p.m., but ask at the Visitors Centre and other arrangements can be easily made. **[Anzac Park, South St. Entry $3/$2.50/$1. For inquiries phone (02) 6740 2230]**

## TANKS FOR THE TIP

**CAIRNS, Qld**    The diesel tanks were decommissioned by the navy in 1987, and five years later the city council spent a year cleaning out the sludge. Now three of the five tanks serve variously as art galleries, amphitheatres, ballrooms and all-out 'party tanks'. Inside Tank 4 you can see the pipes once linked to Pier 10 on the waterfront, as well as a barnacled fuel barge hung in mid-air like some postmodern art installation. Even the shagadelic entrance gates are wrought from wartime iron. Grab a flyer from a cafe in town to see what jazz-cum-film-cum-art-cum-workshop is going down at the Tanks Arts Centre. **[46 Collins St, adjacent to the Flecker Botanical Gardens. Open weekdays 8.30a.m.–5p.m. Entry depends on event, though you can wander round for free. Phone (07) 4032 2349 or visit www.cairns.qld.gov.au]**

**Kalgoorlie (WA)** The YHA Backpackers hostel on Hay St occupies an old bordello. The strip is still the town's red-light zone, with Langtrees on the corner and the infamous 'girl-cages' across the road. Mona, who ran the old bordello, was a legend in local circles, plying her trade until the venerable age of 72.

## DINING CAR

**COBARGO, NSW**    There's a train carriage marooned on the Princess Hwy, trading under the name of the Wattleton Junction Train Stop Cafe. This classic 'red rattler', built in 1926, once swayed along the Bankstown line in Sydney. Diners are warned that 'Plainclothes and Uniformed Police Patrol this Train', which engenders mild paranoia as you demolish a scone. The Internet is also available in the guard compartment towards the street, making this a totally on-line experience. **[Beside the post office. Open daily from 8a.m. Phone (02) 6493 6144]**

## TROPIC REVIVAL

**COOKTOWN, Qld**    In 1873, gold converted this steamy coastal outpost into the state's second largest town after Brisbane. Tents were pitched higgledy-piggledy, occupied by 30 000 optimists. Mines began wherever the shovel fell. Fortunes were made – and drunk just as swiftly. Between the boom and the fizzle, St Mary's Convent was built, a Gothic Revival beauty that outlasted most of the 94 pubs that also materialised. Dogfights above the Coral Sea saw the convent evacuated and the building never resumed as a place of religion. Instead, Captain Cook's cannons – which he ditched in 1770 to lighten the *Endeavour*'s load – came to stay, along with other treasures. **[James Cook Museum, cnr Helen and Furneaux Sts. Open daily 9.30a.m.– 4p.m. Entry $7.50/$2. Phone (07) 4069 5386]**

## UNITED DENOMINATIONS

**COWRA, NSW**    Coins from 106 different countries were melted down to make the Australian Peace Bell. The first such bell, forged by the UN, hangs in New York City and is rung on World Peace Day every September. There are others in major cities around the globe, including Berlin and Hiroshima. Cowra is the only regional town to win the honour, owing to the lasting links forged with Japan since the bloody POW breakout of 1944, when 231 Japanese prisoners were killed during a mass escape attempt. **[Opposite the town library on Darling St. Step inside the shelter, listen to the spiel. Ring the bell]**

Fire and brimstone have been swapped for a fireplace and Stone's Green Ginger Wine at the Pulpit Tavern in **Mt Barker (SA)**. Duck under the ritzy green awning and you'll find yourself in a sober stone vestibule – now flush with beer taps. **[Bonnar Lane, off Hutchison St. Phone (08) 8398 2420]**

## HOME FOR A LOAN

**EDEN, NSW**    The shingles are of split ash, the logs of local stringybark. The cabin's pure prairie design might well have started a craze Down Under if we hadn't been seduced by French windows and the bull-nosed verandah. This little piece of Canada was once home to the local Girl Guides, and was then the shire library for many years (until 2003). Squash your nose against the window and you'll see non-fiction shelves adjoining the stone fireplace. **[Bass St, off Imlay St]**

## FEAT OF CLAY

**EPSOM, Vic.**   As soon as you step into the kiln, the movie (or the 'crock-umentary, as the pottery powers call it) starts. The film tells how George Guthrie dug for gold in 1858, but found white clay instead. So good was the stuff that the ex-potter abandoned his pick and returned to the wheel, establishing Australia's oldest working pottery – now with firing kiln as cinema, for anyone curious enough to enter. **[Bendigo Pottery, Midland Hwy, 6 km from town. Entry to studio free. Museum entry $7/$6/$4, family $18. Free clay-play for kids. Phone (03) 5448 4404 or visit www.bendigopottery.com.au]**

Crime and punishment have been constant themes in the life of the **Burketown (Qld)** Pub. Opening in 1883, the one building has been a troopers' fort, a magistrate's residence, a courthouse and penultimately a prison. Ultimately, it's one helluva pub. **[Cnr Musgrave and Beames Sts. Phone (07) 4745 5104]**

## YOU, CLAUDIUS

**LAUNCESTON, Tas.**   Formerly a squash complex, Aquarius Roman Baths is a little piece of Old Latin in Launceston. Once through the *portus principus*, you can choose between the *tepidarium* (warm bath), the *frigidarium* (guess) or the *ruberium* (massage). Downstairs is the *laconicum* (where patrons don't talk much), and upstairs the gymnasium. You can dunk yourself in lukewarm milk, or try the Cleopatra package (minus asp). This must be how Julius Caesar avoided love handles. **[127–133 George St. Prices vary, from $24 for the *circus basicus*. Phone (03) 6331 2255 or visit www.romanbath.com.au]**

If you want to visit Dhurringile, near **Tatura (Vic.)**, you'll need to know an inmate or commit a minor felony. This 65-room mansion, once one of Australia's biggest homesteads, is now a low-security jail for 170 prisoners. Before accepting crims the manor took in orphans and, further back, German POWs. **[8 km down the Murchison road]**

## SEED CAPITAL

**MULLUMBIMBY, NSW**    Santos Natural Food Store on Burringbar St captures the spirit of Mullum (as citizens know it) like nowhere else. The town began life as a farming hub and over the years evolved into an alternative oasis. The ex-Bank of NSW is now a treasury of sunflower kernels, dandelion coffee and low-sodium Gorilla Munch. Instead of tellers and clientele, the floorboards creak with barefoot earth mothers in kaftans and topknots. Om Gaia Life Force Food occupies the porch. Upstairs, where the manager once slept, is the Byron Environment Centre. **[Cnr Burringbar and Stuart Sts]**

# ODDITIONS

⑥ John L. Swinney took over the service station in **Gundagai (NSW)** a few years ago. Now this may seem a curious venue for an undertaker and monumental mason, but you can get a drive-thru casket quote at this born-again garage on West St.

⑥ An old dairy in **Leura (NSW)** has been made over into a four-star guesthouse. The cream of the cream must be the old milk vat that's now used as an outdoor jacuzzi. **[36 Mount St. Phone (02) 4784 1739 or visit www.oldleuradairy.com]**

⑥ Four tall wheat silos on the Derwent River in **Hobart (Tas.)** were converted into 30 luxury apartments by Geoff Harper in 2000. The precast concrete served as the ideal shell for 10 storeys of four-star living. **[End of Castray Esplanade, Salamanca]**

⑥ Western Plains Zoo in **Dubbo (NSW)** occupies an acreage known as Hand Grenade Range, which was an army camp during World War 2. You can only hope they retrieved all the ammunition. **[Open daily 9a.m.–5p.m. Entry $27/$19/$14, family $70. Phone (02) 6882 5888]**

⑥ What's a chimney stack doing in the Coles supermarket at **Port Augusta (SA)**? It's a hangover from the building's earlier life as a brewery, established in 1893.

⑥ Examine the library wall on Brodie St, in **Hughenden (Qld)**. The dinosaur portrait is an ingenious assembly of old farm equipment salvaged from the local dump by artists Sam Brown and Terry Lindsay.

# ROADSIDE

*(Being a verge of eye-catching eccentricity found
en route to elsewhere)*

## SNAPPY LITTLE VEGEMITE

BEAUFORT, Vic.   Vegemite's inventor, Cyril Callister, came from a one-chook town called Chute, just north of Beaufort on the Raglan road. A sign, larger than the town itself, celebrates the fact. But the true reward for the offbeat traveller is Registered Mail Box 832, which features a Ned Kelly statue with a shotgun in his lap. 'Waiting for the Mail Run', says the caption. [4 km down the road to Raglan. Chute is some 6 km further on]

## THRONE AND KING

BENDIGO, Tas.   Opposite Vintage Talking Tram Stop 2 is a bronze deckchair, an ideal spot from which to watch Australia's oldest running street parade. The first Easter procession was held in 1871, in support of the Bendigo Base Hospital and Mental Asylum. A block downtown from the chair, the statue of George Lansell, Bendigo's first millionaire, remains standing. Look carefully and you'll see a promising quartz chunk in his grip.

## MORE THAN A FILLING

CARDWELL, Qld   Two American tourists, flying home from their Qld holiday in the early 90s, noticed a paper bag sitting on a window ledge in a Japanese airport. Could it be? Yes, the smiling crocodile logo belonging to Cardwell Pies. The visitors had been gobbling at that very company's roadside cart just days before, enjoying Robert Jesse's egg-and-bacon special and the pie-and-pea combo. Since that international fluke, the Cardwell croc has bobbed up in places as far apart as Potsdam and Essex, planted by approving customers. 'I'm going global,' laughs Robert, a veteran of eight years selling pastry on the Bruce Hwy. His dad started the business 37 years back. The cart offers a dozen different fillings, but not crocodile. [Look for the yellow cart with an Australian flag close to the state school]

Each verse of Australia's unofficial national anthem, 'Waltzing Matilda', is symbolised on a nature strip down Elderslie St in **Winton (Qld)**. Three cocked pistols represent three troopers. Stirrup and fob signify squatter a-riding. While a royal wave among the bubbles is the ghost below the billabong's surface. Banjo Paterson, the author, is holding his tongue outside the municipal pool.

## LOITERING PERMITTED

**DONALD, Vic.**    Psst, want to see a 90-year-old stripper from Nullawil? Mind you, she's a bit shopworn and rusty in places. Or maybe you'd prefer the wet pickler from Patchewollock? What's most off-the-wall about the Donald Agricultural Museum is the fact you can enjoy the exhibits from the footpath. Every tree-puller and bag-jumper is caged inside a warehouse flush on the street, giving kerb-crawling a new meaning. **[Hamill St, down from the train park]**

## FOR WHOM THE GATE TOLLS

**GREAT WESTERN, Vic.**    Pigs and goats cost a ha'penny each. Oxen will set you back a penny. While any gig, chaise, coach or chariot constructed on springs and drawn by one horse or other animal will cost the owner a monumental sixpence. All tariff details are spelt out on the 1863 tollgate, tucked away on the Mechanics Hall porch. A reminder that GST belongs to a long tradition of government penny-filching. **[On the Western Hwy, in the heart of town]**

## HORSE LATITUDES

**KULIN, WA**    The Tin Horse Hwy is a 16-km stretch that links the wheat town of Kulin to the Jilakin racetrack where the real gee-gees run. The imagination has run rampant here, the way being lined with oil drums welded into every sort of mare and mustang under the sun – Olympic torch runners, fence-sitters, palomino ballerinas, equine pilots, and zebras. October is the peak season, when the sculptures increase in number to celebrate the bush races. But a punter can marvel at most of the herd regardless of the calendar. Look for a tin horse cowering on top of a tin silo, trying to escape the tin man climbing the tin ladder.

## CORNY BEEF

**LARRIMAH, NT**   Fran Hodgetts' mother-in-law was the daughter of Harold Lasseter, the American bridge-builder who allegedly found his own El Dorado in the outback. That's just one of the yarns awaiting consumers of Fran's famed corned-beef rolls, buffalo pie and home-made ginger beer. She's seen the world pass through her flystripped door, from Manpower to The Wiggles (the first with clothes, the second minus skivvies). **[Fran's Devonshire Tea House has turned the old police station into a no-frills dining-room. Open 8a.m.–5p.m. Phone (08) 8975 9945]**

Most city bus stops are grotty. But one in Vaucluse, **Sydney (NSW)**, is a *grotto*. Catch the No. 325 around the eastern suburbs and you'll see a cute cave on the corner of Fitzwilliam and Wentworth Sts. And just around the corner, up Chapel St, stands a grotto of another kind – the private mausoleum of colonial explorer William Wentworth, mounted on a sandstone boulder.

## DUCATI DETOUR

**MOUNT WHITE, NSW**   Max Moore is not Mad Max. In fact he's quite mellow, but he is the owner of one of the biggest motorbike-magnets in Australia – Road Warriors Café. He says the Mad Max reference is acci-dental: 'Road Warriors just seemed the right name for the place,' he shrugs. Hundred of riders frequent the cafe, especially on weekends when Kwackas and Goldwings go full-throttle along the Old Pacific Hwy. Max's place is the perfect distance – with inky coffee – to punctu-ate a run. The full-suspension barstools are enough to reward a visit. **[1147 Pacific Hwy. Open daily 7a.m.–6p.m. Phone (02) 4370 1122]**

## FAR-OUT PLACE

**RABBIT FLAT, NT**    Bruce and Jacqueline Farrand enjoy each other's company. Just as well, considering the couple run Australia's remotest roadhouse, a petrol stop more than 600 km from Alice Springs, along the Tanami Rd. Bruce can count on one hand the times he's been to the 'big smoke' of Halls Creek, about 300 clicks the other way. It's hardly the place for a drop-in, but after hours of eating dust either way the Rabbit Flat oasis is a sight for sore eyes. Though be warned, the Rabbit has the habit of shutting on the middle three weekdays.

Some 53 km north of **Newman (WA)**, heading towards Karijini National Park, is a memorial garden in the desert. A sign beside a tall white cross announces the patch as Pacey's Place, after truck driver Roy Pacey who met his end here in 1997. 'Be it night or be it morn,' goes the attached verse, 'we will give a wave and sound the horn.'

## FILLED TO THE BRIM

**RENNER SPRINGS, NT**    The roadhouse barman used to wear a pith helmet. An Italian tourist in 2000 liked the look of it, and offered his Tele Italia cap in exchange. Swap done, the cap was hooked to the ceiling. Four-hundred hats later, including a blue beret from East Timor, a panama, and a Barney the Dinosaur visor, this place is more a millinery than an hostelry. **[Desert Hotel, the only pub in town]**

On the road towards Mt Nameless in **Tom Price (WA)**, you'll encounter three fishermen. These tin figures, each with rod and tackle, are a droll means of decorating the town's settling tank (what one citizen describes as 'where the drinking water ends up'). To complete the diorama there is a shark fin poking out of the brown water.

## RARE COMMON

**ST ALBANS, NSW**    Chain gangs built the Great Northern Rd from the Hawkesbury River to the high ridges of Bucketty, and signs along this amazing route point out convict-cut culverts, road ramps and bridges. Another sign, 6 km out of St Albans, marks the beginning of the McDonald Valley, better known as St Albans Common. This is the only official common in Australia, a slab of some 914 ha granted by Queen Victoria for the purposes of grazing. Essentially, the valley's residents, or 'Commoners', are perpetual owners of the turf, with five trustees elected every three years. The sign at the cattle grid requests that you drive straight through the 8 km of exclusive real estate, neither stopping nor straying. As you do so, watch out for the cows: they roam the road as if they own the joint, which is of course pretty much the case.

# ODDITIONS

- There are 15 km of surreal letterboxes between Devonport and **Wilmot (Tas.)**. The carnival starts at Chinaman's Crest, where a Roy Rogers figure awaits the next bill. Then follows a moonshine still, a lawnmower, a doll's house, a motorbike and a Tasmanian tiger . . .

- . . . a rival to this kooky collection stretches between **Wallangra** and **Ashford (NSW)**. Gas cylinders and scrap metal feature prominently in an array of hitchhikers, bikies and helicopters.

- Heading south into **Oatlands (Tas.)** as you pass through St Peters Pass, look out for a fish, a dinosaur, a reindeer and a train. The Oatlands topiary has now been joined by the steel silhouettes (on the eastern side) of five colonial figures.

# ROCK

*(Being an array of rocks that rock, rocks that roll, and other bits of striking stonework)*

## FLINDERS KEEPERS

**ARKAROOLA, SA**   Mt Gee in the Flinders Ranges is the only crystal-quartz mountain in the world. The best way to get close to this rarity is via the white-knuckle Ridgetop Tour out of Arkaroola. The rollercoaster route, famous for The Armchair where numerous TV commercials have captured suburban 4WDs stopping on the brink, follows an old mining road bulldozed during World War 2. With nuclear bombs then all the rage, defence scientists were busily scratching for the right fissionable stuff, as the name Radium Ridge would suggest. Don't be put off, though, for this is one of the most stunning parts of Australia, with chasms, hanging rocks and geo-enigmas at every turn. **[Inquiries on tours and access, call 1800 676 042 or visit www.arkaroola.com.au]**

Sixteen sandstone blocks were set aside and 16 sculptors in the lower **Blue Mountains (NSW)** received a single instruction: 'Make a seed pod'. The result is the Wentworth Falls Lake Sculpture Project at 41–51 Sinclair St. Every pod portrayed is native to the mountains, from the swamp grevillea purse to the waratah's tongue.

## SURF'S UP, JOEY

**DURRAS, NSW**   Durras Lakes National Park can offer you two marvels, both on the same stretch of shore. The first is the prospect of seeing kangaroos surfing on Pebbly Beach – though rangers insist this myth dates back to a photo of a roo belly-deep in the waves trying to flee a dog. The second marvel requires a short walk north at mid to low tide. The name Pebbly Beach won't quite prepare you for several hectares of chalcedony agate with barely a grain of sand in sight.

[Look for the Pebbly Beach turnoff some 10 km south of Termeil. The 8-km road is unsealed]

Back in 1911 the Marine Board of **Burnie (Tas.)** quarried a hill off West Beach, seeking rubble to help build a breakwater. Instead they found the world's finest example of hexagonal basalt. A curse rather than a blessing, in fact, as it meant they had to quarry further away. **[Cnr Marine and North Tces]**

## AMBITIOUS MUD

**HAMELIN POOL, WA**    Geologists in 1954 discovered a rock that breathed. Imagine a mud pie made of algae and living in a salty bath, and you have a stromatolite in the mind's eye. At the dawn of time, these 'rocks' began to manufacture oxygen. Stromatolites are the oldest known living creatures. And they're not stupid: of all the possible locations around the world, the stromatolite has chosen to live only in balmy WA and the Bahamas. NASA scientists have analysed stromatolites in the belief that Mars may have its own colony of these organic boulders, which grow 10 times more slowly than coral. **[Museum at the Hamelin Pool caravan park allows you to inspect these old guys 'breathing' (entry $3). Or you can stroll the pool's edge itself, 300 m away]**

## AGAPE

**HOME HILL, Qld**    There's an agate in Jim Ashworth's gem display, which he has dubbed the Turning Agate. Every other stone on the shelf stays put despite the occasional railway vibration, but this restless rock rotates, by degrees, anticlockwise. This is just one of a thousand staggering stones in Ashworth's Rock Shop. There's a unique soccer ball made of agate hexagons and pentagons, soil super-fused by lightning, and the world's only white-ant nest made of graphite. And I haven't even mentioned the fossilised tyre-tracks. **[164–170 Eighth Ave. Open weekdays 8.30a.m.–5p.m., Sat. 8.45a.m.–noon, Sun. 10a.m.–noon (May–Sep.). Entry to gem display $2.50/$1.50. Phone (07) 4782 1177]**

A massive cube sits on the edge of Ben Buckler, the point at North Bondi Beach. You may notice a cement glob on top where a sculpted mermaid once rested. Yet far more interesting is the plaque affixed on another facet, telling you the story of a massive storm in 1912. So big were the waves they spat this cube out of its seabed.

## ROUGH DIAMOND

**STAWELL, Vic.** If you can build a house using pebbles and slats – without a single nail – then you're clever. But if you can do all that *and* make a harlequin pattern into the bargain, arranging the quartz and brown stones just so, then like John Hearne in 1868 you're blowing your own horn. His Diamond House is an art deco gem before its time. All the stones were fossicked from Church Hill across the road. **[Hearn's house is now the Diamond House Motel and Restaurant, cnr Prince and Seaby Sts. Phone (03) 5358 3366.]**

God lost his pencils 14 km from **Merriwa (NSW)**, along the Denman Rd. They're sitting in a rock cluster known as The Battery. Geologists seem to think the formation arose some 35 million years ago, when cooling lava created 'columnar jointing'. But really, they're God's pencils.

## HIT THE HIGH NOTES

**THANGOOL, Qld**  Mt Scoria could be described as a picturesque place at which to break your ankle. Basalt fragments cover all sides of this extinct volcano. But a vigorous scramble will be rewarded not only by the view but by music as well. Any loose pebble sent down the scree produces a melodic note as it strikes the mountain's stone flanks. Sicily and Scotland are the only other nations on earth to boast such an orchestral landmass, which is the result of basalt columns cooling into interlocking columns. You can either strike (with a piece of metal) one of the columns on the peak or pitch a pebble downhill for a random riff. Wild winds have been known to play their own tunes on the rocks. [7 km west of Thangool, a silo town 10 km south of Biloela. No damage to flora, fauna or geology is permitted]

## INDENTIKIT

**TORRINGTON, NSW**   This is an old tin town north of Glen Innes. Once the tin petered out, fossickers moved in and lucked upon a larder of gems including emerald, beryl, topaz and a risky-sounding stone called arsenopyrite. But the sandstone at the end of Butler Rd, just past Captain Thunderbolt's Lookout, is also beyond price. From the tantalisingly named Mystery Face picnic ground, the round walk is 3.5 km: keep looking up and you'll not only see a massive Easter Island countenance but ducks and tigers and all sorts of natural shapes.

> The biggest meteorite to strike Australia is in a corner of the Western Australian Museum in **Perth (WA)**. The size of a Datsun and 11 tonnes in weight, the Mundrabilla Meteorite was discovered on the Nullarbor Plain in 1908. [**Perth Cultural Centre, James St. Open daily 9.30a.m.–5p.m. Free entry. Phone (08) 9427 2700 or visit www.museum.wa.gov.au**]

## DRY DOCK

**WALGA ROCK, WA**   Measuring 5 km in circumference, this monolith amidst the mallee scrub is home to feral goats and rock wallabies. The cairn on top offers amazing views of endless plains and the crease of Sanford River, but the rock's *real* high point is an art gallery near the northern tip. Among the spirals and wavy lines is a twin-masted sailing ship, painted in white clay by the Wandjina people. The square portholes and distinctive rigging led Dr Ian Crawford, a scholar of Wandjina artwork, to believe the ship is the *Xantho*, the state's first coastal steamer, which sank in 1872. The coast, by the way, is 200 km away. [The rock – its Aboriginal name is Walgahna – is 47 km east of Cue along reasonable unsealed road]

## SPUNKY SPELUNKER

**WYNYARD, Tas.**  Fossil Bluff is a giant claystone sandwich, with tillite and basalt for bread, sitting beside Bass Strait. It is notable for two reasons. First, our oldest marsupial fossil, a huge possum-like character called *Wynyardia bassiana*, dating back some 21 million years, was found here. Second, the discoverer was a marine biologist called Theodore Thomas Flynn, father of Errol. **[3 km west from town centre]**

# ODDITIONS

⊚ Despite their name, thunder eggs are not hatched in heaven. These bizarre balls formed from lava have a crystal core. There's a whopping example in the **Murwillumbah (NSW)** Visitors Centre, complete with the story of its acquisition.

⊚ Regardless of the hour, you can investigate the chunk of rock outside the **Bulahdelah (NSW)** Courthouse Museum on Bombah Point Rd. A souvenir found by road workers building a new freeway stretch, it bears a hundred mollusc fossils.

⊚ It sounds like a compilation album from the 1970s, but Gotta Rock is actually a leasehold granted to N.S. Lawson in 1840. You can't miss the roadside outcrop, which is about 5 km southwest of **Coolah (NSW)**.

⊚ In a mild sea, the blowhole in **Bicheno (Tas.)** can be tame and the rocking rock next-door won't rock. But when Neptune adds pep, where else can you see a 75-tonne boulder rocking with rollers? **[Signposted left on leaving the town, heading south]**

# ROOMS

*(Being a storey of extraordinary chambers and quaint quarters)*

## SLEEP NOW, LITTLE SUZIE

**INVERMAY, BALLARAT, Vic.**   Babyboomers can flash back to their heyday at a remarkable B&B here. Ken and Maureen Vincent have dedicated their back shed, and half the house, to Cruzin The 50s/60s, a live-in monument to the days when swing was a dance and surf was a style of music. Special garages have been allocated to guests arriving in fin-tailed Chevvies. **[9 Handford Crt. Phone (03) 5333 2484 or follow the links at www.ballarat.com/cruzin]**

## LANDLOCKED

**COOBER PEDY, SA**   Pets are welcome at the Underground Motel – except wombats. This two-level warren brings to mind Tora Bora caves where Osama bin Laden is reputed to have lain low. Ceiling fans spin in all rooms. Every living space has been gouged from the hill – from en suite to communal kitchen. And yes, there's undercover parking too. **[Catacomb Rd. Phone (08) 8672 5324 or 1800 622 979 for bookings. Email undergroundmotel@ozemail.com.au for tariffs]**

## BLIND AMBITION

**DARWIN, NT**   Born in Mongolia of missionary parents, Beni Burnett went to Shanghai to study architecture by correspondence. At the age of 47, he found his way to Darwin, and with World War 2 raging was employed to design military quarters. This being the tropics, the key word was cool. Instead of walls, Burnett gave his new-wave bungalows asbestos louvres and sleeping verandas instead of bedrooms. Idle past the rattan chairs and you can almost sniff Raffles on the breeze. **[Burnett House is part of the Myilly Point Heritage Precinct, at the northern extension of Smith St. Open Mon.–Sat. 10a.m.–1p.m., Sun. (for high tea) 3.30p.m.–6p.m. Entry by donation. Phone (08) 8981 0165]**

## CELL AND BREAKFAST

**DUBBO, NSW**   Before Dubbo was even declared a town, there was Dundullimal homestead, reputed to be the oldest slab house in Australia. John Maughan, the original squatter of 1841, based the house's design on the Indian bungalow, with breezy pavilions fanning out like wings. Of more ambiguous origins is the lock-up bedroom off the verandah. Most passersby were welcome to some food and a bed for the night, but if unknown to their host they were ushered to the less-than-cordial chamber on the porch (a cell-like arrangement known as the Stranger's Room). **[Obley Rd, past Western Plains Zoo. Homestead open daily 10a.m.–5p.m. Entry $6/$5/$3 and $15 family. Phone (02) 6884 9984]**

## PRIVATE COVER

**ESPERANCE, WA**   Alan likes to have a joke with guests. When they arrive at The Old Hospital Motel, he gives them the keys to Ward 7 (the former mortuary). 'Just to see the look on their faces.' But seriously, typhoid was rife in this seaside town in the late 1800s. Concerts were held to raise funds for public beds, and several cottage hospitals were built (Taylor's Tea Rooms a block away was once the Leinster Hospital). Nevertheless, coffins soon jammed the corridors and had to be passed out the window via human chains. Those same coffin windows now look upon a birdbath and the Bay of Isles. **[1A William St. Single, family and VIP units available. Phone (08) 9071 3587 – and ask for the duty matron]**

## HERE, MISS, OVER

**KATHERINE, NT**   The world's largest classroom is invisible. Though you *can* get to see where the teachers work, and where many of the kids' collages, stories and paintings end up. Katherine is one of 13 radio hubs that comprise The School of the Air, reciting the five-times table over 800 000 square km. *The Hungry Caterpillar* is beamed to Birdsville and Borroloola, the *Dawn Treader* launched to Argyle Downs and Mistake Creek. Picnics and carnivals allow the far-flung students to have a fling together regularly, but nine days out of 10 this humble cottage is the nerve centre. **[Some 1.5 km down Giles St. Mid-March to end Nov.,**

weekday tours 9a.m., 10a.m. and 11a.m. for $5. Phone 1800 653 142 or visit www.schools.nt.edu.au/ksa]

## SHUT THE GATE

**KILKIVAN, Qld**    When the Union Bank of Australia opened a branch here, it advertised for a manager who could 'ride a horse around the district and visit his clients'. That was 100 years ago. More recently the ANZ, the last banking giant to occupy the Federation-style Queenslander, hopped on its own horse and galloped into the distance. Bruce and Rae Hurley recognised the investment opportunity and opened a cafe and guesthouse under the name The Left Bank. Strongrooms and teller chambers have been converted into restaurant and art gallery. **[10 Bligh St. Phone (07) 5484 1016 or visit www.theleftbank.com.au]**

## END OF THE LINE

**LIGHTNING RIDGE, NSW**    A mini-cyclone fast-tracked civic planning here during the 1950s. A hall, Dick Brown's cafe, and a dozen kero-tin shanties took off, never to be seen again. In 1960 a few gaps were filled with three Sydney trams and the No. 372 tram from St Kilda in Vic. – the first tourist accommodation to appear in this opal outpost. Guests at the Tram-o-Tel can choose from six self-contained rooms in three of the trams (the fourth serves as reception and opal shop.) You'll also be treated to the novelty of air-conditioning, a luxury the original trams never offered commuters. **[5 Morilla St. Phone (02) 6829 0448 or visit www.wj.com.au]**

## ACQUA VITAE

**MEDLOW BATH, NSW**    Retail baron Mark Foy learnt the virtues of spa therapy while in Derbyshire in the early 1900s. Returning home, Foy converted an orthodox guesthouse – the Belgravia – into a sprawling sanatorium called The Hydropathic Establishment. He imported a steam-driven generator from Germany (which lit all 130 rooms) and a doctor from Lake Lucerne. Alas, Dr Bauer was a bit too strict for the antipodean hypochondriac. Foy farewelled the good doctor and renamed the complex the Hydro Majestic. This was the Midas touch: the stream of guests was the A-list of its day and included Olympians, bohemians, Sir Arthur

Conan Doyle, our first PM Sir Edmund Barton (who died here), plus the Rajah of Pudacoota and his wife, Molly Fink. A flying fox ferried groceries from the Megalong Valley. Convalescent Americans got to enjoy the facilities during World War 2, when the Hydro was a wartime hospital. **[Great Western Hwy. Inquiries regarding rooms, tours or dining on (02) 4788 1002, or visit www.hydromajestic.com.au]**

## VISITING HOURS

**MT GAMBIER, SA** Tennis was the sport of choice at Mt Gambier Jail, mainly because the nets made excellent ladders. And a free man could fit a month's supply of hallucinogenic fun into a Slazenger Pro-Bounce tennis ball and lob it over the wall without a guard ever blinking. More exercise yarns are told by Gary Adam, who runs the youth hostel inside the granite walls. Original cells (rooms 1–5) are available, as are bread and water at the restaurant (functions only). **[Margaret St. $52 a double, $22 a dormitory bunk. Tours $3.30/ $1.10. Phone 1800 626 844]**

## OAST WITH THE MOST

**NORTHCLIFFE, WA** *Hansel and Gretel* is not the only instance of a human being lodged in an oven. The Hulcup family's Watermark Homestay offers accommodation overnight in a renovated tobacco kiln. Roof flaps, once designed to regulate the baking temperatures, now operate as skylights. The same farm-stay has several ponds teeming with marron, the world's biggest freshwater crayfish. **[Cnr Karri Hill and Hill Brook Rds. Phone (08) 9776 1513]**

## ALL QUIET ON THE WESTERN COAST

**PEMBERTON, WA** Allan Jones (two L's) is neither the Formula One champ nor the emperor of talk-back radio in Sydney, but the Picture Show Man of Pemberton – once. Jones built the last timber cinema of its kind left in this state. The cinema reeled in the late 1970s, turning into a woodwork studio until 1998. That was the year new owners, the Telfords and the Palmers, used original blueprints (and polished jarrah) to magic the building into a luxury guesthouse. Not only is the cinema feel retained in the art deco leadlights, but the five apartments also reflect the silver screen. Guests can opt to queen-size it in the Dress Circle, the Projection Room or The Lounge. Exhibitionists may tend towards The Stage. **[Cnr Ellis and Guppy Sts. Phone (08) 9776 0258 or view www.oldpicturetheatre.com.au]**

## ME TARZALI, YOU AMAZED

**TARZALI, Qld**   Cassowaries usher their chicks through the man-ferns and drink from the Ithaca River. Staying in luxury treehouses, at canopy level, you're likely to see other species from wampoo pigeons to tree kangaroos. Platypus forage for yabbies in the river shallows. Green-eyed tree frogs cling to the windows, envying your spa. Harry and Sandy Walker's arboreal accommodation offers every mod con in a primitive microcosm. **[Fur'n'Feathers, Hogan Rd. Rates from $280 a double. Kids welcome. Phone (07) 4096 5364 or hover over www.rainforesttreehouses.com.au]**

## ODDITIONS

- ⊚ **Cossack (WA)** offers a derelict turtle-soup factory, a shipwreck, pearling graves – and budget accommodation in the form of the old cyclone-proof police barracks, built in 1897. **[Single rooms $22, families $44. Phone (08) 9182 1190]**
- ⊚ Of nuns, you'll find none in the Old **Cobargo (NSW)** Convent. That's because the sisters flew the nest long ago, leaving the 1917 man-sion in the hands of Bob and Dianne, your B&B hosts. **[Phone (02) 6493 6419 or check out the decor on www.babs.com.au/oldcon-vent]**
- ⊚ Don't know which name is cuter – The Misty Morn Cat Motel or the town in which it's found, **Wonglepong (Qld)**.

# SCANDAL

*(Being an uproar of lurid business, headlining headaches and general brouhaha)*

## LIQUID ASSET

**BERMAGUI, NSW** Which story do you believe? Both start with a bank manager named Rawson. Both insist he lobbied feverishly to save a spotted gum from the Forestry axe during the 1920s. Motive is where the stories differ. In the cleaner version, Mr Rawson is a proto-type greenie, entrusting the tree to Mumbulla Shire for the term of its natural life. In the tawdrier tale, Rawson was in the habit of swerving home from his weekly spree at the Horseshoe Bay Hotel, stopping off at the tree to siphon his bladder. Version B also explains how the gum outgrew all its siblings. **[A picnic shelter on the Cobargo Rd, 5 km from Bermagui marks the (wet) spot]**

## THE BUTCHER'S DAUGHTER

**CEDUNA, SA** The initials MH appear in scrollwork on the cemetery gates. They stand for Mary Hatton, a young girl murdered in 1958 in a crime that might never have left the parish pump had it not been for the overblown trial. An Aboriginal named Rupert Stuart was the accused, and race-based controversy wrenched the nation: he was seen as either a monster or a scapegoat. Newspaper editors were tried for libel. The trenchant stance adopted by Sir Thomas Playford, then SA premier, was seen as contributing to his political downfall. Appeal followed appeal, but ultimately Stuart was found guilty and sentenced to be hanged, which was later commuted to life. The brouhaha is imperfectly captured in the 2002 movie *Black and White* starring Robert Carlyle. The girl's grave is four rows down. **[Smith Rd]**

## THE HOUR OF NEED

**HUGHENDEN, Qld** Scandal or saga – take your pick. But a grave some 72 km out of Hughenden, heading towards Porcupine Gorge, reflects a sorry yarn. In 1888, bullock driver William Crossley was putting rocks beneath a bogged wheel when he felt a sharp pain in his hand. Snake or scorpion – take your pick. Either way, Bill was poorly. His mate Ben Smith galloped all the way back to Hughenden, only for the doctor to request cash before he'd place his toe in a stirrup. Smith rode back out, cadged the 25 pounds and rode into town again. This time the doctor made the trip. Four days had passed from mystery bite to the quack arriving – and Bill died within hours. Bill's death, marked by a roadside grave, was a harbinger of bulk-billing practices.

## ED ON ARRIVAL

**LEONORA, WA**    Edward Sullivan, better known as Doodah, found a promising reef of gold in 1896, close to modern-day Leonora. He and his colleague Cameron travelled south to register the find. The Johannesburg, as they called the lease, proved to be a rich vein that brought about the birth of Leonora and led to other finds nearby. But Doodah never got to see the spoils. 'The Prospector of Leonora' shot himself within the year, so the story goes. Does seem fishy, you have to admit: the owner of untold gold choosing to swallow lead . . . **[The lone grave is 2 km north of Leonora, signposted on the left as you head out of town]**

## MOOR, SHE CRIED

**MARYBOROUGH, Qld**    Floods have been frequent visitors to Maryborough. Those in doubt should take in the water levels painted on the corner of the Old Bond Store on Wharf St, including the whopper in 1893. But sailors being sailors, no flood was going to stem the flow of libido. As the story goes, the Riverside Apartments on Wharf St once housed working girls. At the height of one flood, rivermen allegedly moored their boat to the second-storey veranda posts and spent some time indoors. A child resulting from such a transaction was known in the local slang as a 'brothel sprout'. **[88–90 Wharf St]**

## DARWIN VS GOD

**PENOLA, SA**    Father Julian Edmund Tenison Woods was the parish priest who helped Australia's first saint, Mary Mackillop, set up her school here. But Father Woods had other strings to his bow. He wrote knowledgeably on the fish of NSW and the fossils of Mt Gambier. He travelled to Java in 1883, a month after Krakatoa erupted. And after 40 years of studying nature, this sage man of God confronted Darwin's theory. Did Genesis rule out the concept of evolution – or vice versa? Woods' conclusions await you in all their heretical glory. **[Mary Mackillop Centre, cnr Portland St and Petticoat Lane. Open daily 10a.m.– 4p.m. Entry of $3.50 includes schoolhouse. Phone (08) 8737 2092 or visit www.mackillop-penola.com]**

## KEENER THAN MUSTARD

**PROSERPINE, Qld**   Gunyarrah is a paddock with a plaque. The scandal lies in what the plaque *doesn't* say. When Singapore fell in 1944, the British were itching to test new strains of gas for possible use against the Japanese. So at the Gunyarrah Field Experimental Station scientists built gas chambers and dropped mustard bombs onto Australian guinea pigs – the human kind. They put volunteers Bob Campbell and 15 other servicemen into a steel tank for one and a half hours to measure the results. 'It felt like severe sunburn,' recalls Campbell, as documented in the Proserpine Museum. Later the skin blistered, blackened and peeled off. Barry Butler, another subject, recounts how globs of porridge were sucked from his stomach every 20 minutes to check for a mustard aftertaste. By and large the findings were futile, with war's end just around the corner. **[Site is signposted off the Bruce Hwy, some 10 km south of town. The Proserpine Museum, open every day but Sat., has far more ghastly details]**

## FABULOUS BAKER BOYS

**STANTHORPE, Qld**   Two angels stand above the grave of two young boys, Edward and Keith Baker. The headstone, like their death date, is shared. Their deaths, as the epitaph reads, were attributed to the Bundaberg Serum Tragedy. Between wars, diphtheria was the biggest killer of Australians and the Department of Health was spurred into finding a vaccine for children. Alas, the antitoxin they injected into small arms in January 1928 was closer to toxin, causing seizures, blood poisoning and violent anthrax-like symptoms. The Baker boys, whose bodies were returned to their home soil, were among the 14 children who died within a week. According to the couplet on their headstone: 'Thy purpose Lord, we cannot see. But all is well that's done by thee.' If done by malpractice, however, call a lawyer. **[The cemetery lies at the end of Victoria St, past the high school. The grave lies between the two creeks, away from the school: look for the angels seven rows downhill from the public toilet]**

## RANK AND VILE
**ST MARYS, Tas.**   You can't miss St Patrick's Head poking above the plain. The peak was the easternmost flank of the infamous Black Line march of 1830, when more than 2200 men equipped with muskets and 300 sets of handcuffs spread out across northeastern Tas. from St Marys to Deloraine, with instructions to herd the Indigenous population onto Tasman Peninsula. But the Aborigines knew the art of concealment, and the march's pickings amounted to one frail elder and one young boy.

## PEE & OH
**SYDNEY, NSW**   Back in 1963, shipping giant P&O commissioned a sculptor to create a water feature for their Sydney skyscraper. Tom Bass dreamt up a series of brass niches with a playful trickle in each, but the bad boys of *Oz Magazine*, an undergraduate gazette edited by Richard Walsh, Richard Neville and painter Martin Sharp, saw scope for a spoof. A front cover in the same year showed three men lining up and piddling into the artwork. In 1964, when *Oz* faced several obscenity writs in the Sydney courts, it was the Bass blasphemy that swung the judge. Fearing the prank would provoke an epidemic of urination on the streets, His Honour sentenced Walsh and Neville to six months' hard labour and Sharp to four. Though a public ground swell led to a successful appeal. **[Cnr Hunter and Castlereagh Sts]**

## WHIPPING UP A FRENZY
**TARRALEAH, Tas.**   The old hydro-electric power station is now a cafe-cum-chalet familiar to a multitude of fly fishermen. There was outrage in 2002, however, when the previous tenants (who included Leah, a popular dominatrix from the mainland) hosted a bondage festival here.

They constructed a public discipline cage over the valley's abyss, and hydro-electricity was used to power cattle prods and other behavioural devices. Pilgrims came in chains and trans-gender ensembles. Bad debts and irate puritans saw the hosts vanish before the year was out. **[Halfway between Queenstown and Hobart on the Lyell Hwy. Open daily 8a.m.–8p.m. Phone (03) 6289 1199]**

# SERENDIP

*(Being a mishmash of good fortune, blessed discoveries and accidental eurekas)*

## GOOG AND CLOG

**AUGUSTA, WA**   1930 was a good year for serendipity in Augusta. The same year uncovered two very different treasures in the space of 30 km. The egg (belonging to a Madagascan elephant bird) and the clog (a possible keepsake of the Dutch whaling ships that once frequented this stretch of coast) are on display in the local museum. **[Blackwood Ave. Open daily 10a.m.–noon and 2p.m.–4p.m. in summer and school holidays, 10a.m.–noon at other times. Entry $2/$1.50/50c. Phone (08) 9758 4500]**

## HEY, DOZER FISH

**CANOWINDRA, NSW**   A dozer driver dislodged a sandstone slab in 1955. The rock was reddish, with weird grooves on it. Some time later, a beekeeper named Bill Simpson came across the slab when travelling the road, and rang the Australian Museum in Sydney. Further digging uncovered a fantasia of fish fossils, including the remarkable *Canowindra grossi* whose lobe fins are deemed to be the precursor of the human arm. With a snake-like skull and a full-blown nasal system (allowing the creature to take air on the surface as well as underwater via gills), the fish is seen as a fascinating interloper between evolutionary epochs. The only hazard it couldn't survive was the billabong's evaporation, which happened 360 million years ago. **[Age of Fishes Museum, cnr Gaskill and Ferguson Sts. Open daily 10a.m.–4p.m. Entry $5/$3. Phone (02) 6344 1008 or visit www.ageoffishes.org. au]**

## BYO COFFEE

**CARNARVON, WA**   Digging for coal in 1903, prospectors hit on something else: a constant supply of water. There's only one catch – the flow's constant temperature is a steaming 65°C, enough to brew an

Earl Grey teabag. In the same patch as the key-shaped cauldron of Bib-bawarra Bore is the 'longest cattle trough in the southern hemisphere', though really it's more of a trench. **[About 10 km north of Carnarvon, signposted off Robinson Rd]**

## BUSH TELEGRAPH

COFFS HARBOUR, NSW   A bloke called Dumpy Stride (seriously) was out chopping firewood near Timmsvale, west of town, when he noticed a flash of white in the red timber. To his surprise an old ceramic insulator and its 1927 telegraph wire had been secretly engulfed by the tree. Some 50 years of growth had swallowed the hardware entirely, just waiting for Dumpy's axe in 2003. **[Coffs Harbour Museum, Harbour Dve, a block east of the mall. Open Mon.–Fri. 9a.m.–4p.m., Sun. 10a.m.–4p.m. Entry $2/$1. Phone (02) 6652 5794]**

## FALSE IMPRESSIONS

COOLGARDIE, WA   Two ink bottles back in 1954 began the mania. From that day on, May and Frank Waghorn were hooked and sold their farm to become bottle nomads, prospecting for glassware all over the goldfields. They browsed in Broome, poked in the Pilbara and dug in Dingo Flats. The couple uncovered whisky jugs, perfume vials, pince-nez and vacuum bottles. But May found the ultimate treasure in 1974, when something glittery caught her eye in bushland near Boulder, the sister town of Kalgoorlie. It was a dental plate made of pure gold. As May writes, 'If only they [the teeth] could talk.' **[On display, with said bottles, at Goldfields Exhibition, 62 Bayley St. Open weekdays 9a.m.–4p.m., weekends 10a.m.–3p.m. Entry $3/$1. Phone (08) 9026 6090]**

## PLATE THEORY

FREMANTLE, WA   Dirk Hartog nailed a pewter plate to a post, record-ing his landfall at Shark Bay in 1666. Known as the earliest Euro-relic in Oz (now held in Amsterdam), the plate didn't last for long: Hartog's compatriot, De Vlamingh, visited the beach 31 years later, copied the old plate's text onto a new plate, added his own postscript and freighted the original to the Spice Isles. Enter Hamelin, a Frenchman, in 1801, who nailed the new plate onto a new pole, and left. (Confused yet?) Hamelin's compatriot De Freycinet snuck back in 1818 and swiped both plate and pole. Historians presumed the famous 'Vlamingh plate' missing, until a nosy clerk uncovered the treasure in L'Académie d'Inscriptions during World War 2. In the Armistice spirit, the French government surrendered the pewter to the Great Southern Land, sans apology, sans pole. **[Shipwreck Galleries, Western Australian Maritime Museum, end of Cliff St. Open daily 9.30a.m.–5p.m. Entry by gold coin. Phone (08) 9431 8444]**

## JAW-DROPPING DOOR-STOPPING

**HUGHENDEN, Qld**   In 1987, 14-year-old Robert Walker was wandering the plains 7 km out of town when he came across a nifty rock. One edge had a funky zigzag pattern. 'I knew what it was,' Robert later told the press. 'I figured I'd just hold onto it for safekeeping.' He gave the rock to his mum, who used it as a doorstop. Months later, when word got round, an archaeological team descended on Robert's secret spot and it transpired that Mrs Walker had been using a petrified jawbone to chock her doors. The piece belonged to Mutt, or Muttaburrasaurus, one of the largest dinosaurs to stamp the earth. **[See Mutt in the Flinders Discovery Centre on Gray St. Open daily 9a.m.–5p.m. Entry $3/$1. Phone (07) 4741 1021]**

## ANCESTRAL MOUSE

**INVERLOCH, Vic.**   Nicole Barton was a volunteer digger at Flat Rocks, a fossil site on Bass Strait. In 1997 she found a bony outline in a piece of rock and took it to archaeologist Lesley Kool, who identified it as an ancient, ancient mammal. The rock layers indicated that the creature was some 120 million years old, thrice more ancient than any other Aussie placental. It was named *Ausktribosphenos nyktos*, which loosely translates as 'very old tooth-crunching mouse cousin that spurned daylight' (though Barton claims the 'nyk' is her very own syllable). **[All inquiries to Monash Science Centre on (03) 9905 1370 or the Bunurong Environment Centre in Inverloch on (03) 5674 3738. Also in town, the Sea Shed holds fossils, and the Beach Box Cafe has Brontosaurus Burgers]**

## STRANGE WELCOME

**MOLIAGUL, Vic.**  In 1869 Cornish miner John Deason, with seven lean years behind him, was rinsing and rocking the tailings in his Bulldog Gully claim. Things were grim: already three piles had yielded nil. Legend has it that as Deason stabbed his shovel into the fourth pile he jarred his elbow on a hidden boulder which turned out to be the world's largest nugget of the day, a 66-kg godsend christened The Welcome Stranger. The wily miner and his partner, Richard Oates, sneaked the bonanza home for a knees-up – and later a break-up, as that was the only way the man-sized nugget could fit on the bank scales in Dunolly. The anvil of honour stands outside Dunolly Museum on Broadway. As for Deason's X, where the welcome treasure was buried, look for the signs on Moliagul's main drag.

## VERY SENIOR CITIZEN

**POONCARRIE, NSW**  Old, old, old people have been found beneath the crust of Lake Mungo. Mungo I, or Mungo Lady as she's known, was dug up in 1968. Carbon tests traced her back 26 000 years, making her the world's oldest cremation by 10 000 years. So imagine the geological jubilation when Mungo III came to light 30 years later (Mungo II was only fragments), his age estimated to be in the ballpark of 60 000 years. And even when DNA tests reduced that figure to 40 000 years, he was still the oldest known Australian. **[Park inquiries through www.nationalparks.nsw.gov.au]**

## I LIKE IKEY

**RICHMOND, Tas.**  Bryce Courtenay missed his plane home in 1976. Footloose in Hobart, the novelist took a drive to Richmond to see the oldest existing convict jail in Oz. The name of one inmate – Ikey Solomon – caught his eye, for Solomon was the maiden name of Bryce's wife. He did some exploring and while the prisoner was no relation the research paid dividends. Ikey Solomon, the inspiration for Dickens' Fagin, also became Courtenay's inspiration and the rogue starred as chief character in Courtenay's *The Potato Factory*. **[Cnr Bathurst and Forth Sts. Open daily 9a.m.–5p.m. Entry $5.50/$4.50/$2.50, family $14. Phone (03) 6260 2127]**

# SHOPS

*(Being a mall of eccentric emporiums, bizarre bazaars and devious depots)*

## EXTRAORDINARY APOTHECARY

**BOULDER, WA**   Grumpy local pharmacist Norman Lee was legendary in the Dirty Acre – the squalid end of Kalgoorlie. In tribute, much of his original stock occupies one half of the modern Boulder Pharmacy. In the new sector, you have 30+ block-out cream; in the old, Kwiktan Sun Oil. Wander the historical side and you'll come across Infant's Corrective Cordial, rat paste, Doctor Hope's Catarrh Linctus, and carbolic tooth powder. Goanna oil and Fisherman's Friend seem to be the only two products to have lasted the distance. While the Pharmacy Museum down the track at Coolgardie has more artefacts, the mixing of old with new makes Boulder bolder. **[46 Burt St. Open weekdays 8.50a.m.–5.30p.m., Sat. till 12.30p.m. Free entry]**

## CHAIRMAN MEOW

**PADDINGTON, BRISBANE, Qld**   Charlie was described as a natural diplomat with a strong commitment to the community. He came out of retirement in 2004 to run for state parliament, contesting the urban seat of Upper Latrobe, only to be beaten by a human. You see, Charlie is a cat. His personal spin doctor, a woman named Katina, owns Pussies Galore, a knick-knack shop for all things feline. The open-fronted weatherboard building holds cat lamps, cat paperweights, cat figurines and anything else in the catalogue. You can also buy incense for sex kittens, or cat's ears like the pair Katina wore outside the polling booth. Come the big day, the campaign manager was forced to quash rumours of Charlie's promiscuity (he's neutered), his links to vice (sure, he lives in a cathouse) and the smuggling allegations at Brisbane Airport (since when can you trust a sniffer dog – or *any* dog?). **[139A Latrobe Tce. Open Wed.–Sun. 10a.m.–5p.m. Phone (07) 3217 6758]**

In **Charters Towers (Qld)** you can walk down Bow St, behind the tyre shop, to see a giant vault painted in Beaurepaire blue. The vault once belonged to E.D. Miles, a wealthy mine-owner who kept his hoards safe in one of the largest safes in town. Now Aaron and his mates keep the radials here under lock and key. 'Haven't lost a tyre yet,' they claim.

## AERIAL RELIC

**GAYNDAH, Qld**    This southeastern settlement has the tag-line 'Oldest Town in Queensland'. (The key word here is 'town', so disqualifying cities such as Brisbane and Ipswich.) Mind you, 1849 is pretty ancient in colonial terms. But more to the point, Mellors Drapery and Haberdashery on the main drag testifies to Gayndah's grander days, with yesteryear decor below a cash-dispensing flying fox – one of the few functioning models left in Australia.

## FIRST EDITION

**HOBART, Tas.**    Australia's oldest pharmacy moved digs in 1841, to be replaced (after a lolly shop had come and gone) by Australia's oldest bookstore. Birchalls opened its doors in 1844 and still purveys paperbacks today. Penny-dreadfuls may cost a little more, but the proprietors remain devoted to 'books, stationery and fancy goods arriving by every vessel'. Birchalls also had the distinction of selling the first batch of ballpoint pens on our continent (each cost £25 and came with a five-year guarantee). Look for the Georgian windows – and the latest Harry Potter countdown – at 147 Bathurst St. **[Phone (03) 6234 2122 or visit www.birchalls.com.au]**

## SHELF LIFE

**MARYBOROUGH, Qld**    Bengal curry powder circa 1890. Hang Mee tea from Canton, 1885. Super Rinso Soap Flakes, fourpence off. Just three of the items on George Geraghty's inventory, not that George was quite so organised when it came to itemising merchandise. George ran the shop until his 88th birthday in 1972, a year after the shop's centenary. The shelves still groan with original stock, from quinine wine (popular with the Sisters of Mercy) to 1940s Quik. Out the back is one of few known 'riding saws' in the world, a Cincinnati contraption that proved too flimsy for Aussie ironbark. Curator Ken Brooks grew up next-door and now finds himself the emporium's latest acquisition. **[Brennan and Geraghty Store, 64 Lennox St. Open daily 10a.m.–3p.m. (closed mid-Feb.). Entry $5/$3.50/$2. Phone (07) 4121 2250 or visit www.nationaltrustqld.org]**

Americans call them Mom-and-Pop-stores, those humble family affairs down the end of the street. In **Armidale (NSW)** you have the next best thing: Nana and Pop's West End Niagara Store, complete with a portrait of the wholesome owners, and on the wall a pledge to 'sharpen the senses' and 'sweeten the tooth'. You'll find the place near the corner of Niagara and Dumaresq Sts.

## BOB DE NO-WHEELS

**SARINA, Qld**   Much like a caravan with two open wings, the Sarina pie cart was the first so-called restaurant in town. It plied the streets during the 1930s depression until being parked at the Central St railway crossing. The pie business flourished, the cart becoming a spiritual home for the wayfarer, the rail ganger and the sugar worker. Now it has plywood cladding and permanent benches. Recently a few civic fathers tried to abolish the 'eyesore', but a petition guaranteed the future of Skip's Sunset Kebab. Food is still cooked on a wood-stove in what must be the world's narrowest diner. **[Open weekdays 4a.m.–6p.m., Sat. 4a.m.–10a.m.]**

## RED SPOT SPECIAL

**WILMOT, Tas.**   As a young man, George J. Coles had big dreams. Standing behind his blackwood counter in Wilmot, George imagined bright aisles, deli sections, express lanes, multi-storey car parks and trolleys with recalcitrant wheels. Visit the Original Coles Store, with the same blackwood counter in place, and you'll see how far the Coles–Myer empire has come. G.J. ran the place from 1910 to 1925. Many relics remain, from mohair buttons to pumice soap, along with your modern 2-Minute Noodles. **[Coles fanatics can even stay next-door in G.J.'s own estate, Cradle Manor. Phone (03) 6492 1156, or just drop by for a bag of mixed lollies]**

> Dannae Thorp and her cat, Levi, run Spellbox in central **Melbourne (Vic.)**, a shop that caters to the state's witches. Tarot, palm and psychic readings can be booked upstairs. Arrayed in the shop's main 'cauldron' is a range of wands, talismans and arcane incenses. **[Shop 17, Royal Arcade, off Bourke St Mall. Open daily. Phone (03) 9639 7077]**

## ANTIQUE UNIVERSE

**YASS, NSW**   The town's indoor cricket centre is no more. Nor is Comur St Arcade, for that matter. Both properties have been monstered by Ross's Relics, a 20-room extravaganza that stocks anything from Toby jugs to wicker whatnots. Even Sugar's Coffee Lounge has been swallowed by Ross Lyall's trash-'n'-treasure, though the hamburger prices are still chalked on the blackboard. **[Comur St. Open daily 9a.m.–5p.m. Phone (02) 6226 4900]**

## FRATERNAL LIFE

**YORK, WA**   So who are those two wizened farmers pictured in the Happy Valley Chinese Restaurant? The taller is Lee Lee Chung (or Elder Brother), and the other is Lee Wan (Younger Brother). The two came to York in 1901 and left in 1975, aged 102 and 95 respectively. According to Sister York, a suitably named nurse who visited the market-gardening pair, the brothers' secret to longevity was snake-water and Australian beer. You can find more yarns – and homemade rakes – in the Residency Museum on the other side of the river.

## SMUTT

**YOUNG, NSW**   Travel veteran Bill Bryson 'discovered' this mixed business in his book, *Down Under* (known offshore as *Walkabout*). He classified the place as a pet-and-porno emporium, but the plot thickens if you browse the window. Herrett's Bookshop and Aquarium offers chew toys, fright wigs, live worms, Big Tits, pebble mix, a second-hand *Pet Sematary* and a sealed copy of *Amputee Fetish* magazine. Only a few items – such a patent leather extend-o-leash – could meet both of Bryson's classifications at once. **[213 Boorowa St. Open weekdays 9.30a.m.– 1p.m. and 2.15p.m.–5.30p.m., plus Sat. mornings]**

# ODDITIONS

◎ Don't expect service with a smile at The Grumpy Baker in **Humpty Doo (NT)**.

◎ Central Second Hand Shop on Todd St in **Alice Springs (NT)** is just across from the hospital. Look for the big red hand jutting from the yard, with a second hand waving from its pointer.

◎ Hair salons have a long tradition of hairy puns. But one that really cuts it is the salon occupying a National Trust stable in **Uralla (NSW)**. Its name? Clipperty Crop. The groan can be had on Salisbury St, at the southern end of town.

◎ Toto's on Lygon St in the **Melbourne (Vic.)** suburb of Carlton was the first pizzeria in Australia. Twirling the inaugural dough in 1966 was Signor Salvatore Della Bruna. Almost 40 years on, you can still get a hearty Hawaiian there. **[Phone (03) 9347 1630]**

# SIGNS

*(Being a set of signals both salient and silly,
with a few spectacular ones thrown in)*

## CARRY ON BARGING

**CORINNA, Tas.**   The only way across the Pieman River in the state's wild west is aboard a flat-topped ferry called the Fatman. The official-seeming sign on the riverbank includes the following five-step plan, under the heading, 'How To Get On Barge':

1   Drive up and down Car Park looking for bridge.
2   Park at Information Centre.
3   Then park in Car Park.
4   Drive to Kiosk and ask is Barge Operator still in bed, or how you get across on Barge if there is no Operator?
5   The Quickest and Easiest way is when you are ready, Park on road at STOP SIGN and a Barge Operator will come.

## GLOBAL VILLAGE

**DIMBOOLA, Vic.**   Honolulu is 8983 km from Dimboola, while the North Pole is some 14 033 km away. Meanwhile, Casablanca puts a country mile in the shade. You too can impress your friends with your mileage trivia just by standing under the International Sign Project outside the post office. There's a total of 48 destinations pinned to a tall pole. Originally there were 50, but Destination 49, the South Pole, got mangled and Destination 50 is a mystery.

## VINDALOONY

**HOBART, Tas.**   Horace Watson was an advertiser before his time. Heir to the Keen's Curry Powder fortunes (and formula), Horace purchased a parcel of land on the slopes of Mt Wellington in 1905 and arranged a few hundred white stones. Their message, KEENS CURRY, has occasionally been distorted by overnight manipulators into HELLS CURSE and NO CABLE CAR – the last a lobby against a mooted funicular for the mountain. **[A short drive up Davey St – or Keen's Curry Hill – until the Antill St junction. Look to your right]**

At Etty Bay and Ella Bay, two idyllic inlets close to **Innisfail (Qld)**, you can find one of the rarest wildlife signs – a cassowary silhouette. Snoop around for long enough and you may see the three-D version. Though it may pay to read the other roadside message: 'Cassowaries can be aggressive. Do not feed or approach a cassowary.'

'Long Range Weather Forecast', says the sign at the BP station in **Roebourne (WA)**, which lies in the Pilbara iron-ore belt. 'Hot', 'Hotter' and 'Damned Hot' are the variations. Below is a line reading 'Last Rain', with an empty box to chalk in the latest drought-buster. The final line offers 'Last Snow – The Ice Age'.

## YOU BEAUT ROUTE

MARLA, SA    Marla, an overgrown roadhouse, stands at the western tip of the Oodnadatta Track, a famous desert road of some 850 dust-inhaling kilometres. Only the hardy or heroic take this route, though a billboard in Marla is trying to change all that. Erected by the Oodnadatta Progress Association ('Fair dinkum', admits the sign), the tin panels are a hand-painted manifesto listing the track's many virtues – and the miserable 'colonial attitude' of the state government in allegedly isolating the outpost. Best check out the handiwork before the government gets wind of the polemic and dismantles it. **[Marla lies between Coober Pedy and the Territory border]**

Never mind the misspelling, the warning at the deep end of the Fitzroy Pool in **Melbourne (Vic.)** is here to stay. Heritage Victoria plans to register the Italian message, 'Aqua profunda', as an expression of the city's ethnic diversity (though in Italian 'water' is actually *acqua*). The sign was also a key motif of the 1982 film *Monkey Grip.* [Cnr Alexander Pde and Young St. Open weekdays 6a.m.–8p.m., weekends 8a.m.–6p.m. Phone (03) 9417 6493]

## ROADS TO ENLIGHTENMENT

**SHEFFIELD, Tas.**   The Garden of Eden is 10 miles beyond Paradise, according to the signpost outside the Sheffield tourist office. While No Where Else is a day's walk from Promised Land. Sheffield marks the start of the Tas. 'bible belt', from the Jordan River to the Walls of Jerusalem National Park. But this signpost presents your best wacky photo opportunity. Though pilgrims are advised to leave the figleaf at home – the promised locations are all fleabites.

# ODDITIONS

- Don't blame the *fascinating* people of **West Wyalong (NSW)**. They can't help the surnames of their founding family. As the sign on the highway reads, 'You are now entering the Shire of Bland'.
- The twin doors in the Macleay River Museum in **Kempsey (NSW)** seem to hail from a lost world with an unfamiliar language. The ancient-looking hieroglyphs are actually cattle brands that black-smith Ernie Colling tested out on his decor.
- Taken out of context, a parking sign in **Byron Bay (NSW)** may raise the odd eyebrow: '15 minutes, nose in 7 days'.
- In 1941 the scouts of **Casterton (Vic.)**, carved a fleur-de-lys below Mickle Lookout, a hill adjoining the town. Initially flaming rags were used to highlight the logo, but after numerous total-fire-ban days the civic fathers plumped for electricity.

# SOLIDARITY

*(Being an assembly of unified fronts, tribal action
and mass undertakings)*

## ROLL OUT THE BARRELS

ALBION, BRISBANE, Qld   In 1977, when XXXX beer changed its wooden kegs to stainless steel, the locals at the Breakfast Creek Hotel launched a campaign to return to good old wood and the brewery actually listened. Exhibit A is the photo of Paddy Fitzgerald that appears in the front bar – the Very Merry Face on the Castlemaine label – sharing a drink with the publican, showing that all was forgiven. Exhibit B is the daily ritual of 'throwing up wood', where staff spike the wooden barrels at noon and 5p.m., a traditional pub chore now unique in this metallic world. Just don't overdo the sampling, or you'll be a candidate for the less honoured throwing-up ceremony. **[Kingsford Smith Dve. Phone (07) 3262 5988]**

Hats off to the Seventh Day Adventists of **Manjimup (WA)**. In 1906, a group of devoted parishioners built their own road to convey the faithful to Sabbath services, as many lived on farms scattered about Fonty's Pool and other pockets. Seven Day Rd, as it's known, reaches the main highway 2 km south of town.

## GETTING THE MESSAGE ACROSS

GENOA, Vic.   It's hard to think of another municipal plaque in Oz that salutes the local population for 'opposing bureaucracy'. Such is the message inscribed at the head of Genoa's old trestle bridge. No longer used for cars (or wagons), the bridge has become a quaint promenade complete with period lamps and a park bench. Officialdom tried to scrap the structure when the highway was re-routed 60 m further south, but loyal locals kicked up a stink. The decking was restored in 1997, though the derelict service station on the Melbourne side remains a communal tractor garage. **[Turn left just before the new bridge, heading towards Eden]**

> **Texas (Qld)** went on a communal diet in 2002, obliging the local hamburger joint to serve up a few healthier choices and the butcher to trade his T-bones for heart-smart cutlets. Walking tracks were also installed. Pop in and see if the anti-fat infatuation still carries weight.

## NO NAMES, NO DRILL

**KALGOORLIE, WA**    Back in the early 1990s, several trucking companies tried pressuring the state government to build a bypass linking the Kambalda goldfields to the Great Eastern Hwy. As things stood, road trains were hauling the ore through the suburbs, complete with dust, noise and kerb-riding. Not popular. But the government wasn't convinced it was a priority issue, so a gang of miners-cum-road-builders attacked the problem in one frenetic weekend, lopping trees, grading earth, laying stones and paving a road in less than 72 hours. Thus Anzac Dve was born, eventually being acknowledged by the government with shrugs – and signposts. **[Opposite the WesTrac CAT compound heading out to Perth]**

## HEDGE FUND

**RAILTON, Tas.**    Neil Hurley started the fad, fashioning a farmer and his horse outside the craft shop. Since then topiary has taken over this town in the state's north, with more than 32 creations in some 21 locations, and all growing – slowly. That's the catch. Don't expect a privet paradise just yet. A green nurse near the RSL monument looks almost human, though her three servicemen companions still resemble wire cages. But watch this space. Rare is the town that sets about growing topiary in unison. In encouraging maturity are the plump green cows above the butcher's shop.

In **Wellington (NSW)**, 400 residents aspired to lose a tonne between them inside 12 weeks during 2003. Weekly weigh-ins kept the participants honest. And shazam, the Wellingtonne Challenge caused 1000 kg of humanity to disappear. The challenge's shelf life is reflected in signs and the available food choices, not just in the population's midriffs.

## PUBLIC BAR

RENMARK, SA    When the God-fearing Chaffey brothers gouged irrigation channels into the red mud hereabouts, they hoped the place would stay dry, alcoholically speaking. But the local farmers thought otherwise. In 1897, as new orchards spread across the plain, they combined to open the British Empire's first community hotel, where the work and the profits were shared by all. The pub flourished, gaining two storeys in a jiffy and later a spotter's tower (after the bombing of Darwin in World War 2). Sip by sip, monies raised from the venture went to bankroll the district hospital, parks, gardens and football clubs. This is also the pub where Breaker Morant rode his steed through the main saloon – exactly the kind of horseplay that the pious Chaffeys were trying to avoid. **[Renmark Hotel, Murray Ave. Phone (08) 8586 6755]**

## CALL WAITING

UBOBO, Qld    The phone stands outside the general store, which in itself is worthy of celebration. Halfway through 1999, Telstra attempted to remove the booth in the interests of shareholder return, but Ubobo said no. The entire population of 40 joined forces with local National Party member Paul Neville to face the Goliath down. The nearest alternative phone, they argued, was along 17 km of flood-prone dirt. After they threatened switching to Optus and found a voice on *Australia All Over*, the ABC's weekly national soapbox, the phonebox won a reprieve. So next time you're in Ubobo, be sure to ask for some change at the store. **[South of Gladstone along the Boyne River]**

Sleeves rolled, 120 volunteers set about building a church in 1913. The fruit of their labours was the Church of Christ on 8 Ivanhoe St in Bassendean, **Perth (WA)** – which went up in a single day. Lord knows what the faithful could have achieved with a few nail guns.

## SEEING IS BELIEVING

**WOOLGOOLGA, NSW**   If you fail to see the Guru Nanak Sikh Temple at the southern end of town, I suggest you see your local optometrist. The same applies to the Raj Mahal restaurant, all minarets and elephants, on the Grafton side of the hill. The first Sikhs arrived here in the 1940s, to work on banana farms. Hundreds more followed, and now the streets iridesce with saris as well as lorikeets. At Planet Fruit & Veg you can get very cheap bananas and a free copy of *Indian Link* newspaper. At the RSL Club, Sikhs are the only patrons permitted to persist with headwear, after years of bureaucratic argy-bargy.

# STATIONS

*(Being a succession of rare ranches and rarer railway platforms)*

## OLD FLAMES

**ADELAIDE, SA**   How would you feel, waking up in the wee hours and finding a fire engine at the foot of your bed? With luck, a few heartbeats would make you remember that you're staying at the Fire Station Inn, a luxury guesthouse that occupies an early-20th-century fire station. Rodney and Regina Twiss did the makeover in 1998, filling the smokies' space behind the classic bi-fold doors with helmets, extinguishers and brass-buttoned oilskins. The station began life in 1904, seeing the worst of the Adelaide Hills infernos and countless domestic call-outs. As you'd expect, access from the Penthouse to the Fire Engine Suite is via a brass pole. **[Tynte Rd, North Adelaide. For bookings, phone (08) 8272 1355 or check out www.adelaideheritage.com]**

## WINE ON LINE

**AUBURN, SA**   Eighty years separate the opening of the railway station in Auburn and its refit in 1998. In keeping with the Federation colour scheme, architects for Mt Horrocks Wines have turned the old waiting-room into a dining-room. The ticketing office is now the tasting room for the dry riesling and cabernet merlot. A brass plate decreeing 'Do Not Spit From Car, £20' stands above the tippler's spittoon. **[Open weekends and public holidays 10a.m.–5p.m. Phone (08) 8849 2243]**

**Yass (NSW)** boasts the smallest railway platform in Oz, not counting sidings. Even if the museum is shut, you can still see the platform from the carpark. **[Cnr Lead and Craigs Sts, off Comur St. Open weekends 10a.m.–4p.m. Phone (02) 6226 2169]**

## NEW LINE OF BUSINESS

**BYRON BAY, NSW**   'Drinking Intoxicating Liquor on this Station Is Prohibited', reads a sign. Pure chutzpah when you consider that the adjoining refreshment room is a pub, known as the Railway Friendly Bar, or simply The Rails. There's live music in the forecourt at night, and fishing-club raffles on Fridays. While the innkeeper's motto was 'Why get off at Redfern when you can go all the way at Byron Bay?', in fact trains don't stop here any more. Across from the pub is the stationmaster's house, now the tourist information centre. **[Off Jonson St. Open daily. Phone (02) 6685 7662]**

## PUMP ACTION

**CHILTERN, Vic.**   If a Red Sentry from Fort Wayne, Indiana, means nix to you, then chances are you know nothing about the history of petrol pumps. The fact is, the Red Sentry of 1911 was one of the original bowsers made by S.F. Bowser & Co., who entrusted their surname to the language. You can meet the Red Sentry and friends in Australia's biggest gas-pump collection – behind the only petrol station in Chiltern. **[Phone (03) 5726 1236]**

## OUTPOST

**COOBER PEDY, SA**   Anna Creek is the world's largest cattle station. At 34 000 square kilometres, it's roughly the size of Belgium or half the size of Tasmania. You can visit the fiefdom as part of the unique mail run operating out of Coober Pedy. The same route entails the world's longest fence, the island's pinkest roadhouse (in Oodnadatta), the majestic Algebuckina Bridge, and Australia's first solar phonebox. **[Inquiries on 1800 069 911 or via www.mailruntour.com]**

## STATION SERVICE

**GLENBROOK, NSW**   For 65 years a sandstone cottage was enveloped by a petrol station on the Great Western Hwy. All you could see was a heritage chimney poking from the outhouse. The cottage was built in the 1870s to house a pointsman and his family attached to the Lapstone Zig Zag Railway. But progress and petroleum went and smothered the address until 1995, when the service station was demolished – delicately – by Ampol in cahoots with the National Trust. At present the cottage, a dozen paces from the diesel pump, remains a useful storage room for the ShopStop drinks range. **[Off the Great Western Hwy]**

## TRAIN FOREST

**LAVER'S HILL, Vic.**   Crowe's Buffer Stop is a railway station drowned in bush. Cornelius Crowe owned the land where the state extended a narrow-gauge timber railway that trundled through Beech Forest. The line prospered during the early 1900s, carrying timber to Colac, but lately nature has resumed control. Hidden among the regenerated trees are engine sidings, sheds and inspection pits. To reach the end of the line, hike for a few hundred metres along the old highway that the Great Ocean Rd supplanted. 'Stop Look Listen' reads the sign, and the advice holds good a century down the track. **[Look for the Melba Gully turnoff west of town. Melba Gully boasts the world's biggest Otway messmate stringybark – perhaps the one that got away]**

## TAX HAVEN

**SERVICETON, Vic.**   The low-key wheat town of Serviceton leapt in importance when the railway arrived in 1886. This being before Federation, duties were still collected at border crossings, though hereabouts the exact location of the border was in doubt, as early surveying pegs had somehow missed the meridian by a few miles. Consequently the station and its customs office sat in the middle of a 4.5-km belt of disputed territory, a gilt-edged enticement for smugglers and corrupt officials alike. Every crate of passing freight was literally a borderline case, attracting tax or gaining exemption as whim decreed. (In frontier fashion, the station once fulfilled the role of pub, lockup and morgue!) It took another 27 years until a precise line was drawn, affirming the platform as Victorian. **[Elizabeth St, off the highway west of Kaniva]**

## HOST TRAINS

**SYDNEY, NSW**   Below Central Station is a honeycomb of 'parcel tunnels' along which a swarm of workers once ferried food, freight, trash, mail and coffins. Coffins? Attached to the 27 platforms is the Mortuary

Station, no longer in use though the branch line still leads to Rookwood Cemetery in Sydney's inner west. (You can see the ultimate terminus on the corner of Kensington and Regent Sts.) Platform 1 is reserved exclusively for (live) VIPs, the place where governors alighted and General Macarthur disembarked during wartime. Platforms 26 and 27 were built in anticipation of the eastern suburbs lline, which never reached so far downtown. To be honest, Platform 9¾ is about the only mystery omitted from the monthly tours run until recently by the Australian Railway Historical Society. **[Tours currently suspended. For up-to-date information, phone (02) 9749 5280 or visit www.arhsnsw.com.au]**

In **Bruce (SA)**, the stationmaster's residence attached to the defunct station has been converted into bed-and-breakfast accommodation. At least, the bed part of the equation is in the residence, while the cooked breakfast awaits you in the waiting room. **[Phone (08) 8648 6344]**

## GENERAL HEARSAY

**TEROWIE, SA**  General Douglas Macarthur was the Supreme Commander of the Allied Forces in the Southwest Pacific during World War 2, but on 20 March 1942 he was momentarily stranded in Terowie. The cause of the delay was a switch in rail gauges, and hundreds flocked the platform. Asked about his exit from battle and the infamous death camps in the Philippines, the general pledged, 'I came out of Bataan and I shall return.' He kept his word, returning within two years to Manila, though never once popping back to Terowie. **[A plaque salutes the occasion on Terowie's derelict station]**

## TWO SIDES TO THE STORY

**WALLANGARRA, Qld**  Seriously, what's 30-odd centimetres between friends? Let me rephrase that. Before Federation, when states were colonies, Qld was among several colonies that made a railway with a 1066-mm gauge. Down south, the Cockroach Colony (aka NSW) opted for the wider 'standard' (1435 mm) gauge. At Wallangarra, in

1887, the fettlers realised their folly and the station became known as the Interchange, where the unmatched lines terminated and every last person and chattel crossed the platform. In true parochial style, the neighbours couldn't even see eye to eye on architecture, with the Qld side of the station having a bull-nosed roof while NSW plumped for the skillion look.

## EGG CURRY
**WARWICK, Qld**    On a barnstorming tour of the provinces in 1917, PM Billy Hughes spent 13 minutes on Warwick railway station. He stood on a podium and tried to give conscription a feel-good spin. Nothing doing. The Celtic crowd was hostile – an egg was thrown, dislodging Billy's hat. A melee ensued, during which the PM suffered a nosebleed. He tried to resume his propaganda, but a heckler called Brosnan continued to make trouble. 'Arrest that man,' Hughes ordered the local policeman. But Senior Sergeant Kenny, an Irishman, sided with the mob. He urged the dignitary to carry on. Hughes left at 3.12p.m., two minutes late and steaming. The ugliest 13 minutes of his tenure, known as the Warwick Egg Incident, led to the founding of our federal police force, who jump when the boss says jump. **[A sign stands at the station on Lyons Rd]**

## SECOND DRAFT
**WATHEROO, WA**    Watheroo was once a booming railway town. Its elegant station, built in 1891, was a mid-west hub until the passenger service was given the sword 40 years ago. But Watheroo people are quick to adapt. The community took out a lease from the state railways and they've converted the station into a pub. If your beer starts shivering, it's doubtless just a goods train passing by.

# SURREAL ESTATE

*(Being a precinct of mind-blowing buildings
and unique edifices)*

## WOW WANG TEMPLE

**ATHERTON, Qld**   The Hou Wang Temple is the only Chinese temple in Australia built of corrugated iron. Inside are beams of cedar and black bean. Note the high thresholds to keep out the dragon's breath (or table-land mist) that the Chinese believed carried impish spirits. Unfortunately, vandals (and Cyclone Agnes in 1956) fleeced many of the ceremonial banners, though the rustic feng shui is wholly intact. Symbols on the walls are such a rich mix of Taoist and Buddhist that you might describe the leading denomination in this corner of the world as Confusionism. **[86 Herberton Rd. Open daily 10a.m.–4p.m. Entry $7/$5.50/$2, family $16. Phone (07) 4091 6945 or visit www.houwang.org.au]**

## PHARAOH'S GARDEN

**BALLARAT, Vic.**   Origami turned to glass. That's one description of the Robert Clark Conservatory, designed by architect Peter Elliott. The zigzag glasshouse, with six angular folds on each flank, stands 13 m high in the Botanical Gardens. Inbuilt computers regulate sunlight. Automatic misters moisten the seasonal flower shows. And Robert Clark, the newspaper editor who provided the seed funding, squints in statue form near the door. Westward stand more busts – in the chrono-logical Avenue of Australian Prime Ministers. **[Open daily 9a.m.–5p.m. Entry $3/$2/50c – or free between 24 May and 10 October]**

## A TIP FROM THE TIP

**BAMAGA, Qld**   I've given you the answer before the riddle, but where in Australia can you find stilt houses made from bamboo and banana leaves? Amazingly, the history of Bamaga's residents is even stranger than that of their homes. In 1947, with dwindling fresh water and rising briny, the people of the Saibai Islands (off Papua) were on borrowed time. Chief Bamaga Ginau hatched a plan, leading his people onto

Cape York, first to Muttee Head and then further inland. Aside from its high-rise huts and underground ovens, Bamaga is also distinct for standing on DOGIT land (Deed of Grant in Trust), a unique arrangement under the Torres Strait Act of 1984. It's also our mainland's northern-most town. Frank Jardine, a cattle baron with grand airs, hoped Bamaga (which he knew as Somerset, back in 1863) would grow into Singapore II. Guess what? It never did. **[4WD, and flights from Cairns, are your only ways of reaching Bamaga. Passports not required]**

## SHEAR MAJESTY

**GOSTWYCK, NSW**   Debate surrounds the identity of the woolshed's architect, though nobody argues the building's uniqueness. The likely culprit is John Horbury Hunt, an eccentric Canadian architect who happened to be working up the road in 1872, designing St Peter's Cathedral in Armidale. Hunt lived in Watsons Bay with his bride and a house full of dogs and birds. The woolshed is a three-tiered pagoda, with glass strips (clerestories) dividing each level. Picture a giant beach umbrella standing in a sheep paddock, and there you have Deeargee, the local name for the octagonal wonder. **[On the northern bank of Munsie Bridge, 11 km from Uralla]**

> The Bottle House in **Lightning Ridge (NSW)** is built from mud and long-necked beer bottles, and even boasts a bottle-built kennel. There are frequent tours, with no need to BYO. Mining relics is also preserved among the glassware. **[60 Opal St. Phone (02) 6829 0618]**

## SPECTACULAR SPECIFICS

**HALLS GAP, Vic.**   In front of me I have the building specifications of the Brambuk Aboriginal Cultural Centre, and they do little to suggest the building's marvel. (Sample: 'Ridge beam supports one end of the series of inclined 360 mm x 63 mm LVL rafters . . .') Maybe if I tell you that in the language of local Aborigines *brambuk* means 'white cockatoo'? The bird was clearly foremost in architect Greg Burgess's mind, the building having wings resembling those of a cockatoo in flight. A ramp within, coiling around the axis of a vast stone chimney, evokes the Dreamtime serpent. Earth levees encircling the building suggest Aboriginal ceremony. **[Grampians Rd, south of town. Open daily 9a.m.–5p.m. Free admission. Phone (03) 5356 4452]**

## IT CAME FROM THE SWAMP

**JABIRU, NT**   The hotel's outline is monstrous, no question. In fact, the entire building suggests a crocodile. From snout to tail it measures 250 m, with 110 rooms in its gullet. A closer look reveals the eye-like air vent that glows red at night, and parking bays that mimic the monster's eggs. Ginga, the giant crocodile of the Gagudju people, also brags a billabong foyer, a swimming-pool heart, fire-escape claws and weed-green Colorbond scales. **[1 Flinders St. Freecall 1300 666 747 or phone (08) 8979 9000. The courageous might try www.gagudju-crocodile.holiday-inn.com]**

## DESERT HIGH-RISE

**LITCHFIELD PARK, NT**   Termite mounds – from humble to humungous – dominate Australia's Top End. Cathedral termites, which specialise in 'molten candle' nests, are the rifer species. Rarer are the magnetic termites, whose work is on show near the main entry to Litchfield Park, coming from Batchelor. Their nests resemble parallel headstones. Information boards explain this ant's brilliance – how each nest aligns along the north-south axis, though varying by crucial degrees depending on shade and wind. Handy to know if you're wandering the savannah without a line of breadcrumbs.

You have two chances of seeing a semicircular shearing shed – in Australia or in Argentina. Unless you have the pampas in your sights, I suggest you go to **Isisford (Qld)**. The crescent wonder on Isis Downs 20 km east of town was prefabricated in London by the team responsible for the Sydney Harbour Bridge struts. The shed was shipped in pieces, hauled inland, and erected in 1913.

## MONASTIC CELLS

**NEW NORCIA, WA**    The Spanish monks who arrived on the Victoria Plains knew a thing or two about civic planning. A central axis runs east–west through the town, occupied by the faith's key locations: a hilltop shrine, a cemetery, a church, a monastery…and the eight-sided bee-house. Bishop Salvado released the first bees in the 1870s and the swarms soon repaid the community. Monks would wear nuns' veils when harvesting the honey, until floods wiped out the enterprise in 1967. Nowadays you'll find more flies than bees here, but the restored building remains a monkish icon. **[Follow the river walk to the paddock behind the monastery]**

## JUMBO JETTY

**POINT SAMSON, WA**    You can't walk on the tallest jetty in the southern hemisphere, let alone drop a fishing line. But you can drive to the end of Meares Dve, from where a football-stadiumful of iron ore is tipped into ships bound for Asia and Europe every half-hour. Cape Lambert is owned by Robe River Iron Associates. **[Inquire at the tourist bureau in nearby Roebourne or phone Robe Visitors Centre on (08) 9182 1060]**

The Big Camera is a focal point of **Meckering (WA)**. Electronics whiz and veteran photographer Chic Wadley turned a derelict service station into a camera museum, with lens as front door and flashcube as mock-chimney. **[11 Dreyer St. Phone (08) 9625 1335 or check out www.thebigcamera.com.au]**

## HOBBIT FORMING

**RAVENSHOE, Qld**    Altogether Now was a shop selling crystals, incense and tarot decks. Customers kept asking about houses, spare rooms, and studio spaces in the area, and the owners sensed a niche. In the mid-1990s they established a rental agency among the dream-catchers, which soon mushroomed into Middle Earth Realty, the only all-female (Jean, Jenny and Donna), good-karma Tolkienesque-surreal estate agency in the Land of Oz. **[64 Grigg St. Phone (07) 4097 6900 or visit www.merealty.com.au]**

# ODDITIONS

- ◎ Should you learn that Howard Raven is a real-estate agent in **Longreach (Qld)**, your eyebrows would scarcely arch. But when you learn that all the town's streets are named after birds, from Eagle to Ibis, the whole affair verges on cuckoo.

- ◎ The Clarence River is infamous for its devastating floods. Just take a look at the surreal UFO-like house opposite the Lawrence Tavern in **Lawrence (NSW)**. The spaceship rests on a steel cradle, with enough room underneath for bikes (and floods) to travel.

- ◎ Elephants don't live in **Mullumbimby (NSW)**, though there's an elephant house at the head of Burringbar St – or so goes its nickname. The edifice is actually the Council Chambers, built in 1996, a circular silo with elevated skylight and cog-like brickwork.

- ◎ The Forest Eco-Centre in **Scottsdale (Tas.)** is a building-within-a-building. The outer skin is of louvres and Teflon, cloaking a three-storey block inside, all in the name of energy conservation. **[96 King St. Open daily 9a.m.–5p.m. Free entry. Phone (03) 6352 6466]**

# SURVIVAL

*(Being a raft of remarkable revivals, rallying
and recuperations)*

## GENERATION GAP

**ALBANY, WA**   The Gap is part and parcel of every tourist visit to Albany, but few know the Clarke story attached to this seaside ravine. Late in 2002, father and son – Stuart and Geoff – were taking in the sights when a freak gust blew Stuart into The Gap. Down there, Mother Nature's vitamiser made his chances look slim. But son Geoff, a life-saver, ran to the edge and answered his vocation, plunging 30 m into the ocean. He managed to reach his father, who'd suffered multiple fractures and a punctured lung, and deposit him safely on a ledge to await the rescue helicopters. Both men survived. **[Frenchman Bay Rd, 20 km due south of town centre]**

## DJ SOS FOR KLM

**ALBURY, NSW**   On a wild October night in 1932, a Dutch plane called the *Uiver* ('stork') got lost near the Victorian alps. The wings of the DC-2 (an entrant in the London–Melbourne air-race) began to ice over, so the pilot, Captain Parmentier, dropped the plane below the peaks to look for level ground. Down in Albury, an alert engineer heard the struggling engines and raced to the town's substation. He used the entire grid of streetlights to signal ALBURY in Morse code. An equally alert DJ at the local ABC radio station urged citizens to grab torches, lamps and cars to illuminate the racecourse off Fallon St. Dotting and dashing the city's lights, the engineer spelt out this information, and the KLM giant landed intact. Next day, Captain Parmentier took off again and went on to score a silver medal on handicap. Sadly, only two months later, the *Uiver* crashed in Iraqi desert, killing all on board. **[A replica of the plane and a memorial are found at Albury Airport on Riverina Hwy]**

## WILD GREEN YONDER

**BEAUDESERT, Qld** 'You poor bastards,' were Bernard O'Reilly's first words when he came across the plane wreck. 'What's the score?' replied one survivor, referring to the fifth and deciding Ashes Test of 1937. The story is remarkable: seven men were aboard the plane when it plunged into untracked rainforest, 40 light planes failed to find them and the search was scrapped after six days. Three days later, O'Reilly entered the dense jungle of the Macpherson Ranges, equipped with onions, tea, a map and a pencil. Using as a compass the lichen which clings to a tree-trunk's south side, he found the wreck but only two survivors. The whole story is laid out in the museum, with fobs and fuselage from the crash, as the wreck site remains remote. P.S.: Bradman scored 165 not out, while Bernard's namesake Tiger picked up a bag of wickets. **[Beaudesert Historical Museum, cnr McKee and Brisbane Sts. Open daily 9a.m.–4p.m. Entry $3/50c. Phone (07) 5541 3740]**

## ELIZA DO PLENTY

**BOREEN POINT, Qld** With a name like *Stirling Castle*, the ship was never destined to float too well – as indeed it proved, smashing into Swain Reefs off Rockhampton in 1836. On board were Captain James Fraser and his pregnant wife, Eliza, along with 17 crew, two lambs, a cat and a parrot. Eleven humans survived, floating in two boats for six weeks (Eliza's newborn drowned at sea). Starved and mutinous, the party landed on a sandy spit we now call Fraser Island, where natives allegedly speared the captain and kidnapped Eliza. The 'alleged' side of things is owing to the story Eliza peddled (for sixpence a pop) in a Hyde Park marquee back in London, speaking of cannibalism and wise savages. Another novelised version can be read in Patrick White's masterpiece, *Fringe of Leaves*. Or you can visit an obscure monument to this weird tale, a stone tablet hiding near the Sandy Beach Sailing Club of Boreen Point. **[Just look for the sign telling boatmen to 'Lower Masts', and walk lakeward to a jetty]**

## SKIPPY WHO?

**CANBERRA, ACT** Saturday 18 January 2003 was a version of hell for Canberra residents, the day bushfires destroyed homes, schools, a space observatory and Robert de Castella's marathon medals. But six days after the blaze, rangers at the charred Tidbinbilla Nature Reserve found a sole surviving koala in the reserve's last tree. All Canberra adopted 'Lucky', who became a symbol of recovery for the entire capital, enjoying paparazzi and her own email address. **[Paddys River Rd. Open daily 9a.m.–6p.m. Free entry.** Phone (02) 6205 1233]

> When the German raider HSK *Kormoran* and the HMAS *Sydney II* crossed paths in the Indian Ocean in 1941, the outcome was cataclysmic. Not one of the 645 Australians survived. Of the 397 Germans, 317 survived the encounter, a good many squeezing into the steel lifeboat held at the Railway Station Museum in **Carnarvon (WA)**. To this day the location of both sunken ships is unknown.

## NEW DEPTHS

COOLGARDIE, WA    Candle and lunch packed for his shift, Modesto Varischetti went down the mine shaft to Level 10. Conditions were Spartan in 1907. Oxygen came from a pipe, which on this day seized up. Modesto went to check the problem, to find the main tunnel flooded and the water rising. Trapped in his own air pocket, the Italian used his drill to send distress signals to his boss on the dry Level 9 – and waited. And waited. He prayed, but not for the Devil who rose from the water on Day 3, dressed in canvas with a brass globe for a head. Inside the diving costume was Frank Hughes. Modesto was hysterical. He'd never seen a diver, or the Devil, but he took a life-line from this chirpy Lucifer and left his air pocket when enough water had been pumped clear. [Displays capture the drama at the Railway Station Museum, Woodward St. Open Sat.–Thur. 8.30a.m.–4p.m. Entry by donation. Phone (08) 9026 6001]

## EXPERIMENTAL

KUNUNURRA, WA    Hamburgers, soft beds and Mum were the things most missed by the 62 people who set up a brief utopia in the

Kimberley wilderness in 1999. The Ideal Human Experiment, or IHE, was launched by James Salerno, who called for volunteers across the age and class spectrums, hoping to further man's understanding of harmonious cohabitation – a sort of *Survivor* meets *Big Brother* before either show was invented. People lived in tents, ran a government, held awareness sessions. They paid regular visits to the Wisdom Bank to solve such teasers as dog ownership or squabbling children. The six-month trial lasted four months, the premature pull-out blamed on 'bacterial adjustment'. Salerno maintains that the early conclusion was a symptom of success. 'Most human beings,' he told a Channel 9 reporter, 'if given the right environment can solve every possible social conflict harmoniously.' **[The 'mystery site' was 70 km west of town, towards El Questro on the Gibb River Rd]**

## BABE IN ARMS

**MACKAY, Qld** Back in the 1860s, the local Lindeman people regularly attacked settlers' cattle with spears. District troopers chased some of the marauders up a mountain after one brazen raid. Kowaha, a Lindeman woman, leapt off the cliff with her baby daughter, to escape. Kowaha died, but the baby survived and stayed in the valley until her death in 1925. A statue outside The Leap Hotel commemorates Kowaha's martyrdom. **[20 km north of Mackay, along the Bruce Hwy]**

## WISE WORDS

**MOLE CREEK, Tas.** 'In other portions of this cool retreat,' wrote Andrew Garran in the *Picturesque Atlas of Australasia* in 1888, 'the fibrous traceries seem to mimic lacework . . .' The cool retreat is King Solomon's cave, in Mole Creek Karst National Park, in the state's central north. The traceries are soda straws, frail curls of limestone that survived a robust shaking in 2004, when an earthquake of force 4.7 struck the grotto during a tour. Tourists said it sounded like running water; the guide knew better, but carried on. Nobody was hurt and not a single soda straw snapped. **[Cave is about halfway between Mole Creek and Lake Rowallan. Open most days except Christmas. Tours roughly 10.30a.m.–4p.m. Entry $9/$4, family $22. Phone (03) 6363 5182]**

## ORCA-STRATION

**SEAL ROCKS, NSW**   On 12 July 1992, the lighthouse-keeper on Sugarloaf Point noticed a few out-of-season sunbakers on the beach below him. They turned out to be 49 false killer whales. A naval chopper airlifted the stranded beasts and two days later, after a massive public response, 36 were released from Boat Beach on the other side of the promontory. A plaque on the grass opposite the general store commemorates the rescue. The unsaved whales were buried in the dunes above Submarine Beach, where giant bones are still being exposed by the shifting sands.

## SILKY TERRIER

**ZEEHAN, Tas.**   The handkerchief was a gift to Jim Ryan from his bride and the miner kept it as a charm when working the North Lyell Shaft. In 1912, the shaft caught fire and some 93 men were trapped. Citizens lowered a 300-m rope down the mine, hoping for tugs of life. They pulled up Ryan's hanky instead, and then haunting handwritten notes from the miners, many of which are now preserved in the Pioneer Museum. Four days later, Ryan and 39 others saw daylight again. **[Main St. Open daily 9a.m.–5p.m. Entry $9/$8, family $20. Phone (03) 6471 6225]**

# SWEET

*(Being a chocolate-box of sugary strangeness
and luscious lunacies)*

## ACCIDENTAL IMPORTS

**ALBANY, WA**    Blind Freddy can see the *Amity* on Princess Royal Dve. It's a model of the brig that arrived in 1826, at the helm one Major Edmund Lockyer, sent from Sydney to name the virgin port Frederick's Town. Blind Freddy could, on the other hand, miss the nearby fibreglass boat lying behind the *Amity*, better known as Lifeboat 4. This glorified dinghy hails from the P&O carrier *Haythrop*. Ablaze off Africa in 1971, the *Haythrop* lost her lifeboat and presumed it lost at sea. Not so – it drifted for 10 000 kilometres over 700 days, and washed up at Albany. Its primary cargo, on view in the Eclipse Museum beside the *Amity*, was 29 jars of barley sugar, packed as survival rations. **[The boat is on permanent view. Museum open daily 10a.m.–5p.m. Entry by donation. Phone (08) 9841 4844]**

## DESERT DESSERT

**ALICE SPRINGS, NT**    The Iraqi Barhee is crunchy. The Aussie Undoolya tastes like toffee. While the Red Bungalow is as dry as toast. Taste the spectrum at the oldest date plantation in Australia. Many of the trees have been transplanted from historic camel depots to shade the patrons eating Date-vonshire Teas. **[Palm Circuit, south of town. Open Thur.–Sun. 9a.m.–6p.m. Free entry. Phone (08) 8953 7558]**

## PRESERVE THE RAGE

**HAHNDORF, SA**    This big tin shed is where the Beerenberg brand of preserves was born. Grant and Carol Paech began their sticky business in 1971, selling strawberries from a roadside stall. Now the humble shed exports jam sachets to 23 Asian countries and 300 high-star hotels. What the Paeches don't know about peaches, guava, figs and Satsuma could be written on a mini-jar label. Not just jams, the hangar brags chutneys, marinades, mustards and a wicked grapefruit marmalade. **[On the Mt Barker side of town. Open daily Oct.–May 9a.m.–4.30p.m. for picking ($2 charge for strawberries picked). Phone (08) 8388 7272]**

## MAKE TRACKS

**KAKADU, NT**    Sweet is Patsy's word for good-tasting. If the palm fruit is too green, she describes the taste as 'a little hot'. Animal Tracks is the only tour in Kakadu National Park (and one of few in Australia) where a full-blooded Arnhem Lander takes you on a gourmet safari. You have your choice of magpie goose, file snake or lily bulb. The tour also includes some up-close encounters at a buffalo farm, despite the fact that buffalos don't officially exist in the park any more. **[Day trips leave from Cooinda for $95. Phone 0429 676 194]**

## I SCREAM

**KATOOMBA, NSW**    J.J. Pannell was doing his best to make ice-cream at the Leura Falls Cafe in 1913 when 'his mind unhinged', as the inquest put it. He seized his revolver, waving the weapon in a deranged manner at Mrs Pannell, her scones and her sister, and in the end shot himself. The coroner ascribed Pannell's psychosis to a spinal injury from the past. This story, plus the *real* horror tales of Sophia Maziere, the cafe's temperamental owner during the 1970s and 1980s, plaster the kiosk walls. **[Kiosk attached to Solitary, 90 Cliff Dve, Leura Falls. Open Tues.–Sun. Phone (02) 4782 1164]**

Yappacino is a lactose-free froth-fest offered to deserving dogs by the Jells Park Teahouse in Wheelers Hill, **Melbourne (Vic.).** Epicurean canines can also enjoy spare ribs, rawhide chews and doggie kebabs, as owners opt for the humanly orthodox. **[Off Waverly Rd. Park open daily from 9a.m. Phone (03) 9561 4522 or visit www.jellsteahouse.com.au]**

## AZTEC TECHNOLOGY

**LATROBE, Tas.**    Montezuma, the former emperor of Mexico, isn't tall (five feet in the old money) but he's exceptionally sweet. Totally made of chocolate in fact, and carrying a cacao pod – much as he was when he met Cortes and unleashed its flavour on the chocoholic west. The chocolate Aztec was crafted by Heidi van Gerwen, the sister of Igor who began the sweet-toothed House of Anvers back in 1989. As well as seeing pralines being born, you can luxuriate in the adjoining cafe and garden. **[Bass Hwy. Open daily 7a.m.–5p.m. (to 6p.m. during daylight saving months). Free entry to the chocolate museum. Phone (03) 6426 2958 ]**

## ORIGINAL TO THE CORE

**RYDE, NSW**   Maria Ann Smith is better known as Granny, the cultivator of those crunchy apples found in a million lunchboxes across the world. Maria ran an orchard in the mid-19th century, in the then-rural fringes of Eastwood, Sydney. She also managed to bear 16 kids and moonlight as a midwife. If that wasn't enough, she invented an apple. Yet don't expect any fruity mention on her headstone in St Anne's Church, Ryde. You might be better off munching a Granny Smith on 9 March, the anniversary of her passing. **[Church St, between Victoria Rd and Gowrie St]**

## SWARM GREETINGS

**TANAWHA, Qld**   Only at Superbee can you see a see-through hive of Australian native bees. Unlike their Italian cousins, Aussie bees are stingless. They prefer making honey 'bubbles' instead of hexagons, and they see the world horizontally, designing their hive lengthways rather than vertically. Native bees resemble skinny flies, unlike their plump Italian cousins who dominate the airwaves like Vespas in a piazza. At Superbee you get to taste the full honey gamut from grey gum to alfalfa. In the gardens, kids can swarm the electric cars, or putt balls into fibreglass hives. **[Tanawha Tourist Dve. Open daily 9a.m.–5p.m. Entry free, though beekeeping shows on the hour from 10a.m. cost $6.50. Phone (07) 5445 3544]**

## IDEAL WITH EMU

**TANUNDA SA**   With Galliano in his blood, Fernando Martino (anglicised to Martin) had no trouble imagining quandongs as a potential liqueur. In 1985, on part of the former Seppelts Winery, he drew on a family recipe to make Quandong Mead with wild honey and secret herbs. This elixir hovers between cough mixture and ambrosia. The price per bottle, around $25, is only a little higher than its alcohol ratio. Other fruit-based variations ensued; conventional wines also available. **[Chateau Dorrien, cnr Seppeltsfield Rd and Barossa Valley Way. Open daily 10a.m.– 5p.m., or till 4.30p.m. in winter.** Phone (08) 8562 2850]

## REALLY, THE REAL THING

**TOODYAY, WA**    Word has reached me, writes Roberto Goizuetta, that you are an avid Coke collector. Goizuetta, the CEO of Coca-Cola, had heard right. The letter's recipient, Brian Dawes, has more Coke spin-offs than there are bubbles in a Fanta bottle. The bug bit Brian in Zimbabwe, where he grew up. He recalls the local service station handing out a Coke crate for collecting two dozen Coke bottles. Forty years later, at the back of The Cola Cafe, a bright-red room overspills with Coke keyrings, lighters, yoyos and belt buckles. A Barbie doll is dolled up in a Coke ensemble. Santa waves from a Coke snowdome. **[122 Stirling Tce. Open daily 8.45a.m.–4.30p.m. Entry free.** Phone (08) 9574 4407]

# ODDITIONS

@ The world's largest sugar crystal is in the **Mackay (Qld)** Regional Museum. Hillary Bartholomew, a scientist from the Sugar Research Institute, developed the flashbulb-sized lump drop by sweet drop.

@ Don't expect a giant green tin in **Smithton (NSW)**, the birthplace of the Milo chocolate drink, back in 1934. But you will encounter a giant Nestlé factory that generates most of the 6 billion cups of Milo that the world swallows per annum.

@ Keeping a slice of wedding cake is traditional, but hanging on to the top three tiers? The squirrels in question are Mr and Mrs C. Teale of **Stanthorpe (Qld)**. Ornate to the max, their 1921 cake is shelved in the Heritage Museum. **[12 High St. Open Wed.–Sun.]**

@ A chocolate shop on Rokeby (pronounced rockerbee) in Subiaco, **Perth (WA)**, is called Chokeby (pronounced chockerbee). Mind you, choking to death on chocolates could be a very sweet way to go.

# TIME

*(Being a synchronicity of eccentricity
and momentous moments)*

## AGE BEFORE YOU-BEAUTY

**BEERWAH, Qld** Steve Irwin may be the first human to inspire his own fair-dinkum Muppet character, but the crocodile hunter is still just a young buck compared to Harriet at Steve's Australia Zoo. As this book goes to press the Galapagos tortoise is turning 175, making it the oldest-known living reptile on our continent. Struth. **[Glass House Mountains Tourist Rd. Open daily 9a.m.–4.30p.m. Entry $34/$29/$24, family pass $109. Phone (07) 5436 2000 or check out www.crocodilehunter.com]**

## IF WALLS HAD MOUTHS

**KAKADU, NT** Painted in the Nanguluwr caves are X-ray barramundi, spirit figures, snakes and hand stencils. There's also Algaigho the Fire Woman – and a two-masted ship. The ship image is dated to the mid-1900s, when buffalo hunters ventured forth for fresh meat, while the other stretches back millennia – comparable to the Bayeux Tapestry sharing a wall with digital photos of Kylie Minogue. **[Take the turnoff for Nourlangie Rock, south of Jabiru. Six km in, turn left for Nanguluwur. The 1.7-km walk from the car park can be very hot]**

## WHAT'S THE TIME, MR SHADOW?

**KINGSTON S.E., SA** Driving into Kingston from the west, the order is Lobster, then Shell. (That's giant lobster, followed by Shell service station.) Past the Shell is the Apex Park where your shadow can tell the time, assuming it's day-time and not raining. The Druidic gadget is called an analemmatic sundial. (It's not in my dictionary either.) Basically, it's a dais of inscriptions that allows your shadow to act as an hour hand. Kids need to 'think tall'.

Three churches share a crossroad in **Bendigo (Vic.)** but have no Sunday services scheduled at the same hour. A theory behind the discrepancy points to a creek that once ran down Forest St, the former power source for all three church organs. **[Cnr Forest and MacKenzie Sts]**

## DOWNTIME

**MENZIES, WA**    Two versions exist as to why Menzies' municipal tower went clockless for the best part of a century. The first is romantic, involving the wreck of the SS *Orizaba* in 1905. Allegedly the London-freighted clock sank to the seabed off Fremantle, never to tick in the gold-mining town that indentured it. The second story is bureaucratic. As gold sputtered in Menzies, the Attorney-General of the day deemed it prudent to avoid the expense of ordering a clock for a town whose days were numbered. Whichever the cause, the tower won its timepiece in 1999 – four in fact, known as 'slaves', with the master clock hiding in a steel box in the foyer.

## RADIO DAYS

**PARKES, NSW**    Question: Aside from Somalia, where can you watch the sun set over Somalia? Answer: 26 km north of Parkes, at the radio telescope. Below the massive dish is a geochron clock that traces nightfall across the world. You can stand there imagining twilight in Sri Lanka, or dawn in Vladivostok. (Such omnipresence is created by the shadows that grow precisely across the mounted globe in the dish's forecourt, with Parkes being perfectly aligned on planet Earth to play global timekeeper.) Nestled nearby, as part of the cosmic display, is the high-tech control panel as seen on screen in the 2001 film *The Dish*. **[Open daily 8.30a.m.–4.15p.m. Admission free. Phone (02) 6861 1777 or view www.parkes.atnf.csiro.au]**

## A FAMILIAR FACE

**SALE, Vic.**    Travellers into Sale always saw the clock tower first. The Victorian monolith stood above the post office on the corner of Foster and Raymond Sts. Backlit by gas lamps, the clock was wound each week and kept the township ticking. When road works and expedience saw the landmark demolished in 1964, protest from the punctual citizens was vociferous – and effective. In 1988 the tower was duplicated, minus the post office, and erected in Cunninghame Mall, relying on the original weathervane, balustrades and clock.

Don't trust the clock outside the post office in **Cue (WA)**. Premier of the state, Sir John Forrest, bestowed the timepiece on the old gold town in 1897. The pendulum alone weighs some 50 kg, and only a daredevil with a head for heights would risk winding the pulley attached to the counterweight. These factors, and the excessive heat, tend to make a mockery of chronometry.

## SHADOW OF ITSELF
**SINGLETON, NSW**    Gnomons are those sharp little nubs in the centre of sundials. The gnomon on Singleton's sundial is a fair bit larger, say the size of a howitzer, and throws off shade rather than shadow. It's the biggest sundial in the southern hemisphere, a gift from Lemington Mines, a colliery founded by such 'big-timers' as CSR and Esso. With a face of hexagonal stones, the dial allows you to calculate the time down to the minute, applying the correction chart supplied. Just don't forget to wind the shadow backwards one hour when daylight saving starts. **[Along John St, beside the river]**

## TIRELESS AS CLOCKWORK
**STAWELL, Vic.**    If the time is right, nip down to the Stawell Town Hall to watch the bronze diggers try their luck fossicking the tower's parapets – as they've been doing punctually since 1969. Just before the clock strikes, the mechanical figures crank into action: the striking of the bells decrees the length of their labours, though these poor prospectors seem doomed to scoop and rock, scoop and rock, ad infinitum. **[Downhill from Wimmera St. The blokes set to work at 9a.m., noon and 3p.m.]**

A lump of rock 4 km west of **Ravensthorpe (WA)** has a global role to play. As it happens, the rock marks the 120° meridian of longitude. In plain English, that means that noon in this highway layby is exactly eight hours ahead of noon in Greenwich, England. In solar terms, you're also 16 minutes ahead of Perth, the state capital, though no state capital worth its salt would ever admit as much.

## I'LL HAVE WHAT IT'S HAVING

TOWNSVILLE, Qld   Canadian redwoods and Galapagos tortoises have nothing on a bombie coral. This spherical monster of the Great Barrier Reef, much like a medicine ball with a bad case of acne, may well be the oldest living thing on the planet. Upstairs in the Museum of Tropical Queensland, a drill core taken (harmlessly) from a bombie's heart spells out the creature's antiquity. Just as tree rings denote the passing years, the X-rayed cells of this coral speak of eight centuries. The imprint on the wall outlines the bombie's actual size – thank God these things aren't carnivores. **[70–102 Flinders St East. Open daily 9.30a.m.–5p.m. Entry $9.50/$5.50/$7. Phone (07) 4726 0606 or visit www.mtq.qld.gov.au]**

# ODDITIONS

- In **Goomeri (Qld)**, if someone says 'It's W past F', that means it's 10 past 8. This secret code owes its origins to the memorial clock in the centre of town. Instead of numbers, all four faces bear the inscription 'LEST WE FORGET'.
- The splendid sandstone post office on Margaret St in **Toowoomba (Qld)** has a quirk. For reasons of optimal viewing down Margaret and Ruthven Sts, the clock tower has been built a few metres forward of the main building.
- The floral clock in Kings Park, **Perth (WA)**, has a cute point of difference. The call of an invisible rufous whistler marks the passing of every half-hour.

⊚ Moving westward in **Torres Strait (Qld)**, a boat can thread past Wednesday, Thursday and Friday Islands in the space of an hour.

⊚ An ornate clock in **Wangaratta (Vic.)** commemorates Albert, Charles, Fredrick, Joseph, Reginald, Richard, Robert and William – the eight sons of Mr and Mrs R. Handcock killed in World War I. **[Phone the Wangaratta Historical Society on (03) 5722 2838]**

# TOUGH

*(Being a slugfest of stoical souls
and never-say-diehards)*

## JUST ADD WATER

**BILLINUDGEL, NSW**   In February 1995, Sue Stirton was on the verge of signing a contract to buy the Billinudgel General Store and Hardware, when the river broke its banks and the shop went underwater. Sue helped in the mop-up (boogie boards ferried beer from the pub, and canoeists dropped by for absorbent nappies and smokes) and signed the papers the following day. She's turned the sodden emporium into a sublime deli, BBQ chicken included. Nowadays, when the rain gets heavy, media are quick to call Billinudgel, asking Sue which step the floods have reached. **[Open daily. Phone (02) 6680 1002]**

## DIESEL WOMAN

**COOKTOWN, Qld**   Call her Thora and Toots Holzheimer would mow you down with a semi-trailer. Mother of eight, Toots was a trailblazing trucker of the 1960s. Most weeks she drove through shin-deep mud, her beloved diesel 'Man' a regular sight between Cairns and Weipa. One local recalls Toots hoisting 44-gallon drums two days before she gave birth to a baby girl. Tragically Toots died in an accident at Weipa wharf. Cooktown councillors were quick to pay homage, dubbing the first bridge across the Kennedy River in Lakefield National Park the Thora Holzheimer Bridge. Mind you, Toots would have preferred plain Toots. **[Toots' old Man is parked in the Trucking Hall of Fame in Alice Springs, NT]**

## BOX OF TRICKS

**CRACOW, Qld**   Fred Brophy had two dreams as a kid. One was to own a boxing troupe like his uncle, Selby Moore. The other was to run a pub. The first he achieved with distinction, the outback his oyster as he throws such fighters as Kid Goanna, The Friendly Mauler and the Masked Marvel from Yugoslavia in front of local heroes. Fred Brophy's

Famous Boxing Troupe – a fourth-generation affair – all but lives on the rodeo circuit, while off-season Brophy pours beers in his two-storey pub, which is infested with boxing and boozing memorabilia. If you're lucky, you may arrive in this central Qld town on the night of the Tough Man Competition (details undisclosed) or a boxing night in the bar. As the signs say along the road: 'The Cracow Pub – It's Scary'.

## REINVENTING THE WHEELBARROW

**KARRATHA, WA**   The Dampier Salt Shakers excel in the elite sport of wheelbarrow pushing. The sinewy lads hold the record number of Black Rock titles, a 120-km race from Whim Creek to Port Hedland, and have also dominated the Burra to Broken Hill Barrow Push further east. The team spent $10 000 on the heritage trail that starts behind the Visitors Centre, a robust walk of 3.5 km, sans wheelbarrow. From the lookout you can understand why NASA looked twice at St Paul's steeple, and why the Jaburara people knew Burrup Peninsula as Murujuga ('hipbone sticking out').

> Bungle Bungle sandstone is unique. The rock that makes up the awesome beehives of the Purnululu National Park, 200 km south of **Kununurra (WA)**, can resist immense pressure, up to 5800 pounds per square inch, yet shatters if struck by a pick. The perverse brittleness is due to the rock's unusual lack of binding agent.

## THE COMPLEAT DANGLER

**MATARANKA, NT**   Brian has all 10 fingers and so does Sarah, his wife. Strange, considering that both hang their hands twice daily in a cast-iron tank of water containing two hungry barramundi who snatch a dangling pilchard, or pinkie, with ballistic power. As part of his spiel, Brian will hold up the monsters in his hand and tell you about the fish's transsexuality, and how their sandpaper jaws have a habit of hurting ordinary mortals. [Territory Manor Motel and Caravan Park, Martins Rd. Turn off near the water tower. Free feeding shows at 9.30a.m. and 1p.m. Phone (08) 8975 4516]

## GONE WITH THE CATTLE

NEWCASTLE WATERS, NT    Noel 'Piccaninny' Willett, better known as Pic, led the Last Great Cattle Drive in 1987, from Newcastle Waters to Longreach. At 57, the boss drover had no hassles driving 1200 head over 2000 km, but he couldn't cope with all the media types and their talk-talk-talk. A statue of Pic stands in Drover Park, staring up the road to the Junction Hotel, where drovers let rum do the talking.

## OBSTACLE RACE

PORT MACQUARIE, NSW    Luke Tresoglavic is made of tough stuff. In February 2004, the snorkeller was duckdiving off Caves Beach when a Port Jackson shark bit him on the leg. The shark wasn't huge (only around 60 cm long), nor was it deadly, but it *was* persistent. The shark stayed attached to Luke's leg as he swam ashore, hopped in the car, drove to the surf club and asked for advice. A jet of cold water did the trick, then Luke drove to the hospital (minus shark) for a stitch or two.

## SCAB LABOUR

QUEENSTOWN, Tas.    Walk across the Conglomerate Creek and you'll reach a footy oval like few others in the world. Smelter fumes have scared off the grass. The Gravel, as the pitch is known, is a sweep of sand and stone that's graded instead of mown. But just in case the Queenstown Football Club doesn't seem tough enough, take a look in the footy room of the Eric Thomas Galley Museum – a century of mining teams, and hardly a scabby knee to be seen. **[Museum is in Driffield St]**

## MATES FOR LIFE

SOMERSBY, NSW    In July 2000, a fire ripped through the Australian Reptile Park here, killing a swathe of snakes and lizards. A rare survivor was an alligator-snapping turtle, since called Terminator. As some divine reward for her resilience, a new mate called Leonardo was, not long after, found snoozing in a Sydney sewer, although his natural home is a Louisiana bayou. The pair are taking things slowly, as turtles do, in the Lost World of Reptiles exhibit. **[Off the Pacific Hwy near Gosford. Open daily 9a.m.–5p.m. Entry $20/$10, family $52. Phone (02) 4340 1146 or visit www.reptilepark.com.au]**

## STILL CLINGING

**WILPENA POUND, SA**   Harold Cazneaux had an eye for the extraordinary. The photographic re-toucher tired quickly of studio work in Adelaide, and longed for the scenic beyond. He travelled to the Flinders Ranges in 1937 and found a giant tree in front of which he stood 'in silent wonder and admiration'. What struck him most were the bent fingers of the roots (Wilpena in fact means 'bent fingers') clinging grimly, barely, to a creek bank. For Cazneaux, the tree embodied the spirit of endurance, the eventual title of a photograph which earned him an honorary fellowship of the Royal Photographic Society as well as countless calendar royalties. Three generations later, the Cazneaux Tree still clings to the bank. **[Coming from Hawker, nearing the Pound, pass the T-junction and look for a sign on your left after 200 m]**

# TOWERS

*(Being a rampart of rare turrets, crazy crows-nests
and various other vantages)*

## TOWER OF BABBLE

**ARCHGATE, NSW**   Some 10 km east of Nowra, heading for Calbarra
Beach, is a farm called Lapland. Its owner is Warren Halloran, a wealthy
recluse and top-shelf eccentric. You only need see the Rhenish bell-
tower on his property next-door, Reganville, to suspect the bloke's
belfry may host a few winged residents. The bell, with 'Oh Me Oh My'
inscribed, chimes on the quarter-hour. Chiselled above the doorway facing the Crookhaven River is a second wisdom – 'The Answer is Blowing
in the Wind'. On the day the tower was opened, Christmas Day 2001,
Sussex Inlet was ablaze but the ceremony went ahead regardless.
When the electric bell failed to ring, a member of the crowd, with one
eye on the nearby fires, scampered up the internal stairs and rang the
maiden note with a crisp hammer blow. **[Opposite Archgate Nursery
on the Currarong turnoff. The farm is private property]**

## PIECE OF PISA

**BUNDABERG, Qld**   The East Water Tower, on the corner of Princess
and Sussex Sts, has been described as a 'masterpiece of bricklaying'.
A mason called N.C. Steffenson trowelled the eight storeys into being
in the year of Federation. The 40-m tower lays claim to 40-plus arched
windows, none of which serves any real purpose other than show.
Birds called bottle swallows have made the tower their own private
skyscraper. **[Head out to the Bundaberg Rum distillery, and look left
as you reach Princess St]**

## GREEN LIGHT

**EDEN, NSW**   You won't see a borderline where the Pacific Ocean
meets Bass Strait, but you will see Green Cape lighthouse, south of
Eden. The 29-m beacon has been throwing light to settler ships and
sporting yachties since 1883. These days you can bed down in the

Assistant Lightkeeper's Quarters, and the tariff includes a tower tour and an obligation-free sunset over Disaster Bay. [Inquiries on (02) 6495 5000. See more at www.lighthouse.net.au]

A 17-m chimney built by Cornish masons with grand ambitions stands alone in the hills of **Kilkiven (Qld)**. Its heyday lasted only four years, from 1872 to 1875. The chimney was slated to be a copper smelter, but poor ore and downright remoteness won out. **[To get there, follow a 14-km, half-tar, half-dirt, all-narrow road into the Mt Coora bush just north of town]**

## 241 STAIRS TO HEAVEN

**JIMNA, Qld**    Some serious driving lies between Jimna and the outside world, but the view is worth the motocross rally. A timber town around 70 km northwest of Brisbane and sequestered in deep forest, Jimna boasts the tallest fire tower in the state, one of the most elegant examples in Australia. The 44-m all-wood affair commands an eagle eye over the yowie-rich wilds of Kilcoy and Murgon.

## SKYSCRAPER

**MILDURA, Vic.**    At the time of writing the tower doesn't exist, but you may soon see a 5-km hole awaiting the concrete. That's the kind of foundation that would be needed for the world's tallest tower, a 200-megawatt solar power station proposed by German company Euromission and destined to stretch for a vertical kilometre. The likely location, if the project survives the feasibility studies, is Ned's Corner, 65 km northwest of Mildura. The principle behind this giant snorkel has been described as 'a hydro system in reverse' whereby 32 turbines at the base are driven by the updraft from earth to sky, rather than a torrent pulled downwards by gravity.

## ALL CLEAR TO LAND

**NAGAMBIE, Vic.**    The Observation Deck is a 55-m neo-Bavarian turret that stands stark above Mitchelton Winery. Designed by Robin Boyd in 1974, the tower looks down on a tangle of pampered vines. You can even (just) observe a faint yellowy streak below one vineyard tracing the remains of the old runway that once served the estate. Hence the label downstairs at the cellar door: 'Airstrip Marsanne'. **[Open daily 10a.m.–5p.m. Entry free. Phone (03) 5736 2222 or visit www. mitchelton.com.au]**

Take the spectacular tourist loop west of the **Esperance (WA)** township and you'll encounter Salmon Beach, the site of Australia's first wind farm. At present a lone tower stands on the headland, the survivor of a lapsed installation. More permanent seems the old Salmon Beach propeller mounted on The Esplanade, outside the town's museum.

## MULTIPLE ERECTIONS

NEWCASTLE, NSW   A most curious turret stands on the corner of Brown and Tyrrell Sts. Built as a beacon in 1865, the Leading Light Tower had to be rebuilt 12 years later owing to a 'parsonage erection' that occluded the beam. The double entendre is trebled once you know the local nickname for the port's newest tower, down on Queens Wharf near the railway station. Put it this way – Viagra has expressed interest in a sponsorship deal.

## HOME AMONG THE RANGES

PORT AUGUSTA, SA   Built of boiler plate with a coronet finial (that cute bit on top), the Water Tower Lookout in Port Augusta not only gives you a view of the Flinders Ranges, the Gawler Ranges and Spencer Gulf, it also reveals the pipeline linking Morgan on the Murray River to Whyalla. It was this pipe that made the original 1882 tower redundant after a century of faithful supply to the town below. Who else but R. E. Steele, the district engineer, could open the new vantage point? **[Mitchell Tce, on the west side of town. Free entry]**

Australia's oldest brewery, in **Goulburn (NSW)**, is a shrine to the convict architect Francis Greenway. In the museum you will discover the original blueprints of his most notable project – Macquarie Tower on Sydney's South Head – is a mathematical tribute to a seventh wonder of the Ancient World, the Lighthouse of Alexandria. **[23 Bungonia Rd. Open daily from 11a.m. Phone (02) 4821 6071 or visit www. goulburnbrewery.servebeer.com]**

## BEACHHEAD

**PORTLAND, Vic.**    Wade St sounds like a risky place to build a water tower. But that's what they did in 1930. Thirty years later, improved supply made the tower obsolete and demolishers loitered with an eye to salvaging materials. But diggers – Australian soldiers, that is – jumped the queue and converted the 25-m tower to a war museum over Portland Bay in 1996. Military exhibits occupy each landing on the way up. **[Wade St, off Percy St, east of town. Open 10a.m.–4p.m. Entry $4/$3, kids free. Phone (03) 5523 3938]**

The silver ball mounted on a massive tripod, just east of town, is the obsolete water tower of **Warrnambool (Vic.)**. If there's a crucifix on top, it usually means the date is somewhere between Christmas and Easter. The building beneath, once a wing of the homegrown Fletcher Jones factory, now forms part of the campus of South West TAFE. **[Off Raglan Pde]**

## LAST WORD IN TOWERS

**WOODSIDE, Vic.**    The tallest high-strength steel tower in our hemisphere belongs to the Omega navigation station near Woodside. Stretching up 427 m, the glorified antenna pulses out 10 kilowatts around the clock, helping to lay a 'navigational mesh' around the globe for sea and air traffic. The tower has clones in Japan, Hawaii, Argentina,

North Dakota, Liberia, Norway and a small dot in the Indian Ocean called Reunion. **[Along South Gippsland Hwy, 6 km northeast of town]**

# ODDITIONS

◎ The ashes of John Campbell Miles, the man who stumbled across lead ore in 1923 and started the rush that became **Mt Isa (Qld)**, have been lovingly placed in three ornate barrels that comprise an ad-hoc obelisk on the corner of Marian and Miles Sts.

◎ A sandstone chimney soars behind the old bank at 45 View St in **Bendigo (Vic.)**. So rife was reef gold back in 1859 that the Union Bank smelted its own.

◎ Our tallest concrete silo – the old Noske Flour Mill – soars above the streets of **Nhill (Vic.)**. The tower can hold up to 4000 tonnes of barley.

◎ The clock tower above the **Tenterfield (NSW)** Post Office doesn't seem so high. But imagine the construction foreman in 1881 doing a handstand on top of it, to celebrate the building's completion. Seems a little higher, no?

# TRANSPLANTS

*(Being a surgery of the shifted and shunted,*
*the removed and relocated)*

## MOUNTAIN TO MOHAMMED

**BOREEN POINT, Qld**   Neil Paynter wanted to run a pub on the Sunshine Coast, but he couldn't get a licence in his precinct of choice. So he did the next best thing, buying The Apollonian, a cedar and hoop-pine palace (pub and adjoining concert hall) from Gympie, which was set to be demolished, and shifting the old gal on a stream of semi-trailers. When the pub opened 25 km up the road, Neil invited the loyal Gympie drinkers to christen his new local. **[Laguna St. Phone (07) 5485 3100]**

## MEMORY PROPS

**BUNDABERG, Qld**   If pioneer Oz aviator Bert Hinkler is Bundaberg's favourite son, then Hinkler House must be the city's favourite cottage. Why else would sound-minded Rotarians demolish it brick by brick and transport the resulting rubble from Southhampton in the UK to their very own Botanical Gardens? Well, basically because their own heroic pilot once lived there, and all his bits and pieces needed a shrine Down Under. Hence the bizarre juxtaposition of a broken Avro Baby propeller against rose wallpaper. Or a piston from Bert's plane, the *Southern Cloud*, perched above a tin bath. **[Open daily 10a.m.–4p.m. Entry $5/$2, family $11. Phone (07) 4152 0222 or visit www.bundabergonthe.net]**

## STATION OF THE CROSS

**CANBERRA, ACT**   All Saints Anglican Church in Ainslie was once a railway station attached to Australia's biggest cemetery. The cemetery – Rookwood, in Sydney – had its own branch line from 1868, a service designed to carry both corpses and mourners to the necropolis. Alas, a fire gutted the Gothic Revival platform in 1958, following which the brickwork was numbered, dismantled and trucked to Canberra for a Gothic revival Mark 2. The rebuilding took more than a year, with the bell tower moving from left to right, and the two 'train portals' being fitted with stained-glass windows. **[Junction of Cowper, Bonney and Foveaux Sts]**

## BANK BREAKER

**CLERMONT, Qld**   A concrete tree on Old Drummond St recaptures the horrors of the 1916 floods. Sixty-five people drowned in the deluge as Sandy Creek broke its banks, and 100 more clung to roofs and real trees. A vote by the citizenry decided to shift the town to higher ground, including the L-shaped Commercial Hotel which moved in two pieces from Drummond to Capella Sts. The traction engine on Lime St can take much of the credit.

## RESTLESS FAITH

**DARWIN, NT**   Simpsons of Scotland, the washing machine people, shipped a prefab church Down Under. The chapel was assembled in Adelaide as a trial in 1897, then dismantled and hauled to Darwin (then known as Palmerston) to replace a timber one that a cyclone had dispatched. With steel ties on each corner, the new church survived 18 cyclones, including Tracy, as well as heavy Japanese bombing some decades earlier. After Methodism faltered, the chapel became a squat and later a motorbike showroom. In the nth twist, it was trucked to the Botanical Gardens in 2000 where, God willing, it will remain. **[Just in from the Gardens Rd entrance]**

## MARY'S MASSES

**GEROGERY, NSW**   A weatherboard box called St Mary's Catholic Church was built near Albury in 1934 to serve as a worship hub for weir workers. When the weir was complete the chapel moved closer to town, until in 1974 one Mary Holden purchased St Mary's and trucked it to her farm in Gerogery, 25 km north. Nowadays the church holds a congregation of 2000-plus, though they're generally silent except for a few who have a pull-string on their spines. That's because it's now the Gerogery Doll Museum, boasting the world's tallest Barbie and a walnut-cracking bohemian manikin. **[5 Main St. Open daily 9a.m.– 5p.m. Entry $3/$2/$1, family $5. Phone (02) 6026 0578]**

## IMPROVISATION 101

**MARGARET RIVER, WA**    During the 1920s, Australia bent over backwards to attract new immigrants. In WA the need was so dire that a plan called 'group settlement' was proposed, where entire hamlets, say, were transplanted holus-bolus to the Australian wilds. The best re-creation of this folly stands in the Old Settlement Museum, where the story has to be heard (courtesy push-button audio) to be credited. To build their own hut (or humpy) settlers were issued with tin sheets and nails. But nails could not be used, as they were needed later for constructing the larger 'contract house' for the whole village. Such an edict was enforced by virtue of the larger government-issued roof coming with nail-holes, while the hole-free humpy model demanded a timber frame – held together with scrounged chicken wire. Neither Kafka nor Heller could contrive a richer idiocy. **[Bussell Hwy, north of town. Open Tue.–Sat. Sep.–Jul. 10a.m.–3p.m. (closed Thur. during winter). Entry $6.60/$5.50/$22. Phone (08) 9757 9335]**

## COTTAGE INDUSTRY

**MELBOURNE, Vic.**    Here's an easy way to win $5. Start mumbling within earshot of a trivia tragic that the earliest European building in Australia was constructed in 1755. That's not possible, you'll be told. But your friend is neglecting to consider Captain Cook's Cottage in the Fitzroy Gardens. The house was shipped brick for brick in 1933 from a Yorkshire nook called Great Ayrton. An inscription on the doorway, 'J.G.C. 1755', is apparently the ceremonial graffito of James Cook Senior, father to the man who put Australia on the map – 15 years later.

## STUNNED MULLETS

**TWEED HEADS, NSW**    For decades the four Boyd brothers ran a flourishing mullet industry from an old shed in Boyds Bay. But the shed had another role for much of the 1950s, the era of six o'clock closing: if you needed a beer, you saw the Boyds. In 1954, when the speakeasy was flooded (by water), the boys offered rowboats to customers and kept a floating bar within. Known as Mugil Dobala (after the bountiful mullet), the shed became such an icon that two separate demolition orders were stopped. Eventually, plank by plank, it was moved upriver in

1996 to keep the bootleg spirit alive. **[Tweed River Regional Museum, Pioneer Park, Kennedy Dve. Open Tues., Thur., Fri. 11a.m.–4p.m.; Sun. 1p.m.–4p.m. Entry $4/50c. Phone (07) 5536 8625 or visit www. tweedhistory.org.au]**

## MYSTERY SHED

**WAGIN, WA**    First diphtheria, then typhoid and lastly flu spurred the construction of the quarantine hut in Wagin's hospital grounds. Flu was the worst (the doctor of the day was slammed for having too many graves dug in the local cemetery, in anticipation of the death toll). The shed moved twice in its life, then finally joined the Historical Village. In 2001, while restoring the joint, a builder found a tin epitaph hiding in the wall space. 'Sacred to the memory', read the tin sheet, 'of James Cowie who died while work was proceeding on this building, May 1928.' But who was Cowie? There was no record of the man at the cemetery and the only James Cowie in Wagin was a hale old fella who outlived 1928 by a long chalk. It turns out that James Cowie, a carpenter, had died in Albany, over 200 km away. The tin sheet was a tradesman-like way of saying farewell to a union mate. **[Kitchener St. Open daily 10a.m.–4p.m. Entry $5/$4/$3. Phone (08) 9861 1232 or visit www.waginhistoricalvillage.com]**

# ODDITIONS

◎  A rare thing, a transplanted lighthouse. The Cape Jaffa beacon of **Kingston (SA)** was shifted in 1976 from Margaret Brock Reef some 15 km away. **[Marine Pde. Open during school holidays 2p.m.–4.30p.m. Tours $5/$2.]**

◎  **Ceratodus (Qld)** is a ghost town named after a lungfish. It's also where the disused railway station was shifted to a roadside rest area in 1997. Pull in for a DIY cuppa and stretch your legs in the old waiting-room.

◎  Caged beside some real-life emus in **Erldunda (NT)** are a giant echidna and a frill-neck lizard that aren't so vibrant. The two critters once paraded as mascots of the 1988 World Expo in Brisbane. **[On the Stuart Hwy, just north of the Uluru turnoff]**

# TREES

*(Being a thicket of unique eucalypts, fabulous foliage and staggering stumps)*

## REBEL PLANTERS

**BOULDER, WA**   In the heart of Boulder there's a roundabout. For years its inner circle remained bare. Council debated over how to fill the space: one lobby group favoured a date palm; another pushed for a fountain. Or why not the statue of a miner operating an air-leg drill? This is the Golden Mile, after all. As the arguments persisted, a group known only as the Rebel Planters whacked in a date palm. Council removed it. But seeing the tree in place had secretly swung the community. After another year of motion and counter-motion, the council reckoned a palm could do the trick – but with one proviso. The Rebel Planters had to do the job again. Overnight, they did. The palm *does* look good. While the bloke operating the air-leg drill can only stare green-eyed from outside the Credit Union. **[Cnr Burt and Lane Sts]**

Anyone-who's-someone to visit **Kununurra (WA)** in the last 20 years has been invited to plant a tree in Celebrity Tree Park on Lily Creek Inlet, a shady lobe of Ord River that's getting shadier by the year. Names include such luminaries as Rolf Harris, Dame Mary Durack and HRH Princess Anne. Doesn't get a lot of A-list traffic, Kununurra . . .

## ESCAPE CLAWS

**KOROIT, Vic.**   Draco Malfoy, Harry Potter's *bête noir*, owes his first name to the Greek word for dragon. A tree in Koroit can teach you this, the *Dracaena draco* or dragon tree, one of very few in the world. Native to the Canary Islands, the tree has gnarled branches, clawlike offshoots and bloody sap that must have prompted the analogy. The nation's prime specimen stands beside a car-park toilet block. **[Cnr High and Garden Sts]**

## CRACKED IDEA

**MURCHISON, Vic.**    On the west bank of the Goulburn River in this central Victorian town is the shuttered hulk of Gregory's Hotel. No less grand is the world's largest oriental plane tree, which blocks the pub's facade. The tree, planted in 1913, managed to flourish thanks to a cracked horse trough that stood nearby. It's said the broken masonry inspired the notion of drip-feed irrigation.

Some of our longest gum leaves lurk near **Mt Beauty (Vic.)**. After the big fire of 2002, a boy called Philip Ryder found a whopper on his property – at 82 cm, it's roughly the length of your average bootlace. Several rival beauties are pinned to the walls of the Bogong Hotel in Tawonga, a few km north of Beauty.

## SNAPPY DECISION

**ONSLOW, WA**    Ashcroft Shire is flat, pimpled by ant nests and blistered with salt farms, which made the sole snappy gum sapling stand out all the more. Grader driver Bob McAllay saw it as his moral duty to safeguard the tree, giving it water whenever he passed and ensuring that the access road avoided it. A tribute to the green-thumbed Roebourne boy with Pilbara iron in his blood, who died with Wittenoom asbestos in his lungs, stands below the lone eucalypt 11 km down the road to Onslow.

## TREE OF SPECULATION

**PORT HEDLAND, WA**    Tamarind is a well-known curry ingredient. So either the tree was planted by a pearler of Indonesian extraction, or a tamarind seed passed through an Afghan cameleer spelling his mob at the spring. Either way, the tree pre-dates the town (gazetted in 1896) by a good decade. Aborigines know the giant tamarind as the Tree of Knowledge. Local kids esteemed the tree, for shade and for camouflage. With the school once standing next-door, truants would often disappear into the dense foliage, preferring nature's Tree of Knowledge to the institutional variety. **[Cnr Armstrong and Acton Sts]**

Legend has it that gun shearer Percy Morran, on being recruited for World War 1 duties, stabbed his shears into the red gum outside the community hall, near **Deniliquin (NSW)**. 'I'll collect these when I get back,' he said. But the digger never did either. The rusty blade still juts from the gum – now about 6 m overhead. **[Moraga Community Hall between Deniliquin and Wakool]**

## FAMILY TREE

**TALBOT, Vic.**   Womb-like in shape, the Aboriginal birthing tree outside Talbot is a special place. The only signpost is a stark plaque reading 'MATERNITY'. The river gum has been hollowed over time, webbed by spiders, riddled by wasps, and witness to countless, timeless deliveries by the Indigenous women. **[2 km past Talbot, heading to Maryborough. Turn left on Pollocks Rd after the bridge, then head along the creek some 300 m]**

## JARDIN A TROIS

**TEWANTIN, Qld**   Three amazing trees stand outside the Royal Mail Hotel in this town on the shores of Lake Doonella. A so-called little fig, a red gum and a cupiana tree entwine to form one colossal column sharing one root system. If your appetite is whetted for another arboreal freak, stroll past the two German mines – one for each war – in the RSL Park and head for the bus-stop facing the post office. This giant white fig, which was used by the Gabbi-Gabbi people as a crib to store their dead, once arched the road but has been cropped, and bolstered by cement, to give it a longer chance at life. **[The pub and its three trees stand at 120 Poinciana Ave]**

To see why the banyan is the holy tree of India, visit the ethereal specimen in Queens Park **Maryborough (Qld)**, where A-frames keep the lower boughs from collapsing. In other places, the aerial roots act as columns. The tree seems magnified because of the tiny model steam train that scoots in its shade on the last Sunday of each month. [Close to cnr Sussex and Bazaar Sts]

## BOTANICAL BUZZ

**WALPOLE, WA**    Tingle is not just a nerve sensation, but a sensational tree unique to this area. Tingles lack orthodox taproots and in order to get enough moisture the tree flares its trunk and emits surface roots, often creating massive alcoves among its buttresses. Another side-trip for tree lovers is Nut Rd, even further on. It was roughly here that trailblazing botanist Baron von Mueller souvenired a nut from the red flowering gum *Ficifolia* in 1867 and took it to the wider world. That species now blossoms across the globe, from Morocco to San Francisco. [You can see the giant tingle on Hilltop Rd, east of town, or take the famous Treetop Walk further down the highway]

## GO FIGURE

**YUNGABURRA, Qld**    The Curtain Fig is a grand parabola of roots and vines and cables, just south of town. For good reason this tree draws hordes of tourists every year, but also worth a detour is the lesser-known Cathedral Fig some 20 km on the other side of town, toward Gordonvale. This latter goliath creates a basilica in the Danbulla State Forest, the mazy home to sugar gliders, quolls, amethyst pythons and forest dragons. [Both figs are signposted off the Gillies Hwy]

## ODDITIONS

⑥ Two trees outside the Newcastle University Aquatic Centre (think algae research, not water slides) in King St, **Raymond Terrace (NSW)** have heard their share of vows. Before 1840, when the town lacked a church, the trees deputised as chapel, hosting countless weddings.

◎ **Coober Pedy (SA)** has very few trees, owing to the heat and dust. One tree standing above the town was reputedly the first to grace the district: it's built out of scavenged truck pipes. **[Big Winch Lookout]**

◎ Between Greenough and **Geraldton (WA)**, the trees take a definite lean. Take a look along West Bank Rd to see a whole row on the tilt. So beloved are these slantwise gums that Greenough Shire has adopted the tree as its symbol.

◎ You need 1200 gallons (4542 litres) to fill the water trough in Dalrymple Creek Park, coming into **Allora (Qld)** from Toowoomba. Not bad going for a single 15-m bloodwood log hollowed out by maul and wedge in 1948.

◎ Where else but Wood St in **Tenterfield (NSW)** will you find Australia's largest cork tree? Edward Parker, a Pom, planted the seed in 1861 and the 'old man' has been sprawling ever since.

◎ Near the corner of Johnston and Loch St, outside the Elders' stock and station agency in **Derby (WA)** is a boab tree in the shape of a teapot. To complete the set, a large boab in the park mimics a coffee plunger.

◎ Near Noah Beach in **Daintree (Qld)** National Park you'll find the dried pods of cannonball mangroves. The name says it all, and the likeness is perfect. When cracked, the pods were traditionally used by the Kuku Yulanji people of Cape Tribulation as three-D jigsaws.

◎ A gum tree in **Keyneta (SA)** will be the weirdest bell tower you've seen in a while. Members of St Peter's Lutheran Church placed the bell in the tree in 1874, where it's announced worship time ever since. **[Eden Valley Rd]**

# TRICKS

*(Being a glimpse of pranks and illusions,
dodges and confusions)*

## SIGHTSEEING

**PARKES, CANBERRA, ACT**   It's not what you see at Questacon, the National Science and Technology Centre, but what you *fail* to see, thanks to the Poggendorff Illusion, the Titchener Illusion, the Muller-Lyer Illusion, the Herring Illusion, the Zollner Illusion and the Unreal Triangles. Most are inscribed within the Questacon cafe tables, and/or the brilliant website of www.questacon.edu.au **[The 'real thing' is on King Edward Tce. Open daily 9a.m.–5p.m. Entry $14/$9.50/$8, family $42. Phone (02) 6270 2800]**

## BRIDGE OF CUSSES

**CHARTERS TOWERS, Qld**   On the west bank of the Burdekin River, 20 km east of town along the Flinders Hwy, there's a scary flood-marker. The highest recorded level was almost 22 m, in 1946. Equally noteworthy is the railway bridge – well, bridges – in the near distance. The rusty one in the foreground was an engineering disaster, the piers too weak to carry the ore-laden trains from Mt Isa. Instead of scrapping it, the gangers built a functioning replica 20 m downstream. With both tracks at the same height, a train crossing the river produces an hallucinogenic illusion. **[You can take a closer look down the road to Macrossan Park on the eastern side]**

Don't be fooled. At the rear of the renovated Town Hall in **Wollongong (NSW)** is the facade of the original version, painted onto the wall by Nick Brash and 10 other artists in 1994. Shadows from the balustrades and light fixtures fall across the painting as you'd expect shadows to fall. Two air-conditioner vents have been cunningly incorporated. **[Crown St]**

## SHADOW CABINET

**GAYNDAH, Qld**   Celia, Leila, Elsie and Mildred Wade-Brown were playful girls. Just look at their bedroom door, preserved under Perspex in their Ban Ban Homestead. What resembles tattered paper scraps glued on wood is actually a multitude of human faces, the collage created by the girls early last century. Stare for a minute and you will see the silhouettes of rogues, royals, dags and dowagers. Almost more extraordinary, says Cynthia Berthelsen, a volunteer at the museum, is the fact that subsequent owners of the homestead left the images in place, after the girls departed in 1918. **[The homestead, transplanted in 1975, is part of Gayndah Museum, Simon St. Open daily 9a.m.–4p.m. Entry $3/$1, family $8. Phone (07) 4161 2226]**

## HOOK, LINE AND SINKER

**HUMPTY DOO, NT**   Fish aren't dumb. To trick a barramundi you need an ultrasound welding machine, a spray room, two ball bearings, hooks, minnow bibs and finally a test tank, just to see if your lure swims alluringly. Jeff and Cheryl Reid are elite lure-makers, with one alluring workshop. They finish the tour with the 'big boy's lolly shop' where every little fake fish sits bright and gaudy in Tupperware boxes. 'You have to lure the boys,' laughs Cheryl, 'before you can lure the barra.' **[Reidy's Fishing Lure Factory, cnr Stuart and Arnhem Hwys. Open weekdays 8.30a.m.–5p.m., with tours at 11a.m. and 1p.m. Entry $5.50. Phone (08) 8988 4760 or visit www.reidyslures.com]**

## QUESTIONABLE CONSTABLES

**JERILDERIE, NSW**   The first things Ned Kelly and his gang stole in Jerilderie on 10 February 1879 were police uniforms. Once the genuine cops were handcuffed and deposited in the lockup, Ned and Dan Hart then paraded in uniform down the main street and mustered the population into the dining-room of the Royal Hotel while their accomplices withdrew funds from the bank. In a cheeky touch, at the blacksmith's forge the gang made sure the bill for the ironwork went to the NSW police force. **[If the forge isn't open, ask Gaila or Pete at Dobookinna, a B&B next-door]**

Drivers, be warned. You have perfectly good vision. The problem lies in the 'OPTOMETRIST' sign close to the roundabout between Inglis and Saunders Sts in **Wynyard (Tas.)**. The word's letters are strategically fuzzy. Whether the trick has attracted any new clients for Paprocki and Liley, or just more work for the town's smash repairers, remains to be seen.

## LOCAL ATTRACTION

**PEKINA, SA**   James Bruff had a parcel of land on the ridge, so locals called the lump Bruff's Hill. During the 1930s a passing motorist suffered a puncture and wedged a rock in front of his downhill tyre, only to see his car rolling along the road – uphill. Word got around, and soon Bruff's Hill was known as Magnetic Hill and a pseudo-scientific theory about geophysical force fields and whatnot began to circulate. At Bruff's Bluff a plywood magnet in a paddock lets you know you've found the right slope, as well as orientating you towards the enigmatic stretch. Slip your car into neutral and see how you roll. The fact that locals know the place as Bullshit Hill shouldn't influence your verdict a jot. [Some 6 km from Pekina, which is south of Ororoo, or head west from Black Rock on the B56]

## RA ON THE ROCKS

**SYDNEY, NSW**   Did ancient Egyptians live in Sydney's Rocks district? During a recent dig in the area, along with the usual colonial trinkets (pipes, bowls, false teeth) archaeologists uncovered a small Egyptian amulet dated to around 400BC. They also unearthed a holey Chinese coin traced back to the Kang H'si dynasty, circa 1700. Was this some radical new history waiting to be written? No. The amulet was most likely a shipboard souvenir, and it's odds-on that the coin was a gambling chip for the suburb's illegal fan-tan sessions. [Upstairs at the Visitors Centre, 106 George St. Open daily 9.30a.m.–5.30p.m. Entry free. Phone (02) 9255 1788 or pay a call to www.sydneyvisitorscentre.com]

## BANANA REPUBLIC

**WOODBURN, NSW**    The Marquis de Rays was a scoundrel. He waved a brochure under 340 Venetian noses in 1880, showing a Pacific paradise that was nothing like the reality the Italians subsequently discovered. A hundred of them died en route, and scores more succumbed to fever, scorpions and cannibals on arrival at the fabled destination, Papua New Guinea's Bismarck Archipelago. The survivors fled to New Caledonia, but were refused entry. Australia back then had a softer heart for displaced persons, and offered shelter. Two of the party trekked north, found good land in the banana belt and named the 1220 ha New Italy. It attracted 300 compatriots and *la vida era bella* – until 1955, when the social experiment had run its course. [**13 km south of Woodburn. Open daily 9a.m.–5p.m. Entry by gold coin donation. Phone (02) 6682 2622 or enter via www. new-italy.com**]

# TUNNELS

*(Being a warren of wondrous holes
and sensational subways)*

## CAN'T GO ROUND IT . . .

CANUNGRA, Qld   The Darlington Range was too steep for bullocks to haul logs out from the Lamington forests. And time, even back in 1884, was money. Picks started pecking the stone, and a 100-m tunnel erased the steepest pitch. A tramline was built and gradient specialists were imported from Ohio. For the next 30 years, hoop pines and monkey puzzle trees were felled by the tonne and freighted through the mountain. The tunnel was designated an ammunition dump during World War 2. Now you're free to explore it. **[Just east of town, cnr the highway and Darlington Range Rd. The bowls club occupies the site of the old mill]**

## HUMOROUS UNDERTONES

COFFS HARBOUR, NSW   Flight Lieutenant Gough Whitlam of the RAAF's 13 Squadron, our former PM, once stood inside this World War 2 bunker. Ironically, 50 years on, he is one of few politicians absent from the walls of Australia's first cartoon gallery. The local Rotary Club has been the prime mover in converting the derelict space into a cartoon gallery, and not without trouble. Major leaks plagued the project – a problem not unknown to politicians. **[City Hill Dve, a steep turn off the roundabout cnr Albany and Hogbin Sts. Open daily 10a.m.–4p.m. Entry $2/$1. Phone (02) 6651 7343 or visit www.bunkercartoongallery.com.au]**

On the Old Grafton Rd, halfway between **Glen Innes (NSW)** and the coast, is a tunnel carved by convicts. Flush against the Boyd River, the tunnel is a work of captive art. Look around as you wander through and you'll see the workers' initials in the upper vaults.

## BURROWED TIME

**DARWIN, NT**    Japanese bombers called on Darwin 46 times in 1942. The Aussies opted to bury their oil supplies in the city's headland, and five tunnels were hand-dug, earning the names 1, 5, 6, 10 and 11, just to confuse the Emperor's spies. Nowadays the system pipes in oxygen to ventilate the underground tours. **[Kitchener Dve, below Survivors' Lookout. Open daily in the dry season (May–Sep.) 9a.m.–5p.m.; Tues.–Fri. 10a.m.–2p.m. during the wet (Nov.–April). Closed Feb. and late Dec. Entry $4.50]**

## STIRRING THE POSSUM

**MT HOTHAM, Vic.**    Mountain pygmy possums are the only full-blown alpine mammal in Australia. For years the hand-sized creature was thought to be extinct, until one was found on Mt Hotham in 1966. Happily, breeding has resumed apace, many thanks to the 'Tunnel of Love' constructed along the Dinner Plain Rd. Tucked between the Mt Hotham Ski Company staff quarters and Fountains Apartments is a minuscule corridor for the pygmies to pass unscathed beneath the road.

## MEDIBANK

**MOUNT ISA, Qld**    When Darwin was bombed in 1942, this mineral-rich town feared it might be next on the Japanese hit list. Survival plans included a 32-patient hospital hidden inside a hill, dug by miners with spades and buckets. The E-shaped corridors, designed to cater for general wards, maternity and an operating theatre were in the end only used for air-raid drills. But at regular intervals the sick and lame were dragged into the hillside (those too frail to move were hidden under mattresses and told to pray). Bedpans sat in gelignite boxes, along with kerosene-fired sterilisers. The catacomb's location remained a secret until after the war when a bulldozer, clearing the way for a new wing to the orthodox hospital, rediscovered the men's ward. **[Head for Base Hospital on Joan St, off Deighton St. Open daily 10a.m.–2p.m. Entry $10/$8/$4. Phone (07) 4743 3853]**

## SAME BAT CHANNEL

**MOUNT PERRY, Qld**   Saying Boolboonda Tunnel is in Boolboonda is not that helpful since Boolboonda doesn't really exist, not as a postcode anyway. But the tunnel exists, all 192 m of it. You don't get too many chances to drive through an ex-rail tunnel, and certainly not the longest unlined, unsupported tunnel in the southern hemisphere. Bentwing bats are known to hang around, though the ceiling empties in winter months. Pluckier visitors can navigate the length without resort-ing to headlights. **[30 km west of Gin Gin, the turnoff is a few km north along the Bruce Hwy, or 20 km east of the old mining town of Mt Perry]**

## DAY GLOW

**NEWNES, NSW**   A century ago, Newnes was the Great Black Hope for yielding shale oil. The Commonwealth Oil Corporation laid 56 km of railway through rough country just to reach the deposit. The effort paid dividends, and did so for 30 years till in 1932 Newnes supported several mines, a refinery, a brickworks, a candle factory – in other words, a town. But now there are only ruins (the Newnes Kiosk in the ex-pub) and a million glow-worms. Officially known as 'fungus gnats', these fluoro fliers infest the railway tunnel off Newnes Plateau, north of Mt Victoria. Turn off your torch and wait for a blizzard of bioluminescence. **[Easiest access is a 1-km walk from Newnes Plateau, which is a 34-km drive from Clarence off Bells Line of Road. For more information, contact the Blue Mountains Heritage Centre on (02) 4787 8877 or visit www. nationalparks.nsw.gov.au]**

A tunnel connects the Customs House Waterfront Hotel and the state parliament building in **Hobart (Tas.)**, though historians quibble over which way the traffic mostly flowed. While that particular watering-hole is no longer on the itinerary, you can learn similar alcoholic trivia on the Hobart Historic Pub Tours that run Sun.–Thurs. at 5p.m. **[Phone (03) 6225 4806. Price $22.50. Or just prop up a bar and hypothesise]**

## SHE *WAS* COMING ROUND THE MOUNTAIN

SWAN VIEW, WA    Being mostly flat, WA has few railway tunnels – indeed, for a long time there was only one, on the Mundaring line. So narrow is the tunnel, and so steep the slope, that uphill trains turned its confines into a fume chamber. (A trumpet-like tube was carried by all train staff to suck in the virgin air at ground level.) Then in 1942 there was a bizarre mishap. Twin locomotives had trouble hauling their freight up the slope, and by degrees they ran out of puff. The train began a slow slide backwards, gaining speed below the tunnel, until a cool hand at Swan View station threw a switch to derail the juggernaut, sparing it a fatal plunge into Perth. One life was lost. The line itself was doomed, closing in 1954. **[From Morrison Rd, the turnoff is Pechey Rd at the western edge of John Forrest National Park. Park below the junction and follow the level track for 500 m. Near a seat, veer right through grass trees. At 340 m in length the tunnel only just necessitates a torch]**

## GOOD AS ITS WORD

TUNNEL, Tas.    This rural settlement is so called because it has a tunnel – a real-life railway tunnel you can walk through. Rolling stock uses the track maybe twice a year, during steam-train festivals, but otherwise it's a pedestrian's delight. Built in 1888 and stretching some 400 m, the tunnel looks as if it comes straight from the island of Sodor, where Thomas the Tank Engine and his good mate Percy rule the network. A torch would be handy, but the braver will cope without. **[7 km north of Lilydale, take Tunnel Rd for 2 km and then turn left at Tunnel Station Rd. Walk left along the track. Naturally enough, check for festivals in case there's a light at the end of the tunnel]**

## TUBE STOP

UNDARA, Qld    Give or take a millennium, the Undara volcano erupted 190 000 years ago, carving out the world's longest known lava flow from a single crater. (One tendril followed the Einasleigh River for 160 km, while a sister stream traced the Lynd River for 90 km.) The upheaval's upshot is the world's biggest lava tube, a natural tunnel beneath the earth's crust that wouldn't look out of place in the Paris

Metro. Bayliss, the longest tube, stretches for 1350 m, with enough room to smuggle a commuter train. Horseshoe bats and albino slaters call the caverns home, but don't let that deter you. **[300 km southwest of Cairns, not far from Mt Surprise. Tours daily from 8a.m.: half-day $65, two-hour $37. Phone 1800 990 992 or visit www.undara.com.au]**

## THROUGH THE KEYHOLE

**ZEEHAN, Tas.**    About a kilometre from town, you'll see a left turn to the golf course. But for a different kind of hole, take the right-hand turn after the clubhouse. After another kilometre you'll see a giant keyhole staring back at you. The tunnel's profile was designed to accommodate the skull-shaped steam boilers that miners hauled through the hill to the old silver diggings on the other side. Skinny cars will fit, but walking won't endanger the duco and it's far more atmospheric. **[Built in 1904, Spray Tunnel is 100 m long, 2.2 m wide and 3 m high. Torch optional]**

# TV

*(Being a box of mini-series mementos
and other tubular touchstones)*

## I NAME THEE BAY OF PEARLS

**BARWON HEADS, Vic.** One in every 10 Australians watched the ABC mini-series *SeaChange* (Series 2) in 1999, and most fell in love with the mythical Pearl Bay. (For those born on the moon, the show traced the sexual and municipal affairs of city-fleeing lawyer, Laura Gibson, played by Sigrid Thornton.) The series was filmed in a dozy cove called Barwon Heads – which is rather less tranquil now owing to all the attention. Overnight stays can be had at Laura's cottage, one of the mod-con cabins attached to the Barwon Heads Caravan Park (once 'owned' by Kevin). And should you develop a thirst, head northeast on the Bellarine Peninsula to St Leonards, where the show's own Tropical Star Hotel was based. **[For the caravan park phone (03) 5254 1115]**

## HEELER FAITHFULS

**CASTLEMAINE, Vic.** Most of the town shots for *Blue Heelers* are based in this central Victorian city, though the Channel 7 cop show calls the town Mt Thomas. As for the Commercial Hotel, where P. J. and Maggie (alias Martin Sacks and Lisa McCune) first explored their sexual tension, it's actually three pubs: the Imperial in Castlemaine for exteriors; the Willy Tavern in Williamstown for interiors; and an unnamed pub in western NSW that's inspired every last piece of archetypal decor.

## FROM CHIPPIE TO YUPPIE

**CAMBRIDGE, Tas.** 'To be honest,' wrote Regina Bird, when applying for *Big Brother 3*, 'I am really bloody sick of cooking fish and chips.' So it was, after three months of public farting, that beaming, straight-shooting Reggie bagged the $250 000 jackpot and never had to pare a potato again. Tasmania adopted the reality queen as its new state emblem. ('She's far prettier than the Tasmanian devil,' said Max Markson, an admiring celeb agent.) Reggie spent a slice of her prize on a second honeymoon with fellow fryer Adrian. After nine years of battering flake, the pair reneged on renewing the lease for the Cambridge Kitchen and Newsagency. Owner George Newell put the shop on the market in September 2003, only for the shrine to be snapped up for $310 000 by Noel, Reggie's father-in-law. **[On Cambridge Rd. The 'Go Reggie' signs may still be hanging in the window]**

For 10 weeks of the year, 4 Lagoon Place in **Patterson Lakes (Vic.)**, a southern suburb of Melbourne, belongs to the make-believe suburb of Fountain Gate, the stamping ground of the ABC's Kath and Kim. Pilgrims come in dribs and drabs to see the yard where Kath Day tied the knot with artistic butcher Kel Knight – and where the nuptial horse got into a panic and bolted.

## QUIET ON THE SET
**CARCOAR, NSW**    The day I called on Carcoar, the town was parading as Narandera (*sic*). The misspelling (nowadays it's spelt Narrandera) was painstakingly historical. The town had been made over – with dirt on the road and buggies on the football field – for the mini-series *Jessica*, a twisted love triangle between a tomboy, a dead boy and the tomboy's sister, set in ye olde Narandera. Another mini-series, *Brides of Christ*, was shot in Carcoar in 1990. Once you visit this colonial hideaway, you'll know why the location scouts get so smitten.

## THE TOUR NEXT-DOOR
**MELBOURNE, Vic.**    Marathon soapie *Neighbours*, the show that launched a dozen careers (think Kylie Minogue, Russell Crowe, Guy Pearce, Holly Valance, Natalie Imbruglia), takes place in a mythical suburb called Erinsborough, a 'location cocktail' around Melbourne's east. The hotbed is Ramsay St, which is actually Pin Oak Crt in Vermont South. The connecting road is Weeden Dve, off Springvale Rd. Better still, take a Ramsay St Tour with DVD highlights along the way. **[Call (03) 9534 4755 or visit www.neighbourstour.com.au]**

## BARRAMUNDI ALLA VENEZIA

**MILDURA, Vic.**   In 1974, as a teenager, Stefano di Pieri escaped Venice, eager to flee a regime that wished 'the hammer and sickle to coexist with the crucifix'. What he found instead were the egg-slice and frying-pan of a Mildura kitchen. Don Carrazza, a former bellboy of the Grand Hotel, was now the pub's owner, and Stefano's brand-new father-in-law. After a while preparing steak and salads, Stefano opened a restaurant under his own name. Its quality and style attracted numerous gourmet gongs, and the TV show *A Gondola on the Murray* ensured lasting success. Since the series, Stefano has been running the hotel's main eatery. **[Seventh St. Phone (03) 5023 0511]**

## FLYING HIGH

**MINYIP, Vic.**   Why would the Maternal and Child Health Centre call itself the Royal Flying Doctor Service when it doesn't have a plane to its name? And how come Emma's Internet Cafe has propellers and snakes on the outside wall? The answer is *The Flying Doctors*, the big-budget mini-series that morphed Minyip into Cooper's Crossing. Photos of Dr Callaghan and Nurse Wellings hang in the take-away and the pub. Mind you, as photos go, the brown snake with its head stuck in a VB can has to win the Logie for Best Light Entertainment.

> If *The Sullivans* still holds a niche in your heart, then you may benefit from knowing that Kitty and Uncle Dave did much of their chiacking at The Retreat Hotel in the **Melbourne (Vic.)** suburb of Abbotsford. The art-deco nook is at 226 Nicholson St, off Johnston St.

## OUTLIVE, OUTLAST, OUT THERE

**TULLY, Qld**   The secret is out (it has been for several years now, but the secrecy was huge at the time . . . ). I'm speaking of *Survivor 2 – The Australian Outback*, which wasn't out back at all, but filmed at Goshen Station on the Herbert River. Security guards kept prying reporters at bay. Once they were voted off the show, the American contestants were pampered at another 'secret' location – the luxuriant retreat El

Rancho del Rey in the Tully valley. It is now the Echo Adventure and Cultural Centre, offering rainforest tours and overnight accommodation. Enduring fans could ask around for *Survivor 2* recipes. **[Phone 0428 264 494 or visit www.echoadventure.com.au]**

# ODDITIONS

◉ The town of **Singleton (NSW)** doubled as the fictional community of Brackley in the 2003 mini-series *Marking Time*. Creator of the drama, John Doyle, aka Rampaging Roy Slaven, originally hails from Lithgow, not a thousand km from Singleton.

◉ Is it just me, or does **Palm Beach (NSW)** look more like Summer Bay (the invented inlet of *Home and Away*) every year? This exclusive suburb near Barrenjoey lighthouse is the second home to *Home and Away* film crews.

◉ The original four apartments that appeared in the Channel 9 ratings runaway *The Block* can be found at 67 Roscoe St in Bondi, **Sydney (NSW)**. They called it a reality show, but un-reality struck when Fiona and Adam sold their ground-floor apartment for $751 000.

◉ **Greening (SA)** is home to the pub seen in *Macleod's Daughters*. As for the gals' farm, that remains a secret guarded fiercely by network executives, though we can say the town of **Williamstown (SA)** is warm.

◉ That open-roofed block opposite Luna Park at 22A The Esplanade in St Kilda, **Melbourne (Vic.)**, is where *The Secret Life of Us* was filmed. Numerous snogs, kiddie-pool parties and tango lessons were filmed here al fresco.

# URGHH

*(Being an unnerving knot of nauseous episodes
and stomach-turning situations)*

## MIASMA

**COBDOGLA, SA**  If you want to see the only working Humphrey steam pump in the world, head for this Riverland settlement, between Berri and Barmera on the Sturt Hwy. But be careful when you visit: in the summer of 2002–3, the bone-dry swamp edging the town caused such a pong that residents became stay-at-homes. If the drought persists, the state government is keen to trial a giant, pleasantly scented cut-out pine tree suspended over the hollow. **[Irrigation and Steam Museum, Park Tce]**

## PAILS INTO OBSCURITY

**COOLGARDIE, WA**  'Night soil' is the sweeter term for the week's bodily wastes, making night-soil carts the olden equivalent of septic trucks. But the curators at the Railway Museum here have gone one step further. Their cart is laden with personalised buckets from around the town. Empty, fortunately, the pooh pails belong to Wild Willy, Lady Dianne Waterton, Flyn of the Outhouse, and The 3 Amigos. Though your sense of history takes a battering from the bucket marked Trilene's Video Shop.

Nene Valley, a coastal hamlet south of **Mt Gambier (SA)**, was first known as Magotty Point, in deference to the wrigglers abounding in the stranded seaweed.

## SOFT SPOT

**GERALDTON, WA**  Roadworkers couldn't figure out why one little patch on the Nanson–Howathara Rd was always boggy and occasionally bubbling. Geologists explained that the erupting mud was caused by groundwater being pressed through old volcanic ash (otherwise known as bentonite clay, which didn't help all that much). But the road gave the soggy site a wide berth, and so should your shoes unless you want primeval slime on your soles. **[North of Chapman Valley Winery. The mud is signposted]**

Murray Ross has endured his quota of dubious odours over the last few years, driving the school bus in **Wyuna (Vic.)**, near Echuca. Murray pleaded with the arch-offenders to staple their smelliest socks to a tree by McCoy's Bridge. Since then, the reeky ritual has perpetuated. Further directions are not required – just use your nose.

## GUMDROPS

**GUNNEDAH, NSW**    As the self-proclaimed Koala Capital of the World, this northeastern town knows how to market its advantage. Ramble the Waterways Wildlife Park on Mullaley Rd, or even Anzac Park beside the Visitors Centre, and you'll get a sore neck from tallying the dormant marsupials. Meanwhile, in order to ensure a steady flow of funds for Blinky Bill and his clan, the town is in the business of selling koala kitsch. For only $1 you can buy a tasteful sachet of koala pooh (in fact a liquorice bullet with a distinct eucalypt nose). 'Warning,' reads the packet, 'contents not to be consumed'.

## ORAL HISTORY

**INNISFAIL, Qld**    Forensic scientists would go slack-jawed at the dental evidence on display in the museum here. Local dentist Allan Wakeham is the culprit. Not only did the man spend a lifetime taking plaster moulds of citizens' mouths, he *kept* them! A dozen boxes are stacked with disembodied dentition depicting Lingual Erosion, Thumb Sucker, Open Gate and Utter Neglect. Perhaps the most curious specimen is Over-Eruption, not least because the phrase evokes the Pompeiian relics on display in the other room. **[11 Edith St. Open weekdays 10a.m.–noon, 1p.m.–3p.m. Phone (07) 4061 2731]**

In 1985, the Rotary Club in **Lismore (NSW)** began restoring a paradox known as a dry rainforest. As the lantana weed was lopped, the fig trees flourished, a canopy slowly reforming over the six hectares. But the good works have a smelly side-effect. After rain the stinkhorn fungi pervades this precious pocket with its own unique perfume. **[On Rotary Dve off Bruxner Hwy, heading towards Ballina]**

## SUPER BOWL

**MILDURA, Vic.**   Don't expect to catch a 747 to Singapore at the Mildura International Flight Centre. (In fact the only red-eye you're likely to catch may result from the place's aroma.) But the Flight Centre, otherwise known as the town's sewage farm, is recognised as one of the best bird spots Down Under, with more than 142 species on record. The cess-pond is over a kilometre long and about 150 m wide. Plantation gums and native mallee offer ornithologists ideal cover for spotting freckled ducks and rainbow bee-eaters, neither of which possess a developed sense of smell. Adding alum mineral salt to the pond, according to the Sunraysia Water Authority, reduces a thing called flocculation and attracts birds in their thousands.

## GUT REACTION

**MONTO, Qld**   The old butcher's shop, refitted as the Monto History Centre, is run by Cec and Beryl Bleys – a former butcher and his ebullient wife. What the pair don't know about Monto and its surrounds has yet to occur. The couple sold T-bones for 28 years from the premises, but now prefer to chew the fat with visitors. Just don't ask about the coconuts on the shelf. You might find out they're in fact gigantic hairballs extracted from cow stomachs. **[2 Kelvin St. Open weekdays 10a.m.–4p.m. Donation entry. Phone (07) 4166 1277]**

Young ABC viewers will recognise Split Point Lighthouse in **Aireys Inlet (Vic.)** as the cylindrical home of the Twist family in *Round The Twist*. Just as baby-boomers will twig to the musical reference of nearby Eagle Rock. And regardless of your age, your nose will pick out Smelly Beach, an inlet below the lighthouse and named after a potent strain of algal funk.

## TERRA INFIRMA

**SORELL, Tas.**   God rest David Hildyard of Site 93 in Sorell Cemetery. This humble storekeeper curled up his toes in his 32nd year, back in 1852. But the grave remains open for business, as the shifting earth has split the stonework, giving passersby a chance to peek into the abyss. 'You know not when the time is', as the epitaph reminds us. So don't peek too close. [Part of St George's Church Grounds. Mr Hildyard sleeps close to Fitzroy St]

## DENTAL THERAPY

**STAWELL, Vic.**   Casper's World in Miniature has a midget Eiffel Tower, a dwarfish Dutch windmill and a breezeblock igloo. But once you enter King Tut's pyramid, the bizarreness begins in earnest, for inside the tomb is a dinosaur made of human teeth. Real human teeth. Dentist David Lye combined the unwanted molars of Toorak and Warracknabeal to create crocodiles, rainforests and a gum tree made of denture gums. David calls it 'the largest display of dental leftovers in the world', and so far nobody has contradicted him. [Open daily 9a.m.– 5p.m. Entry $8.50/$7.50/$3.50. Look for the Eiffel Tower]

At Pepe's Paperie in **Phillip (ACT)** you can purchase peculiar parchment pulped from powder-dry pachyderm pooh. A portion of the money you spend on the elephant-dung paper goes to the Millennium Elephant Foundation, a fund set up to preserve jungle habitat and pamper pensioner pachyderms. [**Shop 67, Woden Plaza. Open daily. Phone (02) 6282 0300**]

# VERTIGO

*(Being a summit of giddy heights
and vertical drops)*

## CLIFFHANGERS

**ARMIDALE, NSW**   Halfway between Armidale and Ebor is arguably the highest waterfall in Australia. Wollomombi Falls offer a spooky double-drop of 488 m. The argument surrounds the double-drop element, which geographic pedants view as *two* waterfalls. For the hair-splitters in your party, head north to Lumholtz National Park, near Ingham in Qld, where the Wallaman Falls plummet a singular 278 m.

## ASCENDING ORDER

**BEN LOMOND, Tas.**   The state's only ski resort takes three big zigs and three major zags to reach. The only road into the park, about 60 km northwest of Launceston, travels from Upper Blessington up. The zigzag, which takes the name of Jacob's Ladder, is a 225-m stretch of unsurfaced road that climbs at a 70° angle. (For the mathematically minded, the climb is 1060 m in 18 km, one of the steepest hauls in Oz.) Most humble suburban cars can scale this particular ladder of opportunity, but whether most suburban hearts can hold out is another matter. Chains are essential in winter.

When one astronaut left the US space shuttle *Endeavour* in 1996, intent to fix a hi-tech attachment on the fuselage, another astronaut took his picture for posterity. But for the people of **Denham (WA)**, the photo's appeal is its background. Etched on distant Mother Earth is the unmistakable alligator-jaws form of Shark Bay. **[Public bar of Heritage Resort, cnr Durlacher St and Knight Tce]**

## HIGH-ROLLER

**EXMOUTH, WA**   The Vlaming Head Lighthouse is the only fully restored kerosene-powered lighthouse still operating in Australia. Yet another reason to visit the 1912 beacon is to imagine the minibus that rolled over the lip of the carpark in 2003. Nobody was hurt, as nobody was on board. The wheels began to roll when one tourist returned to the parked vehicle to retrieve her mobile phone. She quickly woke another tourist who'd fallen asleep in the bus – and the pair vamoosed. Patrons in the Lighthouse Caravan Park, directly below the escarpment, nearly dropped their jaffle irons when they saw the bus approaching. **[Check for tour times, and the lighthouse-lighting ceremonies throughout the year, at the Exmouth Visitors Centre on (08) 9949 1176 or visit www. exmouthwa.com.au]**

## STANCHION TO STANCHION

**LAUNCESTON, Tas.**   Europe holds all the trumps when it comes to chairlift records – except one. Cataract Gorge in Launceston brags the longest single chairlift span in the world. In plain English, the 308-m stretch from Pylon A to Pylon B can't be matched. In stopwatch terms: it's six-minutes-plus between poles, though speeds can vary according to the volume of customers. When you finally get to the other side, take a stroll. Just don't step on the peacock tails – the gorge is rife with the creatures. **[Best to catch the First Basin bus from town to maximise hiking options. Open most days 9a.m.–5p.m., the chairlift costs $9/$6 return. Phone (03) 6331 5915]**

The pit of your stomach will get an almighty workout on the Giant Drop in Dreamworld, **Coomera (Qld)**. Billed as the tallest freefall drop-ride in the world, the carriage falls down a 38-storey J-curve at roughly 160 kph. You'll overtake your scream before it leaves your mouth. **[Pacific Hwy. Open daily 10a.m.–5p.m. Entry to entire park $60/$38. Phone (07) 5588 1111 or drop by www.dreamworld.com.au]**

## JUST DROPPING IN

**MAPLETON, Qld**    Should you ever doubt that Australia once belonged to the same rugged landmass as Papua, take a drive along the Obi Obi Rd. Known by locals as 'the goat track', this serpentine road splits into two – one road down, the other up – to allow traffic some breathing space. But that's not the feat in question. Halfway down the ridge, where the downhill dirt curves close to the uphill bitumen, you'll see one of Australia's steepest driveways, an 80-m concrete strip at a 60° angle. Not a place for riding billycarts – it would be a cannonball run.

## IN THE CRAW

**MOLE CREEK, Tas.**    For name alone, you should visit Devil's Gullet, but not if you're prone to fainting. Ancient glaciers have turned the val-ley below from a U to a V – though the introduction of a hydro-electricity scheme has since turned the valley's Fisher River from a torrent to a prostate dribble. Still, the awe quotient is high – as are you, at some 220 m straight up, standing on top of dolerite columns. Pack a jumper. **[13 km of gravel road off the C137 south of Mole Creek]**

You don't get a better Grand Canyon impersonation than the Charles Knife Gorge off the approach road into **Exmouth (WA)**. Entry into Cape Range National Park is a bumpy 11 km, and thoroughly worth the vibrations

## KOALA-CAM

**PEMBERTON, WA**    Australia's tallest trees, the mighty karris and jarrahs of WA, grow in the southwest corner of the continent. The best known is the Gloucester Tree close to the town centre. Lesser known is the Dave Evans Bicentennial Tree, in the Warren National Park. A total of 130 steel bars (your rungs) and an eyrie of four ladders give you a view above the canopy to die for . . . or so it feels. After the first 55 bars, a platform gives you the chance to chicken out. Up top, the tree's crown can sway up to 1.5 m, ensuring a teaspoon of queasiness will mix with a tablespoon of exhilara-tion. **[8 km south of town to Old Vasse Rd, then another 5 km along]**

## HAUTE CUISINE

**THREDBO, NSW**   Eagle's Nest Mountain Hut is the highest restaurant in Australia. Perched on the side of Mt Kosciuszko (our highest mountain at 2228 m), the Thredbo eatery offers crucial pre- and après-ski sustenance in the shape of chocolate fondues, gluhwein and schnapps. On certain summer mornings you can catch a gondola (the aerial variety) up Crackenback to the restaurant and watch the sun rise over your champagne breakfast. **[Phone (02) 6457 6019]**

# VILLAINS

*(Being a gallery of remarkable rogues
and newsworthy nasties)*

## BEYOND REDEEMING

**ALBANY, WA** Lord Dunn, Harry Lawson, Baron Swanston, Albert Williams – not an honours list, but a sampling of aliases adopted by one of Australia's worst serial killers. His real name was Frederick Deeming. His victim tally included his two wives and four of his offspring. Under arrest in Albany in 1892, the psychopath used a bottle shard to remove his moustache lest the chief witness recognise him. Also while there Deeming wrote his autobiography, but the manuscript was destroyed in accordance with a Crown Law injunction against killers gaining profit from their crimes. **[Get all the grisly details in the Old Gaol Museum on Stirling Tce. Open daily 10a.m.–4p.m. Entry, which includes a visit to Patrick Taylor Cottage Museum, $4/$2.50, family $10. Phone (08) 9841 1401]**

## GREEN WITH GOLD IN WHITE

**COOLGARDIE, WA** Elizabeth Gold fled across the tennis court, having been shot by her lover Russell Snodgrass. The trouble had started in 1896 when her husband, Captain Charles Gold, died of a burst appendix and grief-stricken Elizabeth was comforted by Mr Snodgrass, a neighbour. Exceedingly comforted, it would seem, for the two became lovers. But Snodgrass, a jealous type, couldn't countenance his mistress attending a charity ball in honour of the late captain. Immediately after he shot her, Snodgrass rued his rashness and sent a bullet through his brain, the two being found lying cross-like on the lawn. Today, murderer and victim lie 20 m apart in Coolgardie cemetery, with explorer Ernest Giles in between. **[Cemetery is west of town. Mrs Gold is grave C-60, down from Mr Giles, who resides near the ornate anchor on your left. The killer is D-87]**

Brutal bushranger Mad Dog Morgan was shot dead in 1865. To deter future deviants, the corpse was put on public display (where, it's believed, a morbid pilgrim souvenired the scrotum for a purse). According to the law of the time, Morgan was buried outside the graveyard in **Wangaratta (Vic.)**. Ironically, as more citizens died the cemetery expanded, and now the Dog has been let into the yard. **[Tone Rd]**

## OLD-TIME SNAG

MACKSVILLE, NSW    Dave Hoffman is Dangerous Dan, a butcher of the first degree and an even better story-teller. His father, also known as Dangerous Dan, was likewise a butcher and, so one particular story goes, was unblocking the chimney of a cottage near Congarinni, west of town, when he came across the secret sausage recipe of its then-owner, a bushranger known as Dingo. The Jolly Jumbuck, thanks to Dingo, is a blend of lean lamb, warrigal spinach and native mint. In Dangerous Dan's shop on Princess St, parallel with the highway, there are Pork Witchetty and peppery Bushman sausages (and more tall tales) on offer. **[Phone (02) 6568 1036]**

In bushranging circles, the Chutzpah Prize goes to Matthew Brady. The ex-convict had a bounty on his head, set by Governor Arthur in 1825. Unfazed, Brady rode into **Kempton (Tas.)** and nailed a note onto the Royal Oak's door, promising 20 gallons of rum to anyone who could deliver him the governor.

## SUGGESTION BOX

URALLA, NSW    Signs the size of billboards point you off the highway to the grave of 'Captain Thunderbolt' (Frederick Ward), a serial highway robber who terrorised Granite Country in the late 1860s. Few pilgrims probably realise that for many years a biscuit tin sat atop the plot, inviting comments from the public. According to relics from the tin – on show in McCrossin's Mill – Ward was revered and reviled in equal measure. Then again, a taxi driver saw his chance for a free plug, dropping in his business card. **[End of John St, south of town]**

## CHOP AND CHANGE

**WAGGA WAGGA, NSW**   Cutting chops one day in 1866, Tom Castro had a brainwave. He knew the difference between being a butcher and a baronet was a kilo of audacity. The meat merchant shocked the world when he claimed to be Roger Tichborne, a young aristocrat who supposedly drowned between Rio and New York in 1854. The reward for such nerve was the Tichborne fortune. Even Roger's own mother was taken by the ruse, thinking Tom was Roger (though Tom's real name was Arthur Orton and he was a career scammer from Wapping in England). The resultant trials, first for fraud, then for perjury, racked up more court days than any other Commonwealth matter to date. **[A painting of the Tichborne trial hangs in the Museum of Riverina in the historic Wagga Council Chambers on Baylis St. Open Tues.–Sat. 10a.m.–5p.m., Sun. noon–4p.m. Free entry. Inquiries on (02) 6926 9655 or visit www.wagga.nsw.gov.au/museum]**

## FORGING A BLACKSMITH

**WINGHAM, NSW**   Jimmy Governor was a half-caste fence-fixer who was trying to fit into a white society. But the bigotry became too much in 1897, when Jimmy left the rails and murdered one or two landowners and several innocent children. After years of cunning elusion, including fence-walking to eradicate tracks, Governor was nabbed in Wingham in 1900 and hanged in Sydney a year later. His tortured tale was novelised by Thomas Keneally, via the antihero Jimmie Blacksmith. The whole regrettable business resonates in the Manning Valley Museum. And you can see not only the lock-up and the manacles inhabited by Governor, but also – in a separate showcase – a Rugby League blazer once worn by one Tom Keneally, father of Thomas. **[12 Farquhar St. Open daily 10a.m.–4p.m. Entry $3/$2/50c. Phone (02) 6553 4910 or visit www.manninghistorical.org]**

## GIFTS OF THE WISEMAN

**WISEMANS FERRY, NSW**   A dapper gent stands on the crest overlooking the Hawkesbury River. He's identified as Solomon Wiseman (a tautology, you may think), 'Pioneer, Innkeeper, Ferryman'. To that list you can add Lumber Thief, Scammer and Machiavellian. Back in England, Wiseman had stolen a pile of valuable timber and so earned a passage in 1806 to the outdoor prison known as Port Jackson. He gained a ticket-of-leave within four years, and after a dabble in shipping he moved inland and in 1827 ran the Hawkesbury's first ferry. Wiseman also bought up land, knowing that a convict road was coming through, and was soon worth a good deal thanks to money from the government and toil from the convicts. It is said that his headless ghost haunts the ferry and/or his former pub on the hill.

# ODDITIONS

- In ambling distance of **Coolangatta (Qld)** Airport is Ned Kelly's Car Rentals. One pledge made by the imposing billboard is 'No Hold-Ups'.
- Kill, the pivotal verb of Commandment 6, has been dumped from the painted tablet in **Fremantle (WA)** Prison's remarkable church. Why? With the jail's execution policy – that saw 44 miscreants hanged – the chaplain preferred the word 'murder'.

# VISIONS

*(Being a dreamscape of occult sightings
and inspired imaginings)*

## EYES ON THE PRIZE

**BOURKE, NSW**  Thirty-six cyclists assembled around an obelisk in Bourke Cemetery in 2002 to pay homage to the optical crusader Dr Fred Hollows, who was buried there. A lapsed Kiwi, Hollows spent a lifetime eradicating trachomas among Aboriginal communities, as well as hunting cataracts in Africa. The cyclists were embarking on a fund-raiser – the 1200-km pedal from Bourke to Bourke St in Melbourne – that still bears his foundation's name. (And keep your eyes peeled for Australia's first mosque in the same graveyard.) **[On Kidman Way, heading to Cobar. Learn more about the foundation at www.hollows.org]**

The Djab Wurrung people once camped on the slopes of Mt Langi Ghiran. They called the regal silhouette cast by the mountain's ridgeline 'the Sleeping Princess'. The best spot from which to see this supine maiden is One Tree Hill in **Ararat (Vic.)**, looking along the plain to Melbourne. **[Off Golf Links Rd. To the west the Grampians, to the east the princess and Pyrenees]**

## PHANTOM FALLS

**CHARTERS TOWERS, Qld**  Venus Gold Battery is the largest surviving stamping mill in Australia, a place of stone breakers, grinding pans and graphite crucibles dating back to the 1870s. Among the relics, a piece of modern technology stands out. Pioneered by Brian Shirley, the multimedia wizard behind the sound and light show 'Blood on the Southern Cross' at Sovereign Hill, the Water Screen is a curtain of twin cascades on which is projected the 'ghost' of Edmund Plant, the mill's original owner. In a place renowned for ore the uncanny vision inspires plenty of it. [Milchester Rd. Open daily for guided tours from 9.30a.m. (last at 3.30p.m.). Entry $11/$10/$5, family $25. Phone (07) 4752 0314]

## PUBLIC HANGING

DELORAINE, Tas.   Ned Terry, a tiger hunter from Tas., admired a theatre curtain he once saw hanging in Griffith, NSW. He reckoned his own home-town, Meander Valley, could stitch up something just as lavish, and 10 years later his faith was vindicated. Niecy van der Elst-Brown oversaw the sew-a-thon, in which 300 people picked and pulled for 10 000 hours, calling on 200 m of hand-dyed silk. *Yarns*, the result, is an eye-popping, four-season, 57-m embroidery of Deloraine and district. For best results, wander the town before you see the replica. [98–100 Emu Bay Rd. Open every day 9.30a.m.–4p.m. Entry $7/$5. Phone (03) 6362 3471 or visit www.greatwesterntiers.org]

## JUMBO EFFORT

DERRINALLUM, Vic.   Mt Elephant is a dormant volcano that dozes on the state's western plains. The 394-m hill is also known as The Swagman's Lighthouse, so prominent and comforting is the lump. And to prove how highly the landmark is regarded, the people of Corangamite Shire *bought* the mountain in 2000, raising $100 000 to match the equivalent grant from a statutory body known as Trust for Nature. The Elephant rates as one of the few Australian mountains owned by the people who live in its shadow. [Off the Hamilton Hwy west of town]

Morning Glory is the name they give to some peculiar clouds that centre over **Burketown (Qld)** in spring. The worm-shaped vapours roll across the surrounding Gulf Country in the early morning, usually in a cluster of three or four. While the clouds look ethereal, the lead lining is the savage winds that often accompany them.

## CAPE CRUSADERS

FORSTER, NSW   The nation's bicentenary in 1988 was the perfect excuse for many towns to restore their pieces of heritage. Here the project focused on Cape Hawke, a landmass spotted and named by Captain Cook, and the highest point between Newcastle and Camden Haven. (Local Aborigines prefer the name Toocaloo, meaning 'oyster'.) Erosion and lantana had made the cape an eyesore, so volunteers tore out the vines and cut a stepped path to the peak. A job well done, they thought, until – thanks to the renewed supply of sun and air – cabbage palms and red ash (a littoral rainforest) shot from the soil. Suddenly the Bicentennial Lookout couldn't see a thing and a two-storey tower had to be built above the canopy. **[Turn down Cape Hawke Dve near the new high school. The going is steep for both car – about 400 m in second gear – and walker]**

## OUT-THERE ART

MARREE, SA   Some 50 km west of Marree along the Oodnadatta Track, the sight of two upright aeroplanes interrupts the plainness of your view. The installation belongs to 'Planethenge', a freakish sculpture garden devised by Melburnian Robin Cooke. Tin dogs, colossal wildflowers and cosmic abstracts keep the planes company. The artist's vision embraces Dreamtime consciousness and what has been described as 'global trance sculpture', which I don't really understand either.

## HERE BE DRAGONS, MAYBE

MONTO, Qld   Imagination is needed in the Dragon Cave, a short return walk in Cania Gorge National Park. Natural leaching has sketched a Chinese monster in the sandstone overhang, though the shadow pattern could equally be a ginger root or a Qantas kangaroo. Ten times clearer is the big footprint near the park's entrance, at the rear of the camping ground. Obviously the naming brigade was fond of metaphors in the gorge, with Giant's Chair and Two-Storey Cave also on the map. Unfortunately Elephant Rock has been closed to walkers – its hide is too slippery. **[12 km north of Monto along the Burnett Hwy]**

## HOLY MOLY

**OATLANDS, Tas.**   Which is weirder? The pathological attraction among Japanese people to a humble Oatlands church, or an apparition of Christ that was seen in St Paul's front left window during a guided tour? Christ disappeared again as mysteriously as he had come, while the Japanese continue to appear. Peter Fielding was the guide on the day. By night and by appointment, he leads ghost tours by lamplight, vividly recounting the manifestation as well as the multiple hangings in Australia's oldest courthouse. [Tours daily on request. Cost $8 for 1½ hours. All profits to St Paul's Restoration Fund. Phone (03) 6254 1135]

## OUTER LIMIT

**POINT HICKS, Vic.**   Point Hicks, otherwise known as Cape Everard, was the first piece of Australia spotted by Captain Cook and his crew as they sailed in from New Zealand on 20 April 1770. The granite cliffs are named in honour of Lieutenant Zachary Hicks, who did the spotting. As to getting to the point (which I'm vainly attempting), you need a sturdy vehicle to travel the 47 km from Cann River to the mainland's tallest lighthouse.

## BATH TOYS

**SEASPRAY, Vic.**   Okay, so it's just a blip on the horizon, but here is the mainland's clearest glimpse of Australia's first oil rig and one of the first rough-water rigs to be built in the world. (It's also the world's luckiest rig, for Esso's explorations in 1965 hit gas at the first jab.) If it doesn't look like rough water, just wait 10 minutes, Bass Strait being so shallow (the Barracouta platform, some 23 km offshore, is rooted in only 46 m of water) that easterly swells can whip the water much as a toddler can devastate a bathtub. For your reference, Barracouta is 20 m high and those blinking lights to the west are the twin rigs Perch and Dolphin.

Drive to the top of Pilot's Hill in **Harrington (NSW)**, and you'll be looking down upon Australia's only river system with two mouths. Please, no mother-in-law jokes.

## BROMLEY SEEKS LEGAL ADVICE

**ULURU, NT**    Bromley is a teddy bear who's been around. In 1986 he travelled with his host family, the Campbells, who photographed the soft toy in various habitats including Uluru. The snaps became part of a children's book which went on to sell 40 000 copies, a large percentage of these being snapped up in the rock's service town, Yulara. But the Anangu people, the rock's traditional owners, now have the legal right to pulp any merchandise that profanes the rock's image or betrays its sacred aspects, and the National Park management wants the book made unavailable. Bromley's custodian, Alan Campbell, is less than impressed and would want fair compensation. The wrangle continues. **[Check with rangers about the rules of photography, and restricted areas]**

## THE SAND TRADE

**VICTOR HARBOR, SA**    Encounter Bay has two meanings. The original encounter was between Matthew Flinders and Nicholas Baudin in 1802. The more recent rendezvous dates back to 1980 when Chris Tapscott, a teacher at Victor Harbor High School, decided his Year 7 students would benefit from encountering the Anangu people of central Australia. His students, and Anangu students from the Musgrave Ranges near the NT border, learnt the basics of each other's language and culture and then swapped places. A generation later, the program is embedded in the Year 7 syllabus in both places. To celebrate the link, a whale called Kondoli wallows on Kleinig's Hill. Fittingly, the creature hails from a Ngarrindjeri story that deals with transformation. **[Telescope on hand, the whale is also the ideal spot to encounter the genuine article during winter]**

# WALLS

*(Being a precinct of brickwork, upright structures and walls with stories)*

## BREAD AND MORTAR

**ADELAIDE, SA**  Jails have walls – no scoop there. But the curious feature of the old Adelaide jail is the shifty design of its inner perimeter. The outer wall is stone and impassable, but the inner wall is riddled with loose bricks, designed to dislodge during any escape attempt. The lock-up shut its doors for the last time in 1988, though now sleep-overs can be arranged, with bread and water thrown in. Just don't nudge the masonry. **[18 Gaol Rd, Thebarton. Open Sun.–Fri. 11a.m.–3.30p.m., Sat. by appointment. Entry $7/$5.50/$4.50, family $19. Phone (08) 8231 4062 or visit www. adelaidegaol.org.au]**

## SISTINE'S SISTER

**BAIRNSDALE, Vic.**  For six shillings a day, back in 1931, Frank Floreani painted heaven and hell and purgatory in St Mary's Cathedral. He did the saints too, each holding a symbol of his own martyrdom. There's also a smouldering soul trying in vain to clamber onto the balustrade. As one grand vision the fresco, sponsored by an Irish priest named Cornelius Cremin, is neck-wrenching. A current cleric, Father Brendan Hogan, tries to ignore the misery on the walls as he speaks of love and forgiveness. But one face it's hard to look past is the horned she-devil on the altar's right, who, legend has it, is the spitting image of Cremin's housekeeper, who managed to get on both men's goat. **[Next-door to the Visitors Centre on Main St]**

In the centre of **Maitland (NSW)**, down Victoria St, is the first Dominican chapel in Australia, built in 1910. Though in 1989, with the Newcastle earth-quake hitting town, the chapel nearly bit the dust. Hence the wall's extra support in the guise of elegant buttresses. Look carefully at the brick's tones and you'll see the reinforcements quite clearly.

## REBIRTH OF VENUS

BROKEN HILL, NSW    Botticelli didn't paint *The Birth of Venus*, not the one above the Palace Hotel's foyer anyway. This version of the gal-in-the-clam was the brushwork of publican Mario Cellotto, who toiled away for weeks. But the vistas don't stop there. A student of Albert Namatjira named Gordon Wyen arrived in the early 1980s to add to the Palace's gallery, putting stratocumulus clouds on the ceiling and Aboriginal warriors behind the bar. This former coffee palace, built by the optimistic Methodist Temperance Movement in 1888, has been a lively institution ever since the wowsers departed. *Priscilla: Queen of the Desert* lent Mario's murals some exposure in 1994. **[227 Argent St. Phone (08) 8088 1699]**

## WYLAND'S WHALES

BUNDABERG, Qld    The Whaling Wall is not a misspelling but a six-storey downtown mural, for which artist Robert Wyland needed 1000 litres of paint. One of the best viewing points is outside the post office half a block away. In fact if you stand on the bench you might even see the turtle gliding at about mezzanine depth. Wyland had painted 22 eco-murals around the world, but this was his first in our hemisphere. The city council encountered a hitch in 2004, though, when having decided that the painting needed touching up they discovered that as Wyland owned copyright on the seascape, only he could do the work. **[Stand on the corner of Bourbong and Barolin Sts]**

## FIREWALL

HOBART, Tas.    William Davidson was worried for his apricots and any other sun-loving plant. Hobart felt far too chilly. So in 1829 the curator of the Botanical Gardens put up a wall with the aid of a dozen convicts. Three furnaces were 'planted' along its length, the heat ducts running through the bricks and the smoke escaping through chimneys disguised in the pillars. You can still see a fireplace down by the herb garden. The Arthur Wall is Australia's only such wall in a public garden. When you reach TV gardening guru Peter Cundall's vegetable patch, you know you're getting warm. **[Queens Domain. Gardens open daily 8a.m.–5p.m. in winter, closing a little later when warmer. Admission free]**

## WALL-TO-WALL CHARACTER

**MENDOORAN, NSW**   The town was on the ebb. First the hospital shut, then the railway, the pub, both garages and the bank. But Karin Duce decided to buck the trend: she took over the hardware store in 1994, and as well as raising five children and keeping a mixed farm afloat with her husband she studied business by night. The store gained a grocery wing, a cafe annexe in 1999, and a 28-m mural on the outside wall painted by Karin herself. Brush in hand, the ex-cartographer depicted 18 scenes along the main street, including the tennis club and the resuscitated pub. The cafe ceiling is sky-blue, with galahs on the wing. Outside, Karin's river gums look so authentic that real galahs frequently try to land on them, only to head-butt the masonry. **[Bundulla St]**

## SILLY POINT

**SEYMOUR, Vic.**   In 1949 British publisher Walter Hutchison asked his Melbourne office to acquire a painting of Australian cricket. What he ended up with was a couple of stick figures playing tip-and-run against a pub wall. So peeved was Hutchison that he dismissed the art dealer responsible. The canvas, *Cricketers* by Russell Drysdale, is now a national treasure, and the pub (once Moodys) is now the Royal. The wall in question faces west, closest to the beer garden. **[Cnr Emily and Manners Sts]**

> The Barossa Valley Reservoir near **Williamstown (SA)** boasts one of the first concrete-arch dams in the world, a spectacular 140-m arc that cannot keep a secret. Murmur at one end and every syllable will reach your friend's ear on the other side of the dam, as clearly as if you were speaking on a mobile (in fact, 10 times clearer). **[Yettie Rd, 5 km northwest of Williamstown. Open daily 8a.m.–5p.m. Closed during fire bans]**

## BRICK-A-BRAC

**WINTON, Qld**   Opal miner Arno Grotjahn is a grade-A fossicker. When not hunting jewels on the Mitchell plains, he's seeking other gems at the town dump. Sausage-makers, fire extinguishers, woks, jerry cans, generators, petrol bowsers and moonstones – whatever his Landcruiser can carry. The boldest flash of colour on his perimeter wall is a painting of the Eureka flag, a salute to an ancestor who fought in the Ballarat uprising. Through an inset wagon wheel you'll see the same creative frenzy in Arno's backyard. And out the front a flying saucer made of truck springs and a mining drill hovers among a crop of Seuss-style cacti. 'The history of man is the whole history of machines,' says Arno, who hasn't even neglected the kitchen sink. **[Vindex St, behind the North Gregory Hotel]**

## POST-INDUSTRIAL PLOT

**WOLLONGONG, NSW**    Tucked below WIN Stadium, close to Five Islands Brewery, is a steel wall like no other. Long before the stadium existed, the foreshore was set aside as the town's first cemetery. Eventually, in 1969, the lure of the beach saw the graveyard converted into a reserve and most of the graves disappeared under new-laid turf. In 1998, when the park became the plaza for the Entertainment Centre, the last 10 headstones were framed within this unique wall, among the names of the 142 other displaced souls. **[On Marine Dve]**

# ODDITIONS

⑥ On one side of a butchery in **Charleville (Qld)** there's a brilliant mural by David Hinchliffe, which shows a butcher in a glass-bubble helmet lunging after the cow that jumped over the moon. You'll find S. & K. Radnedge Meats on the corner of Wills and Parry Sts.

⑥ If you look long enough at St Patrick's Cathedral on Parkfield St in **Bunbury (WA)**, you begin to see that the steeple's bricks are newer than the others. That's because when the cathedral went up in 1921, it didn't go all the way up as the steeple had sunk in the Bay of Biscay. A substitute spire was added 56 years later.

⑥ The famous blue granite of the Sydney Harbour Bridge hailed from **Marulan (NSW)**, on the Sydney side of Goulburn. Visit the town and you'll find the same cobalt hues adorning several buildings.

⑥ Reputedly the biggest mosaic in the world depicts Anzac apparitions floating upwards from a battlefield. The artwork dominates the

Hall of Memory in the Australian War Memorial, **Canberra (ACT)**.
**[Treloar Cres., top of Anzac Pde, Campbell. Open daily 10a.m.–
5p.m., from 9a.m. in school holidays. Free entry. Phone (02)
6243 4211 or visit www.awm.gov.au]**

⊚ Your senses will be arrested when you see the cop shop in
**Nambucca Heads (NSW)**. Guy Crosley is the prime suspect. He
grubbed the crockery, the heirlooms and the ceramics to fashion
this 60-m mosaic skirting the police station. It's on the corner of
Ridge and Bowra Sts.

# WATER

*(Being a whirlpool of current phenomena
and uncanny creeks)*

## BUCKET BRIGADE

HINDMARSH, ADELAIDE, SA    If taste is any guide, you may be wiser drinking Adelaide's famous beer than its infamous tapwater. For compelling evidence of the foul faucet stuff take a trip to the SA Brewery where visitors can take turns collecting water – via the coin-operated spigot – from four wells beneath the brewery, which draw from the Wilunga aquifer. The sight is sobering – an army of citizens armed with jerry cans, and hard currency, prepared to bypass the domestic tap. [Cnr Port Rd and Adam St]

Newfoundland (Canada) may beat the tides of **Derby (WA)** for height, but few places in the world can equal the flows here for speed. Owing to the funnel shape of King Sound, and its terraced floor, the mudflats become a surging flood before you can blink.

## FASCINATING BORE

BLACKALL, Qld    Nothing too dramatic in the dry history of outback water, but at the aquatic centre you can immerse yourself in the subject, neck-deep. Why settle for a backyard jacuzzi when you can have a landscaped pond fed naturally by artesian water at 58°C, right beside an Olympic pool? Few other aquatic centres in remote Australia think to tap into the land's advantage of bubbling bore water. [Salvia St, last left heading for Tambo. Open daily May–Aug. 10a.m.–6p.m., weekdays Sep.–April 6a.m.–10a.m., 2.30p.m.–6p.m. (weekends 11a.m.–7p.m.). Closed end April, early May. Entry $2.75/$1.40/$1.10 (less in summer). Phone (07) 4657 4975.]

## WHERE ALL THE RIVERS RUN

DENILIQUIN, NSW    Imagine a river running beneath a river. This engineering trick occurs at Lawson's Siphons on the Finley side of town.

Essentially the Mulwala irrigation canal drops 5 m below the Edward River and travels underground for 700 m before reappearing on the other bank. A diagram steps you through the puzzle in the tourist information centre in town, where you'll also need to ask for the key if you care to see the real deal. **[Visitors Centre beside Edward River bridge. Phone 1800 650 712]**

> Nip around the back of the post office in **Babinda (Qld)** and you'll see what looks like a rusty milk can sitting in the corner of the yard. This vessel has been planted by the Bureau of Meteorology, and it's usually the most water-laden rain gauge in Australia. The yearly average tops 4 m.

## THE GRUNTER SIGHS

**KATHERINE, NT**   Bolted into Katherine's railway bridge is a water-level gauge, which ranges from zero to 18 m. This is a frightening indicator, when you consider that the flood of 1998 rose to 20 m. To experience the disaster on an intimate level, visit Rod and Rifle in the Woolworths shopping plaza: a flood line marks the pole opposite the till, high enough to devastate the store but just low enough for the striped grunter to stay in his tank. **[Katherine Tce]**

## PRETZEL CREEK

**MARGARET RIVER, WA**   Meekadarribee ('bathing place of the moon' in Wardandi dialect) has been likened to nature's own freeway ramp. This intimate waterfall, a stroll from the recently restored National Trust property Ellensbrook, has the rare distinction of flowing beneath itself. The initial stream flows across a bridge made of tufa (a volcanic cousin of pumice) and then doubles back anti-clockwise. According to legend Alfred Bussell, the homestead's first occupant, bestowed this unique gift upon his teenage bride, Ellen, during the 1850s, but methinks the moon, and the Nyungar people, would disagree. **[Homestead is on Ellensbrook Rd. Open weekends 9.45a.m.–4.15p.m. Entry $4.40/$2.20, family $11. Phone (08) 9321 6088]**

The sea-baths at Bronte Beach in **Sydney (NSW)** are reputed to be the starting blocks for the swimming style known as 'the Australian crawl'. It's worth noting that it was Alick Wickham, a Solomon Islander, who concocted the stroke in 1898 during a handicap event.

## WETTEST CASE SCENARIO

**MOORA, WA**   They called it the once-in-300-years-flood. So high and so quickly did the waters of the Moore River rise in March 1999 that the entire town had to be repatriated to a Perth hostel 170 km south. Slowly the river returned to its channel, and the salvage job began. But the Moore (appropriately enough) wasn't done, returning in May the same year and again in August. The saga is captured on the wall of Makit Hardware – a painting of the first deluge showing the hardware store and nearby Lewis For Tyres a metre under water. The mural is based on a photo taken by Greg Reilly, the hardware owner, the camera held above his head. You can also stand beside the drainpipe and measure up against Floods 1 and 2. **[Cnr Clinch and Midlands Sts]**

Marsh Estate in **Pokolbin (NSW)** is named after chief winemaker Andrew Marsh, not for ooze underfoot. The wines from this vineyard (on Deasys Rd, phone (02) 4998 7587) are unique in that none of their grapes have been irrigated. Part of the Marsh manifesto is a variation of *vino veritas* – they produce the wine the season decrees.

## DEMOCRITUS TOURS

**WALPOLE, WA**   Gary Muir calls it the Moses Line. It's more pronounced after heavy rain, when the tannin-rich rivers confront the Southern Ocean influx, the result a meeting of brown and blue in Walpole Inlet, with a seam of foam marking the division. Gary runs the wilderness cruise to the heart of Walpole Nornalup National Park, and his patter is mesmerising.

How can one mortal squeeze such ingenious stories of Norwegian shipwrecks, Caspian terns, bungled bank robberies, quokka pogroms and Leo Tolstoy into two and a half hours of boating? 'Democritus,' says Gary, halfway through explaining Gondwana's drift using a rubber spider and a stuffed fox, 'said life is to be enjoyed.' This is an offbeat tour for all ages. [Basic boat trip costs $30, $12 for under-14s, free for under-5s. Profit shares go to ecological causes. Book on (08) 9840 1111 or visit www.wowwilderness.com.au]

# ODDITIONS

◎ Singapore has a rainbow fountain, and **Rockhampton (Qld)** has the only other one in the world. After dark, the jets play the palette with variegated floodlights on the corner of Murray St and the Bruce Hwy.

◎ **Cloncurry (Qld)** has posted the hottest temperature (over 51°C) in Australia. That's why the billboard on the town outskirts promises you a warm welcome. It's also why Robert O'Hara Burke's water bottle in the Mary Kathleen Museum is bone-dry. [McIlwraith St. Open weekdays 8a.m.–noon, 1p.m.–4.30p.m.; weekends May–Oct. 9a.m.–3p.m. Closed Dec.–Jan. Entry $7/$5/$3, family $20. Phone (07) 4742 1361]

◎ One reason why **Sale (Vic.)** was slow to attract new settlers was the town's original name, back in 1844. Founding father, Archibald McIntosh, christened the town Flooding Creek.

◎ About 6 km south of **Tamworth (NSW)**, the country of country music, is a guitar-shaped swimming pool. You'll find this curio, with strings attached, at The Allendale Motor Inn on the New England Hwy.

◎ The sea has sculpted a perfect figure 8 on the Palm Jungle Loop Track, in the Royal National Park south of **Sydney (NSW)**. The rockpool can only be seen at low tide: take a short signposted detour near Burning Palms Beach.

◎ The town of **Waratah (Tas.)** encircles its own private waterfall. The Bischoff Hotel on Main St is the ideal perch from which to contemplate this Australian novelty.

# WHEELS

*(Being a revolution of pivotal contraptions,*
*from things that turn to cars that burn)*

## TRUCKING HEAVEN

ALICE SPRINGS, NT   The world's only all-wheel-drive eight-wheeler (built in Middlesex, England, in 1934) is parked in the Road Transport Hall of Fame. The AEC ( the sexy acronym for the Associated Equipment Company) vehicle was found by a camel driver, Noel Fullerton, in a Darwin rubbish tip. It's really the world's first road train, having two gearboxes and a 40-tonne payload. Its turntables are World War 1 gun turrets. The hall teems with wonders for either sex. **[Norris Bell Ave., South Stuart Hwy. Open daily 9a.m.–5p.m. Entry $8/$5, family $22. Phone (08) 8952 7161 or visit www.roadtransporthall.com]**

## LAPPING IT UP

BATHURST, NSW   When most people think Bathurst, they think motor racing. But many visitors to town don't realise there's a chance to drive Australia's only permanent public-road racing circuit. Keeping to the speed limit, of course, you can hack The Esses and The Dipper. For those with a motorhead history, it verges on surreal to vroom (slowly) across Brock's Skyline straight past a letterbox or a sign saying 'Eggs 4 Sale'. And once you've won your fantasy lap, go downtown to stroll the chequered flagstones on the corner of Russell and William Sts, where the real winners are engraved. **[Follow William St to its western end, then turn left into Panorama Ave]**

## VERY VINTAGE CARS

BIRDWOOD, SA   A French priest named Padre Verbiest put together a steam car for the Emperor of China in 1672. Karl Benz got up to similar tricks 200 years later. And in Australia the trailblazer was a plough-maker called Shearer, from Mannum on the Murray, whose steam carriage of 1899 is recognised as the first such vehicle Down Under. He loaded up his family and turned every head on his trek to

Adelaide. Once there, he charged the public a shilling per ride till the police told him his contraption was scaring the horses. [National Motor Museum, Shannon St. Open daily 9a.m.–5p.m. Entry $9/$7/$4 or $24 a family. Phone (08) 8568 5006 or follow links at www.history. sa.gov.au]

A funeral parlour in **Toowoomba (Qld)** has modified a Moto Guzzi motorbike to give their deceased clients that last sense of freedom before being committed to God's care. Brian and Judith Coulqhoun have the baby-boomer boom trade firmly in mind. [Call (07) 4634 9946 for all sidecar queries]

## VAN FOR ALL SEASONS
**BUANGOR, Vic.**    Kevin Wilde has 8000 sheep and 100 caravans. The first take up most of his time. The vans, including Australia's oldest, take up much of his farm. Things are pretty ramshackle, but you can't quibble with the history. The oldest caravan, which hides near the gem-fossicking cabinets, is a collapsible box built by a Stawell blacksmith in 1910. [Between Beaufort and Ararat, 5 km down Warrak Rd, off the Western Hwy. Open by appointment. Entry $5 per car. Phone (03) 5354 3236]

## A MAN, A PLAN, DUNALLEY
**DUNALLEY, Tas.**    Egypt has her Suez, Panama has her Panama, and Australia, well, we have our Dunalley. This prestigious ditch, allegedly the continent's only man-made saltwater canal, was dug by hand in 1905. A weatherboard booth on the mainland side of the Arthur Hwy swings the bridge open in a few seconds. Compare that to the rusty wheel outside the pub on the opposite bank, a giant that needed six minutes to free the way between Marion and Lime Bays – back in the days when the world was time-rich.

## TURNER LANDSCAPE
**GRIFFITH, NSW**    Stand under the spinning prop of the Fairey Firefly plane, bang in the centre of town, and you'll see another spinner – the

Dethridge wheel, a world-first invented locally to measure irrigation flow. Holding your ground, you'll also see the Banna Ave roundabout, designed by Canberra's planner, Walter Burley Griffin, a man whose fetish was the radial street grid. Of course, Griffin's many wheels within wheels can be admired from the Scenic Dve – at the (ahem) Rotary Lookout.

## LADY AND GENTLEMEN, START YOUR ENGINES

**LONGFORD, Tas.**    From 1953 to 1968, the glamour lads of Formula One drove hell-bent around the Country Club Hotel. And one female too: a farmer's wife called Diane Leighton, whose Triumph TR2 Oscar is parked on permanent display in the pub window. Inside the hotel is an F1 museum, including a Maserati steering wheel over the fireplace, once gripped by Argentine legend, Juan Manuel Fangio. **[Country Club Hotel, cnr Union and Wellington Sts. Open from 11a.m. most days. Phone (03) 6391 1155]**

## OLD CURIOSITY

**MARYSVILLE, Vic.**    Grey nomads, eat your hearts out. If you think your four-berth caravan with air-con, BIRs and auto-flush WC is top of the line, have a look at the Romany Vardo in the Marysville Museum. Sculpted by C.J. Spooner, a master of merry-go-round mermaids, this ornate gypsy caravan (*vardo* is just gypsy-talk for wagon) was the cynosure of English turnpikes. Today's Romanies don't drift about in the sort of splendour afforded by this 1895 specimen – the only one of its kind, with a hand-chiselled dragon, intricate garlands, a bow-shaped ceiling and inbuilt double bed. **[49 Darwin St. Open daily 10a.m.–4.30p.m., closed Tues. Entry $8/$6/$5. Phone (03) 5963-3777]**

**Hervey Bay (Qld)** can lay claim to forming the first scooter club in Oz. Not those fold-up jobs that kids favour, but the electric buggies that infirm 'older kids' go for. So watch your step as you navigate the streets. Those mobility aids are likely to attack you from all angles.

## SON OF CANE

**MOURILYAN, Qld**   It's 1926. You live in a small sugar town called El Arish with no automotive engineers, and you have a low-slung steel-wheeled tractor. Every time you drive along the seed beds of your cane plantation, your tractor's underbelly mauls the young shoots. What do you do? Switch to pumpkins? Returned soldier Percy Benn had a better idea. He increased each tyre's height by attaching wooden sheaths, much as snow-chains fatten a car wheel. Such ingenuity recommended Benn to the eventual posting of mill director. [**Australian Sugar Museum, cnr Bruce Hwy and Peregrine St. Open Mon.-Sat. 9a.m.-5p.m., Sun. till 3p.m. May–Oct.; weekends 9a.m.-5p.m. Nov.–April. Entry $8/$6/$3, family $22. Phone (07) 4063 2656 or visit www.sugarmuseum.org.au**]

## HOME MEETS TRUCK

**NURIOOTPA, SA**   On a driving holiday in 1928, Pop Kaesler and his family had to sleep the night in a stranger's tin shed. Three years on, the experience spurred the Tanunda wheelwright to fashion one of the world's first motorhomes. The vehicle came with compass, altitude barometer, beds, toilet, spotlight and rifle. It's encased in a see-through garage outside the Barossa Valley Tourist Park. Where else? [**Penrice Rd, adjoining the football oval**]

## HURRY TO THE PURREY

**ROCKHAMPTON, Qld**   Bordeaux steam trams were not a bestseller, though Rockhampton ordered an entire fleet in 1909. For 30 years the little Purreys (named after their engineer, Monsieur Valentin Purrey) rattled and hummed along the town streets for sixpence a ride. (Number 15 was involved in three separate fatalities, forcing the depot to change its name, for superstitious reasons, to Number 9.) Nowadays only one remains – the last operating Purrey in the world. You can visit the novelty during the week at the Steam Tram Museum, though Sunday is when you can take a joyride. [**Cnr Archer and Denison Sts. Open Sun.-Fri. 10a.m.-4p.m., closed Sat. Entry $5.50/$3.30/$2.20. Phone (07) 4922 2774**]

## TRAVELLING LIGHT

**YORK, WA**    There's a fibreglass bicycle in the Motor Museum, the brainchild of a Briton called Benjamin Bowden. Weighing in at around 20 kg, the bike wasn't picked up by the world at large and the prototype fizzled in the early 1960s. By a strange coincidence, Bowden was the engineer behind the Austin-Healey car, but had nothing to do with a compatriot called Sir Frank Bowden who pioneered the far more successful Raleigh bicycles. **[Avon Tce. Open every day 9.30a.m.–3p.m. in summer, till 4p.m. in winter.** Phone (08) 9641 1288]

# ODDITIONS

- If you order eye fillet with Moreton Bay bugs at The Wagon Wheel Restaurant in **Cloncurry (Qld)**, you ask not for Surf & Turf or Reef & Beef, but Hide & Tide.
- Necessity sparks invention, as the saying roughly goes. A case in point is the wheelbarrow in **Bega (NSW)** Pioneers Museum. The contraption is made from iron cast around a tree fork. **[87 Bega St. Phone (02) 6492 1453]**
- A car rental company in **Broome (WA)** gets the ribbon for cutest name. Their Japanese models race about town sporting the company decal, Broome Broome.

# WINDOWS

*(Being a truckload of stained panes, leading leadlights
and peculiar portholes)*

## FACE THE MUSIC

BALLARAT, Vic.   The Origin Energy shop on Sturt St was once the highest building in Ballarat. Back then, in 1891, it was Sutton's Music Store. For proof, look no further than the window above the verandah, where you'll see Wolfgang Amadeus in profile. And while on the subject of windows, turn around 180°. See the face formed by the Irish Murphy's facade across the street? If you're struggling, perhaps a pint of Ireland's best will help you see the image. **[31–33 Sturt St, a block downhill from the Visitors Centre]**

## AN ABBEY ABERRATION

BUCKLAND, Tas.   There's no question about it, the church was built in 1846. The mystery surrounds its feature window. So much silver-yellow glass, not to mention the grisaille pattern, points to the piece being 400 years older than the building around it. Certain chips and scratches suggest a rough past, perhaps a bumpy sea voyage to the colonies. Legend links the window to Battle Abbey in Sussex, where perhaps it was hidden from Cromwell's marauders and later sent Down Under for safekeeping. The Reverend F.H. Cox, who preached at the time of the window's appearance, took the answer to the riddle to the afterlife. **[Entry donation according to your conscience]**

## SHARD TO BELIEVE

CABOOLTURE, Qld   The Wars of the Roses (1455–85) were much like State of Origin III, with a bit more riding on the result. To celebrate the House of York's victory and the resulting rise of the Tudor monarchy, Elizabeth of York commissioned the royal glazier, William Neve, to create a window depicting a Jesse Tree (a family tree for Christ) which linked Christ to the new regime. Except for a few panels, the window was destroyed during the English Civil War of 1640. In the 20th century, a social history collection that included those panels found its way first to Egypt, then to Sri Lanka and finally (in 1956) to the Sunshine Coast. So it is that a priceless 15th-century pane sparkles in the Qld sun, among Mayan daggers, stone axes and Tang ceramics. **[Abbey Museum of Art and Archaeology, Abbey Pl., off Bribie Island Rd. Open Mon.–Sat. 10a.m.–4p.m. Tours of the Abbey Church are held Tues. and Thur. at 11a.m. Entry $8/$5.50/$4.50, family $18. Phone (07) 5495 1652 or gaze upon www.abbeymuseum.asn.au]**

## GEOGRAPHICAL GLAZING

**FRASER ISLAND, Qld**    Window, barrage, perched – what's the link? If you guessed that they're all types of lakes, you must have peeked ahead. Or maybe you're a lacustrinologist. If so, hasten to Fraser Island, which boasts all three varieties for lake experts to love. Lake Boomanjin is actually the biggest perched lake in the world, a 200-ha peat saucer preventing an expanse of water from disappearing into the planet's largest sand island. As for window lakes, such as Yankee Jack or Ocean Lake, these occur where the ground has dropped below the water table and the sandy floor then acts as filter, giving the water that crystal-blue look of a picture window. And last of all, the barrage: the sand dunes creep up on a lake (Lake Wabby, say, the deepest of the island's lakes) and block its escape to the sea. Class dismissed.

## THE JUMBUCK STOPS HERE

**KYNUNA, Qld**    Guillotine windows are those service hatches once used to divide posh drinkers from the blue-singlet brigade in the adjoining bar. And it's through such a window in the Kynuna Hotel (now called the Blue Heeler) that chilled champagne was passed by publican Mick Fahy to the graziers and shearers in 1894. The booze-up was historic. Only hours before, in the so-called Battle of Dagworth, troopers had fired on striking shearers and the station woolshed went up in flames, killing 143 jumbucks and inspiring poet (and strike negotiator) Banjo Paterson to write a song called 'Waltzing Matilda'. Up the road, Banjo boffin Richard Magoffan OAM at his Matilda Expo has chapter and verse on the song's origins.

Take a closer look at those three windows on the first storey of the Courthouse in **Bacchus Marsh (Vic.)**. Despite the glass, there's no aperture behind each purported portal, just stone. The trick was hatched by the architect, W. Jackson, back in 1859, just to bring some extra elegance to the district.

## STABLE CRASHER

NEW NORFOLK, Tas.    Inside the Anglican Church of St Matthews there's one extra angel. Look at the nativity scene depicted in the principal window and you'll see Nancy Shoobridge standing behind the manger. Her face is unmistakable. Every other person in the scene seems to stem from generic bible illustrations, whereas young Nancy seems a photofit. The young girl drowned near Sri Lanka in 1890 on her way to a new life in the colonies. Wealthy hop farmers, her parents bankrolled the stained glass on the proviso that Nancy lives forever in Bethlehem. [Bathurst St, close to the river]

## WHARF WATCH

PORTLAND, Vic.    The Customs House in **Portland (Vic.)** is the oldest government building in Australia still used for its original purpose. The bluestone cottage was built in 1850, when Portland was part of NSW. Strangely, so the story goes, the windows face away from the port to deter staff from observing ship traffic from the comfort of their office chairs. [1 Cliff St. A working building]

## A LOUVRE MASTERPIECE

PROSERPINE, Qld    Owen Gray was a furniture joiner in this sugar town. He spent his days slicing and dicing timber, but owing to the dust and fumes from passing trucks Gray was obliged to shut his lane-side windows every time a timber truck appeared, so making his shop an oven. So in 1932 he applied his joinery know-how to glass, inventing the Everlite Adjustable Glass Louvre ® and selling his idea to the world. [Patent papers and a proto-window are in the Proserpine Museum on the Bruce Hwy. Open Mon.–Fri. 9a.m.–4p.m., Sun. 10a.m.–4p.m. May–Sep. Entry $4.50/$2.50. Phone (07) 4945 3969]

## CHURCH KNAVE

**ROMA, Qld**   So St Paul's of Roma is not as *magnifico* as St Peter's, Roma, but for a regional church it is *fabulissimo*. The grandeur is aided by a medley of 45 stained windows, ranging from a stark crucifixion (1876) to a resplendent honeyeater (circa last century). But the offbeat offering is part of a display beside the vespers candles, which shows a crusader-like figure on horseback. The window, a relic from the original wooden St Paul's, is devoted to Charles Nutting, the horseback trooper responsible for arresting notorious cattle thief Harry Redford, alias Captain Starlight, in 1872. **[Cnr Bungil and Arthur Sts. Open for tours Tues. and Thur. 9a.m.–10.30a.m. Phone (07) 4622 4623 or visit http://home.ripnet.aunz.com]**

## PUSS IN BOATS

**SYDNEY, NSW**   Who am I? Given little hope by landlubbers, I sailed around Australia in 1801 in the *Investigator*. After my triumphant return to Port Jackson, I set my sights for England. Alas, French officials waylaid me in Mauritius, where I later died in captivity. If you guessed Matthew Flinders you've ignored Trim, his precious cat, to whom the same biography applies. To this day, many wayfarers overlook the beloved moggy that stands on the window-sill of the Mitchell (aka State) Library in Macquarie St, directly behind his master. 'The best and most illustrious of his race,' wrote Flinders of Trim in his journal.

# ODDITIONS

⑥ Ever wondered if pubs are the secular equivalent of churches? Designers of the Victoria Hotel in **Port Fairy (Vic.)** think so, going by their massive stained-glass feature window.

⑥ Either book a tour, or take your chances walking into the Town Hall in central **Sydney (NSW)**. Tell the foyer staff you're hoping to see the window depicting Captain Cook and his telescope – they will more than likely oblige with directions.

# WORSHIP

*(Being a congregation of chosen churches
and adoration variations)*

## SISTERLY SECRETS

**ALICE SPRINGS, NT**   The Araluen Arts Centre is designed around a 300-year-old cork tree. Nip out the back door into the sculpture garden and you'll meet Yaye, the elder sister starring in the Arrernte women's stories. Yaye is the small hill edging the gallery's garden, while the cork tree next to you secretly relates to her story. A warning sign guards the hill, telling all non-Arrernte people to keep out. A frill-necked lizard made of barbed wire is the cork tree's guardian. **[Cultural Precinct, Larapinta Dve. Open daily 10a.m.–5p.m. Entry $9/$6, family $25, for all eight attractions in the Precinct. Phone (08) 8951 1120]**

## GOD IN A BOX

**BENDIGO, Vic.**   St Kilians began life as a tent in 1852. A flag ran up the pole to signal the start of Mass, and parishioners needed oilskins when the rain set in. One year later, bark slabs added a touch of luxury, and then came the stone and mortar. The slapdash masonry was condemned in 1888, though, and replaced by a weatherboard barn. This arrangement lasted until the magnificent Sacred Heart cathedral was finished at the other end of town. But the stop-gap address, the 'holy barn of Bendigo' with its poppet-head bell-tower, wins the blue ribbon for being the largest wooden church in Australia. **[Cnr Chapel and McRae Sts. In sight of the Golden Dragon Museum]**

## ROCKCHOPPERS WELCOME

**CARAPOOEE, Vic.**   Warren Rumble is not a fight scene from *Watership Down*, but the rector of a remarkable church. Known as the pebble church, St Peter's of the St Arnaud district has a rice-bubble quality thanks to a million quartz pebbles. Officially opened in 1874, the church embraces all denominations that recognise God as their Rock. **[From St Arnaud, head south for Avoca, peeling right after 6 km towards Dunolly]**

# HOLY SPIRIT

**COOBER PEDY, SA** Christians in ancient Rome headed for the catacombs below the city to worship with impunity. In Coober Pedy, believers also go underground – but only to escape the infernal heat. The opal town has five subterranean churches, from the cruciform Catholic chapel on Hutchison St to the Serbian Not-So-Orthodox. Anglicans congregate in the Catacomb church on Catacomb Rd, where a mining winch serves as altar. When high summer strikes, the Revival church on Crowders Gully Rd could well be dubbed the Survival church.

> Down behind the grain silos in the port of **Albany (WA)** is a rock that balances like a rugby ball on a goal-kicker's tee. Both ball and tee are known as Mass Rocks, the site of the first Catholic service conducted in WA. The priest of the moment, back in 1838, was chaplain from the French ship *l'Héroïne*. To celebrate the event, there's an altar fashioned from jetty timber.

# CORAL SERVICE

**DENHAM, WA** Coquina is the fancy term for the cemented shell blocks used as a building material around Shark Bay. (The stuff is a product of local cockles being glued together by ancient rain.) In Denham, you can visit The Old Pearler restaurant to see the effect, but the real pearler is St Andrew by the Sea, built in 1954. Not only is this coquina chapel the westernmost church on the Australian mainland, it's also the shelliest on God's earth. Step inside the north-facing vestibule (reoriented to avoid the vehement southwesterlies) and you'll confront the largest shell of all, a honey-coloured bailer serving as the baptismal font. [Cnr Hughes and Brockman Sts]

# CHANTS R US

**EUDLO, Qld** Commentators call it suburban sprawl. Another phrase is 'Caboolture coolture', the plague of tyre shops, food barns, auto service centres, billboards, The Big Loganberry, retirement enclaves, time-share condos, overnight vans, golf showrooms, spaghetti junctions and Wacky Worlds that cover the Sunshine Coast. One means of escaping the sprawl is Eudlo, a cool school of Tibetan monks up in the hills, on 57 panoramic hectares, offering all-comers the chance to heal and meditate. The air alone is salutary, enriched by the vegetarian momo balls and the umpteen oms you'll hear in cooee. **[Chenrezig Institute, 33 Johnsons Rd. Open daily 9.30a.m.–4.30p.m. Phone (07) 5445 0077]**

## COCKING A SNOOK

**MARYBOROUGH, Qld**　Doves are a dime a dozen around churches, but roosters? Take a gander outside St Mary's Church (stand near the main entry), and you'll see a concrete cockerel standing proud on the ridge of the roof. The bird commemorates Father Paul Tissot, the parish's first priest, a Frenchman who harvested his own grapes for the altar wine. A sandwich board near the rear pew adds an extra footnote: 'In France the cock is seen to perch/Upon a roof of many a church./On St Mary's Church this bird stands high/A tale to tell its passersby./A French priest in 1872/First built this church for me and you.' **[Top end of Adelaide St, opposite the main post office]**

## MEETING THE PEOPLE HALFWAY

**MULLEWA, WA**　Monsignor John Hawes was a gifted architect, as his heritage trail of chapels and churches across the state's midwest will suggest. (Booklets are available at the Visitors Centre in Geraldton.) But God's draughtsman scaled things down when doing his missionary best to reach the Indigenous people of Mullewa in the 1920s. His Mass Rock, a conglomerate outcrop with a shelf for altar, is Hawes at his purest and simplest. Grander plans were rumoured, with mention of a mission bell and archway to be added, but Hawes in the end opted for plainness on the plain. **[Turn left on a dirt road immediately after the major grain depot, just east of town heading for Mt Magnet. Then turn left again, 100 m in]**

## THE SHIP IN WORSHIP

**PAYNESVILLE, Vic.**    Jesus Christ and fish go way back. Peter, one of the first disciples, was fond of wetting a line, and Christ opted for loaves and fish when catering for the crowd. Such associations are embraced by St Peter by the Lake, the Anglican church in Paynesville. The ferry-shaped building is 'moored' on the banks of Lake Victoria. A tin lighthouse serves as spire. Joe Bull, a boat-builder from Metung, fashioned the prow-like pulpit. A brass bell scavenged from the steamship *Dargo* is the baptismal basin within a bollard-style font. As for stained glass, the pre-eminent tone is aquamarine. **[Newlands Dve]**

Back in 1872, a chapel was built on private land for the sake of settlers in **Mt Barker (WA)**. This calm and curious church, known as St Werbergh's Chapel, rises above the sheep droppings on Saint Werbergh's Rd. Either collect the Heritage Trail guide at the Mt Barker Visitors Centre, or follow the signs down the hill from the TV tower. Though on private land, the chapel is open to passersby.

## DRINK THIS, THE BLOOD OF CHRIST

**SEVENHILL, SA**    Go on, confess. You've always wondered where altar wine comes from? Well, a major source is Sevenhill Monastery, a Jesuit vineyard on Tiber Creek just south of Clare. Founded by an Austrian, Father Aloysius Kranewritter, in 1851, the monastery eked out its funds in early days by carting butter to Burra in a barrow. Then, hallelujah, wine took over. The stone vault beneath St Aloysius church eerily evokes a wine cellar, with the earthly remains of Father Jacobus, Brother Hubertus and other brethren stowed away like last year's vintage. **[College Rd, 7 km south of Clare. Cellar door open weekdays 9a.m.–5p.m., weekends 10a.m.–5p.m. Phone (08) 8843 4222]**

## ROCK OF AGES

**STAWELL, Vic.**    On Bunjils Cave Rd, a sign points out that Bunjil's Cave is not a cave but a shelter. Semantics aside, the granite niche is a sacred place, an al-fresco altar with kangaroos for curates. On the wall, the Buddha-like figure of Bunjil, or Pund-jel, is the All-Father figure revered by Aboriginal peoples of central Victoria. Beside the god gambol his two celestial dogs. Oral history from a man named Mukjarawaint, recorded back in 1904, helped anthropologists rediscover the outcrop in 1957. **[11 km south, off the Pomonal Rd. Ignore the Barrong Speedway turnoff]**

## DIVINE SCOOP

**SYDNEY, NSW**   The dollop of vanilla ice-cream above Sydney's northern beaches is one of seven Baha'i temples in the world. The faith, a compassionate cocktail of the world's religions, was founded by a Persian aristocrat called Baha'u'llah during the 19th century. (The temple's nine sides symbolise its various peoples and creeds.) A travelling salesman named Hyde Dunn helped spread the Baha'i message in Australia around the 1920s. The temple, built in 1961, is one spectacular outcome of his groundwork. Services are held every Sunday morning, with worshippers of any stripe welcome. **[173 Mona Vale Rd]**

## SPANNER FROM HEAVEN

**TENNANT CREEK, NT**   Flying doctor John Flynn designed an enclosed porch on the Australian Inland Mission to keep out the flies. The one pest he didn't anticipate was Dr Clyde Fenton, a roguish colleague from Katherine. When flying into town, Clyde was in the habit of dropping rocks and spanners onto the mission's roof, an uncivil means of summoning a car to the airstrip. The Inland Mission is now the Uniting Church, but look heavenward and you'll see Fenton's indents still glinting in the galvanised iron. **[Paterson St, a few doors south of Peko Rd]**

## GRAND MOTHER CHURCH

**WINDSOR, NSW**   Designed by convict maestro Francis Greenway, St Matthew's Anglican church is a well-documented Georgian corker. Its offbeat elements include the spire's cross, which isn't original: the first one rotted and was replaced (with the help of an RAAF chopper) in 1963. The shingles are original, though they were briefly replaced by slate in 1857 (the slate became too heavy, causing the roof to bow and enforcing the shingles' return). Inside, one of the most verbose plaques in Australia relates the tale of Captain William Blake, who expired in Africa. There's also a chunk of New Zealand greenstone, given in memory of the church's consecrator, Samuel Marsden, the man who imported Christianity to NZ. And I haven't even got round to the windows or the pioneer cemetery. **[Cnr Moses St and Greenway Cres. Open daylight hours]**

## DHARMA-RAMA

**WOLLONGONG, NSW**    Ten thousand tiny Buddhas occupy the niches in the main shrine of the Nan Tien Temple. You'd need a lifetime (or two) to focus on each one. Here, at the largest Buddhist temple in the southern hemisphere, you can let the freeway hum do the intoning for you. This is a soulful palace of Kremlin proportions, with an eight-tiered pagoda looking down on a lotus pond. Dharma wisdom dots the corridors, as do the rules of respect: no shoes, no phones, no hats, no chewing gum. 'Keep the noble silence', says the placard in the grand meditation hall. Whatever your beliefs, you will be amazed. **[Leave freeway at Five Islands Rd and follow the signs. Open Tues.–Sun. and Mon. public holidays 9a.m.–5p.m. Free entry. Phone (02) 4272 0600]**

# ODDITIONS

- Nominee for Prettiest Church in Australia (Qld sector) goes to St Mary's by the Sea, which she literally is. The original of this **Port Douglas** chapel was smashed by the 1911 cyclone and rebuilt inches from the waters of Trinity Bay, in sheer defiance.
- West of **Ballina (NSW)**, a church in Tintenbar has been converted into a restaurant. Fittingly, both lunch and dinner menus – framed behind a lectern – begin with breaking bread over dipping sauces. **[Church Cafe, cnr Tintenbar and Fernleigh Rds. Open Thur.–Sat. 6.30p.m., Sun. from noon. Call (02) 6687 8221]**
- Off Bangalore Rd in **Bexhill (NSW)** is a turnoff to an open-air cathedral. Climb past the cemetery and you'll find yourself above the world, with invisible walls and psalm numbers around you. The project began on Palm Sunday in 1958, and 'opens' only for a sunrise service and Eucharist during Easter.

# WRECKS

*(Being a carnage of ruins
and ravaged remains)*

## SEAFLOOR TILES

BERRARA, NSW   *Titanic* is surely the most famous ship of the White Star Line, but spare a thought for the luckless *Walter Hood*. The clipper spent 17 unscathed years yo-yoing between England and Australia, until a stormy April in 1870 when she hit rocks (bestowing the name Wreck Bay on the nameless inlet) and sank. Of the 32-man crew, one-third drowned. All cargo was lost, including a load of mosaic tiles intended for St Mary's Cathedral in Sydney. While you can't see the wreck without diving, you can see a monument over Monument Beach. On stormy sequels to that fatal day, beachcombers occasionally find a few blue and yellow tiles washed up on the sand. **[Within Conjola/Cudmirrah National Park, south of Sussex Inlet. Follow Bendalong Rd, then Eedar Rd. More information at the Department of Environment and Conservation office, Coller Rd, Ulladulla. Phone (02) 4454 9500]**

> You may have to wait for Sunday worship (at 9a.m.) if you wish to inspect the pews inside the Uniting Church of **Dongara (WA)** that have been fashioned from shipwreck timber. While you're waiting, have a look at the bell near the door, which was tolled to tell ticket-of-leave convicts in the 1860s that it was time to return to Fremantle Jail.

## SPAR BATH

BYRON BAY, NSW   The rusty spar poking from the waves on Main Beach belongs to a Glaswegian steamer known as the *Wollongbar*. Once the pride of the northern coast, the 2000-tonne greyhound ran butter, bananas and passengers between Byron and Sydney from 1911 to 1921. Her premature end came when a gale cut her ties to Byron's former jetty and sent her skidding broadside across the sand. She stopped where she now lies. A sister ship was built (the *Wollongbar II*) but her fate was even more forlorn (see Déjà Vu). **[Across from Fishheads Cafe at the end of Johnson St]**

## SLOW TO DEAD TRACK

CARPENTER ROCKS, SA   In 1859, the saw-like Carpenter Rocks ripped open the *Admella*. Aboard were 113 people and six horses. Passengers clung to the steamer more than a kilometre offshore, while the horses hoofed it. Night by night, living off dried milk and almonds, the survivors lost their grip. Rescuers assembled on the beach, but couldn't reach the reef. Eight days on, a Portland lifeboat made the trip, saving the last two dozen hangers-on. Meanwhile The Barber, an equine survivor, ran in the Champion Sweepstakes – a precursor to the Melbourne Cup – and finished, forgivably, off the pace. **[See the deadly reefs off the Cape Banks lighthouse, a 2-km drive west of Carpenter Rocks]**

When the SS *Mildura* hit the reef off **Exmouth (WA)**, it was every man and bullock for himself. The Kimberley ship was buffeted by a cyclone in 1907 and now stands on the coral as a regular fixture. All the crew survived, but none of the 461 oxen, making it a field day for reef sharks. Years later, the same hull doubled as a target for homegrown bombing practice.

## SLICK RESPONSE

CERVANTES, WA   Captain Eleftherios Efstathopoulos lost 20 000 tonnes of crude oil in the Indian Ocean when his ship, the *Kirki*, lost her bow in heavy seas in 1991. Nan Halfweeg, a crisis consultant from Rotterdam, flew to Cervantes to help contain the gunk. With some success – the surplus oil was transferred to a BP ship in the nick of time. The slick mustered, the only deterrent for aspiring swimmers hereabouts is the massive drifts of seaweed along the beach. **[The story, a drastic photo and two life jackets are on the wall of the Ronsard Bay Tavern on Alva St]**

## DRAMATIC STACK

CHARTERS TOWERS, Qld    Towers Hill, the lonely knoll above town, used to be even more conspicuous from a distance. A tall chimney of Cornish bricks once stood below the crest, connected to the local pyrites-extracting plant. The American military using the town as a Pacific base during World War 2 objected to the chimney's potential as a Japanese target. They accordingly detonated the smokestack and the Cornish bricks went flying. 'Only damn thing the Americans hit all war,' smirks one cynic at ground level. **[The road up Towers Hill is at the end of Rainbow St. The same hill holds mineshafts, munition bunkers, a seismological station and a colony of rock wallabies. The chimney ruins lie about 200 m beyond the bitumen, following the dirt road downhill]**

Opportunity knocked twice for the builders of the Caledonian Inn in **Robe (SA)**. During the pub's construction in 1857, two ships foundered in Guichen Bay. Timber was snagged from both wrecks – the *Phaeton* and the *Koning Willem* – to go into rafters and joinery for the alehouse. Upstairs, two ship's doors are still swinging.

## INSTANT BALLAST

COSSACK, WA    Cement and water mix wonderfully, should you be building a house. But it's not a cocktail recommended in a ship's hold. In 1935 a barge called the *Silver Star* barged into a jetty in Cossack, splitting her stem post. The river rushed aboard and mingled with the boat's cargo of cement. Slowly the lighter defied its name and sank. Its shell is now stuck on the riverbank, 100 m downstream from the picnic shelter.

At the east end of the Old Great Western Bridge in **Port Augusta (SA)**, you'll see the skeleton of a barge. Fittingly, her last cargo was the water pipes used in building the bridge. Built of Oregon and hardwood, Barge Number 4 (as she's so lovingly known) will be hanging around for some time yet.

## GARDEN LINER

**GRAFTON, NSW**   Winston Churchill once rode the SS *Induna*, now a sorry hull beside the Clarence River. Then an august steamer, the *Induna* whisked Churchill from a Pretoria prison in 1899, when the future British PM was earning his stripes as a Boer War scribe. From that point on, things went up for Churchill and down for the *Induna*. She ended up ferrying goods and chattels across the Clarence until being incorporated by the bank (the river bank) when the bridge monopolised traffic. You can see the wreck up-river from the bridge's under-walkway. Or better still, thread through the she-oaks on the southern side to see the hull in the guise of a garden bed.

## SANDBANK DEPOSIT

**NARRANDERA, NSW**   When the Murrumbidgee River is low, you can see the skeleton of the PS *Wagga Wagga*, the last of the packet steamers. Coming from town, peel right off the Newell Hwy before the river bridge (not the canal bridge). Follow the dirt road for more than a kilometre. After the second gate, take a stroll through to Morgan's Beach and look for the rusty leftovers. In town, at the excellent Parkside Museum, you can see a pink scroll, a skipper's approximate river map that may have led to the sandbar mishap. **[Museum is on Twynam St. Open Wed.-Sun. 2p.m.-5p.m. Entry $2. Phone (02) 6959 1372]**

Mock-antiquity adorns the corner of Swanston and Latrobe Sts in central **Melbourne (Vic.)**, with a half-buried library jutting from the pavement outside the extant State Library. The latter, built in 1911, once claimed the largest reinforced concrete dome in the world. Even now, it's still worth a wander upstairs.

## GREEK TRAGEDY

**PORT WILLUNGA, SA**   Friday the 13th gained one more bogey point in 1888 when a wild storm dragged the *Star of Greece* onto rocks at Port Willunga, south of Adelaide. The 70-metre iron ship, filled with wheat for England, had nowhere to hide and 11 of her 28-strong crew drowned. A wooden post marked the site for years, slowly losing its battle against termites. At low tide, the ship's bow juts from the water. For venturesome snorkellers, a plaque is positioned 3 m below the surface (I needed four breaths to read the whole story). Above the beach the Star of Greece Cafe embodies a few pieces of wood and iron salvaged from the ship. There's a mass grave for the ship's lost in the cemetery attached to the Uniting Church in nearby Aldinga.

## QUEUE JUMPERS

**SCOTTS HEAD, NSW**   The first person to know about the visitors was the baker. He arrived at work near dawn on 11 April 1999, to find a knot of Chinese gentlemen dressed in suits and carrying bundles of US banknotes. Down at the beach, a tugboat named the *Zhou Gan Tou,* with a cargo of 60 illegal immigrants, was stranded on her belly. The fugitives were rounded up, the tug's blue funnel was erected as a relic outside the surf shop on Adin St, and the anchor now stands in the lawn-bowls carpark. The rest of the vessel was dragged to Newcastle for scrap, though in 2003 the local primary school constructed a cardboard replica for a re-enactment. **[As for the wreck site, take the rough track 600 m north of the surf club]**

# XTREME

*(Being an excess of specialised sports
and off-the-scale specifications)*

## DEVIL FOX

**CAIRNS, Qld**   A.J. Hackett, the NZ innovator of bungee jumping, has long been part of the Cairns landscape. His 50-m bungee tower, nestled in the jungle of Saddle Mountain 15 km north of town, draws thousands of buzz-junkies every year. The same locale now offers the Minjin, an xtreme flying fox that accommodates up to three astronauts. The Minjin, which can clock over 100 kph, is named after a mythical 'devil cat' that once terrified the early white population. Some things don't change. **[Prices start from $45 per person, with unlimited package deals. Bookings (07) 4057 7188 or 1800 622 888 or fly by www. ajhackett.com.au]**

## THE BARTON LYNCH MOB

**COOLANGATTA, Qld**   Gold Coast surfers will murder me for telling you this, but the longest wave in the world starts off Point Danger and rolls, rolls, rolls as far as Kirra Groyne over a kilometre away. Conditions need to be right, of course. With a northerly swell, those with good balance can glide from Snapper Rocks across Rainbow Bay (a spot called Marleys) and hop out at the Kirra takeaway – roughly a four-minute ride. The perfect spot to see this record-breaking breaker is the aptly named R.T. Peak Memorial Park, an eyrie overlooking the coast. Eyrie is the right word too, as a rusting steel eagle balances off twin girders while U watch. **[End of Garrick St, on the headland south of Kirra]**

## TRAIN SPOTTING

**DAMPIER, WA**   The longest private railway in Australia stretches from the Pilbara coast into the ore-rich heartland. Running along the longest private line are some of the longest, heaviest trains in the world. To get a good look at these 226-wagon juggernauts, each train weighing over 23 000 tonnes, you could do a lot worse than loiter on the Dampier

Rd bridge, using the nearby information bay for shade in the interim. Alternatively, ask for train times at Port Hedland Visitors Centre on (08) 9173 1711 and set up punctual camp on Wallwork Rd bridge, just out of South Hedland.

> The biggest water slide in Australia is Mammoth Falls at Wet 'n' Wild at Oxenford on the **Gold Coast (Qld)**. No grubby sponge mats here, but a six-person tube in a wide trough dips and twists for more than 200 m, ending with a triple-jump precipice called the Mammoth Plunge. **[M1 Pacific Motorway. Open daily from 10a.m. Entry $38/$24 (less if purchased online). Phone (07) 5573 2255 or visit www.wetnwild.com.au]**

## KING TIDE

**DERBY, WA**    The only thing to rival the 2 million litres of seawater spewing through a crevice is your body's own adrenaline rush as you ride the Horizontal Waterfalls at Talbot Bay on the Buccaneer Archipelago. Renowned naturalist David Attenborough labelled the torrent as among the world's greatest wonders. The phenomenon occurs on each tidal switch, when gigalitres get penned behind a narrow cleft dividing two islands and then burst in a fan-like flood of rapids and whirlpools, with an overall drop of some 4 m. You can view this marvel from the air, or go with the flow in a twin-hulled speedboat. **[For seaplanes that drop you on-site, call Derby Visitors Centre on (08) 9191 1426 or visit www. derbytourism.com.au]**

## RINSE CYCLE

**PIMPAMA, Qld**    A few years ago, New Zealanders Dwane van der Sluis and Andrew Akers were thinking about balls. Big balls. Soft balls. The sort of ball a man might crawl inside and roll down a hill with impunity. They dreamt up a zorb, like a transparent beach ball within a transparent beach ball but weighing 80 kg and rolling at 50 kph. The first test roll was at One Tree Hill in Auckland. At Pimpama, the only purpose-built zorb slalom in the world, you can harness-zorb, triple-zorb or hydro-zorb (adding 25 litres of warm water for a sloshier journey). Despite the gradient, the 'zorbonaut' only revolves once every 10 m or so, creating more a bizarre than a queasy effect. **[232 Old Pacific Hwy. Exit 54 off M1, not far from Dreamworld. Park entry free. Triple-zorb from $17 per person (kids must be over 3). Phone (07) 5547 6300 or visit www.zorb.com.au]**

If the tide is right and the sense of lunacy high, you can watch a band of local surfers from the jetty in **Port Campbell (Vic.)**. On big-surf days the grommets go ballistic off the point. On lumpier occasions they surf inshore, weaving like trainee kamikaze pilots between the jetty's pylons.

## FLYING IN HARGRAVE'S FOOTSTEPS

**STANWELL TOPS, NSW**   Lawrence Hargrave is seen as the forefather of manned flight, by Australians at least. While the Wright Brothers may have pipped our box-kite boffin into the record books, Hargrave was being hoisted by his own contraptions as early as 1889. He wrote more than 25 papers on his 'soaring machines', experimenting at the beach here with monoplanes, engines, weights and kites. More than a century later his legacy can be seen in the shape of hang-gliders leaping off Bald Hill, 70 m above the famous beach. If you feel the urge, you can take that extra step with Peter Armstrong, a freestyle champion and aerial veteran of 25 years. Short of learning the art, tandem flying is the perfect way to relive Hargrave's great adventure. **[Bald Hill is off Lawrence Hargrave Dve. Look for the windsock when you leave the F6 for Stanwell Park. Bookings essential. Phone Hangglide Oz on 0417 939 200 or visit www.hangglideoz.com.au]**

## WHIRLPOOL CIRCUIT

**SYDNEY, NSW**   Empathising with a French fry may not top your agenda, but at Penrith Whitewater Stadium you can grab a raft, a canoe or a kayak and enter the merry hell known as the Deep Fryer. Built for the Olympics, the 320-m U-shaped torrent could fill 50 Olympic pools in less than a minute. An adjacent warm-up lake is sucked up by five pumps and spat down the chute for your heart-in-mouth pleasure. A conveyor belt whisks you and your vessel from the lower pool back to the mountaintop. Guided and unguided cruises are available. [McCarthys Lane, off Great Western Hwy; or take the Mulgoa Rd turnoff on the M4. Open daily, $66 for 90 minutes, age limits apply. Bookings essential. Phone (02) 4730 4333 or visit www.penrithwhitewater.com.au]

# ODDITIONS

⑥ Forest Flying is what it says it is. Strapped into a harness, you can glide and slide for over 350 m through a rainforest canopy in Finch Hatton (Qld). [Phone (07) 4958 3359 or check out www.forestflying.com]

⑥ The straightest stretch of railway track in the world lies across the Nullarbor Plain (SA/WA). Safe to say that during this 478 curve-free km, passengers on the Indian-Pacific can sip a hot coffee with reduced risk . . .

⑥ . . . meanwhile drivers on the same vast expanse face their toughest curve-free test between Caiguna (WA) and a vague kink east of Balladonia, a total of 148 km, the longest such stretch in Oz.

⑥ Not only does Marrawah (Tas.) brag the world's cleanest air, but the same coastal nook can serve up some awesome waves. At Temma Harbour, the average day's swells of 5–8 m attract troppo surfies and death-wish wave-sailors.

⑥ Not that I've travelled the continent with a tape measure, but they say the main street of Trundle (NSW) is the widest in Australia, at a whistle-worthy 30 m. The width was in deference to U-turning bullock trains.

# YIKES

*(Being an x-file of eternal edginess
and general heebie-jeebies)*

## SCHOOL SPIRIT

**BEGA, NSW**   Teachers and students at the high school here are cool with their poltergeist. Much like a Year 9 student on muck-up day, the spirit enjoys flicking off lights in the assembly hall and moving chairs to random corners overnight. Just another ghost yarn, you're thinking, but Bega's bogey has reasonable grounds. The school sits on top of the town's first cemetery. Constant flooding early last century compelled the shire to relocate their loved ones, though many ancestors knocked back offers of exhumation. We can all do with a bit more education, pre-sumably was the logic, even in the afterlife. **[Cnr Upper and Eden Sts]**

## PARLIAMENTARY X-FILES

**CANBERRA, ACT**   Elvira is black and cool and curvaceous – and a 1967 Cadillac hearse. Tim the Yowie Man, a self-claimed 'cryptonatu-ralist' who likes to hunt for Brindabella bigfoots in his spare time, joins Allan the Hearse Whisperer as your Destiny Tours hosts. The pair will recount tales of a War Memorial poltergeist, disembodied screams in the embassy, the death train, the car-friendly lake, the skeleton in Duntroon's closet, a spy-riddled funeral parlour and the prime ministe-rial ghost who can't seem to find the pub's exit. Elvira, in fact, offers the ride of your life. **[Tours operate on the last Fri. and Sat. of each month, except Dec. Cost $49 for a 90-minute marvel. Phone Allan Levinson, who also runs Elvira (plus the grey cadillac Morticia) around Sydney's spookier sites, on (02) 9402 5676 or 0414 232 224]**

## MASKED AVENGER

**DUBBO, NSW**   Robert Rice Howard was a handsome man who drove hansom cabs in Woolloomooloo, until tragedy struck. Howard fell off his carriage and became horribly disfigured. Poor wretch lost his nose, and gained the nickname Nosy Bob. Too grotesque for cab duties,

Nosy Bob became hangman at the jail here during the 1870s. The mask he wore seemed tailor-made – two eyes and no nose. It hangs, as you'd expect, within the jail's museum. **[Macquarie St. Open daily 9a.m.–4.30p.m. Entry $7/$5.50/$3.50. Adults-only tours also available at night. Phone (02) 6882 8122]**

## SECRET CODEINE

**LATROBE, Tas.**  Don't even think about loitering at Glaxo Smith and Klein. This Bond-esque fortress, where you almost expect to be accosted by special agents with Uzi rifles, is where most of the state's opium poppies are converted to codeine. As for the opium farms, your best bet is cruising nearby Forth in midsummer when the vivid purple offers a natural high. But keep it moving, please, keep it moving, nothing to see here... **[Henry St, off Bass Hwy 10 km south of Devonport]**

In the Visitors Centre at **Newman (WA)**, a collection of bottled bugs emphasises how everything is that much bigger in the outback. On show are centipedes, wolf spiders, crickets and cockroaches that each warrants its own horror movie. The giant of the pack, though, is the well-named buffalo beetle.

## BEER KRAIT

**MARRAWAH, Tas.**  Dippy Flint caught the granddaddy of snakes in 1990. His 2-m tiger snake hangs above the pub's fireplace, and those with a serpentine bent can also marvel at the pickled varieties behind the bar, freaks and foetuses included. So rapt in snakes was the former publican that the Marrawah Hotel has become a fork-tongued focal point. Just ask about the king brown the ex-owner kept in the deep-freezer. You'll look at the phrase 'crowd management' in a brand-new light. **[Come Back Rd, Green Point. Phone (03) 6457 1102]**

## HELL AND HIGH WATER

**OGMORE, Qld**  Can you think of a more infernal address than the Styx River Hotel on Charon's Ferry Rd? As a tourist town Ogmore has yet to join the mainstream, but that may change if public access is granted to see Australia's most dramatic tidal bore. The phenomenon, a knee-high surge racing up the Styx and disgorging onto the floodplain, occurs every full moon. Publican Gordon Campbell, he of the diabolical address, says the tidal wave turns outback desert into wetlands in a blink. But unless a few farmers soften on the 'tourism threat', Hell looks a more plausible stopover. **[Take dirt-road turnoff about 190 km south of Mackay]**

## ON THE BEACH

**PORT MACDONNELL, SA**    The first wreck in this area, the Southern Ocean coast south of Mt Gambier, occurred before the port existed. A wooden schooner, the *J. Lovett*, ran aground in 1852. Prey to looting, the ship sat stranded for 14 months, guarded by her disgraced captain. His sentry duties ended in 1853 when two locals with a penchant for port wine took a razor to the skipper's throat. Three years later, in the interests of greater vigilance, the port was conceived. In fact, the town's lighthouse (built in 1860) was often the first sign of Australia visible to immigrants travelling the 'Great Circle' route via Antarctica.

## BATS OUT OF HELL

**ROCKHAMPTON, Qld**    Bentwing bats have faces (and habits) that only a bentwing mother could love. So don't expect a beauty pageant when 80000 of the little critters flash past your nose at the Bat Cleft, in Mt Etna National Park. The cave is the creche for more than three-quarters of Australia's bentwings. Around twilight you can grab a safety line and peer into the storm's heart, an experience no horror movie can duplicate. You'll even see the odd infanticide, as diamond pythons and tree frogs gorge on the daycare's release. **[Caves are 24 km north of town, off Bruce Hwy. Tours run Nov.–Feb. only, on Mon., Wed., Fri. and Sat., for $7.45/$4.90/$3.70, family $22.20. Rigorous walking involved. Inquiries (07) 4936 0511]**

## THE EXPLORER'S EYE

**YASS, NSW**    Milton Niemenen is the Yass and District Museum's main curator, and he swears by the roving eyes of Hamilton Hume. A portrait of our first home-grown explorer hangs in the rear section. No matter where you stand, says Milton, old Hamilton is watching you. He's also watching the so-called yowie wool also on display. [Open Sat. and Sun. 10a.m.–4p.m., or when Milton's in town. Entry $2/50c. Phone (02) 6226 2315]

# ODDITIONS

⊚ Next time you want to let rip on the green, head for Nostalgia Town at **Pacific Paradise (Qld)**, where the whole putt-putt course is designed on a cemetery theme.

⊚ Skill meets skull at the Boadicea Shop and Gallery in **Augathella (Qld)**, where a shelf-load of painted sheep skulls await your caress. **[Main St. Phone (07) 4654 5116]**

⊚ On the wall at the Fishermen's Club in **Eden (NSW)** is a thresher shark with a human arm jutting from its jaws.

# ZANY

*(Being a circus of lovable loonies
and fantabulous funsters)*

## ROCKS IN HIS HEAD

**ATHERTON, Qld** Dutchman Renee Boissevain has farmed mink in Norway and hunted crocs in the outback. But his greatest exploit has been to create his own universe, the Crystal Caves, an artificial grotto that extends beneath the streets of this far-north town. Using egg-cartons for insulation, polystyrene for stalagmites and a dazzling collection of blue topaz, petrified wood, fossils, stunning water agate and a 525-kg boulder of rose quartz, Renee and his wife Nelleke have given 'Down Under' a whole new spin. **[Fascinating Facets, 69 Main St. Open weekdays 8.30a.m.–5p.m., Sat. 8.30a.m.–4p.m., Sun. 10a.m.–4p.m. Entry to the caves $12.50/$6/$10, family $37. Phone (07) 4091 2365, or visit www. crystalcaves.com.au]**

## THE LIZARDS OF OZ

**EULO, Qld** Australia stops on the first Tuesday in November for the Melbourne Cup, while things tend to keep going on the last Sunday in September (give or take a week) during the Cunnamulla–Eulo World Lizard Racing Championships. The event has been running for almost 40 years, its most renowned thoroughbred being Destructo the cockroach, who won line honours in an inter-species showdown with Wooden Head the bearded dragon back in 1980, only to be squashed by a sozzled punter. All lizards gathered for the day are tagged, and later returned to their habitat. Shinglebacks, which resemble a tyre retread with legs, usually kick off the meet, with the pedigree dragons spared for the feature race. **[Inquiries at Eulo Queen Hotel on (07) 4655 4867]**

## GROTESQUERIE

**FREMANTLE, WA** UMVWAWA (Ugly Men's Voluntary Workers' Association of Western Australia) once ran a funfair called Uglieland opposite Fremantle's railway station. Every year the association held a penny-per-vote ballot to discover the ugliest bloke in the state. (Wives were forbidden to nominate husbands.) The sideshows have long gone, but an 'ugly' membership badge is on show at the Fremantle History Museum, in the old lunatic asylum – now called the Arts Centre. **[1 Finnerty St. Open weekdays 10a.m.–4.30p.m., Sat. 1p.m.–5p.m., Sun. 10.30a.m.–4.30p.m. Entry by donation. Phone (08) 9430 7966]**

## THE EYES DON'T HAVE IT

**MELBOURNE, Vic.**   No lighters, no torches, no matches and no luminous watches. Them's the rules at Black Out, a restaurant that offers diners no view at all. Your single chance to read the menu is in the lit foyer. After that, unless you're spotted waving your hands by the night-goggled waiters, the only other light source you'll experience is in the WC. Blind dining was inaugurated by a Zurich restaurateur who was blind, as were his waiters. Losing their eyes, patrons found acuter senses of taste and smell. This place is popular with celebrities desperate to be seen, so you never know who you might bump into. **[604 St Kilda Rd. Phone (03) 8530 1850]**

About 6 km from the coal-mining town of **Collie (WA)**, heading for Boyup Brook, you'll come across Betty Rd on your right. Take that road for 400 m and you'll encounter 40 miners' helmets arranged at a bus-stop. Little in the way of explanation is offered. Could the helmets belong to pit retirees? Are they company spares? The most that most locals seem to know is the place's name – Helmut's Corner.

## CRAZY DAISY

**MOOBALL, NSW**   Jeff and Jodi Pryer liked the idea of a semi-tropical retreat. Then in 1998 the Ampol service station here became available. Cow-mad, the entrepreneurs painted every pole in town black on white. They camouflaged the garage, the bowsers, the planter boxes, the jeep. A weatherboard collage of a Friesian bull and cow in congress was the landmark for their Moo Moo Cafe, until rustlers intervened in 2001. But otherwise the place is bovine to the max, with moo-acinos, moo-moo burgers and hot cow-pats. The pinball machine moos, the cutlery box is labelled Cattlery. Hard to say which is more excruciating – the puns or the colour scheme. **[Tweed Valley Way. Open daily. Phone (02) 6677 1230]**

## DALI LIVED HERE

**NANNUP, WA**   Surrealism is the *soupe du jour* at House of Dada. Run by artist Tyrone Stanley and his wife, Debbie King, this gallery has a rotating collection of local stuff within the old medical surgery. Though it's the garden that first catches the eye, with two bored demons as gateposts, a bedspring gate, and for a pet the skeleton of an upright goat (*Capricorn erectus*) which Tyrone calls The Scapegoat. **[Cnr Warren and Struther Sts. Open most days]**

## UNPREDICTABLE

**ROCKHAMPTON, Qld**   As the beef capital of Australia, this city has long had its share of bull statues. There are in fact six dotted round town, from a Brahman near the university to a Droughtmaster at the airport. (Get your bull map from the tourism office to find the whole herd.) Since the first triennial Beef Expo in 2000, there's even been a gold bull, dubbed Bullion of course, standing atop Morgan Stockbrokers at 26 Denham St. Valu-bull grazes the awning of Heron Todd White at 250 Quay St. And the statue above the Great Western Hotel on Stanley St, a beast smashing his head through the panel of a door? Simply Adoora-bull.

A stretch of the Great Eastern Hwy between **Midland (WA)** and Mundaring is known as Greenmount Hill. Your engine will notice it. The gradient is stiff and the hill is long. (Coming down, trucks have a choice of 'arrester beds' to kill their speed should low gear fail.) But spare a thought for the first generation of motorists: with gravity-fed engines, the maiden batch of cars had to be reversed up the hill.

## DINER ON THE EDGE

**STRATFORD, Vic.**   The specials blackboard should sound your first warning. The Junk Yard Flaming Grill is as likely to offer diners 'Daisy the Cow' as 'Sauteed Retreads'. Inside, the kookiness continues. Hubcaps blister the feature wall. Vices are bolted to dining booths. Underpants said to belong to Bill Clinton sport the kiss-prints of a certain White House intern. Other mock captions join a mock-museum in the corner, including the homicidal history of Frisbees. 'We cater for vegetarians,' brags the meat-heavy menu, 'because we love them. I myself could almost eat a whole one . . .' **[48 Tyers Rd. Open Thur.–Sat. 6p.m. till late. Phone (03) 5145 6335]**

## NOSES ON PEEL

**TAMWORTH, NSW**   A punter can't breathe for country-music shrines hereabouts. If it's not the Roll of Renown on Goonoo Goonoo Rd, or the Hands of Fame Park on Kable Ave, or the songwriter plaques out-side the Visitors Centre, then it's the wax figures at the Golden Guitar. There's a refreshing twist on conventional C&W memorabilia out back of Joe Maguire's Pub (aka Tattersall's Hotel) at 148 Peel St. There the beaks of various showbiz celebs have been poked into wet cement to create the Country Music Noses of Fame. Gina Jeffreys' schnozz wins the prize for Most Petite, while Pixie deserves to be renamed Rhino. **[Phone (02) 6766 2114]**

## COPPER ART IT AIN'T

**WOODBURN, NSW**   Free-spirited sculptor Will Ponweiser has created his own zoo at Copper Art Gallery and the garden resembles a 'Wild Side' cartoon in colour. A crocodile is cemented to the kerb. A dragon weathervane twitches. Two dolphins arc over the birdbath. The menag-erie spills out from the house, and across the road a sickle-shaped tree supports a kookaburra carrying a rubber snake. You can visit the stu-dio where more animals lurk, but don't be too alarmed by the Alsatian on the porch – he's a statue too. **[61 River Rd. Studio entry $1/50c. Phone (02) 6682 2477]**

# ODDITIONS

◎ A garden on the corner of Farrelly and Pyrites Sts in **Charters Towers (Qld)** has two mining manikins dressed in full regalia. The dummies wave from beneath two windmills and a poppet-head. Behind the men is a laden kibble cart – and petunias.

◎ Three statues clutter the footpath at 74 Vulcan St in **Moruya (NSW)**. The first – a Eurobodalla Aboriginal holding spear and mulloway – is permanent. The other two – a turnpike trooper with pistol at the ready, and a motor mechanic with Hitler moustache – belong to Silly Willy's Superstore, and vanish out of hours.

◎ The Udder Cow, a funkadelic cafe in **Comboyne (NSW)**, has gone ga-ga for moo-moos. You won't be able to swing a cat without demolishing the cattle clutter. Phone (02) 6550 4188 or visit www. uddercow.com.au

◎ At 1 Brooking St in **Goolwa (SA)** the front 'lawn' is a map of Australia. Blue gravel mimics ocean. A black swan waddles in the west. A garden boulder denotes Uluru. Retired farmer Max Kairl created the continent with an astronaut's perspective.

◎ Mid Coast Ford on Manning River Drive in **Taree (NSW)** doesn't sell seashells. The big oyster on the roof is a 1990 hangover from two Hungarian brothers who thought the giant shell could put Taree on the offbeat map.

# SOURCES

In a sense, I've been writing this book since primary school. Thirty years ago, staring out a window in General Studies, I started musing about specific places like Woy Woy, Bong Bong and Kurri Kurri and what made them special special.

Penniless, without a car, a licence, a long-enough holiday, I was forced to rely on travel and trivia books to tell me more about Abercrombie Caves and Zuytdorp Cliffs, the A-Z of *Australia mysteriosa*. A lot of those books are still floating around my office today, along with two or three skip-loads of newspaper snippets and yellowy back issues. In fact, I'm pressed to name a single newspaper in Australia that *hasn't* helped me write *Cassowary*, as have the likes of more orthodox guides such as the Lonely Planet series, Explore, Rough Guides, Let's Go and Fodors. In addition to these staples, my office is insulated by umpteen brochures, flyers, dog-eared magazines, microfiche printouts, research notes, website lists and the odd apple core.

Below is an inventory of that unholy mess, a tribute to the many books and other sources that have helped inform this book, and the curious kid inside.

## BOOKS

Andrews, Malcolm, *Great Aussie Trivia*, Horwitz Grahame Books, 1985
——, *The Ultimate True Blue Trivia Book*, ABC Books, 2002
Barca, Margaret (ed.), *Explore Historic Australia,* Viking, 2002
Baglin, Douglass and Austin, Yvonne, *Australia's Museums*, Child & Henry, 1980
Barnao, Anthony, *Violent Crimes That Shocked A Nation*, QB Books, 1985
Barrow, Graeme, *Walking from the Mountains to the Sea*, Dagraja Press, 2002
Beatty, Bill, *Tales of Old Australia*, Ure Smith, 1966
——, *Here in Australia*, Cassell, 1959
——, *A Treasury of Australian Folk Tales and Traditions*, Ure Smith, 1968
Biggs, Ronald, *Odd Man Out*, Pan Macmillan, 1994
Blaikie, George, *Scandals of Australia's Strange Past*, Rigby, 1976
Blake, Philip and Mary, *Secret Tasmania*, New Holland, 2002
Brasch, R., *Permanent Addresses*, Angus & Robertson, 1995
Bryson, Bill, *Down Under*, Black Swan, 2001
Clark, Alan, *A Collection of Shoalhaven History*, Leader Printery, 1994
Clarke, David, *Big Things*, Penguin, 2004
Clarke, Frank, *The Big History Question*, Kangaroo Press, 1998
Cockington, James, *Mondo Bizarro*, Mandarin, 1994
——, *Mondo Weirdo*, Mandarin, 1992
——, *Secret Sydney*, New Holland, 1999
——, *History Happened Here*, ABC Books, 2003
Coupe, Sheena, *Historic Australia*, Golden Press, 1982

Cripps, Cecil, *Racetracks Ring-ins and Rorts*, Vetsport Promotions, 1990

Crocker, Jenny and Collingwood, Julia, *Free and Low-Cost Sydney*, Choice Books, 1999

Crowe, David, *The Sydney Beach Guide*, Mandarin, 1996

Dale, David, *The 100 Things Everyone Needs To Know About Sydney*, Pan Macmillan, 1997

Darwin, Chris and Amy John, (eds.), *The Ultimate Australian Adventure Guide*, Pan Macmillan, 1995

Dean, Lois, *Historic Mount Gambier*, Corporation of the City of Mount Gambier, 1986

Drinnan, Neal (ed.), *the Rough Guide to Gay and Lesbian Australia*, Rough Guides, 2001

Duffy, Helen (ed.), *Best of Victoria*, Pan Macmillan, 1998

Farwell, George, *Ghost Towns of Australia*, Rigby, 1974

Frank, Rivka, *Kids' Activities Melbourne*, RFA, 1999

Fray, Peter, Tony Rodd and Arthur Woods (eds.), *Country Australia: The Land and the People*, Reader's Digest, 1989

Gardam, Faye, *Shifting Sands*, Devonport Maritime Museum, 2001

Hayes, Mike, *The Complete Book of Aussie Yarns,* ABC Books, 2001

Healey, John (ed.), *SA's Greats*, Historic Society of South Australia, 2001

Hepburn, Alec, *Strange Tales of Australia*, Rigby, 1982

Hickey, Alan (ed.), *Postcards – On the Road Again*, Wakefield Press, 2002

Hornadge, Bill, *The Hidden History of Australia*, Imprint, 1997

Hunter, Bill, *Bill Hunter's Thousands of Great Australian Facts*, Boab Press, 1997

Isaacs, Jennifer, *Quirky Gardens*, UQP, 1995

Jones, Graham, *People, Places & Things of the North East*, Charquin Hill, 1979

Jones, Howard C., *Good Old Albury*, self-published, 2002

Knightley, Phillip, *Australia: Biography of a Nation,* Vintage, 2001

Lane, Jacqui (ed.), *The Great Australian Gazetteer ™*, Focus Publishing, 2001

Liddy, Peter, *The Rainbird Murders*, Peacock Publications, 1993

Lloyd, Clem, *The National Estate: Australia's Heritage*, Cassell, 1977

Luck, Peter (ed.), *This Fabulous Century*, Circus Books, 1981

——, *Australian Icons*, William Heinemann, 1992

McCann, Joy, *A Lot in Store*, NSW Heritage Office, 2002

McKay, Mark, *On Tap*, Wakefield Press, 1999

McLagan, David, *Melbourne Trivia Book*, Hyland House, 1996

McNamara, Ian, *Australia All Over*, ABC Books, 1992

Morton-Evans, Michael, *The Australian Book of Lists*, Cassell, 1980

Nicholson, Margaret, *The Little Aussie Fact Book*, Penguin, 2002

Peach, Bill, *Outback with Bill Peach*, Southdown Press, 1989

Read, Ian G., *Continent of Extremes*, University of NSW Press, 1998

Reed, AW, *Place Names of Australia*, Reed Books, 1984

——, *Aboriginal Stories of Australia*

Reed, Nicholas, *The Dinkum Aussie Dunny Companion*, MaxiBooks, 1992

Richardson, Matthew, *The Penguin Book of Firsts*, Penguin, 1997

Robertson, Patrick, *The Guinness Book of Australian Firsts*, Collins, 1987

Ross, John (ed.), *Chronicle of Australia*, Penguin, 2000

Shears, Richard, *Ripley's' Believe It Or Not Book of Australia and New Zealand*, Ripley Books, 1983

Smith, Malcolm, *Bunyips and Bigfoots*, Millennium Books, 1996

Smith, Russell, *Curiosities of South Australia (1* and *2)*, Smithbooks, 2000

Spindler, Graham, *Sydney Strolls: Eastern Suburbs* and *Sydney Strolls: Lower North Shore*, New Holland, 1999

Stepnell, Kenneth and Esther, *Kryall Castle*, Rigby, 1976

Talbot, Don and John Larkin, *Toowoomba Strange and Unusual Tales*, self-published, 2003

Tim the Yowie Man, *The Adventures of Tim the Yowie Man,* Random House, 2001

Tipping, Richard, *Signs of Australia*, Penguin, 1982

Van Oudtshoorn, Nic and Daphne, *Oddly Australian*, Bay Books, 1984

Van Tiggelen, John, *Mango Country*, Pan Macmillan, 2003

Wade, Margaret, *Canberra's Secrets*, self-published, 2003

Wannan, Bill, *Australian Folklore*, Lansdowne Press, 1970

White, Charles, *History of Australian Bushranging*, Rigby, 1975

Wilson, Robert (ed.), *Discover Australia: Our Highways and Byways*, Lansdowne Press, 1990

Wood, Anne, *More Tales from our Streets*, self-published, 2000

## GENERAL WEBSITES

www.aussie-travel.com.au

www.getaway.ninemsn.com.au

www.walkabout.com.au

(. . . and countless others mentioned throughout the book)

## NEWSPAPERS, MAGAZINES, MISCELLANEOUS SOURCES

*Australia Post*, 1961–78

*Australia's Heritage*, parts 1–96

*Australian Geographic*

*Bulletin* magazine

*Bunbury: I Remember When . . .'* series

Coast & Country

First and Oldest (Maryborough Queensland), 2000

Focus – Australian Doctor Magazine

*Living Australia* magazine, 1986–87

*40° South* (Tasmania) magazine

*Outback* magazine

RACV touring guides (2003–2004, all states)

*Ralph* (*Outback* Special), October 2002

*Royal Auto* magazine

*This Australia* quarterly, 1982–86

*Time* magazine (Australian Journeys), 2 December 2002

# ACKNOWLEDGEMENTS

I don't which is more daunting – to write a book about a large strange land, or hope to record all those savvy people who helped me along the way. Naturally, both tasks are a folly, but I've had a crack nonetheless.

Before I go beyond my own patch, trying to name those who breathed life into this book, let me first thank Bill Tikos, my imaginative agent who 'got' the Cassowary idea long before the project took flight. Ali Watts and Sarah Dawson, the two Empress Penguins who adopted this author, were also vital to the book and my psychic welfare: Ali for her faith and exuberance; and Sarah, her stamina, style and care.

Other people involved in the book's production were just as inspiring. I'd like to make a special fuss over Jo Hunt for dreaming up the cover, fact-checker Barbara Sweeney for re-enacting my trip via a cordless phone, and Fay Donlevy for wrapping the index around her little finger.

I'd also like to acknowledge Virgin Blue for flying me and my ratty notebooks around this big island. And yes, I can recite the safety presentation by heart.

Further afield, saints like Sue Finnegan in Brisbane, Amber Cross in Gosford, Adelphe King in York, Ian 'Lewey' Lewis in Port Hedland, Erica Reid in New Norfolk, or Susan Philips in Charters Towers . . . (seriously, this is impossible) . . . recommend themselves for inspirations beyond the cause.

Even now, there's sure to be someone saying 'Hey, I went a mile for this blessed book. How come I missed out on star billing?' Here's hoping you'll be soothed by finding your name among the legendary legion below.

As for that splendid old lady in Orroroo, the one to show me the polar bear's head mounted in the shire hall – I'm sorry, I never caught your name. Was it Molly? Millie? To others whose names I knew but subsequently forgot or mislaid in the paper storm, my shamefaced apologies.

## ACT

Lauren Fanning, Claire Hurford, David Peake

## NSW

Stuart Allardice, Armidale; Usha Castillon, Bellingen; Tracey Sherlock, Bermagui; Dinitee Haskard, Broken Hill; Ruth Fagan, Cowra; Matthew Colahan, Paul and Jo Sutton, Dubbo; Richard Barwick, Forbes; Wendy Fahey, Fred Blair, Glen Innes; Gaila Smith, Jerilderie; Kerry Fryer, Stuart Richardson, Katoomba; Kym Coulton, Merriwa; Caroline Stallion, Pam Gibbs, Newcastle; Bob 'Windy' Geale, Nowra; Heidi Duckworth, Pokolbin; Wendy Dell, Con Young, Port Macquarie; Wayne Johnson, Mike Cufor, Sydney; Kent Mayo, Uralla; Vera Cvetkovski, Wollongong.

**NT**

Meredith Mitchell, Nita Milne, Alice Springs; Paul Clark, Kelly Dickins, Darwin; Greg Miles, Kakadu; Bill Daw, Katherine; Roddy Calvert, Nigel Skelton, Tennant Creek.

**QLD**

Madonna Cameron, Jon Kenyon, Toni Malone, Brisbane; Kylie Burton, Bundaberg; Lyn Cooley, Caboolture; Dion Eades, Cairns; Cath Stewart, Caloundra; Renee Wright, Cardwell; Ray Evans, Chinderah; Margie Barnes-Maynar, Gladstone; GT Deakin, Emily Harrison, Longreach; Pam Brooks, Tracey Heathwood, Mackay; Carmel Murdoch, Maryborough; Judy Evans, Mena Creek; Wayne Erickson, Mount Isa; Ranger Shayne O'Sullivan, Peel Island; Geoff Robins, Rockhampton; Peter Keegan, Roma; David Bell, Tanawha; Garry Rose, Toowoomba; Rebecca Harries, Danielle Bombardeiri, Natascha Duerr, Stephen Wilson, Townsville.

**SA**

Michial Farrow, Pat Gobell, Adelaide; Underground Elsa, Coober Pedy; Rachael Elliott, Hahndorf; Sharon Morris, Mintaro; June Kain, Mount Gambier; Susan Gray, Penola; Chris Goodman, Peterborough; Rose Boxall, Yorke.

**TAS**

Charles Cameron, Burnie; Helena Swift, Copping; Angela Williams, Currie; Faye Gardam, Judy Moore, Bob Vellacott, Devonport; Shirley Lincoln, George Town; David Bellamy, Mary Brownell, Anne McVilley, Samantha Meyer, Hobart; Steven French, Chris Preston, Launceston; Stephanie Burbury, Peter Fielding, Oatlands; Gloria Andrews, St Helens; Patricia DeSouta, Sheffield; Kelli Skipper, Mole Creek; Richard Davey, Strahan.

**VIC**

Julie Bishop, Sharon Oliva, Ballarat; Kathryn Mackenzie, Rachel McCullough, Bendigo; Michelle Coxall, Buninyong; Bryan Moroney, Castlemaine; Rachel Donovan, Camperdown; Jane Roads, Hamilton; Chris McClure, Horsham; Colin Scott, Macarthur; Laura Cavallo, Doris Jinks, Tracy O'Shaughnessy, Boris Aragorn, John Lamerand, Melbourne; Alan Cameron, Kristina Harrington, Mildura; Kerri Dakin, Mornington; Margaret Collins, Port Fairy; Customs Officer Steve McCabe, Portland; Charlene Stratton, Shepparton; Shane Tresider, Traralgon; Lyn Brooke, Suasannah Woodward, Warrnambool.

**WA**

Joy Matla, Albany; Nerreda Hillier, Broome; Stephanie Painter, Carnarvon; Chris Clark, Cossack; Graham Gundy, Dongara; Joe Smith, Esperance; Ron Campbell, Exmouth; Denise Riley, Lisa Williams, Kerryn Olvide, Fremantle; Pat Rowell, Geraldton; Tim Hewson, Gwalia; Megan Sadler, Norma French, Kalgoorlie; Peter Rigby, Margaret River; Terry Proctor, Mount Barker; Jason Nelthorpe, Nannup; Peter Murfit, Northam; Lynette Kemp, Onslow; Peter Hill, Jodie Semini, Kate McGurk, Nick Bailey, Caryn Nery, Perth; Gordon Thomson, Shark Bay; Derren Foster, Walpole.

# REGIONAL GUIDE

## TOWNS BY STATE AND TERRITORY

## NSW
### Southeast

Abercrombie Caves
Adaminaby
Albury
Alectown
Archgate
Ardlethan
Avoca
Batemans Bay
Bathurst
Bega
Bermagui
Berrara
Berry
Blayney
Blue Mountains
Bookham
Boorowa
Bowning
Bowral
Braidwood
Branxton
Brooklyn
Bulahdelah
Cabramurra

Canberra
Canowindra
Carcoar
Cessnock
Cobargo
Collector
Coolah
Cowan
Cowra
Culburra Beach
Durras
Eden
Ettamogah
Forbes
Gerroa
Glenbrook
Goulburn
Greenethorpe
Guildford
Gundagai
Huskisson
Jervis Bay
Junee
Katoomba
Kiama
Lake George
Lake Macquarie
Leura
Lithgow
Lucknow
Marulan
Medlow Bath
Merimbula
Merriwa

Minnamurra
Mirrool
Mollymook
Molong
Morpeth
Moruya
Moss Vale
Mt White
Mt Wilson
Mt Victoria
Narooma
Newcastle
Newnes
Nowra Hill
Nowra
Oberon
Palm Beach
Parkes
Parramatta
Phillip
Picton
Robertson
Ryde
Sofala
Somersby
St Albans
Stanwell Tops
Sydney
Tarcutta
Tathra
Thredbo
Tilba Tilba
Trundle
Tumut

Ulladulla
Vincentia
Wagga Wagga
Wamberal
West Wyalong
Windsor
Wisemans Ferry
Wollombi
Wollongong
Woollamia
Woy Woy
Yass
Young

### Southwest

Coleambally
Conargo
Darlington Point
Deniliquin
Gerogery
Griffith
Jerilderie
Jindera
Narrandera
Pooncarie

**Northeast**

Alstonville
Armidale
Ashford
Ballina
Bangalow
Bellingen
Bexhill
Billinudgel
Binnaway
Bowraville
Byron Bay
Chinderah
Coffs Harbour
Comboyne
Coramba
Dorrigo
Dubbo
Dungog
Emmaville
Forster
Glen Innes
Gostwyck
Grafton
Gunnedah
Guyra
Harrington
Hawks Nest
Herons Creek
Hunter Valley
Kempsey
Kendall
Laurieton
Lawrence
Lightning Ridge
Lismore
Macksville
Maclean
Maitland
Manilla
Mendooran
Mooball
Mudgee
Mulli Mulli
Mullumbimby
Murwillumbah
Muswelbrook
Nabiac
Nambucca Heads
Nana Glen
Nimbin
Pokolbin
Port Macquarie
Port Stephens
Raymond Terrace
Scone
Scotts Head
Seal Rocks
Singleton
Smithtown
South Tweed Heads
South-West Rocks
Tamworth
Taree
Tenterfield
Teven
Tiona
Torrington
Tweed Heads
Uralla

Walcha
Wallangra
Wauchope
Wellington
Wingham
Woodburn
Woodenbong
Woolgoolga

**Northwest
[includes Hunter Valley]**

Bourke
Broken Hill
Silverton
Tibooburra

**NT
South**

Aileron
Alice Springs
Erldunda
Finke
Henbury
Kings Canyon
Kulgera
Stuarts Well
Ti-Tree
Uluru

**Central**

Daly Waters
Dunmarra
Newcastle Waters
Rabbit Flat
Renner Springs
Tanami Desert
Tennant Creek
Wauchope
Wycliffe Well

**North [Top End]**

Batchelor
Darwin
Hayes Creek
Humpty Doo
Jabiru
Kakadu
Katherine
Larrimah
Litchfield Park
Mataranka
Noonamah
Parap

**QLD
Southeast**

Augathella
Ballandean
Beaudesert
Beerwah
Biggenden
Blackall
Bli Bli
Bonargo
Boreen Point
Brisbane
Bucca
Bundaberg
Caboolture
Canungra
Ceratodus
Caloundra
Charleville
Childers
Chinchilla
Condamine
Coolangatta
Coomera
Cracow
Dalby
Darling Downs
Eidsvold
Eudlo
Fraser Island
Gayndah
Gold Coast
Goomeri
Goondiwindi
Gympie
Hebel
Hervey Bay
Ideraway
Injune
Isisford
Jimna

Kilcoy
Kilkivan
Killarney
Kingaroy
Kolan South
Mapleton
Maroochydore
Maryborough
Maryvale
Monto
Mt Perry
Nindigully
Nobby
Noosa Heads
Noosa
Pacific Paradise
Pimpama
Pomona
Roma
Stanthorpe
Surfers Paradise
Tambo
Tanawha
Tewantin
Texas
Toowoomba
Ubobo
Wallangarra
Warwick
Wonglepong

**Southwest**

Betoota
Birdsville
Eulo
Hungerford

**Central east**

Aramac
Ayr
Bajool
Barcaldine
Bowen
Cardwell
Carmila
Charters Towers
Chillagoe
Clermont
Emerald
Emu Park
Finch Hatton
Gladstone
Halifax
Home Hill
Hughenden
Ingham

Mackay
Marian
Mirani
Mt Morgan
Ogmore
Prairie
Proserpine
Rockhampton
Sarina
Thangool
Townsville
Undara
The Caves

**Central west**

Boulia
Cloncurry
Kynuna
Longreach
Mackinlay
Mt Isa
Richmond
Winton

**Far North**
**[includes Cape York]**

Atherton
Babinda
Bamaga
Booby Island
Burketown
Cairns,
Cooktown
Daintree
Gordonvale
Hebel,
Helensvale
Herberton
Innisfail
Kuranda
Laura
Lower Wonga
Malanda
Mena Creek
Mourilyan
Normanton
Port Douglas
Ravenshoe
Tarzali
Torres Strait
Tully
Wangan
Weipa
Yungaburra

**SA**
**South**
**[includes Adelaide Hills,**
**Barossa Valley]**

Adelaide
Ambleside
Angaston
Ardrossan
Auburn
Barmera
Beachport
Birdwood
Blanchetown
Bordertown
Bruce
Burra
Carpenter Rocks
Ceduna
Cobdogla
Cowell
Eudunda
Gawler
Goolwa
Hahndorf
Hallet
Kangaroo Island
Kapunda
Keith
Keyneton
Kingston S.E.
Langhorne
Millicent
Mintaro
Monarto
Mt Barker
Mt Gambier
Murray Bridge
Naracoorte
Nullarbor Plain
Nuriootpa
Orroroo
Pekina
Penola
Peterborough
Port Lincoln
Port MacDonnell
Port Victoria
Port Willunga
Renmark
Robe
Salt Creek
Sevenhill
Tantanoola
Tanunda
Terowie
Victor Harbor
Whyalla
Williamstown
Yankalilla

**Central**

Arkaroola
Cockburn
Lyndhurst
Marree
Parachilna
Port Augusta
Roxby Downs
Wilpena Pound
Woomera

**North**

Coober Pedy

**TAS**
**South**

Buckland
Cambridge
Copping
Dunalley
Eaglehawke Neck
Hamilton
Hobart
Kempton
New Norfolk
Plenty
Port Arthur
Richmond
Sorell

**Central**

Avoca
Bicheno
Campbell Town
Coles Bay

Oatlands
Queenstown
Renisen Bell
Ross
Strahan
Swansea
Tarraleah
Triabunna
Zeehan

**North**

Beauty Point
Ben Lomond
Burnie
Corinna
Deloraine
Devonport
Forth
George Town
Grassy
King Island
Latrobe
Launceston
Legana
Longford
Marrawah
Mole Creek
Promised Land
Pyengana
Railton
Scottsdale
Sheffield
Sidmouth
Smithton
St Marys
Tunnel
Ulverstone
Waratah
Westbury
Wilmot
Wynyard

**VIC**
**South**

Aireys Inlet
Anakie
Bacchus Marsh
Bairnsdale
Barwon Heads
Beveridge
Buninyong
Cowes
Cranbourne
Darnum
Fish Creek
Genoa
Healesville
Inverloch
Lakes Entrance

# INDEX OF PLACES

# GENERAL INDEX